# WRITINGS OF
# LEON TROTSKY
## [1937-38]

**Writings of Leon Trotsky** is a collection, in twelve volumes, of pamphlets, articles, letters, and interviews written during Trotsky's third and final exile (1929-40). They include many articles translated into English for the first time. They do not include the books and pamphlets from this period that are permanently in print, nor most of the unpublished material in the Trotsky Archives at Harvard University Library. Five of the volumes cover Trotsky's residence in Turkey (1929, 1930, 1930-31, 1932, 1932-33); two in France (1933-34, 1934-35); one in Norway (1935-36); and four in Mexico (1936-37, 1937-38, 1938-39, 1939-40).

# WRITINGS OF LEON TROTSKY

## [1937-38]

PATHFINDER PRESS, INC.
NEW YORK

This volume is dedicated to
the memory of VINCENT R. DUNNE (1889-1970)

Edited by Naomi Allen and George Breitman

First edition, 1970
Second edition, 1976

Pathfinder Press, Inc.
410 West Street
New York, N.Y. 10014

# CONTENTS

*Published here in English for the first time.

Leon Trotsky in Mexico.

# PREFACE

This volume covers the period from the end of October 1937 to mid-September 1938, when Leon Trotsky was living at Coyoacan, a suburb of Mexico City. It is one of a series collecting Trotsky's writings during his last exile (1929-40) which are not otherwise available in books or pamphlets permanently in print.

This was a time when all the great powers were rearming and in other ways preparing for the impending war. The Japanese militarists were forcing their way into China. German and Italian troops joined Franco's assault on the Spanish republic, which was sinking slowly to its death. Hitler's armies marched into Austria and occupied it without resistance. The British and French governments, having accepted Hitler's advances in Spain and Austria, seemed unable to find a reason why they should fight over his demands for the dismemberment of Czechoslovakia, which were soon to lead to the infamous agreement at Munich. Roosevelt had recently delivered his "quarantine the aggressors" speech at Chicago, which served notice to all concerned that they would have to reckon with the might of U.S. imperialism in the coming redivision of the world. The Kremlin maintained its policy of peaceful coexistence with the imperialist democracies, but it was preoccupied with its bloody purges of dissidents at home, and met little success in its drive to cement an alliance with Britain, France, and the U.S. against the Axis powers.

For Trotsky too this was a period of preparation for the war. Specifically, it meant the preparation of the international revolutionary movement so that it would be able to meet the supreme tests that the war and its concomitant revolutions and colonial uprisings would bring.

The so-called Trotskyist movement began in 1923, when Trotsky organized the Left Opposition in the Soviet Union to fight for Leninist internationalism and proletarian democracy. It became the International Left Opposition (ILO) in 1930, after Stalin exiled Trotsky to Turkey. In 1933, after the Stalinists capitulated to Hitler without a struggle in Germany, the ILO decided that the Communist International and its affiliates could no longer be reformed and that it was necessary to build a new International and new revolutionary parties throughout the world. To express this change in orientation, the ILO changed its name to the International Communist League (ICL). In 1936 the ICL held an international conference, but its delegates disagreed with Trotsky's advice that they should establish the Fourth International at that conference; instead, they postponed founding it and renamed themselves the Movement for the Fourth International (MFI).

At the end of 1937 Trotsky was convinced that founding the Fourth International could be put off no longer; the approaching war required the speedy consolidation of all revolutionary forces inside a common international party united around a common Marxist program, even if at first it would be a small International. This was his major political preoccupation during the period of this volume—demarcating and challenging indecisive and wavering elements in and around the MFI, and preparing its cadres politically, ideologically, and psychologically for the coming war and for their new responsibilities.

Trotsky's efforts to build the Fourth International, which he considered the most important part of his life's work, was generally ignored or belittled by Isaac Deutscher in *The Prophet Outcast* (1963). The present volume, containing many previously unpublished letters about the preparation of the founding conference of the Fourth International, and the recently published *Transitional Program for Socialist Revolution* (second edition, 1974), containing the central programmatic document Trotsky wrote for that conference and stenograms of all the discussions he had on the subject before and after writing it, will enable readers to judge for themselves how seriously Trotsky took the building of the Fourth International and what he did to influence its founding conference.

The main personal event of this period was the death of Trotsky's beloved son and comrade, Leon Sedov, at the hands of GPU agents in a Paris hospital. There is hardly anything more moving in the whole realm of political literature than Trotsky's tribute to Sedov, reprinted here. Another personal and political blow was the kidnaping and murder in Paris of another cherished comrade who had been Trotsky's secretary in Turkey and France, the young German refugee Rudolf Klement, who was in charge of technical preparations for the founding conference.

One of the major events of the period was the third Moscow

trial, involving Bukharin, Rykov, and nineteen other defendants, in March 1938. Trotsky and Sedov had done more than anyone in the world to expose the frame-up character of the first two Moscow trials (1936 and 1937). Now, before the shock of Sedov's death had worn off, Trotsky threw himself into the mammoth job of reaching world public opinion with a day-by-day refutation of the falsifications and contradictions presented in the Moscow courtroom. With the aid of his secretaries and working almost around the clock for ten days, he wrote and sent out more than a score of articles in three languages that were printed in some of the biggest daily papers in the world, and are reprinted here. (A vivid account of how this was organized and carried out is in Joseph Hansen's introduction to Trotsky's *My Life* [Pathfinder Press, 1970].)

As usual, he wrote about different things for different audiences. He made skillful use of the capitalist press to break through the isolation and ostracism by which the Stalinists tried to gag him, but most of his writing was addressed to radicals. His article assessing the *Communist Manifesto* on its ninetieth anniversary, his letter to the British Labour Party's paper on the Mexican oil expropriations and the consequent British boycott, and his statements on freedom of education, art, the press, and the right of asylum were designed to influence labor and radical opinion. In addition he wrote articles for the MFI, the most numerous of all, which can be divided into two parts: those that were meant for the members as a whole and were printed in the internal bulletins of the various national sections (such as two polemical replies on the class character of the Soviet Union that answered criticisms by French and American comrades, a letter on democratic centralism, criticism of the party press, etc.); and the letters that Trotsky sent to leaders of the national sections or to the International Secretariat, usually on confidential matters. Some of these, it should be noted, were sent in English, in which Trotsky's choice of words was not always exact, so that in the text of this volume there is some unevenness between the English used by Trotsky and the English of translators and editors in 1938 or since.

In the first editions of the *Writings,* Trotsky's forty-three-month stay in Mexico was covered in three volumes—designated 1937-38 (although that volume actually began four days before 1937), 1938-39, and 1939-40. Since their publication, a vast number of Trotsky's articles and letters from the Mexican period have become available, many of them never published before. This has made it necessary, in the second editions, to reorganize and expand the number of volumes for the Mexican period from three to four, which are now designated by title as 1936-37, 1937-38 (the present volume), 1938-39, and 1939-40.

The second edition of this volume differs from the first in the following ways:

1. Of the 129 selections in this volume, 52 are here published for the first time in English. These include 40 that were written or transcribed in English but never before published, and 12 that were written or published in other languages and had to be translated into English for this volume.

2. It covers a shorter time span (October 1937–September 1938) than the first edition (December 1936–April 1938), and therefore does not include material from the first edition dated October 1937 and before or September 1938 and after, which has been transferred to the appropriate places in the second editions entitled 1936-37 and 1938-39. It also does not include the article "Behind the Kremlin Walls," dated January 8, 1938, which has been transferred to *Political Portraits* (Pathfinder, 1977).

3. The first edition was divided by theme into twelve sections, each arranged chronologically. All the articles in the second edition are arranged chronologically.

4. Unlike the first edition, the second is annotated.

5. Some dates mistakenly used in the first edition have been corrected here, and passages missing from certain articles in the first edition have been restored.

Many articles in this volume were signed by pen names or were unsigned when first published, usually for security reasons; the use of pen names, especially in the stenograms, explains why in some cases Trotsky speaks of himself in the third person. The date preceding each selection indicates when it was completed; if that is not known, the date when it was first published is given. Translations originally made in the 1930s and 1940s have been revised to correct obvious errors and achieve uniformity in spelling of names, punctuation, style, etc. Acknowledgments about the articles and translations, and explanatory material about the persons and events mentioned in them, will be found in the section entitled "Notes and Acknowledgments." A list of Trotsky's 1937-38 books, pamphlets, and articles not included in this volume because they are in print and available elsewhere will be found in the section entitled "Other Writings of 1937-38."

For expansion of this edition and improvements in its contents, special thanks are due to the Harvard College Library, for its permission to examine and use material in the "open" section of the Trotsky Archives; to James P. Cannon, who opened his archives to us before his death in 1974; and to Louis Sinclair, for the help provided by his *Leon Trotsky: A Bibliography* (Hoover Institution Press, 1972).

The Editors<br>April 1975

# CHRONOLOGY

## —1937—

October 30–November 1—Second congress of the POI, French section of the Movement for the Fourth International (MFI), held in Paris.

November 2—Trotsky calls for an offensive against Stalinism.

November 6—Fascist Italy signs anti-Comintern pact.

November 25—Trotsky writes on the class character of the Soviet state, as contribution to discussion preceding founding convention of Socialist Workers Party (SWP) in U.S.

December 13—Dewey Commission of Inquiry releases text of its "not guilty" verdict on charges against Trotsky and Leon Sedov in Moscow trials.

December 31—Four-day convention, to form SWP as U.S. section of MFI, opens in Chicago.

## —1938—

January 15—Trotsky analyzes renewed debate over Kronstadt uprising of 1921.

February 16—Leon Sedov dies under mysterious circumstances in a Paris hospital.

February 23—Stalinist-dominated CTM (Mexican Confederation of Workers) adopts a resolution condemning Trotskyism presented by Lombardo Toledano.

March 2-13—Twenty-one Old Bolsheviks, including Bukharin and Rykov, become defendants in third Moscow trial, which ends in their conviction.

March 11—Hitler annexes Austria.

March 20-25—A delegation of SWP leaders meets with Trotsky to discuss international and national problems.

April—Trotsky writes the Transitional Program, for submission to founding conference of Fourth International, and signs contract with Harper for biography of Stalin.

April 23—Trotsky defends the Mexican government's nationalization of British- and American-owned oil industry.

May 31—Trotsky insists on clear-cut founding of Fourth International at coming international conference.

July—Trotsky, Andre Breton, and Diego Rivera write a manifesto on revolutionary art.

July 13—Rudolf Klement, one of Trotsky's secretaries, is kidnaped by Stalinist agents in Paris; his body is found a few days before the FI's founding conference.

July 19—Trotsky protests French police cover-up in Sedov's death.

August 30—Trotsky assesses the significance of the coming conference of the FI.

September 2—FI is founded at an international conference in France.

September 6-12—Stalinist-controlled trade union congress and congress against war and fascism are held in Mexico.

# NINETY YEARS
# OF THE COMMUNIST MANIFESTO[1]

## October 30, 1937

It is hard to believe that the centennial of the *Manifesto of the Communist Party* is only ten years away! This pamphlet, displaying greater genius than any other in world literature, astounds us even today by its freshness. Its most important sections appear to have been written yesterday. Assuredly, the young authors (Marx was twenty-nine, Engels twenty-seven)[2] were able to look further into the future than anyone before them, and perhaps than anyone since them.

As early as their joint preface to the edition of 1872, Marx and Engels declared that despite the fact that certain secondary passages in the *Manifesto* were antiquated, they felt that they no longer had any right to alter the original text inasmuch as the *Manifesto* had already become a historical document, during the intervening period of twenty-five years. Sixty-five additional years have elapsed since that time. Isolated passages in the *Manifesto* have receded still further into the past. We shall try to establish succinctly in this preface both those ideas in the *Manifesto* which retain their full force today and those which require important alteration or amplification.

1. The materialist conception of history, discovered by Marx only a short while before and applied with consummate skill in the *Manifesto*, has completely withstood the test of events and the blows of hostile criticism. It constitutes today one of the most precious instruments of human thought. All other interpretations of the historical process have lost all scientific meaning. We can state with certainty that it is impossible in our time to be not only a revolutionary militant but even a literate observer in politics without assimilating the materialist interpretation of history.

2. The first chapter of the *Manifesto* opens with the following

words: "The history of all hitherto existing society is the history
of class struggles." This postulate, the most important conclusion
drawn from the materialist interpretation of history, immediately
became an issue in the class struggle. Especially venomous
attacks were directed by reactionary hypocrites, liberal doctrinaires, and idealistic democrats against the theory which
substituted the struggle of material interests for "common
welfare," "national unity," and "eternal moral truths" as the
driving force of history. They were later joined by recruits from
the ranks of the labor movement itself, by the so-called
revisionists, i.e., the proponents of reviewing ("revising") Marxism in the spirit of class collaboration and class conciliation.
Finally, in our own time, the same path has been followed in
practice by the contemptible epigones of the Communist International (the "Stalinists"): the policy of the so-called People's Front
flows wholly from the denial of the laws of the class struggle.[3]
Meanwhile, it is precisely the epoch of imperialism, bringing all
social contradictions to the point of highest tension, which gives
to the *Communist Manifesto* its supreme *theoretical* triumph.

3. The anatomy of capitalism, as a specific stage in the
economic development of society, was given by Marx in its
finished form in *Capital* (1867). But even in the *Communist
Manifesto* the main lines of the future analysis are firmly
sketched: the payment for labor power as equivalent to the cost of
its reproduction; the appropriation of surplus value by the
capitalists; competition as the basic law of social relations; the
ruination of intermediate classes, i.e., the urban petty bourgeoisie
and the peasantry; the concentration of wealth in the hands of an
ever-diminishing number of property owners, at the one pole, and
the numerical growth of the proletariat, at the other; the
preparation of the material and political preconditions for the
socialist regime.

4. The proposition in the *Manifesto* concerning the tendency of
capitalism to lower the living standards of the workers, and even
to transform them into paupers, had been subjected to a heavy
barrage. Parsons, professors, ministers, journalists, Social
Democratic theoreticians, and trade union leaders came to the
front against the so-called "theory of impoverishment." They
invariably discovered signs of growing prosperity among the
toilers, palming off the labor aristocracy as the proletariat, or
taking a fleeting tendency as permanent. Meanwhile, even the
development of the mightiest capitalism in the world, namely,
U.S. capitalism, has transformed millions of workers into

paupers who are maintained at the expense of federal, municipal, or private charity.

5. As against the *Manifesto,* which depicted commercial and industrial crises as a series of ever more extensive catastrophes, the revisionists vowed that the national and international development of trusts would assure control over the market, and lead gradually to the abolition of crises. The close of the last century and the beginning of the present one were in reality marked by a development of capitalism so tempestuous as to make crises seem only "accidental" stoppages. But this epoch has gone beyond return. In the last analysis, truth proved to be on Marx's side in this question as well.

6. "The executive of the modern state is but a committee for managing the common affairs of the whole bourgeoisie." This succinct formula, which the leaders of the Social Democracy looked upon as a journalistic paradox, contains in fact the only scientific theory of the state. The democracy fashioned by the bourgeoisie is not, as both Bernstein and Kautsky thought,[4] an empty sack which one can undisturbedly fill with any kind of class content. Bourgeois democracy can serve only the bourgeoisie. A government of the "People's Front," whether headed by Blum or Chautemps, Caballero or Negrin,[5] is only "a committee for managing the common affairs of the whole bourgeoisie." Whenever this "committee" manages affairs poorly, the bourgeoisie dismisses it with a boot.

7. "Every class struggle is a political struggle." "The organization of the proletariat as a class [is] consequently its organization into a political party." Trade unionists, on the one hand, and anarcho-syndicalists, on the other, have long shied away—and even now try to shy away—from the understanding of these historical laws. "Pure" trade unionism has now been dealt a crushing blow in its chief refuge: the United States. Anarcho-syndicalism has suffered an irreparable defeat in its last stronghold—Spain. Here too the *Manifesto* proved correct.

8. The proletariat cannot conquer power within the legal framework established by the bourgeoisie. "Communists openly declare that their ends can be attained only by the forcible overthrow of all existing social conditions." Reformism sought to explain this postulate of the *Manifesto* on the grounds of the immaturity of the movement at that time, and the inadequate development of democracy. The fate of Italian, German, and a great number of other "democracies" proves that "immaturity" is the distinguishing trait of the ideas of the reformists themselves.

9. For the socialist transformation of society, the working class must concentrate in its hands such power as can smash each and every political obstacle barring the road to the new system. "The proletariat organized as the ruling class"—this is the dictatorship. At the same time it is the only true proletarian democracy. Its scope and depth depend upon concrete historical conditions. The greater the number of states that take the path of the socialist revolution, the freer and more flexible forms will the dictatorship assume, the broader and more deepgoing will be workers' democracy.

10. The international development of capitalism has predetermined the international character of the proletarian revolution. "United action, of the leading civilized countries at least, is one of the first conditions for the emancipation of the proletariat." The subsequent development of capitalism has so closely knit all sections of our planet, both "civilized" and "uncivilized," that the problem of the socialist revolution has completely and decisively assumed a world character. The Soviet bureaucracy attempted to liquidate the *Manifesto* with respect to this fundamental question. The Bonapartist degeneration of the Soviet state is an overwhelming illustration of the falseness of the theory of socialism in one country.[6]

11. "When, in the course of development, class distinctions have disappeared, and all production has been concentrated in the hands of a vast association of the whole nation, the public power will lose its political character." In other words: the state withers away. Society remains, freed from the straitjacket. This is nothing else but socialism. The converse theorem: the monstrous growth of state coercion in the USSR is eloquent testimony that society is moving away from socialism.

12. "The workingmen have no fatherland." These words of the *Manifesto* have more than once been evaluated by philistines as an agitational quip. As a matter of fact they provided the proletariat with the sole conceivable directive in the question of the capitalist "fatherland." The violation of this directive by the Second International brought about not only four years of devastation in Europe, but the present stagnation of world culture.[7] In view of the impending new war, for which the betrayal of the Third International has paved the way, the *Manifesto* remains even now the most reliable counselor on the question of the capitalist "fatherland."

Thus, we see that the joint and rather brief production of two young authors continues to give irreplaceable directives upon the most important and burning questions of the struggle for emancipation. What other book could even distantly be compared with the *Communist Manifesto*? But this does not imply that after ninety years of unprecedented development of productive forces and vast social struggles, the *Manifesto* needs neither corrections nor additions. Revolutionary thought has nothing in common with idol-worship. Programs and prognoses are tested and corrected in the light of experience, which is the supreme criterion of human reason. The *Manifesto,* too, requires corrections and additions. However, as is evidenced by historical experience itself, these corrections and additions can be successfully made only by proceeding in accord with the method lodged in the foundation of the *Manifesto* itself. We shall try to indicate this in several most important instances.

1. Marx taught that no social system departs from the arena of history before exhausting its creative potentialities. The *Manifesto* excoriates capitalism for retarding the development of the productive forces. During that period, however, as well as in the following decades, this retardation was only *relative* in nature. Had it been possible in the second half of the nineteenth century to organize economy on socialist beginnings, its tempos of growth would have been immeasurably greater. But this theoretically irrefutable postulate does not invalidate the fact that the productive forces kept expanding on a world scale right up to the world war. Only in the last twenty years, despite the most modern conquests of science and technology, has the epoch of out-and-out stagnation and even decline of world economy begun. Mankind is beginning to expend its accumulated capital, while the next war threatens to destroy the very foundations of civilization for many years to come. The authors of the *Manifesto* thought that capitalism would be scrapped long prior to the time when from a relatively reactionary regime it would turn into an absolutely reactionary regime. This transformation took final shape only before the eyes of the present generation, and changed our epoch into the epoch of wars, revolutions, and fascism.

2. The error of Marx and Engels in regard to the historical dates flowed, on the one hand, from an underestimation of future possibilities latent in capitalism, and, on the other, an overestimation of the revolutionary maturity of the proletariat. The revolution of 1848 did not turn into a socialist revolution as the *Manifesto* had calculated, but opened up to Germany the possibility of a vast future capitalist ascension.[8] The Paris Commune proved that the proletariat, without having a tempered

revolutionary party at its head, cannot wrest power from the bourgeoisie. Meanwhile, the prolonged period of capitalist prosperity that ensued brought about not the education of the revolutionary vanguard, but rather the bourgeois degeneration of the labor aristocracy, which became in turn the chief brake on the proletarian revolution. In the nature of things, the authors of the *Manifesto* could not possibly have foreseen this "dialectic."

3. For the *Manifesto,* capitalism was—the kingdom of free competition. While referring to the growing concentration of capital, the *Manifesto* did not draw the necessary conclusion in regard to monopoly, which has become the dominant capitalist form in our epoch and the most important precondition for socialist economy. Only afterwards, in *Capital,* did Marx establish the tendency toward the transformation of free competition into monopoly. It was Lenin who gave a scientific characterization of monopoly capitalism in his *Imperialism.*[9]

4. Basing themselves on the example of "industrial revolution" in England, the authors of the *Manifesto* pictured far too unilaterally the process of liquidation of the intermediate classes, as a wholesale proletarianization of crafts, petty trades, and peasantry. In point of fact, the elemental forces of competition have far from completed this simultaneously progressive and barbarous work. Capitalism has ruined the petty bourgeoisie at a much faster rate than it has proletarianized it. Furthermore, the bourgeois state has long directed its conscious policy toward the artificial maintenance of petty-bourgeois strata. At the opposite pole, the growth of technology and the rationalization of large-scale industry engenders chronic unemployment and obstructs the proletarianization of the petty bourgeoisie. Concurrently, the development of capitalism has accelerated in the extreme the growth of legions of technicians, administrators, commercial employes, in short, the so-called "new middle class." In consequence, the intermediate classes, to whose disappearance the *Manifesto* so categorically refers, comprise even in a country as highly industrialized as Germany about half of the population. However, the artificial preservation of antiquated petty-bourgeois strata in no way mitigates the social contradictions, but, on the contrary, invests them with a special malignancy, and together with the permanent army of the unemployed constitutes the most malevolent expression of the *decay* of capitalism.

5. Calculated for a revolutionary epoch the *Manifesto* contains (end of Chapter II) ten demands, corresponding to the period of direct transition from capitalism to socialism. In their preface of

1872, Marx and Engels declared these demands to be in part antiquated, and, in any case, only of secondary importance. The reformists seized upon this evaluation to interpret it in the sense that transitional revolutionary demands had forever ceded their place to the Social Democratic "minimum program," which, as is well known, does not transcend the limits of bourgeois democracy. As a matter of fact, the authors of the *Manifesto* indicated quite precisely the main correction of their transitional program, namely, "the working class cannot simply lay hold of the ready-made state machinery and wield it for its own purposes." In other words, the correction was directed against the fetishism of bourgeois democracy. Marx later counterposed to the capitalist state, the state of the type of the Commune. This "type" subsequently assumed the much more graphic shape of soviets. There cannot be a revolutionary program today without *soviets* and without *workers' control.* As for the rest, the ten demands of the *Manifesto,* which appeared "archaic" in an epoch of peaceful parliamentary activity, have today regained completely their true significance. The Social Democratic "minimum program," on the other hand, has become hopelessly antiquated.

6. Basing its expectation that "the German bourgeois revolution . . . will be but a prelude to an immediately following proletarian revolution," the *Manifesto* cites the much more advanced conditions of European civilization as compared with what existed in England in the seventeenth century and in France in the eighteenth century, and the far greater development of the proletariat. The error in this prognosis was not only in the date. The revolution of 1848 revealed within a few months that precisely under more advanced conditions, none of the bourgeois classes is capable of bringing the revolution to its termination: the big and middle bourgeoisie is far too closely linked with the landowners, and fettered by the fear of the masses; the petty bourgeoisie is far too divided and in its top leadership far too dependent on the big bourgeoisie. As evidenced by the entire subsequent course of development in Europe and Asia, the bourgeois revolution, taken by itself, can no more in general be consummated. A complete purge of feudal rubbish from society is conceivable only on the condition that the proletariat, freed from the influence of bourgeois parties, can take its stand at the head of the peasantry and establish its revolutionary dictatorship. By this token, the bourgeois revolution becomes interlaced with the first stage of the socialist revolution, subsequently to dissolve in the latter. The national

revolution therewith becomes a link of the world revolution. The transformation of the economic foundation and of all social relations assumes a permanent (uninterrupted) character.

For revolutionary parties in backward countries of Asia, Latin America, and Africa, a clear understanding of the organic connection between the democratic revolution and the dictatorship of the proletariat—and thereby, the international socialist revolution—is a life-and-death question.

7. While depicting how capitalism draws into its vortex backward and barbarous countries, the *Manifesto* contains no reference to the struggle of colonial and semicolonial countries for independence. To the extent that Marx and Engels considered the social revolution "in the leading civilized countries at least," to be a matter of the next few years, the colonial question was resolved automatically for them, not in consequence of an independent movement of oppressed nationalities but in consequence of the victory of the proletariat in the metropolitan centers of capitalism. The questions of revolutionary strategy in colonial and semicolonial countries are therefore not touched upon at all by the *Manifesto*. Yet these questions demand an independent solution. For example, it is quite self-evident that while the "national fatherland" has become the most baneful historical brake in advanced capitalist countries, it still remains a relatively progressive factor in backward countries compelled to struggle for an independent existence.

"The Communists," declares the *Manifesto,* "everywhere support every revolutionary movement against the existing social and political order of things." The movement of the colored races against their imperialist oppressors is one of the most important and powerful movements against the existing order and therefore calls for the complete, unconditional, and unlimited support on the part of the proletariat of the white race. The credit for developing revolutionary strategy for oppressed nationalities belongs primarily to Lenin.

8. The most antiquated section of the *Manifesto*—with respect not to method but to material—is the criticism of "socialist" literature for the first part of the nineteenth century (Chapter III) and the definition of the position of the Communists in relation to various opposition parties (Chapter IV). The movements and parties listed in the *Manifesto* were so drastically swept away either by the revolution of 1848 or by the ensuing counterrevolution that one must look up even their names in a historical dictionary. However, in this section, too, the *Manifesto* is perhaps

closer to us now than it was to the previous generation. In the epoch of the flowering of the Second International, when Marxism seemed to exert an undivided sway, the ideas of pre-Marxist socialism could have been considered as having receded decisively into the past. Things are otherwise today. The decomposition of the Social Democracy and the Communist International at every step engenders monstrous ideological relapses. Senile thought seems to have become infantile. In search of all-saving formulas the prophets in the epoch of decline discover anew doctrines long since buried by scientific socialism.

As touches the question of opposition parties, it is in this domain that the elapsed decades have introduced the most deepgoing changes, not only in the sense that the old parties have long been brushed aside by new ones, but also in the sense that the very character of parties and their mutual relations have radically changed in the conditions of the imperialist epoch. The *Manifesto* must therefore be amplified with the most important documents of the first four congresses of the Communist International, the essential literature of Bolshevism, and the decisions of the conferences of the Fourth International.[10]

We have already remarked above that according to Marx no social order departs from the scene without first exhausting the potentialities latent in it. However, even an antiquated social order does not cede its place to a new order without resistance. A change in social regimes presupposes the harshest form of the class struggle, i.e., revolution. If the proletariat, for one reason or another, proves incapable of overthrowing with an audacious blow the outlived bourgeois order, then finance capital in the struggle to maintain its unstable rule can do nothing but turn the petty bourgeoisie ruined and demoralized by it into the pogrom army of fascism. The bourgeois degeneration of the Social Democracy and the fascist degeneration of the petty bourgeoisie are interlinked as cause and effect.

At the present time, the Third International far more wantonly than the Second performs in all countries the work of deceiving and demoralizing the toilers. By massacring the vanguard of the Spanish proletariat, the unbridled hirelings of Moscow not only pave the way for fascism but execute a goodly share of its labors. The protracted crisis of the international revolution, which is turning more and more into a crisis of human culture, is reducible in its essentials to the crisis of revolutionary leadership.

As the heir to the great tradition, of which the *Manifesto of the Communist Party* forms the most precious link, the Fourth

International is educating new cadres for the solution of old tasks. Theory is generalized reality. In an honest attitude to revolutionary theory is expressed the impassioned urge to reconstruct the social reality. That in the southern part of the Dark Continent our cothinkers were the first to translate the *Manifesto* into the Afrikaans language is another graphic illustration of the fact that Marxist thought lives today only under the banner of the Fourth International. To it belongs the future. When the centennial of the *Communist Manifesto* is celebrated, the Fourth International will have become the decisive revolutionary force on our planet.

# IT IS HIGH TIME TO LAUNCH A WORLD OFFENSIVE AGAINST STALINISM[11]

## An Open Letter to All Workers' Organizations

### November 2, 1937

The world socialist movement is being consumed by a terrible disease. The source of contagion is the Comintern, or to put it more correctly, the GPU, for whom the apparatus of the Comintern serves only as a legal cover.[12] The events of the last few months in Spain have shown what crimes the unbridled and completely degenerate Moscow bureaucracy and its hirelings from among the declassed international scum are capable of. It is not a case of "incidental" murders or "incidental" frame-ups. It is a case of a conspiracy against the world labor movement.

The Moscow trials[13] could, of course, have taken place only under a totalitarian regime, where the GPU dictates alike the conduct of defendants, of the prosecution, and of the defense. But these judicial frame-ups were from the outset designed as a starting point for a crushing offensive against the opponents of the Moscow clique on the world arena. On March 3 Stalin delivered a speech at a plenum of the Central Committee of the CPSU [Communist Party of the Soviet Union] in which he declared that "the Fourth International consists two-thirds of spies and diversionists." This brazen and truly Stalinist declaration already indicated quite clearly at what the Kremlin Cain was aiming. His designs are not confined, however, to the framework of the Fourth International. In Spain the POUM,[14] which was itself in an irreconcilable conflict with the Fourth International, was enrolled among the "Trotskyites." After the POUM came the turn of the anarcho-syndicalists and even of the left Socialists. And now, all those who protest against the repression of the Anarchists are being enrolled among the Trotskyites. The frame-ups and crimes are mounting at a fearful rate. Isolated and especially scandalous details may, of course, be accounted for by excessive zeal on the part of individual agents. But the activity as a whole is rigidly centralized, and is being conducted in accordance with a plan elaborated by the Kremlin.

On April 21 an emergency plenum of the ECCI [Executive Committee of the Communist International] convened in Paris, at which the most trusted representatives of the seventeen most important sections participated. The sessions were strictly secret in character. The world press carried only a brief dispatch mentioning that the deliberations of the plenum were devoted to an international struggle against Trotskyism. The instructions came from Moscow, directly from Stalin. Neither the discussion nor the decisions have been published. As is evident from the information at our disposal, and from all the ensuing events, this mysterious plenum was *in reality a conference of the most important international agents of the GPU for the purpose of preparing a campaign of framed accusations, denunciations, kidnapings, and assassinations against the adversaries of Stalinism in the labor movement the world over.*

At the time of the Zinoviev-Kamenev trial[15] (August 1936) there was still some wavering in the ranks of the Comintern. Despite the efforts of hoary hirelings of the GPU like Jacques Duclos in France,[16] even the inured cadres of the Comintern were loath to prostrate themselves in the mud which was soaked with fresh blood. But within a few months, the resistance of the waverers was broken down. The entire press of the Comintern, which Stalin keeps in a dog-collar of gold, was drawn into an orgy of slander unprecedented in vileness and cruelty. The guiding role was assigned, as it always is, to the emissaries of Moscow like Mikhail Koltsov, Willi Muenzenberg, and other scoundrels.[17] *Pravda* confidently promised that the purge in Spain would be conducted with the same ruthlessness as in the USSR. Its words were followed with deeds: framed documents against the POUM, assassinations of Anarchist writers, the murder of Andres Nin, the kidnaping of Erwin Wolf, the kidnaping of Mark Rein,[18] dozens of less prominent stabbings in the back or murders from ambush, incarcerations in Stalin's extraterritorial prisons in Spain, confinement in these prisons in special cells, beating and infliction of all sorts of physical and moral torture—all this under the cover of continuous, crude, poisonous, and truly Stalinist slander.

In Spain, where the so-called Republican government serves as a legal shield for Stalin's criminal gangs, the GPU found the most favorable arena for fulfilling the directives of the April plenum. But matters were not confined to Spain alone. The French and British military staffs, as appears from the press of the Comintern itself, were supplied with some sort of mysterious documents pertaining to "Trotsky's meeting with Rudolf Hess."[19] The Czech military staff was handed forged correspondence intended to establish a connection between the Gestapo and an old German revolutionist, Anton Grylewicz.[20] Jacques Duclos tried to link up the "Trotskyites" with mysterious terrorist acts in Paris, concerning which the GPU could doubtless have supplied some information to the French police. On September 4, in Lausanne, Ignace Reiss was murdered, only because, horrified at the crimes of Stalin, he had publicly broken with Moscow.[21]

Some of Reiss's assassins have been arrested. They are members of the Comintern and agents of the GPU recruited from among Russian White Guards.[22] The investigation of the French and Swiss court authorities provides every ground for the assumption that this very gang had committed a whole series of hitherto unrevealed crimes. White Guards serve Stalin as assassins, just as they serve him in the guise of prosecutors (Vyshinsky), publicists (M. Koltsov, Zaslavsky, etc.), or diplomats (Troyanovsky, Maisky, and the rest of the fraternity).[23]

No sooner did military activities begin in the Far East than Stalin launched a crushing offensive against his revolutionary opponents in China.[24] The method is identical with that applied in Spain. Stalin sells to Chiang Kai-shek,[25] as to Negrin, products of Soviet industry at high prices, and with the income thus obtained pays his falsifiers, journalistic swindlers, and hired assassins. On October 5, a cable dispatch from Shanghai appeared in the New York *Daily Worker,* accusing Chinese "Trotskyites" in Kwangsi of an alliance with the Japanese general staff. The *Daily Worker* is an organ of the GPU published in New York; its Shanghai correspondent is a GPU agent who fulfills the decisions—of the April plenum. Informed Chinese sources have in the meantime ascertained that there was and is no Trotskyist organization in Kwangsi (*Socialist Appeal,* October 16). But this does not alter the situation: the Shanghai cable signifies that in China there has opened the chapter of framed documents, kidnapings of "Trotskyites," and murders from ambush. The prisons of Chiang Kai-shek have already in them not a few impeccable revolutionists. Their lives are now being directly threatened by Stalin.

The Canadian Communist Henry Beatty, who participated as a volunteer for four months on the Spanish front, and who was then sent back to his own country as an agitator by the militiamen themselves, has recently recounted in the press how the party of Canadian Stalinists had compelled him to say at public meetings that Trotskyites in Spain "shot wounded militiamen." For a while, Beatty, according to his own statement, fulfilled this monstrous order, "submitting to party discipline," i.e., to the decision of that same secret plenum directed by Stalin. Today, after Beatty escaped from the poisoned atmosphere of the Comintern into the clear air outside, he is of course branded as a spy and a diversionist, and it is even possible that there is a price on his head. When it comes to such understandings Stalin is not stingy: the technical expenses alone for the murder of Ignace Reiss amounted to 300,000 francs!

To cover up or justify these crimes, dozens of foreign bourgeois journalists of the Walter Duranty–Louis Fischer school[26] are kept on the payrolls of the GPU. It has long been no secret to those able to read between the lines that the amiable-critical-equivocal dispatches and articles from Moscow signed by "independent" names, often accompanied with a notation "uncensored," are in reality written under the dictation of the GPU and have as their aim to reconcile world public opinion with the sinister figure of the Kremlin Cain. "Independent" journalists of this type differ from Messrs. Duranty only in that they come at a higher price. But the reporters are not the only ones mobilized. Writers with high-sounding or famous names like Romain Rolland, the deceased Barbusse, Malraux, Heinrich Mann, or Feuchtwanger[27] are in effect pensioners of the GPU, which pays liberally for the "moral" services of these friends through the medium of the State Publishing House.

There is a somewhat different but not greatly improved situation with regard to the leaders of the Labor and Socialist International. Out of considerations of diplomatic or internal political character Leon Blum, Leon Jouhaux, Vandervelde,[28] and their compeers in other countries have organized, in the full sense of the term, a conspiracy of silence around the crimes of the Stalinist bureaucracy both in the USSR and on the world arena. Negrin and Prieto[29] are direct accomplices of the GPU. All this they do—under the guise of defending "democracy"!

We know that the enemy is powerful; he has a long reach; gold clinks in his pockets. He covers himself with the authority of the revolution which he is strangling and dishonoring. But we also know something else: however powerful the enemy may be, he is not omnipotent. Despite the Kremlin's treasury and apparatus and legion of "friends," truth is beginning to cut a path for itself into the consciousness of the labor masses of the world. Drunk with impunity, Stalin has grossly overstepped that boundary which caution dictates even to the most privileged criminal. It is possible to dupe so brazenly only those who want to be duped. Not a few of the dubious luminaries belong to this category. But the masses do not want to be deceived. They need the truth. They are striving for it, and they will attain it.

No longer bound by any principles, Stalin has overstepped the final boundary. Precisely therein is his weakness. He is still able to kill. But he cannot halt the truth. More and more worker-Communists, Socialists, and Anarchists are being seized by alarm. Even Stalin's allies in the Second International are beginning to cast fearful glances at the Kremlin. Many literary "friends" have already cautiously withdrawn to the sidelines under the pretext of "neutrality." But this is only the beginning.

Ignace Reiss was not the last to bring us his revelations. The murderers of Reiss, apprehended in Switzerland and France, may disclose a good many things. Thousands of revolutionary volunteers in Spain will spread the truth about the hangman of the revolution throughout the globe. Thinking workers are asking themselves: "To what end is all this? What aim is this endless chain of crimes serving?" And the answer is hammering its way into their minds: Stalin is preparing his "coronation" over the ruins of the revolution and the corpses of revolutionists.

The Bonapartist coronation of Stalin must coincide with his political death for the working class movement. It is necessary to rally the efforts of all revolutionists, all honest workers, all true friends of the proletariat, to purge the horrible contagion of Stalinism from the ranks of the emancipatory movement. There is only one way to attain this: by disclosing to the workers the truth, without exaggerations, but also without any embellishment. The program of action thus flows well-nigh automatically from the situation itself.

We must definitely establish and make public the names of all the national delegates who participated in the recent Paris plenum, as the men directly responsible for the organization of frame-ups, kidnapings, and murders in the respective countries.

We must definitely establish and make public the names of all foreign Stalinists who either held or are holding any kind of military, police, or administrative posts in Spain. All these individuals are agents of the GPU, implicated in the crimes committed in Spain.

We must carefully follow the international Stalinist press, as well as the "literary" activity of the avowed and undercover friends of the GPU, inasmuch as from the character of the fumes they emit it is often possible to forecast what new crimes Stalin is preparing.

It is necessary to institute in all labor organizations a regime of rigid mistrust of everyone directly or indirectly connected with the Stalinist apparatus. One must always expect any kind of perfidy on the part of the agents of the Comintern who are the spineless tools of the GPU.

We must tirelessly gather printed material, documents, testimonials of witnesses concerning the criminal work of the agents of the GPU-Comintern. We must periodically publish in the press rigorously substantiated conclusions drawn from these materials.

It is necessary to open the eyes of public opinion to the fact that the honeyed and lying propaganda of many philosophers, moralists, aesthetes, artists, pacifists, and labor "leaders" in defense of the Kremlin, under the guise of "defense of the Soviet Union," is paid for liberally in Moscow gold. These gentlemen must be covered with the infamy they so richly have earned.

Never before has the labor movement had in its own ranks so vicious, dangerous, powerful, and unscrupulous an enemy as Stalin's clique and its international agents. Remissness in the struggle against this enemy is tantamount to betrayal. Only windbags and dilettantes but not serious revolutionists can confine themselves to pathetic outbursts of indignation. It is necessary to have a plan and an organization. It is urgent to create special commissions which would follow the maneuvers, intrigues, and crimes of the Stalinists, warn the labor organizations of danger in store, and elaborate the best methods of parrying and resisting the Moscow gangsters.

It is necessary to publish appropriate literature and collect funds for its publication. In each country a book should be issued, exposing completely the respective section of the Comintern.

We possess neither a state apparatus nor hired friends. Nevertheless we confidently fling our challenge to the Stalinist gangs before all mankind. Our hands will not lie idle. Some among us may still fall in this struggle. But its general outcome is predetermined. Stalinism will be laid low, crushed, and covered forever with infamy. The world working class will march out onto the open road.

# ONCE AGAIN:
# THE USSR AND ITS DEFENSE[30]

## November 4, 1937

### Craipeau Forgets the Principal Teachings of Marxism

Comrade Craipeau wants to persuade us once again that the Soviet bureaucracy as such is a class. It is not a question, however, for him of pure "sociology." No. All he wants, as we shall see, is once and for all to mark out a free and straight path to his kind of internationalism, an internationalism, alas, which is not at all sure of itself. If the bureaucracy is not a class, if the Soviet Union can still be recognized as a workers' state, it is necessary to support it during the war. How then can one remain in irreconcilable opposition to one's own government, if the latter is allied to the Soviets? There you have a terrible temptation to fall into social patriotism! No, it is preferable by far to make a radical sweep of the field: the Stalinist bureaucracy is an exploiting class, and in case of war, we hardly need to distinguish between the Soviets and Japan.

Unfortunately, this terminological radicalism does not advance things very much. Let us admit for a moment that the bureaucracy is really a *class,* in the sense of Marxist sociology. We then have a new form of class society which is identical neither with feudal society nor with capitalist society, and which never was foreseen by Marxist theoreticians. Such a discovery is worthy of a little more attentive analysis.

Why does capitalist society find itself in a blind alley? Because it is no longer capable of developing the productive forces, either in the advanced countries or in the backward countries. The world imperialist chain was broken at its weakest link, Russia. Now we learn that in place of bourgeois society there has been established a new class society. Craipeau has not yet given it any name nor analyzed its internal laws. But that does not prevent us from seeing that the new society is progressive in comparison

34

with capitalism, for on the basis of nationalized property the new possessing "class" has assured a development of productive forces never equaled in the history of the world. Marxism teaches us, does it not, that the productive forces are the fundamental factor of historic progress. A society which is not capable of assuring the growth of economic power is still less capable of assuring the well-being of the working masses, whatever may be the mode of distribution. The antagonism between feudalism and capitalism and the decline of the former has been determined precisely by the fact that the latter opened up new and grandiose possibilities for the stagnating productive forces. The same applies to the USSR. Whatever its modes of exploitation may be, this new society is by its very character superior to capitalist society. There you have the real point of departure for Marxist analysis!

This fundamental factor, the productive forces, also has its reflection in the ideological domain. While the economic life of capitalist countries no longer teaches us anything except different forms of stagnation and decay, the nationalized and planned economy of the USSR is the greatest school for all humanity aspiring to a better future. One must be blind not to see this difference!

In the war between Japan and Germany on one side, and the USSR on the other, there would be involved not a question of equality in distribution, or of proletarian democracy, or of Vyshinsky's justice, but the fate of the *nationalized property and planned economy.* The victory of the imperialist states would signify the collapse not only of the new exploiting "class" in the USSR, but also of the new forms of production—the lowering of the whole Soviet economy to the level of a backward and semicolonial capitalism. Now I ask Craipeau: When we are faced with the struggle between two states which are—let us admit it— both class states, but one of which represents imperialist stagnation and the other tremendous economic progress, do we not have to support the progressive state against the reactionary state? Yes or no?

In his entire thesis, Craipeau speaks of the most diverse things, and things furthest away from the subject, but he does not mention a single time the decisive factor of Marxist sociology, the development of the productive forces. This is precisely why his entire construction remains suspended in air. He juggles with terminological shadows ("class," "nonclass") instead of grasping the reality. He believes that it suffices to attribute the term "class" to the bureaucracy in order to avoid the necessity of analyzing what place the new society occupies in the historic rise of humanity. Wishing to force us not to distinguish between a society which is absolutely reactionary, since it fetters and even destroys the productive forces, and a society which is relatively progressive, since it has assured a great upsurge in economy, Craipeau wants to impose upon us the policy of reactionary "neutrality." Yes, Comrade Craipeau, reactionary!

## But Is the Bureaucracy a Class?

One sees from the preceding that we could very well dispense with again analyzing this theoretical question, that is to say, the question preoccupying Craipeau, which in itself is far from being decisive for our policy in time of war. But the problem of the bureaucracy's social character is, despite everything, very important from a more general viewpoint and we do not see any reason to make the slightest concession to Craipeau on this level. Our critic changes his arguments without putting himself to any inconvenience. This time he draws his smashing argument from a statement in *The Revolution Betrayed* to the effect that "all the means of production belong to the state, and the state belongs, *in some respect,* to the bureaucracy" (my emphasis). Craipeau is jubilant. If the means of production belong to the state, and the state to the bureaucracy, the latter becomes the collective proprietor of the means of production and by that alone, the possessing and exploiting class. The remainder of Craipeau's argumentation is almost purely literary in character. He tells us once again, with the air of polemicizing against me, that the Thermidorean bureaucracy is evil, rapacious, reactionary, blood-thirsty, etc.[31] A real revelation! However, we never said that the Stalinist bureaucracy was virtuous! We have only denied it the quality of class in the Marxist sense, that is to say, with regard to ownership of the means of production. But there is Craipeau forcing me to disown myself, since I recognized that the bureaucracy treats the state as its own property. "And that's the key to the enigma!"

By this oversimplified argument Craipeau shows a deplorable lack of dialectic sense. I have never stated that the Soviet bureaucracy was equal to the bureaucracy of the absolute monarchy or to that of liberal capitalism. Nationalized economy creates for the bureaucracy an entirely new situation and opens up new possibilities—of progress as well as of degeneration. We more or less knew this even before the revolution. The analogy between the Soviet bureaucracy and that of the fascist state is much greater, above all from the viewpoint that interests us. The fascist bureaucracy likewise treats the state as its property. It imposes severe restrictions upon private capital and often provokes convulsions within it. We can say, by way of a logical argument: if the fascist bureaucracy succeeded in more and more imposing its discipline and its restrictions on the capitalists without effective resistance on the part of the latter, this bureaucracy could gradually transform itself into a new ruling "class" absolutely analogous to the Soviet bureaucracy. But the fascist state belongs to the bureaucracy only "in some respect" (see quotation above).

Those are three little words Craipeau deliberately ignores. But they have their importance. They are even decisive. They are an integral part of the dialectical law of the transformation of quantity into quality. If Hitler[32] tries to appropriate the state, and by that means, appropriate private property completely and not only "in some respect," he will bump up against the violent opposition of the capitalists; this would open up great revolutionary possibilities for the workers. There are, however, ultralefts who apply to the fascist bureaucracy the reasoning that Craipeau applies to the Soviet bureaucracy and who place an equal sign between the fascist and Stalinist regimes (some German Spartacists, Hugo Urbahns, certain Anarchists, etc.).[33] We have said of them what we say of Craipeau: their error is in believing that the foundations of society can be changed without revolution or counterrevolution; they unwind the film of reformism in reverse.

But it is here that Craipeau, still jubilant, quotes another statement from *The Revolution Betrayed* regarding the Soviet bureaucracy: "If these relations should be stabilized, legalized, become the norms, without any resistance or against the resistance of the workers, they would end up in the complete liquidation of the conquests of the proletarian revolution." And Craipeau concludes: "Thus Comrade Trotsky envisages the possibility (in the future) of a passage without military intervention (?) from the workers' state to the capitalist state. In 1933, that used to be called unrolling the film of reformism in reverse." That is called the same thing in 1937. What for me is a purely logical argument, Craipeau considers a historical prognosis. Without a victorious civil war the bureaucracy cannot give birth to a new ruling class. That was and that remains my thought.

Besides, what is now happening in the USSR is only a preventive civil war, opened up by the bureaucracy. And nevertheless, it has not yet touched the economic foundations of the state created by the revolution which, despite all the deformation and distortion, assure an unprecedented development of the productive forces.

Nobody has ever denied the possibility—especially in case of prolonged world decay—of the restoration of a new possessing class springing from the bureaucracy. The present social position of the bureaucracy which by means of the state holds the productive forces in its hands "in some respect" is an extremely important point of departure for this process of transformation. It is, however, a question of a historic possibility and not of an already accomplished fact.

## Is a Class the Product of Economic or Political Causes?

In *The Revolution Betrayed* I attempted to give a definition of the present Soviet regime. This definition comprises nine paragraphs. It is not very elegant, I'll admit, this series of descriptive and cautious formulas. But it attempts to be honest with regard to reality. That's always an advantage. Craipeau doesn't even mention this definition. He doesn't oppose another one to it. He doesn't say if the new exploitive society is superior or inferior to the old one, and he doesn't ask himself if this new society is an inevitable stage between capitalism and socialism or if it is merely a historic "accident." However, from the point of view of our general historical perspective, as it is formulated in the *Communist Manifesto* of Marx and Engels, the sociological definition of the bureaucracy assumes capital importance.

The bourgeoisie came into the world as an element born of the new form of production; it remained a historic necessity as long as the new form of production had not exhausted its possibilities. The same assertion can be made with regard to all previous social classes: slave-owners, feudal lords, medieval master-artisans. In their time they were all the representatives and leaders of a system of production which had its place in the advance of humanity. How, then, does Craipeau appraise the historical place of the "bureaucracy-class"? He doesn't say anything on this decisive question. Nevertheless, we have repeated many times, with the aid of Craipeau himself, that the degeneration of the Soviet state is the product of the retardation in the world revolution, that is to say, the result of political and "conjunctural" causes, so to speak. Can one speak of a new . . . "conjunctural" class? I really doubt that. If Craipeau will consent to verify his rather hasty conception from the point of view of the historic succession of social regimes, he will surely recognize himself that to give the bureaucracy the name of a possessing class is not only an abuse of terminology, but moreover a great political danger which can lead to the complete derailment of our historic perspective. Does Craipeau see sufficient reasons to revise the Marxist conception on this capital point? As for myself, I do not see any. That is why I refuse to follow Craipeau.

However, we can and must say that the Soviet bureaucracy has all the vices of a possessing class without having any of its "virtues" (organic stability, certain moral norms, etc.). Experience has taught us that the workers' state is still a state, that is, a product of the barbaric past; that it is doubly barbaric in a backward and isolated country; that under unfavorable conditions it can degenerate to the point of becoming unrecognizable; that it may require a supplementary revolution in order to be regenerated! But the workers' state nonetheless remains an inevitable stage on our road. This stage cannot be overcome except by the permanent revolution of the international proletariat.

## And Where Is the Dialectic?

I cannot follow the entire argumentation of Comrade Craipeau point by point; for that it is really necessary to recapitulate the entire Marxist conception. The trouble is that Craipeau does not analyze the facts as they are, but rather collects logical arguments in favor of a preconceived thesis. This method is in its essence anti-dialectic and therefore anti-Marxist. I will give some samples of this.

a) "The Russian proletariat lost all hope of political power many years ago. . . ." Craipeau takes care not to say exactly *just when*. He merely wants to create the impression that our tendency has nurtured illusions for "many years." He forgets to say that in 1923 the bureaucracy was quite shaken up and that only the German defeat and the discouragement of the Russian proletariat which followed it restabilized its position.[34] During the Chinese revolution (1925-27) the crisis was repeated with similar phases. The first five year plan and the great rumblings in Germany which preceded Hitler's rise (1931-33) once again threatened the bureaucracy's domination.[35] Finally, can we doubt for an instant that if the Spanish revolution had been victorious and if the French workers had been able to develop their May-June offensive of 1936 to its conclusion,[36] the Russian proletariat would have recovered its courage and its combativity and overthrown the Thermidoreans with a minimum of effort? It is only a succession of the most terrible and depressing defeats throughout the entire world that has stabilized Stalin's regime. Craipeau opposes the result, which is quite contradictory in itself, by the way, to the process which produced it and to our policy, which was the reflection of this process.

b) In order to refute the argument that the bureaucracy manipulates the national resources only as a corporation guild, an extremely wobbly one at that, and that the isolated bureaucrats do not have the right to freely dispose of state property, Craipeau replies: "The bourgeois (?) themselves had to wait for a long time before they could transmit to their descendants title to property over the means of production. At the dawn of the guilds, the boss was elected by his peers . . ." etc. But Craipeau leaves aside the trifle that precisely at the "dawn of the guilds" the latter were not yet divided into classes and that the boss was not "bourgeois" in the modern sense of the word. The transformation of quantity into quality does not exist for Craipeau.

c) "Private property is being restored, inheritance reestablished. . . ." But Craipeau avoids saying that it is a matter of property over objects of personal use, and not of the means of production. He likewise forgets to mention the fact that what the bureaucrats, even those in high places, possess in private property is nothing in comparison with the material resources opened up to them by their posts, and that precisely the present "purge," which by one stroke of the pen throws thousands upon thousands of the families of the bureaucrats into the greatest poverty, demonstrates how entirely fragile are the links between the bureaucrats themselves—and all the more so between their families—and state property.

d) The preventive civil war being conducted at present by the ruling clique demonstrates anew that the latter cannot be overthrown except by revolutionary force. But since this new revolution must develop on the basis of state property and planned economy, we have characterized the overthrow of the bureaucracy as a political revolution in contradistinction to the social revolution of 1917. Craipeau finds that this distinction "remains in the domain of casuistry." And why such severity? Because, you see, the recapture of power by the proletariat will also have social consequences. But the bourgeois political revolutions of 1830, 1848, and September 1870 also had social consequences insofar as they seriously changed the division of the national income. But, my dear Craipeau, all is relative in this world, which is not a creation of ultraleft formalists. The social changes provoked by the so-called political revolutions, serious as they were, really appear to be secondary when they are compared with the Great French Revolution, which was the bourgeois *social* revolution par excellence. What Comrade Craipeau lacks is a sense of proportion and the concept of relativity. Our young friend is not at all interested in the law of the transformation of quantity into quality. And yet that is the most important law of the dialectic. It is true that the authorities of the bourgeois academic world find that the dialectic in itself is in the "domain of casuistry."

e) It is not by chance that Craipeau is inspired by the sociology of M. Yvon.[37] The personal observations of Yvon are honest and very important. But it is not by accident that he has found refuge in the little haven of *La Revolution proletarienne*.[38] Yvon is interested in the "economy," in the "workshop"—to use Proudhon's word—and not in "politics," that is, in *generalized economy*. He belongs, in form, to the Proudhonist school; this permitted him precisely to remain neutral during the struggle between the Left Opposition and the bureaucracy; he did not understand that the fate of the "workshop" depended on it.[39] What he has to say about the struggle "for the heritage of Lenin" without distinguishing the social tendencies—even today, in 1937!—clearly reveals his altogether petty-bourgeois conception, entirely contemplative and not at all revolutionary. The notion of class is an abstraction for Yvon which he superimposes over the abstraction "workshop." It is really sad that Craipeau does not find any other source of theoretical inspiration!

## Defense of the USSR and Social Patriotism

This whole sociological scaffolding, unfortunately very fragile, only serves Craipeau, as we have said, to flee from the necessity of distinguishing between the USSR and the imperialist states during the war. The two last paragraphs of his treatise, which deal with this subject, are particularly revealing. Craipeau tells us: "Every European or world war is resolved in our day by imperialist conflicts and only the Stalinist and reformist fools can believe that, for example, the stakes of tomorrow's war will be the fascist regime or the democratic regime." Mark well this magisterial thesis: somewhat simplified, it is true, but nevertheless borrowed, this time, from the Marxist arsenal. Immediately after this, in order to characterize and to flay the USSR as the "champion of the imperialist war," Craipeau tells us: "In the camp of Versailles, its (the USSR's) diplomacy now plays the same animating role as Hitlerite diplomacy in the other camp." Let us admit it. But is this imperialist character of the war determined by the provocative role of fascist diplomacy? Not at all. "Only the Stalinist or reformist fools can believe it." And I hope that we others are not going to apply the same criterion to the Soviet state. One is a defeatist in the imperialist countries—isn't that so?—because one wants to crush the regime of private property and not because one desires to castigate some "aggressor." In the war of Germany against the USSR, it will be a matter of changing the economic base of the latter, insofar as the imperialists are concerned, and not of punishing Stalin and Litvinov.[40] And then? Craipeau has established his fundamental thesis solely in order immediately to take the opposite road. The danger, the real danger, consists, according to him, in that the social patriots of every caliber will take the defense of the USSR as the pretext for a new treachery. "In those conditions any equivocation in our attitude becomes fatal." And in conclusion: "Today it is necessary to choose: either the 'unconditional defense' of the USSR, that is (!!!), the sabotage of the revolution in our country and in the USSR, or defeatism and the revolution."

There we are. It is not a matter at all of the social character of the USSR—what does that matter?—since, according to Craipeau, the defense of a workers' state, even when it is most authentic, implies that the proletariat of the allied imperialist country concludes a sacred union with its own bourgeoisie. "And there is the key to the enigma," as others say. Craipeau believes that in the War—the war with a capital W—the proletariat should not be interested in whether it is a war against Germany, the USSR, or against a Morocco in rebellion, because in all these cases it is necessary to proclaim "defeatism without phrases" as the only possibility of escaping the grip of social patriotism. Once again we see, and with what clarity, that ultraleftism is always an opportunism which is afraid of itself and demands absolute guarantees—that is, nonexistent guarantees—that it will remain true to its flag. This type of intransigent calls to mind that type of timid and weak man who, becoming furious, shouts to his friends: "Hold me back, I'm going to do something terrible!" Give me hermetically sealed theses, put impenetrable blinkers over my eyes, or else . . . I'm going to do something terrible! Really, we have found the key to the enigma!

But in any case does Craipeau, for instance, doubt the

proletarian character of the Soviet state between 1918 and 1923 or at least, in order to make a concession to the ultraleft, between 1918 and 1921? In that period the Soviet state maneuvered on the international arena and sought temporary allies. At the same time, it is precisely in that period that defeatism was made a duty for the workers of all the imperialist countries, the "enemies" as well as the temporary "allies." The duty of defending the USSR has never meant for the revolutionary proletariat giving a vote of confidence to its bourgeoisie. The attitude of the proletariat in the war is the continuation of its attitude in time of peace. The proletariat defends the USSR by its revolutionary policy, never subordinated to the bourgeoisie, but always adapted to the concrete circumstances. That was the teaching of the first four congresses of the Communist International. Does Craipeau demand a retrospective revision of this teaching?

If Blum, instead of proclaiming the perfidious "nonintervention"—always obeying the orders of finance capital—had supported Caballero and Negrin with their capitalist democracy, would Craipeau have renounced his irreducible opposition to the "People's Front" government? Or would he have renounced the duty to distinguish between the two camps fighting in Spain and of adapting his policy to this distinction?

The same holds for the Far East. If Chiang, following England, should tomorrow declare war against Japan, is Craipeau going to participate in a sacred union in order to help China? Or will he, on the contrary, proclaim that for him there is no difference between China and Japan that can possibly influence his policy? Craipeau's alternative: either the defense of the USSR, of Ethiopia, of Republican Spain, of colonial China, etc., by concluding sacred union, or thoroughgoing defeatism, hermetically sealed and cosmic in scope—this fundamentally false alternative will crumple into dust at the first test of events and open the doors wide for the crassest sort of social patriotism.

"Our own theses on the war," Craipeau asks, "are they exempt from any equivocation on this question?"[41] Unfortunately not! Analyzing the necessity of defeatism, they underline that *"in the character of the practical actions there may be considerable differences provoked by the concrete situation in the war."* For instance, the theses point out, in case of a war between the USSR and Japan, we must "not sabotage the sending of arms to the USSR"; consequently we must avoid instigating strikes which sabotage the manufacture of arms, etc. One can hardly believe one's eyes. The events have confirmed our theses on this point remarkably, with an indisputable force, and especially in France. Workers' meetings for months vibrated with the cry: "Airplanes for Spain!" Imagine for a moment that Blum had decided to send some. Imagine that at this particular moment a strike of longshoremen or of sailors was in process. What would Craipeau have done? Would he have opposed the cry: "Airplanes for Spain"? Would he have counseled the workers on strike to make an exception for this cargo of airplanes? But the USSR really did send airplanes (at quite a high price and on the condition of support for the capitalist regime, I know that very well). Should the Bolshevik-Leninists have called upon the Soviet workers to sabotage these shipments? Yes or no? If tomorrow the French workers learn that two boatloads of ammunition are being prepared for shipment from France, one to Japan and the other to China, what will Craipeau's attitude be? I consider him enough of a revolutionist to call upon the workers to boycott the boat destined for Tokyo and to let through the boat for China, without, however, concealing his opinion of Chiang Kai-shek, and without expressing the slightest confidence in Chautemps. That is precisely what our theses say: "In the character of the practical actions there may be considerable differences provoked by the concrete situation in the war." Doubts were still possible, concerning this formula, at the time when the draft theses were published. But today, after the experience of Ethiopia, Spain, and the Sino-Japanese war,[42] anyone who speaks of equivocation in our theses seems to me to be an ultraleft Bourbon who wants to learn nothing and to forget nothing.

Comrade Craipeau, the equivocation is entirely on your side. Your article is full of such equivocations. It is really time to get rid of them. I know very well that even in your errors you are guided by your revolutionary hatred of the oppression of the Thermidorean bureaucracy. But sentiment alone, no matter how legitimate, cannot replace a correct policy based on objective facts. The proletariat has sufficient reasons to overthrow and to chase out the Stalinist bureaucracy, corrupt to the bone. But precisely because of that it cannot directly or indirectly leave this task to Hitler or to the Mikado. Stalin overthrown by the workers—that's a great step forward toward socialism. Stalin crushed by the imperialists—that's the counterrevolution triumphant. That is the precise sense of our defense of the USSR. On a world scale, analogous, from this point of view, to that of our defense of democracy on a national scale!

# AN 'ATTEMPT' ON STALIN'S LIFE[43]

## November 4, 1937

The new Moscow statement about the attempts on Stalin's life, this time in Abkhasia, Caucasus, represents a police fabrication of the same quality as all the preceding ones. The comment of the papers that it is the "first known attempt" on Stalin is false. The trial of Zinoviev-Kamenev and the trial of Pyatakov-Radek[44] unveiled a picture of a series of analogous "attempts" on Stalin's life. Berman-Yurin and Fritz David were to have assassinated him at the Comintern Congress.[45] But it happened that there were "too many people" at the congress, whereas the terrible terrorists hoped to be alone with the victim. Then he was to have been assassinated on a May Day demonstration but there again was failure—the terrorist was too far away from his victim. Alleged terrorist groups with alleged bombs were allegedly found in a pedagogic institute in Gorky, where the defendant Olberg prepared a lot of bombs against Stalin.[46] But all these bombs turned out to be inefficient; at any rate, nobody heard their explosion. The Caucasian terrorist revealed the same lack of efficiency. In the first case, when Stalin was on the water in a boat, the terrorist was too far away. In the second case, when he was on earth, the terrorist came too late. All in all this would have the appearance of a vaudeville show were it not for the bloody denouement.

The chief organizer of the conspiracy in Abkhasia was allegedly Nestor Lakoba, the head of the beautiful little subtropical republic on the coast of the Black Sea. I knew Lakoba very well. He was a little man, a genuine hero of the civil war, very taciturn because almost totally deaf. Every one of the higher dignitaries, beginning with Stalin, spent some weeks every year in Sukhum, the capital of Abkhasia, as a guest of Nestor Lakoba. His brother, Mikhail Lakoba, was the chief of the Abkhasia police. The personal authority of the taciturn Nestor was very high. Had he had a plan to assassinate Stalin or other leaders, he could have accomplished this purpose without any difficulty with a dagger or by putting poison in the food. All the possibilities were open to him. But, according to the GPU, he chose the most incredible and inefficient one.

However, Nestor was not to be found amidst the defendants: he was shot before, without any trial. The reason is clear. This little man with an iron will refused, as did many others, to confess to crimes he never committed. The trial of his younger brother Mikhail and all the others was arranged post factum in order to justify "juridically" the assassination of Nestor.

The statement, naturally, says that I personally created an "anti-Soviet organization" in Abkhasia in 1923. If you remember that in 1923 I was a member of the Politburo, the chief of the army and navy, and a member of the Soviet Executive Committee, you will need to admit that it was a strange enterprise for me: to build an illegal "anti-Soviet organization." But anachronisms are inevitable parts of all frame-ups.

In a more general political plan, the extermination of the leading group of the Abkhasian Republic is a part of the bloody crusade against all the "nationalist" heads of all the Soviet republics. The bureaucratic centralization which stifles the life of the Russian central republic became totally incompatible with any kind of national autonomy of the scores of big and little peripheral republics. The danger is that they can, through the new elections, give political expressions to their discontent. That is why on the eve of the elections all these republics, without exception, were decapitated. But the ruling clique, which forced everybody to confess, cannot itself confess that the real reason for the purge is the fight for its self-preservation. Terrible crimes must be imputed to the victims. Thus the world learns with astonishment that the governments of the twenty-five republics planned to assassinate the "beloved" Moscow leaders and sell their own fatherland to foreign countries. Whoever can believe such tales, let him believe them.

# AMERICA'S SIXTY FAMILIES[47]

## November 8, 1937

My Dear Farrell:

I received your letter and a bit later the book of Lundberg's. Heartiest thanks for both. As yet I have only partially read the book, but have covered enough in order to say that it is a remarkable work in every respect: serious, honest, and courageous. The fact that the author is not a Marxist but comes from the bourgeois literary milieu makes the book doubly and triply precious for every Marxist. The question as to whether social antagonisms are sharpening or attenuating played a great role in socialist literature for the past decades. The reformists attacked the "impoverishment theory" of Marx as totally outdated. Now Lundberg shows that this theory is absolutely correct in relation to the richest country of our day. The political mechanics of reformism is *democracy*. Lundberg shows that it is. The conclusions of his descriptions and analyses coincide totally with the assertions of the *Communist Manifesto* (ninety years old!) and with the most important decisions of the first four congresses of the Communist International. . . . If class antagonisms are sharpening, if democracy is only a camouflage for the dictatorship of sixty families, then the revolutionary perspective cannot be avoided. I do not find anything about this by Lundberg. He abstains from political conclusions. That is his right as an author. But in connection with the economic crisis, Lundberg speaks of the probable catastrophe of capitalist society. This question of *catastrophe* or *gradual evolution* was a subject for discussion between reformists and revolutionary Marxists beginning from 1897! I am not sure that Lundberg knows the respective literature, but no matter; he gives his own answer and it is correct.

I believe that only [one] political tendency is now capable of appreciating Lundberg's book—its real value—and it is our tendency. And if Lundberg should search for political conclusions he will find the road toward the Fourth International.

I always read your articles in the *Socialist Call* with great pleasure.[48] [Will they] now after the split permit you to attack the Stalinists with such vigor? In any case they will not permit you to take up the defense of the "Trotskyites."

I will wait now with great interest for the first issue of the *Partisan Review*.[49] Are you connected with this magazine?

Natalia and I send our best friendly greetings to Hortense and yourself.

Yours,
Leon Trotsky

# LETTER ON AMERICAN PROBLEMS[50]

## November 14, 1937

Dear Comrade Cannon:

I received your letter of November 10.

If you need to write me an entirely personal letter you can send it in the same manner as the last one. You can rest assured that the letter will reach my hands directly.

Concerning the question of a third comrade, I leave the matter totally to the National Committee.[51] The "advantages" of Milton are that he is not married and knows Spanish a bit.[52] I don't know how these things stand with Comrade Stone in either respect. On the other hand, the characteristics you give Stone are very attractive. I think also that Milton, thanks to his activity in Spain, is for the next period more important for political work in the States. Personally I do not know either of them. The National Committee knows both. You can judge better than we. That is, I repeat, why we leave the matter totally to your decision.

If you decide upon Stone, some inconvenience would arise from the fact that I have already addressed Milton. But I wrote him that the decision rests in the hands of the National Committee, and you can give the very important argument that the Spanish question in the next period will play a very important role in your activity and that you need Milton in the States.

Your personal letter I shall answer with the help of Joe[53] and with his "solemn oath" not to communicate to any third person the contents of my letters. I understand very well that some indiscretion, even without the slightest bad will, can in some cases produce supplementary difficulties for the National Committee. I am naturally ready to do everything in my power to avoid such occurrences. You understand, of course, from your side that the presence or the absence of one or the other comrade in our home cannot have the slightest influence on my approach to the questions which interest us.

I cannot conceal from you a certain astonishment that a long

49

series of my letters and other communications to you remain unanswered. What is the reason? Your apprehension over some indiscretion? If so, I hope this reason is now eliminated by the new arrangement concerning our correspondence. You understand it would be very difficult for me to give my opinion on some question which arose unexpectedly for me. I should be kept conversant with all the happenings in the party.

You didn't answer our suggestions concerning the conference. Here the preparations for the Latin American conference go on energetically.[54] The most important theses are elaborated and now are in translation. We will send the first of them to you during the next week. I agree totally with Diego Rivera[55] that New York and California should pay incomparably more attention to Latin America than heretofore. The working class of the States is called upon because of its situation to play the role of a guide for the semicolonial peoples of Latin America. It is very important to have articles in the paper from time to time about Latin America. These could be usefully translated here into the Spanish language. I will write about this very important question more amply in the near future.

I hear from some comrades that the mood in your ranks is a bit "pessimistic" and only a minority is really active. Possibly it is only a transitional phenomenon corresponding to the passage from one form of activity to another. But it is also possible that a number of good comrades who have been with us almost ten years are a bit tired at the too slow development of the organization. I have observed analogous phenomena many times. In this case it is necessary to introduce fresh blood into all the leading bodies of the party and generally select systematically young elements for the party cadres.

I am very interested in the position of comrades on the USSR matter. The sentimental reaction against the indescribable crimes of the bureaucracy in the USSR, in Spain, and elsewhere and its counterrevolutionary role in the international working class movement generally must inevitably influence the sociological and psychological appreciation of the USSR. I believe we should remain firm on this question but also be pedagogically tolerant to the inevitable exaggerations in our own ranks. We have the possibility of wielding a club against the Oehlerites[56] and other people of the same kind outside the party. I am ready to write an article on this question for the *Socialist Appeal* if you send me the necessary Oehlerite, Anarchist, and similar material.

Hansen [Trotsky]

# LETTER TO COMRADE WASSERMAN[57]

## November 14, 1937

Dear Comrade Wasserman:

1. It is not necessary for me to tell you how highly I appreciate the activity of Pioneer Publishers.[58] It would not be an exaggeration to say that it is now the only publishing house of revolutionary Marxist literature in the entire world. Pioneer Publishers has international importance. The enterprise must be developed at any cost if we want to educate new Marxist cadres and build up a new International. No sacrifices are too great in supporting and developing Pioneer Publishers.

2. I understand very well your insistence upon the Kronstadt matter,[59] but if I come back to this question for the second time it should be done in an absolutely exhaustive manner. I do not have at the moment either the necessary materials or the time for such an article. I advised my son to prepare a pamphlet on the question including all the necessary facts, documents, and so on. On the basis of this material I would willingly write an article for the *Socialist Appeal* or for the *New International.*

My best greetings,
L. Trotsky

# COMING TRIALS TO REVEAL
# SECRET PLANS OF GPU[60]

## November 16, 1937

In France and in Switzerland sensational trials are imminent over the criminal activities of the GPU upon the world arena. The inquiry is apparently being conducted with energy. A series of facts have already been conclusively established. One of the new facts is the painstaking preparation of an attempt upon the life of Leon Sedov, my son living in Paris.[61] The Swiss woman, Renata Steiner, has made a precise deposition on this affair, totally confirmed by the evidence. As an agent of the GPU Renata Steiner participated, as is known, in the assassination of Ignace Reiss near Lausanne. But for more than a year before this assassination, Renata Steiner and a Russian White Guard accomplice, Smirensky, were occupied in shadowing Leon Sedov: they prepared the theft of my archives and attempted the kidnaping of Sedov himself. Smirensky and Renata Steiner rented an apartment next door to that of Sedov (Rue Lacratelle 28) where the respective balconies were only three feet apart from each other.

On November 7 of last year, Smirensky, together with other agents who will be named in time, stole 187 pounds of my archives stored by Sedov with the Institute of Social History.[62] The crime remained unsolved in spite of the fact that the French police did not have the slightest doubt that all threads led to Moscow.

In January of this year, the GPU terrorists tried to arrange a trap for Leon Sedov at Mulhouse (Muehlhausen) analogous to the one they arranged for Ignace Reiss in Lausanne. Under cover of the name of my Swiss attorney, who is occupied with a suit over slanders made by the Comintern, the conspirators repeatedly urged Leon Sedov by telegraph and telephone to come to

Mulhouse for a conference. Only accidental circumstances prevented Sedov from going to Mulhouse, where he was awaited at the railroad station by Renata Steiner and Smirensky. The confession of Steiner shows from what danger Sedov was saved in January. It was just at the moment that Moscow prepared the second great trial (Pyatakov-Radek).

The shadowing of Sedov went on uninterruptedly until last August when Steiner, Smirensky, and others received an unexpected order from above to find and kill Ignace Reiss. The Kremlin considered this assassination as the most urgent, in view of the threatening disclosures from the former trusted agent. The new enterprise was, as is known, successful: Reiss was assassinated September 4. But the subsequent arrest of Steiner led to the uncovering of the terrorist GPU organization in France.

It is beyond doubt that the judicial authorities will find the solution to a whole series of hitherto unsolved crimes (the assassination of the Russian economist Navashin in the Bois de Boulogne in Paris; the kidnaping of General Miller, and so on).[63] These crimes were committed by the same organization that stole my archives, assassinated Reiss, and attempted to trap Leon Sedov. It is in connection with all these crimes that I recommended by cable to the French authorities that they submit to interrogation, at least as a witness, Jacques Duclos, member of the Politburo of the French Communist Party, vice-president of the Chamber of Deputies, for many years an agent of the GPU.[64]

Permit me to add that such "Friends of the USSR," who are in reality friends of the GPU, should prepare themselves for very disagreeable revelations in the coming months.

# HOW TO STRUGGLE AGAINST WAR[65]

## November 17, 1937

Dear Friends:

You suggest that I take part in your campaign against war. Allow me to confine myself to a few words.

In order to fight against war, it is necessary to understand clearly the factors that cause war. It is necessary to know the laws of development of contemporary, i.e., imperialist society. The Marxist analysis of war and of the ways of fighting against it were expressed in the programmatic pamphlet of the International Secretariat,[66] *War and the Fourth International*. This pamphlet should be made the object of careful and serious study in youth circles.

The struggle against war is inseparable from the class struggle of the proletariat. Irreconcilable class consciousness is the first condition for a successful struggle against war. The worst wreckers of class consciousness and the worst saboteurs of the revolutionary struggle at the present time are the so-called "Communists." These people are "fighting" against war only in Germany, Italy, and Japan, i.e., in those countries where they are insignificant; whereas in the so-called democratic countries, i.e., where the bourgeoisie allows them to exist undisturbed, the "Communists" are at the present time the foremost agitators in favor of imperialist war.

These gentlemen hold pacifist conferences, banquets, and parades to cover up their treacherous work. Together with parliamentary careerists, priests of various churches, and bored liberal ladies, they from time to time offer up prayers to heaven for peace. This pacifism of the drawing-room and church bazaar can evoke nothing but disgust in every thoughtful member of the working class. That is why the struggle against war must begin and end with the unmasking of the treacherous role of the

Comintern, which has finally become an agent of the imperialist bourgeoisie. The Second International is, of course, no better. But it is more compromised and therefore less dangerous. It now leaves the most cynical and shameful work to the Comintern, which in Spain is already emerging as the direct and open butcher of revolution.

To fight against war means above all to build the new International, to consolidate its ranks, and to temper its cadre.

I warmly wish you success in this work.

# BERTRAM WOLFE
# ON THE MOSCOW TRIALS[67]

## November 25, 1937

Bertram Wolfe writes the following in regard to the stenographic transcript of the hearings in Coyoacan (the *New Republic*, November 24, 1937): "The writer owns that his previous position was to give credence rather to Stalin than to Trotsky, but a rereading of the Moscow confessions together with the present work (*The Case of Leon Trotsky*), or rather its closing speech, carried literally overwhelming conviction that Trotsky could not have done the things charged against him in the Zinoviev-Kamenev and Radek-Pyatakov trials."

Such an acknowledgment attests that Bertram Wolfe is somewhat conscientious. If Wolfe were a bourgeois jurist or a mere psychologist, one could be satisfied with this acknowledgment. But Wolfe considers himself a Marxist and is, to my knowledge, a member of a political group. A Marxist should first of all have asked himself how, during a number of years, he could have been so deeply mistaken about questions of the highest importance, since it is not at all a question of Stalin's personal accusations against Trotsky but of the struggle between two historical tendencies—bureaucratic and proletarian. The Moscow trials were a surprise only to bourgeois and petty-bourgeois philistines. In reality, the trials were being prepared openly, before the eyes of the whole world, during a period of no less than thirteen years. The documents collected by me in my book *The Stalin School of Falsification* bear partial witness to that. Neither can one be silent about the fact that the group of Brandler-Lovestone,[68] to which Bertram Wolfe belongs, has been reared in this school of falsification, and Lovestone himself, by no means a model of conscientiousness, has done his bit in the preparation of the Moscow trials.

This judicial frame-up, unprecedented in human history, is a result of the historically unprecedented reaction against the first proletarian revolution. Falsification—philosophical, historical, biographical, political, literary, judicial—is the inevitable ideological superstructure over the material foundation of the usurpation of state power and the exploitation of the conquest of the revolution by the new aristocracy. A Marxist who openly declares that the Moscow trials were an enigma to him until the appearance of the report of the Coyoacan hearing thereby admits that he has not understood the most important events and processes of contemporary history.

We would not begin to upbraid Wolfe a posteriori for this lack of understanding had he drawn the necessary *political* conclusions from his tardy discovery, i.e., had he reexamined the position he has taken during the past thirteen years. But Bertram Wolfe behaves in exactly the opposite manner. Having come to the conclusion that the Moscow accusations are a frame-up and that they thus confirm the prognosis of the Left Opposition about the degeneration and the decay of the Thermidorean bureaucracy, Wolfe demands that . . . *we* reexamine our outlook. Unbelievable as this sounds, that is, nevertheless, what he demands. The Moscow trials and the subsequent development placed me—don't you see?—before a "new dilemma." I pointed out to the commission and to the press that Stalin consciously brought several dozen former revolutionists to moral prostration and physical ruin with but one aim: that with their corpses he might deal a blow to the Fourth International and to me in particular. "Now it is becoming clear that he (Trotsky) has been made into a devil largely to make a case against *others*—leaders of a new opposition which has grown up against Stalin and his methods among his closest supporters."

This is completely correct. Long before now we were aware of this "dialectic" of the frame-up. Stalin had to sacrifice dozens of his former comrades in order to create a fantastic figure of the counterrevolutionary arch-conspirator Trotsky. And then he used this figure in order to destroy all his adversaries. There were more of them than Stalin had thought. Their number is growing. It is exactly the coldly prepared bloody frame-up of innocent people, the builders of the Bolshevik Party, which cannot help causing the ranks of the bureaucracy itself to shudder.

There is nothing unexpected in all this. From 1931 we, the "Left Opposition," more than once foretold that the Thermidorean bureaucracy would come into deeper and deeper conflict with the development of the country and that this contradiction would decompose its own ranks. Organized control of the masses, like the democratic discipline of the party, has long since ceased to exist. Only the completion of the Bonapartist regime can overcome the centrifugal forces within the bureaucracy. The new constitution prepares this completion. *After the elections there will follow, in one form or another, the "coronation" of Stalin.* Philistines will reduce all this to love of personal power. In reality, the Thermidorean regime has no perspective other than that of a Bonapartist coronation. But it is exactly now, when our prognosis receives an irrefutable confirmation, that Bertram Wolfe makes his completely unexpected demand—that we reexamine our views.

"What then happens," he writes, "to Trotsky's central theory that the entire military and police and party and state machinery were so degenerate that no opposition (?) could any more arise within the party, and that a new revolution was necessary as the only road to renovation?"

We have never said that "no opposition" could ever arise within the "party." On the contrary, we have affirmed that the so-called "party," i.e., the political organization of the bureaucracy, will, due to the centrifugal tendencies, further and further decompose. The right—not Rykov-Bukharin, but the actual restorationist tendencies—are immeasurably stronger in it than are the left. Under the label of "Trotskyite," Stalin is now shooting not only the remnants of the revolutionary generation but also the extremely impatient partisans of the bourgeois regime. The traditions of the October Revolution undoubtedly live in the masses. The hostility to the bureaucracy is growing. But the workers and peasants, even those who formally belong to the so-called party, have no channels and levers through which they can influence the politics of the country. The present trials, arrests, exiles, judicial and extrajudicial shootings, represent a form of *preventive civil war* which the bureaucracy as a whole leads against the toiling masses and which the more consistent Bonapartist wing of the bureaucracy leads against the other less firm or less reliable elements. If the ruling clique manifestly approaches completed Bonapartism, then it is clear that every serious Left Oppositionist movement cannot help taking the road of a new revolution. But Wolfe concludes that inasmuch as Stalin is shooting many people, that shows the possibility . . . of a *peaceful* reorganization of the regime.

Bertram Wolfe saw a little piece of truth but, as has been said already, he saw it from a formally judicial and individually psychological point of view. That shows that he belongs to that generation of Marxists which is deft in organizational maneuvers and chess moves but completely unlearned in a Marxist approach to great problems. We value the sincerity of Wolfe's acknowledgment, and we say this without the least irony. But it is exactly because of this that we advise Wolfe to throw off the petty considerations of clannishness, to approach the problem without that cynicism which characterizes Brandler-Lovestone, to study anew the problem of the Soviet revolution, and to reexamine his position from beginning to end. Otherwise Wolfe will, with a delay of some years, have to make new discoveries. And time, meanwhile, does not wait. The problems are big. Important work is to be done.

# NOT A WORKERS'
# AND NOT A BOURGEOIS STATE?[69]

## November 25, 1937

### Political Form and Social Content

Comrades Burnham and Carter [70] have placed a fresh question mark over the class character of the Soviet state. The answer which they give is, in my opinion, completely erroneous. But inasmuch as these comrades do not attempt, as do some ultraleftists, to substitute shrieking for scientific analysis, we can and should seriously discuss with B. and C. this exceptionally important question.

B. and C. do not forget that the main difference between the USSR and the contemporary bourgeois state finds its expression in the powerful development of the productive forces as a result of a change in the form of ownership. They further admit that "the economic structure as established by the October Revolution remains basically unchanged." They deduce from this that it is the duty of the Soviet and world proletariat to defend the USSR from imperialist attacks. In this there is complete agreement between B. and C. and us. But no matter how great the degree of our agreement, it by no means covers the whole issue. Though B. and C. do not solidarize themselves with the ultralefts, they nevertheless consider that the USSR has stopped being a workers' state "in the traditional (?) sense given to this term by Marxism." But since the "economic structure . . . still remains basically unchanged," the USSR has not become a bourgeois state. B. and C. at the same time deny—and for this we can only congratulate them—that the bureaucracy is an independent class. The result of these inconsistent assertions is the conclusion, the very one the Stalinists draw, that the Soviet state, in general, is not an organization of class domination. What, then, is it?

Thus we have a new attempt at revising the class theory of the state. We are not, it goes without saying, fetishists; should new historical facts demand a revision of the theory, we would not stop at doing so. But the lamentable experience of the old revisionists should in any case imbue us with a salutary caution. We should, ten times over, weigh in our minds the old theory and the new facts before we attempt to formulate a new doctrine.

B. and C. themselves remark in passing that in its dependence on objective and subjective conditions the rule of the proletariat "is able to express itself in a number of different governmental forms." For clarity we will add: either through an open struggle of different parties within the soviets, or through the monopoly of one party, or even through a factual concentration of power in the hands of a single person. Of course personal dictatorship is a symptom of the greatest danger to the regime. But at the same time, it is, under certain conditions, the only means by which to save that regime. The class nature of the state is, consequently, determined not by its political forms but by its social content; i.e., by the character of the forms of property and productive relations which the given state guards and defends.

In principle B. and C. do not deny this. If they nevertheless refuse to see in the USSR a workers' state, it is due to two reasons, one of which is economic and the other political in character. "During the past year," they write, "the bureaucracy has definitively entered the road of destruction of the planned and nationalized economy." (Has only "entered the road"?) Further we read that the course of development "brings the bureaucracy into ever-increasing and deepening conflict with the needs and interests of the nationalized economy." (Only "brings it"?) The contradiction between the bureaucracy and the economy was observed before this, but for the past year "the actions of the bureaucracy are actively sabotaging the plan and disintegrating the state monopoly." (Only "disintegrating"? Hence, not yet disintegrated?)

As stated above, the second contention has a political character. "The concept of the dictatorship of the proletariat is not primarily an economic but predominantly a political category. . . . All forms, organs, and institutions of the class rule of the proletariat are now destroyed, which is to say that the class rule of the proletariat is destroyed." After hearing about the "different forms" of the proletarian regime, this second contention, taken by itself, appears unexpected. Of course, the dictatorship of the proletariat is not only "predominantly" but

wholly and fully a "political category." However, this very
politics is only concentrated economics. The domination of the
Social Democracy in the state and in the soviets (Germany 1918-
19) had nothing in common with the dictatorship of the
proletariat inasmuch as it left bourgeois property inviolable. But
the regime which guards the expropriated and nationalized
property from the imperialists is, independent of political forms,
the dictatorship of the proletariat.

B. and C. "in general," as it were, admit this. They therefore
have recourse to combining the economic with the political
contention. The bureaucracy, they say, has not only definitively
deprived the proletariat of political power, but has driven the
economy into a blind alley. If in the previous period the
bureaucracy with all its reactionary features played a compara-
tively progressive role, it has now definitively become a
reactionary factor. In this reasoning there is a healthy kernel,
which is in complete conformity with all former evaluations and
prognoses of the Fourth International. We have more than once
spoken of the fact that "enlightened absolutism" has played a
progressive role in the development of the bourgeoisie only
afterward to become a brake upon this development; the conflict
resolved itself, as is known, in revolution. In laying the
groundwork for socialist economy, we wrote, "enlightened
absolutism" can play a progressive role only during an incomparably shorter period. This prognosis is clearly confirmed before
our very eyes. Deceived by its own successes, the bureaucracy
expected to attain ever bigger coefficients of economic growth.
Meanwhile it ran up against an acute crisis in the economy,
which became one of the sources of its present panic and its mad
repressions. Does this then mean that the development of
productive forces in the USSR has already stopped? We would not
venture to make such an assertion. The creative possibilities of
nationalized economy are so great that the productive forces, in
spite of the bureaucratic brake upon them, can develop for a
period of years although at a considerably more moderate rate
than heretofore. Along these lines it is scarcely possible at the
moment to make an exact forecast. In any case, the *political*
crisis which is rending the bureaucracy asunder is considerably
more dangerous for it today than the perspective of a stoppage in
the development of the productive forces. For the sake of
simplifying the question, however, let us grant that the bureaucracy has already become an absolute brake upon the economic
development. But does this fact in itself mean that the class
nature of the USSR has changed or that the USSR is devoid of

any kind of class nature? Here, it seems to me, is the chief mistake of our comrades.

Up until the First World War bourgeois society developed its productive forces. Only during the past quarter of a century has the bourgeoisie become an absolute brake upon economic development. Does this mean that bourgeois society has ceased being bourgeois? No, it means only that it has become a *decaying* bourgeois society. In a number of countries, the preservation of bourgeois property is possible only through the establishment of a fascist regime. In other words, the bourgeoisie is devoid of all forms and means of its own direct political domination, and must use an intermediary. Does this mean then that the state has stopped being bourgeois? To the extent that fascism with its barbaric methods defends private property in the means of production, to that extent the state remains bourgeois under the fascist rule.

We do not at all intend to give our analogy an all-inclusive meaning. Nevertheless, it demonstrates that the concentration of power in the hands of the bureaucracy and even the retardation of the development of the productive forces, by themselves, still do not change the class nature of society and its state. Only the intrusion of a revolutionary or a counterrevolutionary force in property relations can change the class nature of the state.*

But does not history really know of cases of class conflict between the economy and the state? It does! After the "third estate" seized power, society for a period of several years still remained feudal. In the first months of Soviet rule the proletariat reigned on the basis of a bourgeois economy. In the field of agriculture the dictatorship of the proletariat operated for a number of years on the basis of a petty-bourgeois economy (to a considerable degree it does so even now). Should a bourgeois counterrevolution succeed in the USSR, the new government for a lengthy period would have to base itself upon the nationalized economy. But what does such a type of temporary conflict between the economy and the state mean? It means a *revolution*

---

*The London *New Leader,* under the editorship of Fenner Brockway, writes in an editorial, dated November 12 of this year: "The Independent Labour Party does not accept the Trotskyist view that the economic foundations of socialism in Soviet Russia have been destroyed."[71] What can one say about these people? They do not understand the thoughts of others because they do not have any of their own. They can only sow confusion in the minds of the workers.—L.T.

or a *counterrevolution*. The victory of one class over another signifies that it will reconstruct the economy in the interests of the victors. But such a dichotomous condition, which is a necessary stage in every social overturn, has nothing in common with the theory of a classless state which in the absence of a real boss is being exploited by a clerk, i.e., by the bureaucracy.

## Norm and Fact

It is the substitution of a subjective "normative" method in place of an objective, dialectical approach to the question which renders it difficult for many comrades to arrive at a correct sociological appraisal of the USSR. Not without reason do Burnham and Carter say that the Soviet Union cannot be considered a workers' state "in the traditional sense given to this term by Marxism." This simply means that the USSR does not correspond to the norms of a workers' state as set forth in our program. On this score there can be no disagreement. Our program has counted upon a progressive development of the workers' state and by that token upon its gradual withering away. But history, which does not always act "according to a program," has confronted us with the process of a degenerating workers' state.

But does this mean that a workers' state, coming into conflict with the demands of our program, has ceased thereby to be a workers' state? A liver poisoned by malaria does not correspond to a normal type of liver. But it does not because of that cease to be a liver. For the understanding of its nature, anatomy and physiology are not sufficient; pathology too is necessary. Of course it is much easier upon seeing the diseased liver to say: "This object is not to my liking," and to turn one's back upon it. But a physician cannot permit himself such a luxury. Depending upon the conditions of the disease itself, and the resulting deformation of the organ, he must have recourse either to therapeutic treatment ("reforms") or to surgery ("revolution"). But to be able to do this he must first of all understand that the deformed organ is a sick liver, and not something else.

But let us take a more familiar analogy; that between a workers' state and a trade union. From the point of view of our program, the trade union should be an organization of class struggle. What then should be our attitude to the American Federation of Labor?[72] At its head stand manifest agents of the bourgeoisie. Upon all essential questions, Messrs. Green, Woll, and Company carry out a political line directly opposed to the interests of the proletariat. We can extend the analogy and say that if until the appearance of the CIO,[73] the AFL accomplished somewhat progressive work, now that the chief content of its activity is embodied in a struggle against the more progressive (or less reactionary) tendencies of the CIO, Green's apparatus has definitely become a reactionary factor. This would be completely correct. But the AFL does not because of this cease to be an organization of the trade unions.

The class character of the state is determined by its relation to the forms of property in the means of production. The character of a workers' organization such as a trade union is determined by its relation to the distribution of national income. The fact that Green and Company defend private property in the means of production characterizes them as bourgeois. Should these gentlemen in addition defend the income of the bourgeoisie from attacks on the part of the workers; should they conduct a struggle against strikes, against the raising of wages, against help to the unemployed; then we would have an organization of scabs, and not a trade union. However, Green and Company, in order not to lose their base, must within certain limits lead the struggle of the workers for an increase—or at least against a diminution—of their share of the national income. This objective symptom is sufficient in all important cases to permit us to draw a line of demarcation between the most reactionary trade union and an organization of scabs. Thus we are duty bound not only to carry on work in the AFL, but to defend it from scabs, the Ku Klux Klan, and the like.

The function of Stalin, like the function of Green, has a dual character. Stalin serves the bureaucracy and thus the world bourgeoisie; but he cannot serve the bureaucracy without defending that social foundation which the bureaucracy exploits in its own interests. To that extent does Stalin defend nationalized property from imperialist attacks and from the too impatient and avaricious layers of the bureaucracy itself. However, he carries through this defense with methods that prepare the general destruction of Soviet society. It is exactly because of this that the Stalinist clique must be overthrown. But it is the revolutionary proletariat who must overthrow it. The proletariat cannot subcontract this work to the imperialists. In spite of Stalin, the proletariat defends the USSR from imperialist attacks.

Historical development has accustomed us to the most varied kind of trade unions: militant, reformist, revolutionary, reactionary, liberal, and Catholic. It is otherwise with a workers' state. Such a phenomenon we see for the first time. That accounts for our inclination to approach the USSR exclusively from the point of view of the *norms* of the revolutionary program. Meanwhile the workers' state is an objective historical *fact* which is being subjected to the influence of different historical forces and can as we see come into full contradiction with "traditional" norms.

Comrades B. and C. are completely correct when they say that Stalin and Company by their politics serve the international bourgeoisie. But this correct thought must be established in the correct conditions of time and place. Hitler also serves the bourgeoisie. However, between the functions of Stalin and Hitler there is a difference. Hitler defends the bourgeois forms of property. Stalin adapts the interests of the bureaucracy to the proletarian forms of property. The same Stalin in Spain, i.e., on the soil of a bourgeois regime, executes the function of Hitler (in their political methods they generally differ little from one another). The juxtaposition of the different social roles of the one and the same Stalin in the USSR and in Spain demonstrates equally well that the bureaucracy is not an independent class but the tool of classes; and that it is impossible to define the social nature of a state by the virtue or villainy of the bureaucracy.

The assertion that the bureaucracy of a workers' state has a bourgeois character must appear not only unintelligible but completely senseless to people stamped with a formal cast of mind. However, chemically pure types of state never existed, and do not exist in general. The semifeudal Prussian monarchy executed the most important tasks of the bourgeoisie, but executed them in its own manner, i.e., in a feudal, not a Jacobin style. In Japan we observe even today an analogous correlation between the bourgeois character of the state and the semifeudal character of the ruling caste. But all this does not hinder us from clearly differentiating between a feudal and a bourgeois society. True, one can raise the objection that the collaboration of feudal and bourgeois forces is immeasurably more easily realized than the collaboration of bourgeois and proletarian forces, inasmuch as the first instance presents a case of two forms of class exploitation. This is completely correct. But a workers' state does not create a new society in one day. Marx wrote that in the first period of a workers' state the *bourgeois* norms of distribution are still preserved. (About this see *The Revolution Betrayed*, the section "Socialism and the State," p. 53.) One has to weigh well and think this thought out to the end. The workers' state itself, as a *state*, is necessary exactly because the bourgeois norms of distribution still remain in force.

This means that even the most revolutionary bureaucracy is to a certain degree a *bourgeois organ* in the workers' state. Of course, the *degree* of this bourgeoisification and the general tendency of development bears decisive significance. If the workers' state loses its bureaucratization and gradually falls away, this means that its development marches along the road of socialism. On the contrary, if the bureaucracy becomes ever more powerful, authoritative, privileged, and conservative, this means that in the workers' state the bourgeois tendencies grow at the expense of the socialist; in other words, that inner contradiction which *to a certain degree* is lodged in the workers' state from the first days of its rise does not diminish, as the "norm" demands, but increases. However, so long as that contradiction has not passed from the sphere of distribution into the sphere of production, and has not blown up nationalized property and planned economy, the state remains a workers' state.

Lenin had already said fifteen years ago: "Our state is a workers' state, but with bureaucratic deformations." In that period bureaucratic deformation represented a direct inheritance of the bourgeois regime and, in that sense, appeared as a mere survival of the past. Under the pressure of unfavorable historical conditions, however, the bureaucratic "survival" received new sources of nourishment and became a tremendous historical factor. It is exactly because of this that we now speak of the *degeneration* of the workers' state. This degeneration, as the present orgy of Bonapartist terror shows, has approached a crucial point. That which was a "bureaucratic deformation" is at the present moment preparing to devour the workers' state, without leaving any remains, and on the ruins of nationalized property to spawn a new propertied class. Such a possibility has drawn extremely near. But all this is only a possibility and we do not intend beforehand to bow before it.

The USSR as a workers' state does not correspond to the "traditional" norm. This does not signify that it is not a workers' state. Neither does this signify that the norm has been found false. The "norm" counted upon the complete victory of the international proletarian revolution. The USSR is only a partial and mutilated expression of a backward and isolated workers' state.

Idealistic, ultimatistic, "purely" normative thinking wishes to construct the world in its own image, and simply turns away from phenomena which are not to its liking. Sectarians, i.e., people who are revolutionary only in their own imagination, guide themselves by empty idealistic norms. They say: "These unions are not to our liking, we will not join them; this workers' state is not to our liking, we will not defend it." Each time they promise to begin history anew. They will construct, don't you see, an ideal workers' state, when God places in their hands an ideal party and ideal unions. But until this happy moment arrives, they will, as much as possible, pout their lips at reality. A very big pout—that is the supreme expression of sectarian "revolutionaryism."

Purely "historical," reformist, Menshevik, passive, conservative thinking busies itself with justifying, as Marx expressed it, today's swinishness by yesterday's swinishness. Representatives of this kind enter into mass organizations and dissolve themselves there. The contemptible "friends" of the USSR adapt themselves to the vileness of the bureaucracy, invoking the "historical" conditions.

In opposition to these two casts of mind, dialectical thinking—Marxist, Bolshevik—takes phenomena in their objective development and at the same time finds in the internal contradictions of this development a basis for the realization of its "norms." It is of course necessary not to forget that we expect the programmatic norms to be realized only if they are the generalized expression of the progressive tendencies of *the objective historical process itself.*

The programmatic definition of a union would sound approximately like this: an organization of workers of a trade or industry with the objective of (1) struggling against capitalism for the amelioration of the conditions of the workers, (2) participating in the revolutionary struggle for the overthrow of the bourgeoisie, (3) participating in the organization of economy on a socialist basis. If we compared this "normative" definition with the actual reality, we should find ourselves constrained to say: there does not exist a single trade union in the world today. But such a counterposing of norm to fact, that is to say, of the *generalized* expression of the development to the *particular* manifestation of this same development—such a formal, ultimatistic, nondialectical counterposing of program to reality is absolutely lifeless and does not open any road for the intervention of the revolutionary party. In the meantime the existing opportunistic unions, under the pressure of capitalist disintegration, *can*—and given correct policies on our part in the unions *must*—approach our programmatic norms and play a progressive historical role. This, of course, presupposes a complete change of leadership. It is necessary that the workers of the United States, England, France, drive out Green, Citrine, Jouhaux and Company.[74] It is necessary that the Soviet workers drive out Stalin and Company. If the proletariat drives out the Soviet bureaucracy *in time*, then it will still find the nationalized means of production and the basic elements of the planned economy after its victory. This means that it will not have to begin from the beginning. That is a tremendous advantage! Only radical dandies, who are used to hopping carelessly from twig to twig, can lightmindedly dismiss such a possibility. The socialist revolution is too tremendous and difficult a problem for one to lightmindedly wave one's hand at its inestimable material achievement and begin from the beginning.

It is very good that Comrades B. and C., in distinction from our French comrade Craipeau and others, do not forget the factor of the productive forces and do not deny defense to the Soviet Union. But this is completely insufficient. And what if the criminal leadership of the bureaucracy should paralyze the growth in the economy? Can it be possible that Comrades B. and C. in such a case will passively allow imperialism to destroy the social bases of the USSR? We are sure this is not the case. However, their non-Marxist definition of the USSR as neither a workers' nor a bourgeois state opens the door for *all kinds* of conclusions. That is why this definition must be categorically rejected.

## Simultaneously a Ruling and an Oppressed Class

"How can our political conscience not resent the fact," say the ultraleftists, "that they want to force us to believe that in the USSR, under Stalin's rule, the proletariat is the 'ruling class' . . . ?!" This assertion phrased in such an abstract manner can actually arouse our "resentment." But the truth is that abstract categories, necessary in the process of analysis, are completely unfit for synthesis, which demands the utmost concreteness. The proletariat of the USSR is the ruling class in a *backward* country where there is still a lack of the most vital necessities of life. The proletariat of the USSR rules in a land consisting of only one-twelfth part of humanity; imperialism rules over the remaining eleven-twelfths. The rule of the proletariat, already maimed by the backwardness and poverty of the country, is doubly and triply deformed under the pressure of world imperialism. The organ of the rule of the proletariat—the state—becomes an organ for pressure from imperialism (diplomacy, army, foreign trade, ideas, and customs). The struggle for domination, considered on a historical scale, is not between the proletariat and the bureaucracy, but between the proletariat and the world bourgeoisie. The bureaucracy is only the transmitting mechanism in this struggle. The struggle is not concluded. In spite of all the efforts on the part of the Moscow clique to demonstrate its conservative reliability (the counterrevolutionary politics of Stalin in Spain!), world imperialism does not trust Stalin, does not spare him the most humiliating flicks and is ready at the first favorable opportunity to overthrow him. Hitler—and therein lies his strength—simply more consistently and frankly expresses the attitude of the world bourgeoisie to the Soviet bureaucracy. For the bourgeoisie—fascist as well as democratic—isolated counterrevolutionary exploits of Stalin do not suffice; it needs a complete counterrevolution in the relations of property and the opening of the Russian market. So long as this is not the case, the bourgeoisie considers the Soviet state hostile to it. And it is right.

The internal regime in the colonial and semicolonial countries has a predominantly bourgeois character. But the pressure of foreign imperialism so alters and distorts the economic and political structure of these countries that the national bourgeoisie (even in the politically independent countries of South America) only partly reaches the height of a ruling class. The pressure of imperialism on backward countries does not, it is true, change their *basic* social character since the oppressor and oppressed represent only different levels of development in one and the same bourgeois society. Nevertheless the difference between England and India, Japan and China, the United States and Mexico is so big that we strictly differentiate between oppressor and oppressed bourgeois countries and we consider it our duty to support the latter against the former. The bourgeoisie of colonial and semicolonial countries is a semiruling, semioppressed class.

The pressure of imperialism on the Soviet Union has as its aim the alteration of the very nature of Soviet society. The struggle—today peaceful, tomorrow military—concerns the forms of property. In its capacity of a transmitting mechanism in this struggle, the bureaucracy leans now on the proletariat against imperialism, now on imperialism against the proletariat, in order to increase its own power. At the same time it mercilessly exploits

its role as distributor of the meager necessities of life in order to safeguard its own well-being and power. By this token the rule of the proletariat assumes an abridged, curbed, distorted character. One can with full justification say that the proletariat, *ruling* in one backward and isolated country, still remains an *oppressed* class. The source of oppression is world imperialism; the mechanism of transmission of the oppression—the bureaucracy. If in the words "a ruling and at the same time an oppressed class" there is a contradiction, then it flows not from the mistakes of thought but from the contradiction in the very situation of the USSR. It is precisely because of this that we reject the theory of socialism in one country.

The recognition of the USSR as a workers' state—not a type but a mutilation of a type—does not at all signify a theoretical and political amnesty for the Soviet bureaucracy. On the contrary, its reactionary character is fully revealed only in the light of the contradiction between its antiproletarian politics and the needs of the workers' state. Only by posing the question in this manner does our exposure of the crimes of the Stalinist clique gain full motive force. The defense of the USSR means not only the supreme struggle against imperialism, but a preparation for the overthrow of the Bonapartist bureaucracy.

The experience of the USSR shows how great are the possibilities lodged in the workers' state and how great is its strength of resistance. But this experience also shows how powerful is the pressure of capitalism and its bureaucratic agency, how difficult it is for the proletariat to gain full liberation, and how necessary it is to educate and temper the new International in the spirit of irreconcilable revolutionary struggle.

# FOR A REVOLUTIONARY
# PUBLISHING HOUSE[75]

## November 29, 1937

According to all indications, the present crisis should bring about tremendous changes in the whole world and perhaps first of all in the USA. The crisis of 1929 has already dealt a serious blow to the traditional ideologies of Americanism and created the necessity for a new orientation.

The economic revival of the past year has, it is true, somewhat dampened theoretical and social criticism. Hopes arose that the process of economic growth interrupted by the crisis would again be reestablished. But sooner than one could have expected the hour of a new crisis struck. It started from a lower level than the crisis of 1929 and is developing at a more rapid tempo. This demonstrates that it is not an accidental recession nor even a conjunctural depression but an organic crisis of the whole capitalist system. That is why one can with assurance predict that in all fields of human ideology—in economics, politics, philosophy, literature, art—there will open an epoch of bold criticism, liquidation of old prejudices, searches for new systems, courageous creation.

Revolutionary thought in America, with immeasurably more stability and vigor than hitherto, will begin to study different social doctrines in order to resolve the question of the fate of the United States and of the capitalist system as a whole.

On the other hand, one can expect that the bourgeois publishing houses, which from time to time printed radical works in the firm belief that the U.S. was immune to the actions of "destructive" ideas, will in the coming years become more cautious, i.e., reactionary, and will completely ostracize revolutionary theoretical thought.

It is impossible to place the slightest hope in this respect in the publishing activity of the so-called Communist Party. With time it becomes ever more hostile to theory. No wonder: every page of the revolutionary classics is an accusation against the present politics of the Comintern. Frame-up and falsification have become its basic method in all fields. It is impossible to trust any book, any article, any quotation issued by the Comintern press. Sooner or later all these works will be placed on a special Index under the general title, "The library of pseudo-Marxism and lies."

As far as the Socialist Party is concerned, one cannot in general speak about it in relation to the problems of theoretical thought. This party lives on vulgar commonplaces. Its leaders are ingrained with an organic aversion to scientific analysis. Concern over revolutionary theory appears to their eyes as an unmistakable sign of sectarianism, if not a form of lunacy.

Under these conditions, the necessity for a revolutionary publishing house, independent both from capital and from the Soviet bureaucracy, is completely evident. *Pioneer Publishers* from the very beginning set itself the task of bringing out a serious library of revolutionary thought for advanced workers and radical intelligentsia.

During the last few years the first steps along this road have been taken. They have been met with manifest and encouraging sympathy. But there yet remains immeasurably more to be done than has been accomplished. There is weight in the idea that the center of social-revolutionary and revolutionary-philosophical thought will shift in the next period to America. Under the blows of the crisis and social shake-ups there will here arise a generation of revolutionary theoreticians capable of saying a new word. All the more necessary is it to create for this awakening social criticism a stable base in the form of a publishing house not bound by any other considerations and obligations outside of the objective to open to humanity a new road of development. *Pioneer Publishers* can accomplish a great historic task. Our common duty is to help them.

# MOSCOW-AMSTERDAM 'UNITY'[76]

## November 29, 1937

The unification of the world trade union organization, in the present case the adherence of the Soviet Union to the Amsterdam International,[77] could bring great advantages to the working class—under only one condition: that there are actually unions in the USSR. But there are none there. There is a trade union apparatus totally dependent upon the ruling clique and dominating the working masses. Thus, during the last bloody purge, which is, moreover, far from being ended, the central Council of Trade Unions was totally reorganized without the so-called unionized masses knowing more than what appeared in the official press. The purge of the trade union apparatus was done by the GPU upon the direct order of Stalin.

The former trade union leader, the old revolutionary Tomsky,[78] was driven into suicide by a campaign of slanders and vicious persecution. His place was taken, without the least consultation with the membership, by Shvernik, who isn't and never was anything more than a bellhop in the personal service of Stalin.[79] The renovated apparatus occupies itself in its turn with purging the factories and the offices, hunting and trapping whoever is discontented, critical, or makes demands. Thus the so-called unions represent an organization of industrial police, an appendage of the GPU, and not at all an autonomous organization of workers.

It is not a question then of the unification of the working masses, but of a diplomatic accord between the Amsterdam apparatus, moderately conservative, and the police apparatus of Moscow.

The heads of the British trade unions would like well enough to orient the foreign policy of their country toward a rapprochement with France, the United States, and the USSR. The French policy, that of the People's Front, is based upon the support of Moscow. Jouhaux, the head of the French union, while proclaiming the "independence" of his trade unions, belongs in reality to the People's Front. It is this political conjuncture, nationally and internationally, which has determined the rapprochement of the Amsterdam trade union bureaucracy with the pseudo-trade union bureaucracy of Moscow.

We must add still another element which is not without importance. For some years now, practically since 1924, precisely through the intermediary of the so-called trade union apparatus Stalin has purchased the "sympathies" of various trade union leaders abroad, commencing with England. We are able to cite some cases of British trade union heads on the regular Moscow payroll. Others have benefited through exceptional privileges, or their wives have received presents in gold or in platinum. This practice of demoralizing the workers' leaders was, let it be said in passing, one of the principal points of my struggle against Stalin's clique.

When I became aware of this practice in the spring of 1925, I protested vigorously. "But why?" Stalin countered. "Does not the bourgeoisie buy the workers' leaders?" "One can buy somebody," I answered, "in order to corrupt him, but not in order to make him a fighter for the emancipation of the oppressed." This practice has since that time taken on gigantic proportions. We must not forget that the gold industry has made great progress in the USSR. The industry of bribery and of corruption has made still greater progress.

Many of the so-called "friends" of the USSR who have nothing in common with the Russian people, its revolutionary traditions, its sufferings, and its aspirations are no more than interested friends of the ruling clique of the Kremlin. Some of them are paid directly with gold. Others depend in their personal political aims upon the aid of the powerful international apparatus of Moscow.

I do not doubt that Stalin, Yezhov,[80] and Shvernik will utilize the so-called trade union unification in order to enlarge their hold upon the number of leaders with a supple spine and conscience. What will be the reaction of the working class against these practices? We shall see in the coming years.

# AN FBI AGENT'S STORY[81]

## December 1, 1937

Dear Comrade Weber:

The story you tell me in your letter of November 28 is a bit enigmatic, like all the stories from the no-man's-land between police and revolutionaries. For my part I can propose a hypothesis. The G-man was connected with the Stalinists before his becoming involved in the secret service. It is possible also that he formed connections with them after his engagement. If his friends the Stalinists knew that he was a G-man they could maneuver to orient him in a certain direction. If they didn't know of him as a secret agent, but knew of his connection with certain Trotskyites, they tried to win him for their plans. I believe with you that the police are more cautious and silent with their secret plans. But with the Stalinists the plan of slandering, framing, and exterminating the "Trotskyites" is not a secret but an open topic in their activity. Thus I believe that the three and six months' plans formulated by the G-man to the steelworker express directly not the plans of the government but the aspirations and inspirations of the Stalinists. If this hypothesis is true it limits the weight of the announced three and six months' plans practically. But I will not at all deny that this weight which is today a Stalinist aspiration—totally in the line of bourgeois reaction—can become a reality, at least to a half or a third, if not in three or six months, then in a year. That is why I believe that the open denunciation of these plans is not only necessary but urgent. In my mind they should be denounced not as Washington's plans (it is very improbable) but as the combined plans of the Stalinists and of the most reactionary elements of the police in order to terrorize the White House and to force its hand. Here, as for example in Spain, the Stalinists have a common game with the most reactionary elements in order to subjugate a "too democratic" government. It seems to me that the story should be reported for public opinion under this political aspect.

So far as you can reveal your sources, the revelation can come from San Francisco, but this is a purely technical question of secondary importance.

That the three and six months' plans are very seriously taken by the Stalinists is proved by the recent happenings here. *Machete* published an article accusing me of preparing a fascist coup d'etat with General Villareal, General Cedillo, and the reactionary professor Vasconcelos, now residing in the United States.[82] We laughed. But some days later the walls of the city were covered with innumerable posters revealing the terrible conspiracy.

At the celebration of the anniversary of the revolution, November 20, Laborde,[83] the notorious Stalinist agent, pronounced in the presence of [Mexican President Cardenas] a speech in the same sensational style. Friends who were present at the meeting told me that no one applauded this revelation and that the president ironically smiled. I wrote a letter to the president, asking him for an authoritative body before which I could prove that the accusation is a new frame-up of the GPU in order to deprive me of Mexican hospitality. I received a personal letter from the president assuring me that the government hasn't any doubt of my legality and that I can further use Mexican hospitality "with all the consideration due" to me. The president showed in this case as he has in others that he is not only profoundly sincere in his general plans but that he is also a very courageous and honest man.

*El Universal* published a statement from me (sent to the *Socialist Appeal*) and a conversation between Diego Rivera and General Villareal unmasking the conspiracy. We are sending the respective clippings to the national office. Thus you see that the too brisk attack of the Stalinists is politically repulsed and that we are at the moment on the offensive. But the situation can change every week and every day.

The meeting of the [Dewey] Commission and the announcement of the verdict[84] can play a very important role in the fight against the Stalinists' gangsterism in general if the meeting is immediately followed by a very intensive campaign connecting the definite GPU frame-up [in Moscow to the slander by the Mexican Stalinists] and eliminating one through the other. So far Mexican public opinion is absolutely opposed to the absolutely fantastic plot, Trotsky-Villareal-Cedillo. It is a very appreciable lesson on the real sense of the Moscow trials.

On the Milton-Stone matter, we cabled yesterday that the trip be postponed for two months. On the first of December the vacations in Mexico begin, and we can have for the next two months a Mexican comrade, a teacher or a student, in our house as a guard. In view of the very difficult financial situation we believe this solution is the wisest one. After two months we can see.

On the Russian question I wrote a more extensive article which, as the comrades here hope, can help to clarify the matter. The article in English translation has already been sent today by airmail.

I am working with Rae in Russian very well. She makes real progress and Sara should not be at all desperate over her lack of success up until this time.[85]

Our best greetings to you both.

# A FEW WORDS
## ON LUTTE OUVRIERE[86]

### December 2, 1937

A few words on *Lutte ouvriere*. I may have been wrong in not paying the necessary attention to the national "climate," but I find both the layout and the presentation absolutely unnatural. You imitate the big newspapers—and not the best of them, *Le Temps*, for example—by using big headlines, by sacrificing a third of your space to technical fireworks, which in my opinion only make the paper less readable than it was before. People who buy *Lutte ouvriere* certainly do not do so because of its headlines. Moreover, you have completely dropped the theoretical, the educational, and even the basic political articles. True, you have once again promised to reestablish *Quatrieme Internationale* (I am somewhat skeptical about this in view of the past).[87] But even if you keep your word this time, the problem with *Lutte ouvriere* is still the same.

A paper is a unified whole. It must not only exhort its readers and urge them on; it must also educate them by giving them a theoretical grounding and by opening up a political perspective for them. A small weekly paper is all right if it has no white space showing, if the headlines are reduced to a minimum, if the columns are entirely filled in, and if the text is edited two or three times so that every idea is expressed as precisely as possible and with the greatest possible economy of words.

You say nothing about the numerical composition of the party, which I consider a bad sign. The same goes for the youth. The reason, it seems to me, is that you have almost entirely dropped the doctrinal aspect, that is, you have stopped demonstrating your theoretical and political superiority over all the other tendencies. Then how can you hope to draw close to the broad masses? Not by big headlines, in any case.

I don't know whether you have any system for practical work, or whether you expend too much energy in a vacuum, instead of concentrating it for a certain time on a certain task, in a certain neighborhood, even in a certain factory. I have tried to direct our friends' attention to this many times. But I have never gotten the slightest response. Correct ideas are not enough in and of themselves. They must be presented properly.

Forgive these rather "ill-tempered" remarks, but given the situation in France, it would be gratifying to see more palpable results.

# THE FUTURE OF
# THE DUTCH SECTION[88]

## December 2, 1937

Dear Comrade Sneevliet:

I didn't answer your very belated last letter concerning Reiss directly because we are separated not only by this tragic individual question but by all other important political issues, I could say by the whole conception of revolutionary activity and political solidarity.

This totally unhealthy situation has lasted years, as many years as your group has adhered to our international organization. Many younger comrades better acquainted with the political line and the organizational methods of the Dutch section have insisted, beginning with 1934, upon the necessity of openly clarifying our profound theoretical, political, and practical differences. Through letters and conversations I opposed these proposals. Not that I was in agreement with your political line— never—but I feared that a premature opening of a general discussion without a preparatory period of common experience could only provoke an irreparable split. I was guided by the idea that your organization has a very different prehistory and a different education from all the others. That is why I recommended with insistence to our comrades to give your organization more time for a reorientation, a reeducation. Naturally we were hoping not only to "teach" our Dutch comrades but also to learn from them.

I must say that the hopes I placed in this cautious and patient method proved to be false. The Dutch party, or, better to say, its leaders, intervened in our international life and in the life of every section with vigor and sometimes with extreme brutality. Such was their attitude at the entrance of our French section, then the Belgian, and later the American section, into the

81

respective Socialist parties.[89] Such was their attitude toward the German comrades. The Dutch party, or, better to say, its leaders, never hesitated to support a small minority in a foreign section against the majority. It never hesitated to openly oppose the most important decisions of the whole international organization and act independently as in the case of Spain. At the same time you considered the Dutch party as taboo to all the other sections. Every critical word concerning your general, or more specifically your trade union policy was considered a crime. With other work you asked a totally exceptional position for the Dutch section.

When I wrote a letter to our International Conference,[90] in which I expressed some critical considerations upon your political line, you used this letter as a pretext for not participating in the conference. You declared later that you don't recognize the formally elected International Secretariat. In all questions you act absolutely independently from the international organization. In the Reiss question you acted without the knowledge and participation of the Russian comrades and I believe that this absolutely incomprehensible attitude contributed to the tragic outcome. I write you this with full frankness because I consider this letter as personal. I am making my last attempt to save your connection with the Fourth International and at the same time the future of the Dutch party.

You must finally understand that nobody in our international movement is inclined to further tolerate the absolutely abnormal situation under which the Dutch party covers itself with the banner of the Fourth International and conducts a policy which is flagrantly contradictory to all our principles and decisions.

The NAS has definitely become a stone around the neck of the party, and this stone will drag you to the bottom.[91] A party which doesn't participate in the real mass unions is not a revolutionary party. The NAS exists only thanks to the toleration and financial support of the bourgeois government. This financial support is dependent upon your political attitude. That is the genuine reason why the party didn't, in spite of all our insistence, elaborate a political platform. That is also the reason why you as parliamentary deputy never gave a genuine revolutionary speech which could serve for propaganda in Holland as well as abroad. Your activity has a diplomatic and not a very revolutionary character. You are bound through your NAS position by the hands and feet. And the NAS itself is not a bridge to the masses but a wall separating you from the masses.

When we criticize false trade union politics in other countries, people answer: "And your Dutch organization?" When we criticze the Menshevik and totally fatal policy of the POUM leadership, you intervene in order to give them support against us and you do it under the banner of the Fourth International. Do you believe that any serious revolutionary organization can tolerate indefinitely such a situation? We are very patient, but we cannot sacrifice the elementary interests of our movement.

I personally am ready to do everything in order to help to reintegrate the Dutch party into the ranks of the Fourth International. From Cannon's letter I know that he has the same disposition. I doubt that anyone on our side wishes or even accepts the idea of a split. But at the same time we will free ourselves from equivocation. In any case I say in my own name, openly: If you don't accept common rules for collaboration and active solidarity; if you renounce participating normally, like every other section, in the International [Founding] Conference; if you will continue with the totally ambiguous attitude—in words with the Fourth International, in deeds against it—then it is better to undergo an open and honest split. You will then remain with the NAS and we with the Fourth International. We will create a section in Holland and we will try to realize through an open fight what we were unable to realize through patient collaboration and comradely discussion.

I hesitated for a long time before writing you this letter because, permit me to say it, I know your impulsiveness and your readiness to make the most important decisions under the influence of personal impulses. It is possible also that this letter will provoke in you a reaction contrary to the intention with which it is written. It is possible that you will use this frank warning in order to accelerate the split. But I have no other choice. The denouement, especially after the Spanish experience and the Reiss incident, cannot be postponed any longer. The hour of the last decision is at hand. The future of our relations depends entirely upon your attitude to the coming conference. That is why I make this final appeal to your sense of revolutionary responsibility. The day when I receive a cable or letter from you announcing that your party will participate in the conference on the same grounds as every other section will be a very good day not only for me but for the Fourth International and especially for the Dutch party. If you decide otherwise each of us will know what to do.

> With best comradely greetings,
> L. Trotsky

# A LETTER
# TO THE NEW YORK TIMES[92]

## December 3, 1937

To the Editor of the *New York Times:*

In your issue of November 28 you printed an article by Nathaniel Pfeffer, "Is China Beaten or Has the War Only Begun?" The author, well acquainted with the Far East, gives an excellent analysis of the general situation. His conclusion is: Japan can gain a long series of particular victories, but cannot win the war. China has on her side space, time, human masses, the nationally liberating character of the war.

The author is completely correct when he says that against mass guerrilla warfare on the part of China, Japan will prove in the end powerless and will suffer, we can add, not only a financial and economic but a social catastrophe.

Unfortunately, there is one important political element lacking in this picture, namely, the interrelation between the Chinese government and the nation. In order to turn the war into a national one—to mobilize and direct the initiative and self-sacrifice of the millions of Chinese workers and peasants—it is necessary that the government trust its people or that it at least fear its own armed workers and peasants less than the Japanese aggressors. Is this condition present? We can doubt this.

The author does not mention one other important factor, that is to say, the politics of the Soviet government. Moscow supplied arms to Spain, demanding in exchange the suppression of the initiative and independence of the mass organizations. The results are evident. Franco did not gain a victory, but Stalin-Negrin suffered a defeat.

There is every reason to fear that Moscow is applying the same politics at the moment in China. That is why one has to bring into the conclusions of your contributor an essential limitation. The Mikado will meet a terrible catastrophe if Chiang Kai-shek and Stalin do not save him.

Leon Trotsky

# DEFEATISM VS. DEFENSISM[93]

## December 6, 1937

Dear Comrades:

I have just now received your "Declaration of Principles" and your statement regarding the defeatists within the party. Of course, I have not yet succeeded in studying your "Declaration of Principles." But I have read through your statement attentively twice, and since this has an independent significance I wish to express myself immediately on this point.

The statement is devoted to defending the "right" of defeatists to remain in the party and to carry on defeatist propaganda. The very approach to the question is totally abstract, it seems to me, and at any rate not timely.

Both of you declare yourselves to be defensists on the question of the USSR. A discussion is now going on in the party. The question has tremendous significance. Every organization which occupies a false or wavering position on this question will be shattered by the march of events. It is important for our party to have a clear and distinct position. Is it proper, correct, timely under these conditions to occupy oneself with purely formal abstract juridical discourses as to the "right" of defeatists to defend their false position even after the party comes to a conclusion on the question? Such an approach converts you yourselves from *political* advocates of defensism into *juridical* advocates of defeatism. Thus, regardless of your will, you merely help the defeatists to strengthen their manifestly false position and you prepare the inevitability of a break with them.

"That means that you stand for an immediate organizational break with the defeatists?" you ask me. No, I reply. I stand for an immediate political break with defeatism. This is the first and chief problem. At the same time I favor taking all necessary measures in order to facilitate for the present defeatists their future assimilation into the party. We should give them the necessary time to think over the question seriously. Some of them will undoubtedly and very quickly renounce their point of view, which is in essence anti-Marxian. But others, on the contrary, will make out of their ultraleft mistake an everlasting platform. Of course, with the latter a break will prove inevitable. The whole course of the world workers' movement, beginning with July 1914, demonstrates that defeatists and defensists cannot remain in the same party, if the concept of a party has in general any sort of sense. The basic task of the present discussion consists in demonstrating the full political incompatibility of defeatism in relation to the USSR with membership in a revolutionary proletarian party. Only such an energetic—a Marxist and not a lawyer's—campaign against defeatism is capable of compelling the better part of the defeatists to reexamine their viewpoint.

You invoke, in a defense of your juridical but not political position, the principles of party democracy. Insofar as I can judge, your discussion is being carried on now with a strict adherence to the norms of democracy in essence and in form. But democracy presupposes, first of all, a common programmatic base under our feet. It is true that democracy presupposes likewise an attentive and patient attitude on the part of the majority toward the minority (so far as such a "patient" attitude is authorized by the course of the events themselves and so far as it is justified by the conduct of the minority). But party democracy does not at all signify transforming the party into an arena for the free exercises of sectarians, blunderers, or aspiring individualists. Party democracy does not signify the right of the minority to upset the work of the majority. A revolutionary party is not a debating club but a militant organization. The problem of war, next to the problem of revolution, is the touchstone of a revolutionary party. Here no kind of equivocation is permissible. The principled decision is clear beforehand: *defensism and defeatism are as incompatible as fire and water.* It is necessary to say *this* first of all. *This* truth must be taught the members of the party. It is necessary to convoke a conference on *this* basis. It is necessary to establish *this* idea in the resolution of the conference. At the same time we can and must display the most attentive attitude to each sincere mistaken comrade. Only in this manner can we guard the party from befuddledness and chaos and, in passing, reduce to a minimum the number of those ultraleftists who [some] day sooner or later will find themselves outside of the party, sinking into political nonexistence (on the order of the Oehlerites, Weisbordites, Fieldites, and their sort).[94]

With sincere comradely greetings,
L. Trotsky

# A SUGGESTION ON BURNHAM[95]

## December 6, 1937

Dear Jim:

As the result of a conversation here, I thought it might be well to ask what you think about the following considerations:

The discussion regarding the nature of the USSR seems to us down here to be much sharper than is warranted and to possibly presage results out of proportion to the issues. Were the atmosphere somehow eased, the tension slackened, the entire discussion might result more favorably and with maximum gains in the education of the comrades, etc.

What do you think of Burnham visiting us here? In getting away from New York for a period, even though short, he would have a chance to leave what seems to us a tense atmosphere, and from a distance perhaps formulate a viewpoint more coolly. Carter meanwhile would have a chance to take things easy pending the results of Burnham's visit. It might well be that leaving the somewhat factional atmosphere would have a beneficial effect upon both.

In addition [to] what psychological value such a trip might have, a thorough and amicable discussion with us down here might be conducive to a healthier tone generally. Certainly away from New York in the peaceful backwaters of the south a discussion could be carried on with a much less tense atmosphere and consequently with greater possibilities for more coolly analyzing the problem.

In arranging for such a trip, what do you think would be the best method? Is a suggestion from you or from Max[96] or from some other comrade sufficient or desirable? Or would you prefer a cable or letter of invitation from here? The latter alternative can be arranged on the basis of the long interest in Burnham, the desire to further strengthen the friendship and relation, the added opportunity provided by the present question which is of great importance and can only be thoroughly resolved in discussion rather than through the more clumsy and less satisfactory method of correspondence, etc.

It occurs to me that it is possible during the Christmas holidays to take such a trip without interference with jobs, school, or whatever might prevent his coming otherwise. But then the convention! Could he get back in time? And would the trip down here come soon enough for maximum value?

In any event you know the situation and the comrades and what would be best in resolving the matter. Let us hear from you concerning your opinion and whether you think it best to send an invitation from here.[97]

I send a copy of this letter to Max.

Warmest greetings,
Joe [Trotsky]

# ON DEMOCRATIC CENTRALISM[98]

## A Few Words about the Party Regime

### December 8, 1937

To the Editors of *Socialist Appeal:*

During the past months I have received letters in regard to the inner regime of a revolutionary party from several apparently young comrades, unknown to me. Some of these letters complain about the "lack of democracy" in your organization, about the domineering of the "leaders" and the like. Individual comrades ask me to give a "clear and exact formula on democratic centralism" which would preclude false interpretations.

It is not easy to answer these letters. Not one of my correspondents even attempts to demonstrate clearly and concretely with actual examples exactly wherein lies the violation of democracy. On the other hand, insofar as I, a bystander, can judge on the basis of your newspaper and your bulletins, the discussion in your organization is being conducted with full freedom. The bulletins are filled chiefly by representatives of a tiny minority. I have been told that the same holds true of your discussion meetings. The decisions are not yet carried out. Evidently they will be carried through at a freely elected conference. In what then could the violations of democracy have been manifested? This is hard to understand. Sometimes, to judge by the tones of the letters, i.e., in the main instance by the formlessness of the grievances, it seems to be that the complainers are simply dissatisfied with the fact that in spite of the existing democracy, they prove to be in a tiny minority. Through my own experience I know that this is unpleasant. But wherein is there any violation of democracy?

Neither do I think that I can give such a formula on democratic centralism that "once and for all" would eliminate misunderstandings and false interpretations. A party is an active organism. It develops in the struggle with outside obstacles and inner contradictions. The malignant decomposition of the Second and Third Internationals, under the severe conditions of the imperialist epoch, creates for the Fourth International difficulties unprecedented in history. One cannot overcome them with some sort of magic formula. The regime of a party does not fall ready-made from the sky but is formed gradually in the struggle. A political line predominates over the regime. First of all, it is necessary to define strategic problems and tactical methods correctly in order to solve them. The organizational forms should correspond to the strategy and the tactic. Only a correct policy can guarantee a healthy party regime. This, it is understood, does not mean that the development of the party does not raise organizational problems as such. But it means that the formula for democratic centralism must inevitably find a different expression in the parties of different countries and in different stages of development of one and the same party.

Democracy and centralism do not at all find themselves in an invariable ratio to one another. Everything depends on the concrete circumstances, on the political situation in the country, on the strength of the party and its experience, on the general level of its members, on the authority the leadership has succeeded in winning. Before a conference, when the problem is one of formulating a political line for the next period, democracy triumphs over centralism. When the problem is political action, centralism subordinates democracy to itself. Democracy again asserts its rights when the party feels the need to examine critically its own actions. The equilibrium between democracy and centralism establishes itself in the actual struggle, at moments it is violated and then again reestablished. The maturity of each member of the party expresses itself particularly in the fact that he does not demand from the party regime more than it can give. The person who defines his attitude to the party by the individual fillips that he gets on the nose is a poor revolutionist. It is necessary, of course, to fight against every individual mistake of the leadership, every injustice, and the like. But it is necessary to assess these "injustices" and "mistakes" not by themselves but in connection with the general development of the party both on a national and international scale. A correct judgment and a feeling for proportion in politics is an extremely important thing. The person who has propensities for making a mountain out of a molehill can do much harm to himself and to the party. The misfortune of such people as Oehler, Field, Weisbord, and others consists in their lack of feeling for proportion.

At the moment there are not a few half-revolutionists, tired out by defeats, fearing difficulties, aged young men who have more doubts and pretensions than will to struggle. Instead of seriously analyzing political questions in essence, such individuals seek panaceas, on every occasion complain about the "regime," demand wonders from the leadership, or try to muffle their inner skepticism by ultraleft prattling. I fear that revolutionists will not be made out of such elements, unless they take themselves in hand. I do not doubt, on the other hand, that the young generation of workers will be capable of evaluating the programmatic and strategical content of the Fourth International according to merit and will rally to its banner in ever greater numbers. Each real revolutionist who notes down the blunders of the party regime should first of all say to himself: "We must bring into the party a dozen new workers!" The young workers will call the gentlemen-skeptics, grievance-mongers, and pessimists to order. Only along such a road will a strong healthy party regime be established in the sections of the Fourth International.

L. Trotsky

# TWO DEFECTIONS IN ONE WEEK[99]

## December 9, 1937

In the course of one week, two prominent Soviet figures have broken with the Moscow government. They publicly accused it of organizing fake trials and murdering hundreds of old revolutionaries, including prominent Soviet diplomats. The first of these two figures, Alexander Barmin, was a volunteer during the civil war and, towards its end, a brigadier general and protege of the general staff. After demobilization, he went on to the department of foreign trade, and then into the foreign service. In the recent period, Barmin has functioned as the Soviet minister in Greece. The second, Walter Krivitsky,[100] has nineteen years of party and Soviet work. In the recent period, he was chief of the research institute of war industry. This institute is the brain of war technology. All inventions, improvements, and technical secrets pass through the research institute. Barmin and Krivitsky, in their own words, long ago began to doubt the political correctness of the Stalinist government. Both of them were closely associated with scores of figures who suddenly were declared spies, arrested, and shot. Barmin and Krivitsky could not believe this accusation since they knew very well the honesty and devotion to duty of their former superiors and co-workers.

Many people wondered why Soviet diplomats, military attaches, and trade representatives, one after another, voluntarily returned at Moscow's demand into the arms of the GPU. Barmin and Krivitsky explain the reasons for such submissiveness. To refuse to return meant being assassinated, like Ignace Reiss, an important foreign agent of the Comintern and the GPU. After wavering, Barmin and Krivitsky decided, however, on a complete break with Moscow. Unlike Reiss, they did not try to live incognito. On the contrary, they both appealed to the French government and to world public opinion with an open declaration about their break with Moscow and their decision to become political emigrants. This bold step gave them vitally important protection. World public opinion learned of Ignace Reiss only after he was killed. In contrast, Barmin and Krivitsky are now well known to the whole world. The GPU will have to think it over ten times before it decides on a new crime.

There is no need to explain that the greatest anxiety now reigns inside all the Soviet government agencies abroad, especially in the secret organizations of the GPU. The example of Barmin and Krivitsky can be highly contagious. One can confidently predict that the immediate period will see a whole series of new breaks with Moscow. Thus cracks are showing and holes appearing in the Chinese wall which Stalin has built between the USSR and the rest of the world, with the help of police dogs and privileged frontier guards. Barmin and Krivitsky were deeply committed to the cause of the October Revolution and to the Soviet people. Unlike mercenary "friends," they demonstrated this through their whole lives' work. Confronted with the necessity of making a choice, after wavering, they took a stand in defense of the people against the Stalinist clique. The symptomatic importance of this fact is enormous. It confirms what we said a year and half ago, that the death agony of the Stalinist regime began with the Moscow trials.

# TELEGRAM
# TO THE DEWEY COMMISSION[101]

## December 9, 1937

The commission condemned nobody to death or to prison. Yet it is impossible to imagine a more terrible verdict. The commission says to the rulers of a great country: *"You committed a frame-up for the purpose of justifying the extermination of your political adversaries. You tried to deceive the toilers of the world. You are unworthy to serve the cause which you invoke."*

The commission, which includes people of different political views, could not follow our political aims. But its verdict has an immeasurable political importance. The methods of lies, slander, and frame-up, which contaminate the inner life of the USSR and the workers' movement of the world, today received a terrible blow. Let the official friends of the USSR and the other pseudoradical bigots say that the verdict will be used by reaction. Untrue! Nowhere and never did the truth serve reaction. Nowhere and never is progress fed on lies. The commission, it is true, delivers a blow to the Moscow bureaucracy. But this bureaucracy has become the main brake upon the progress of the Soviet Union. Aiming to serve the truth, the commission served the liberating struggle of all mankind. From now on the work of the commission as well as the names of its participants belongs to history.

# STATEMENT TO JOURNALISTS
# ON THE DEWEY VERDICT[102]

## December 13, 1937

First of all, allow me to express my warm appreciation for your kindness and attention in responding to the invitation to this private meeting concerned with the verdict of the commission. The press has not only the right, but also the duty to form a clear opinion of whether a person who is enjoying this country's hospitality is in fact guilty of such terrible and despicable crimes as his political opponents have accused him of.

Second, allow me to apologize for my Spanish. My great teacher Karl Marx once remarked to his German disciple Wilhelm Liebknecht:[103] "What, you don't know Spanish? What a pity! You can't read *Don Quixote* in the original." Gentlemen, this is precisely my predicament. Up till now, I have only read *Don Quixote* in translation.

My Spanish is very rudimentary. This is the first time that I have ever attempted to make a public statement in the language of your country.

I have prepared my statement with the help of my friends. Of course, the responsibility for my pronunciation, especially for my accent, cannot rest with my friends. My linguistic errors are my own.

I do not wish to abuse your patience. My statement consists of two parts: First, a short general comment on the meaning and importance of the verdict. Second, my replies to questions from journalists and friends.

Now for the statement.

The decision of the International Commission upon the Moscow trials is known to you. Permit me consequently to limit myself to a few comments.

First of all, I give the definite conclusions of the commission. They are very brief, two lines in all.

"(22) We therefore find the Moscow trials to be a frame-up.

"(23) We therefore find Trotsky and Sedov not guilty."

Two lines in all! But there are few lines which have such weight in the library of humanity. If the commission had limited itself to these words: "Trotsky and Sedov are not guilty," there would remain the formal possibility of admitting a juridical error.

The commission has found itself sufficiently armed in order to close the door once and for all to such an interpretation. "We therefore find," says the verdict, "the Moscow trials to be a frame-up."

By such a declaration the commission took upon itself an enormous moral and political responsibility. It should have evidence not only convincing and sufficient, but irresistible and crushing in order to determine upon such a conclusion in the face of the entire world.

I ask you, gentlemen of the press, to study attentively the list of the members of the commission in New York and in Paris. This list is in your hands. It speaks for itself.

The list contains seventeen names. With the sole exception of Rosmer, representative of France,[104] I have never before had personal relations with one of the members of the commission. You find among them scientists with world renowned names, leaders of the Second International and the workers' movement in general, eminent jurists and publicists, and the authoritative representative of anarcho-syndicalist thought.

But among the seventeen names there is not one member of the Fourth International. I can even say that they are all, though in different degrees, my political adversaries, and some of them have publicly demonstrated their negative attitude toward so-called Trotskyism even during the inquiry. All members of the commission have behind them dozens of years of political, scientific, or literary activity. All have names without blemish. If there had been one person who could be bought, he would have been bought a long time ago. My enemies have millions at their disposition for this end and they are not misers.

As for myself and my son, we did not have at our disposition even the means necessary to cover the technical expenses of the investigation. The modest funds of the commission have been furnished by collections among the workers and by personal donations.

The commission insistently invited the representatives of the

Soviet government, the Comintern or its national sections in the United States and in Mexico, the "Friends of the USSR," finally individuals closely linked with Moscow such as the English lawyer, Mr. Pritt, Mr. Lombardo Toledano, and others,[105] to participate in its work with equal rights. The commission has searched, candle in hand, for an authoritative Stalinist or a Stalinist sympathizer who would not limit himself to machinations in the cellars of the GPU, or to calumnies and insinuations in publications without responsibility or honor, but who would have the courage to openly submit the Moscow accusations to the control of critics. It did not find a single person save the former employee in the official Soviet telegraphic agency Tass, Mr. Carleton Beals.[106] But it appeared shortly that Beals was pushed into the commission only in order to explode it from the interior. When Beals's questions, impregnated with the spirit of the GPU, that of provocation, had received adequate response, he fled from the field of battle.

The commission has worked more than nine months without interruption in New York, in Mexico, in Paris, in Prague, and in other European capitals. It has studied thousands of original documents, letters, minutes, articles, and books, verbal and written depositions of numerous witnesses.

You have received also a brief resume of the work of the commission which contains only twenty-four pages. The complete verdict will soon be published in a book of 80,000 words. It contains the most meticulous analysis of all the confessions of the unfortunate defendants and of the assertions of the prosecuting attorney Vyshinsky, the first lieutenant of Stalin in all this juridical falsification. Permit me to advise you in advance that it is impossible to wait for any articulate reply from the falsifiers. The only reply which remains to them, and which they use often enough, is the shot of a revolver or the blow of a knife. With such an argument one can annihilate an opponent, but not assassinate the voice of the world's conscience. The decision of the commission cannot be affected by revolver or knife. It cannot be drowned in water.

The most important task is now done. The verdict is pronounced. Stalin and the GPU are branded forever as the perpetrators of the greatest crimes in history.

In face of the verdict of the commission, none of the agents and lackeys will be able to succeed in escaping his responsibility.

The drawing-room chatterers, disguised as revolutionaries, the male and female votaries of the solemn anniversaries of the

Soviet bureaucracy, the lawyers who make their careers upon the shoulders of the workers—is it necessary to give their names?— and all the other intriguers and charlatans who have permitted themselves to play with my political honor and even to make capital for themselves in this manner, all these gentlemen, one after the other, will be called to order by public opinion. Their great protectors will not be able to save them from merited contempt any more than they have been able to save themselves.

The hour of truth has struck. No one will be able to turn the wheel of justice backward. Every new revelation will reinforce the crushing verdict and extend the radius of its action.

With the chairman of the commission, Dr. Dewey, we can repeat once more the excellent sentence of Emile Zola: "Truth is on the march and nothing can stop it."[107]

Gentlemen of the press, you have the opportunity to actively participate in the triumphal march of truth. Do not let this precious opportunity escape.

You will receive copies of the verified text of the statement in Spanish as well as in English.

I mentioned that I received a number of questions about the verdict before this meeting. I wrote out my answers to the most important and pressing of these. With your permission, I will give you my replies.

*Q:* If we are to admit that the Moscow trials represent a frame-up, then how could Stalin have decided upon such a crime?

*A:* We have to distinguish in this matter two aspects, the social and the individual. The bureaucracy arrived at judicial frame-ups not at one stroke but gradually, in the process of the struggle for domination. Lying and frame-up are lodged in the very essence of the Soviet bureaucracy. In words, it fights for communism. In actuality, it fights for its income, its privileges, its power. With the fright and maliciousness of a social upstart, it exterminates all oppositionists. To justify this mad terror to the people, it is forced to attribute to its victims ever more monstrous and fantastic crimes. Such is the *social* basis of the Moscow crimes.

However, not by accident has Stalin become the leader of the Moscow bureaucracy. His personal qualities correspond to its political needs. In March 1921 Lenin had already given the advice not to choose Stalin as the general secretary since, as he put it, "This cook will prepare only peppery dishes." In his testament (January 1924) Lenin advised that Stalin be removed from the post of general secretary, invoking the fact that Stalin is rude, disloyal, and has propensities for misuse of power. These personal qualities have greatly developed in Stalin in proportion to the growth of the power and appetite of the bureaucracy. Thus the Kremlin "cook" came to the most peppery "dishes" in the form of the Moscow trials.

One could raise the objection: But a frame-up of such dimensions could not help being revealed in the end; how then could the "cautious" Stalin decide upon such risky actions? To this I answer: (a) he had no other choice; (b) from lesser frame-ups, he gradually went over to big ones; (c) with all his political perspicacity and shrewdness Stalin is very limited and believes in the omnipotence of police violence; (d) Stalin does not know either foreign languages or foreign life. He seriously takes the voices of his agents and every kind of paid friend abroad for the voice of world public opinion. Thus in the end he becomes the victim of his own system.

*Q:* You say that Stalin has become a victim . . . but meanwhile the victims appear to be others.

*A:* Completely correct. Stalin still has the possibility of exterminating his opponents, and not only in the USSR but also abroad. For the past year the agents of the GPU have committed a series of murders in Spain, in Switzerland, and in France. One can expect such actions in a series of other countries. These murders, as the recent exposures demonstrate, are also very risky undertakings; however, Stalin has no other choice than to add new victims to the old ones. In that sense your remark is correct. However, in a broader sense, Stalin is the victim of his own system. Those ideas against which he fights gain ever more defenders. The opponents slandered and murdered by Stalin will be rehabilitated in world public opinion. For Stalin there is no rehabilitation. It is not a question of the severity of his measures but of their inner falsity and putridness. His system is condemned. Stalin will leave the stage covered with disgrace.

*Q:* What, in your opinion, are the possible political consequences of the verdict of the commission?

*A:* I do not, it is understood, expect that the sound of a trumpet, even though it be the trumpet of truth, will immediately cause the walls of Jericho to fall. But considered from a more lengthy perspective, the decision of the commission will have tremendous political consequences in relation both to the Comintern and to the Soviet bureaucracy.

The Comintern will suffer in the first place. It is necessary to clearly understand that the apparatus of the Comintern consists of people exactly the opposite of the type of a revolutionist. A real revolutionist has his own self-conquered opinion, in the name of which he is ready to make sacrifices, including even the sacrifice of his life. The revolutionist prepares for the future and because of that it is easy for him to endure all sorts of difficulties, deprivations, and persecutions during the present. In counterposition to this, the bureaucrats of the Comintern are full-blown careerists. They have no kind of opinion and subordinate themselves to the orders of the authority which pays them. Since they are agents of the omnipotent Kremlin, each of them feels himself a small "superman." Everything is permitted them.

They lightly libel the honor of others since they have no honor of their own. This organization, completely degenerated and demoralized to the marrow, maintains itself in radical public opinion, including the workers', only through the authority of the Kremlin as the alleged builder of socialist society. The exposure of the role of the Kremlin oligarchy will deliver an irreparable blow to the authority of the Comintern.

On the other hand, the power of Stalin continues not only through violence and bureaucratic inertia but also through his artificial authority as a supposed "leader of the world proletariat." To uphold this reputation in the eyes of the Soviet workers, the Comintern is necessary to Stalin. The downfall of the Comintern will deliver a severe blow to the positions of the oligarchy inside the USSR.

*Q:* Who, in your opinion, can replace Stalin?

*A:* First of all, I will answer this negatively: in no case *bourgeois democracy.* Before our eyes bourgeois democracy is tottering even in those countries where it has behind it a long tradition. There can be no talk about its revival in the USSR. If the Stalinist bureaucracy should be overthrown *from the right,* then its place will be taken by the most savage and unbridled fascism, alongside of which even the regime of Hitler will look like a philanthropic institution. Such an overturn is possible only as a result of long convulsions, economic chaos, the destruction of the nationalized economy, and the reestablishment of private ownership. If on the contrary Stalin will be overthrown *from the left*, i.e., by the working class, then *Soviet democracy* will take the place of the bureaucracy. Nationalized economy will be preserved and reformed in the interests of the people. Development toward socialism will receive a powerful new impetus.

*Q:* Which of these two is the more probable?

*A:* I prefer on this account not to occupy myself with guesses. The outcome will be decided in the struggle. The verdict of the commission becomes from now on one of the elements of this struggle. It is hard to overestimate its significance. In the eyes of the whole world this verdict clears the Left Opposition of the USSR of these disgusting slanders and by that token helps the working class in its struggle against the bureaucracy. The verdict thus heightens the chances for a progressive uprising. In this lies its greatest historical service.

*Q:* From the stenographic report of the Coyoacan sessions and from the verdict of the commission, it follows that a series of crude contradictions and incongruities occurred in the Moscow trials. If Stalin himself, the chief judge of the court, Ulrich, prosecutor Vyshinsky, the head of the GPU, Yezhov, and their helpers occupied themselves with organizing the juridical frame-up, then how could they allow such crude mistakes?

*A:* All these people, beginning with Stalin, have become depraved through impunity and lack of control. In the articles and speeches of Stalin we meet at every step not only political contradictions but also the crudest factual distortions, not to speak of the errors in grammar. Since no one dares to criticize him, Stalin has gradually lost the custom of controlling himself. The same is true of the remaining bureaucrats. They do not learn, they do not think, they only order. A totalitarian regime assures the apparent success of orders. The chief judge of the court, the prosecutor, the accused, the defense attorneys, the witnesses—all executed an assigned lesson. The newspapers subordinate themselves to the ring of the telephone. There is no discussion, there is no criticism. The people have the right only to give thanks. Under such conditions the stimulus for good work falls to the ground, even in the sphere of frame-ups.

To this there is added another circumstance of no less

importance. The construction of a scheme of alleged conspiracy involving hundreds of people, and not people we meet for the first time, but people known to the whole world, with their own past, with their definite political make-ups, with their intricate personal ties and relationships—the construction of such a scheme without crude contradictions in a police office is a completely insoluble problem. Of course, if we assign such a task to a dozen people of the type of Shakespeare, Cervantes, Goethe, Freud, then they would carry out the task in a much more competent manner than Stalin, Vyshinsky, and Yezhov. But people of genius, as a general rule, do not occupy themselves with frame-ups. In any case, there have not remained even capable people at the disposal of Stalin. Vyshinsky and Yezhov are miserable nonentities. Stalin himself is only a grandiose mediocrity, and at that the grandiosity is due to his historical position and the mediocrity to his own personality. It is not surprising that these people proved doubly impotent before a problem which is insoluble in itself.

*Q:* What is the position of Soviet Ambassador Troyanovksy in relation to the New York commission?

*A:* His position is little to be envied. Diego Rivera told me Saturday: "Troyanovsky has lost his career and, together with the career, perhaps his head." I think that my friend is right. It is true that Troyanovsky has a great advantage: during the revolution he was in the camp of the Whites. But this alone is not sufficient. The most important problem that faced Troyanovsky for the past year was to compel American public opinion to believe in the justice of Stalin. However, nothing came of this. Stalin, as always, needs a scapegoat. One should not be surprised if Troyanovsky were invited to Moscow for "explanations."
Incidentally, if you publish the answer to your question, you can do Troyanovsky a serious service since it will not be easy for Stalin to act in strict accordance with the prediction of Diego Rivera.

*Q:* Do not pessimistic conclusions in regard to socialism flow from the Moscow trials and from the verdict of the commission?

*A:* No, I do not see any basis for pessimism. It is necessary to take history as it is. Humanity moves forward as did some pilgrims: two steps ahead, one step back. During the time of the backward movement, all seems lost to skeptics and pessimists. But this is an error of historical vision. Nothing is lost. Humanity has developed from the ape to the Comintern. It will advance from the Comintern to actual socialism. The judgment of the commission demonstrates once more that the correct idea is stronger than the most powerful police force. In this conviction lies the unshakable basis of revolutionary optimism.

# PERMISSION TO USE ARTICLES[108]

## December 14, 1937

Editor, *Forward*
Glasgow, Scotland
Dear Comrade Hughes:

Thank you for your friendly letter of November 29 and for the review of *The Case of Leon Trotsky*. I have had the possibility in the past of reading the *Forward* only episodically. I believe that we agree on some questions but disagree on many others. This cannot prevent me from writing in your weekly.

My friend Sumner[109] sent me your letter to him where you raise the question of royalties. It is true that I publish from time to time in the bourgeois press and that my literary agent tries to secure a corresponding payment: that is the only possibility for assuring our sustenance. But nine-tenths of my time is devoted to articles, pamphlets, letters for the revolutionary publications or for individual comrades, and the revolutionary papers are so poverty-stricken that there can be no question of royalties.

I will send you all the articles I send to the other working class papers in different countries. You can use everything you find of interest to you. If your paper is capable of paying some modest royalties you can send them to my son in Paris. His address is "*Biulleten Oppozitsii,* Librarie du Travail, 17 Rue de Sambre et Meuse, Paris, 10-2, France." But it is not a condition on my part for the publication of the articles.

Today I am sending you an article concerning a conversation with journalists on the verdict of the Commission of Inquiry. If sometime you should want an exclusive article for the *Forward,* you should indicate to me the topic presenting a special interest for your readers at the time.

With best greetings,
Yours sincerely,
Leon Trotsky

# HOW TO CONDUCT
# A POLITICAL DISCUSSION[110]

## December 15, 1937

Dear Comrade Burnham:

Your letter of December 9 is of the greatest interest to me. It is naturally too easy to be superwise at a great distance from the battlefield and to say to each of the combatants they "exaggerate a bit." But in your controversy with Shachtman I am tempted to play this not very attractive role.

It is difficult not to exaggerate in a clash of opinion. But it is very dangerous to schematize the exaggeration. I know of the position taken by Comrade Shachtman only through your interpretation. As a general rule I believe that it is not correct to begin a discussion with a threat of severe organizational consequences. A discussion is a discussion. It is an attempt to convince one another. The balance sheet of the discussion can reveal irreconcilable views and lead to organizational measures. But it is absolutely clear that the perspective of such measures cannot be considered as an argument.

You quote comrades who say that "the slightest deviation from Bolshevism involves a break from all of Bolshevism." Such an assertion is absurd. A living party can approach a relatively correct policy only by successive approximations; that is, by [successive] deviations to the right and to the left. The same is true for every party member, individually. If we should analyze the history of the entry into the Socialist Party, the work in it, and the break with it, we would find scores of examples illustrating this idea. The vigor of the party and the skill of its leadership are tested by their capacity to assimilate the partial deviations in time and not permit them to lead to a complete break with Marxism.

I agree with you also that organizational practice follows from general politics only in the *last instance*. In other words, that it has, within certain limits, an independent importance; that it can, consequently, influence for good or for bad the general policy.

But here begins the point where, if I correctly see the situation, I disagree with you. The party regime will be elaborated, corrected, improved during years and years in connection with a correct policy. A false position on the defense of the USSR can lead to a total breakdown of the party in the near future. I cannot put both questions on the same plane. At the present time the mature elements of the party should concentrate all their efforts on the most important and acute question: the unmasking and overcoming of the sectarian danger. In your place I would fight at this stage in full solidarity with the National Committee against the defeatists and inside the National Committee oppose premature or avoidable organizational measures. This "proportion" between the political and the organizational fight seems to me at least, from afar, more in correspondence with the real situation in the party today.

You can object to my position with words from your letters; namely, that you are now "finishing up a foundation which will determine the character of the building. A slight mistake now means disaster later on." But here is precisely the weakest point of your position. You reject, and rightly, the assertion that the "slightest deviation from Bolshevism involves necessarily a break from all of Bolshevism." But you repeat on the next page absolutely the same assertion only in relation to the organizational question. You wish with one stroke to provide a perfect foundation for party-building, and this aim dominates you with such power that you are ready to renounce not only a "perfect" Marxist policy but even a common fight in order to approach such a policy upon one of the most important questions of this historical period. Your conception lacks in this point the necessary inner proportions.

I should be very glad to have the possibility sometime of discussing all these questions with you personally. I remember very well how great an impression your article in the *Symposium* produced upon me at Prinkipo, and with what insistence I asked Max Eastman about you in order to clarify for myself the possibility of further collaboration with you.[111] I was very happy when I learned that you came to the Fourth International together with the American Workers Party. I follow with the greatest interest your writings in the party and I should like very much to meet you sometime personally. Don't you believe that it would be possible?

# LETTER TO THE
# NEW INTERNATIONAL[112]

## December 15, 1937

Dear Comrade:

The translation of my article on the *Manifesto* ["Ninety Years of the *Communist Manifesto*"] contained some meaning-distorting errors. We corrected them here with the greatest attention in collaboration with Joe. The text was retyped and sent November 17 to Comrade Shachtman as well as to all the other destinations in different countries. Now I see with stupefaction that the old, uncorrected text is published with a scandalously erroneous footnote.[113] I know the possible apologies: "We are so busy," and so on. My dear comrades, we are also *busy*. But we have enough respect for the *New International* and its readers in order to devote a working day of our common time solely for a good correction of the translation. Not the lack of time is responsible for such things but the lack of careful editing. The staff must have somebody who is totally responsible for the good technical editing of the *New International*. In any case I must know with whom personally I must deal before I send any new articles to the *New International*.

L. Trotsky

P.S.—We note that the title of the article is correct in the body of the magazine. This must indicate that you received the corrected manuscript in time to make editorial corrections even if you had the old copy set up in type.

P.P.S.—We have crossed with a red check those corrections which we categorically insist must be published in the next issue of the *New International*.

# GREETINGS TO NORWAY[114]

## December 19, 1937

Dear Comrades,

I have received your warm telegram of November 7. It was strong moral compensation for another telegram, or more correctly radiogram, that the great socialist Trygve Lie sent to my fascist overseer, Jonas Lie, on January 1, 1937.[115] On board the tanker, I asked myself: "This minister of justice was a member of the Third International just a few years ago and, in this sense, a comrade of mine?" I cannot conceal the fact that on thinking of this I spat in the Atlantic Ocean.

But now I see that there are comrades in Norway of a completely different sort. The new selection of revolutionaries is doubly valuable because the new cadres are forming not around a victorious workers' state, but around a persecuted program. In the present world situation, your little *Oktober* is more significant by far than the big dailies of the Second or Third International. With or without the permission of Mr. Konstad[116] or his Trygve Lie, I wish you the best revolutionary success.

With fraternal greetings,
L. Trotsky

# ANSWERS TO QUESTIONS
## OF MARIANNE[117]

## December 20, 1937

You have asked me a number of very "thorny" political questions. No doubt my answers to these questions differ by 180 degrees from the views of your newspaper. For this reason, I can reply to your questions on the sole condition that my answers be reproduced in their entirety and with no alteration. I daresay that this is also in the interests of your readers; if they are in any way able to show interest in my ideas, it will of course only be possible if my ideas are not cut or mutilated.

My position is that of the Fourth International, the only revolutionary organization of our epoch. The fundamental elements of our analysis of the world situation are as follows:

Since the last war, capitalism has definitively entered a stage of decline and decay. Humanity is now more impoverished than in 1913. The advancement of science and technology under the conditions of decaying capitalism means only an increase in "technological" unemployment, the ruination of the middle classes, and an enormous concentration of wealth. The present crisis began at a lower level than did the last crisis, and is developing at a faster rate. In its decline, capitalism drags bourgeois democracy down with it: it could only afford this luxury in the epoch of its ascendancy. It would be absurd to say that the "traditions" or the particular "national character" of France or England are able to save them from fascism. The fundamental factor in human history is neither "tradition" nor "national character," but the development of the productive forces. Where this development ceases, the institutions and honored traditions crumble into dust. This fact is attested to by the entire history of human civilization.

Modern technology has finally exceeded the framework of the

private ownership of the means of production and the boundaries of the national state. The productive forces of humanity are suffocating in these fetters. It is exactly this fact that determines the character of our epoch as an epoch of social upheavals, of wars big and small, of revolutions and counterrevolutions. Our planet will not find peace so long as the productive forces and the means of production do not become social property and are not organized according to a scientific plan, first on the national, then on the Europe-wide, and finally on the world scale. Such a reorganization is inconceivable without the expropriation of the capitalists, that is, without a social revolution.

In Belgium, Mr. De Man promised to bring about a planned economy without revolution or uprisings.[118] From the start, we characterized this promise as political charlatanism. A harsh appraisal, but events have clearly confirmed it. Mr. De Man has become some minister or other for decadent capitalism.

The fate of Mr. Leon Blum is hardly better. He proposed to "postpone" the idea of social revolution (politicians of this sort always go slowly on the most pressing issues) and to busy himself "in the meantime" with a program of great social reforms. At that time I wrote that this policy, which follows the line of least resistance, is the blindest, most utopian policy. Decaying capitalism can no longer provide social reforms, and for this reason it has to take back with one hand what it gives with the other. The Blum government was a bankrupt, reformist government, and nothing else. In July 1936, a socialist politician, certainly not a very serious one, wrote in *Le Populaire,* "Everything is possible." This was absolutely true. The Blum government, thanks to the powerful offensive of the masses and to the complete disarray of the capitalists, would have been able to realize the nationalization of the economy with a minimum of upheavals or of victims. But obviously this was a purely theoretical "possibility," for it presupposed a homogeneous and courageous revolutionary government, and not a coalition of parliamentary rationalizers. It is no surprise that this great historic opportunity was missed. The foreign policy of Mr. Blum, especially with regard to Spain, was permeated with the same principle: procrastinate, and thereby let the problems accumulate. That was called the "fight for peace." The result was that the Blum government succeeded in preparing a new period of internal and external crises.

The so-called People's Front can do no better. The Radicals, despite their old clothing and outdated mannerisms, represent the left wing of finance capital, and nothing else.[119] They are capable of all the reforms that . . . do not threaten the domination of capital. In other words, they are no longer capable of any reforms. The Socialists, even if they wanted to, can contribute nothing more than the Radicals have agreed to contribute. As for the so-called Communists, I find it very hard to find an expression sufficiently parliamentary to characterize this party: it is impossible to find in history another example of such a mixture of demagogy and servility. In sum, the People's Front is a bloc of the bourgeoisie and the proletariat. When two forces tend in opposite directions, the diagonal of the parallelogram approaches zero. This is exactly the graphic formula of a People's Front government.

In Spain the Caballero-Negrin-Stalin government has strangled the socialist revolution with some success; in doing so, Caballero-Negrin-Stalin have not only trampled on democracy, replacing it with the shameful dictatorship of the GPU, but have also ensured a series of important victories for Franco. Once again, allow me to refer to what I wrote in April 1931: "The Spanish revolution cannot stop at the democratic stage; it will be concluded either by the dictatorship of the proletariat or by the triumph of fascism." To my mind, events have not disproved this prediction.

The politics of the People's Front in France, as in Spain, is fundamentally indistinguishable from the politics of the German Social Democracy, which also untiringly built its "People's Front" with the democrats and the Catholic center. It is precisely this policy of internal weakness and marking time (with a result equal to zero) that led to the triumph of Hitler.

Certainly, in that period (why it was called the "third" period no one knows)[120] the so-called Communists did not want even to consider united actions of any kind with other workers' organizations. Stalin's doctrine said, "Social Democracy and fascism are twins, not opposites." They considered Daladier, Leon Blum, and even Zyromsky as fascists.[121] Since then the Comintern has completely reversed its stand: the "fascists" have become "anti-fascists." But that is hardly better. The Comintern of yesterday sabotaged the struggle of the proletariat by blocking any regroupment of its forces. The Comintern of today sabotages its struggle by submitting the proletariat to the control of the bourgeoisie. The methods are different; the result is the same.

The powerful growth of the unions in France reflected the confused aspirations of the masses for a change in the social conditions. The bureaucracy of Mr. Jouhaux, with the support of the Stalinists, directed all the efforts of its apparatus toward halting the natural and inevitable development of the struggle and has thereby prepared future upsurges. It has been found that the pretended "independence" of the unions has served only to submit the unions to the control of the Radicals, and to push society even deeper into an impasse.

The general conclusion is this: Europe, more than any other part of the world, will see in the coming years national and international explosions. All the parties of order, all the parties of reform, all the forces of "democracy" and "pacifism" are agreed, it seems, on unleashing international anarchy and civil war. This is precisely wherein the historical impasse of capitalism is expressed! The infamous Moscow trials tried to present me as the organizer of a "plot" aimed at provoking a world war. In truth, if indeed I was aiming at such a goal, I do not know what help I could have added to the work of the forces of imperialism, with the direct or indirect cooperation of the Second and Third Internationals and the International Federation of Trade Unions.

All three of these organizations survive, just as bourgeois democracy and capitalism have survived. They are all destined to collapse. The Fourth International is the party of the international socialist revolution. Its strength lies in having no illusions about the future march of history. Its fundamental rule is: openly tell what is. It also tries to predict what will happen, and, as the facts show, not without success. The Fourth International is educating new revolutionary cadres and is helping them meet the tasks of our epoch. The bankruptcy of the Second and Third Internationals prepares the conditions for the rapid growth of the Fourth. In the course of the next ten years it will become a decisive historical force.

You ask whether Stalin, despite everything, has realized his *domestic* goals by his judicial falsifications. I do not think so. The trials themselves were the expression of intolerable internal contradictions. I go into all the necessary details of these in my last two books, *The Revolution Betrayed* and *Les Crimes de Staline* (published by Grasset).[122] Without a doubt, Stalin had not foreseen that his judicial falsifications would bring just as terrible a shock to the whole system of government. But he had no choice. The growing scale of the "purges" shows that even in the ranks of the bureaucracy discontent is spiraling. When the number of victims (shot, imprisoned, and deported) reaches the tens of thousands, then hundreds of thousands and millions of people cannot fail to know the truth. The verdict of the International Commission in New York, which declared that the Moscow trials were judicial frauds, cannot fail to penetrate the USSR; by radio, by foreign newspapers received in Soviet editorial offices, by Soviet citizens abroad, by foreign visitors to the USSR. Ever new revelations will reinforce the commission's verdict. The truth will find a way around all obstacles.

Having answered your questions, let me ask you one: do you know how the chairman of the League for the Rights of Man, Mr. Basch, and his incomparable lawyer, Mr. Rosenmark, felt after the verdict of the commission?[123]

# INTELLECTUALS
# AND THE PARTY MILIEU[124]

## December 21, 1937

Dear Jim:

I thank you for your explanatory letter concerning the "B" case. I sent you a copy of my last letter to him. It is not a formal invitation to come here but an expression of my personal interest in him and of my appreciation of his extraordinary intellectual qualities. I don't believe that such a letter can be prejudicial. In the Russian party we had some representatives of the same type, for example, three history professors, Pokrovsky, Rozhkov, and Cheraskov.[125] Rozhkov passed from Bolshevism to Menshevism. Cheraskov is now in France with Kerensky. Pokrovsky died as a Stalinist but was totally disqualified by the Stalinists themselves after his death. They came from a different milieu to the party, not as young men, and they could never adapt themselves totally to the party milieu. Lenin expended innumerable efforts in order to save them for the party in spite of all the difficulties and to find for them adequate place and work. He succeeded at least in respect to Pokrovsky, the most important of the three.

Don't you believe that "B" could concentrate on the *New International* and as a chief of the scientific propaganda of the party, including the direction of a higher party school? It would be possibly good to introduce him also into international work in order to bring him in more direct contact with leading comrades from different sections. The International Conference or the new International Secretariat should name a commission for the elaboration of the program of the Fourth International and include in this commission, among others, "B" and me. During his vacations he could come here in order to edit with me the first draft for the commission. This would give us the possibility of amply and intimately discussing all the theoretical and practical problems of the revolutionary movement. I believe that by the combination of all the above-sketched measures, we can help "B" during the difficult process of adaptation to a new milieu. Everything should be done in order to save such a first-class force for our movement.

The blow given to the Stalinists by the commission's verdict is tremendous. In the next period the proletarian vanguard will be the first beneficiary in spite of all the reservations and objections of Dr. Dewey and other liberals. Our American comrades accomplished a magnificent work.

Now the question of defense for Stalin's victims in the USSR and abroad remains in full force. I don't know what is the final decision concerning the defense committee. But should it be dissolved or transformed we must immediately have a new committee with a long-range perspective. I read your excellent memo concerning the Robinson case.[126] But this case shows again the necessity of a permanent inquiry and defense body.

My best greetings to Rose and to you,

Hansen [Trotsky]

# LETTER TO AUSTRALIANS[127]

## December 23, 1937

Dear Comrades:

You will surely excuse the delay in my answering your so interesting and important letter. We have all been very busy here at this time with the Dewey Commission and other very urgent matters. Now I can answer your letter only briefly.

It is necessary in my opinion to distinguish strictly between two matters: (a) the Chinese-Japanese war; (b) your relationship to your government.

A Japanese victory will serve reaction. A Chinese victory would have a progressive character. That is why the working class of the world supports by all means China against Japan. But this doesn't at all signify that you can trust your government with the mission of supporting China in your name. It is incomparably more probable that the Australian government will use its armed forces against its own toiling masses than against Japan. Even in the case of military conflict between Australia and Japan the Australian government would be glad to arrange the matter on the back of China. It would be a crime for a workers' party to give any political support to a bourgeois government in order to "help China." But from the other side it would be no less a crime to proclaim a working class organization neutral in face of the Chinese-Japanese war.

We can with all the necessary modifications apply the same reasoning to the question of Australian independence. Naturally no Australian worker or farmer wishes to be conquered and subjected to Japan. For a revolutionary party it would be suicidal to say simply we are "indifferent" to this question. But we cannot give to a bourgeois and essentially imperialist government the task of defending the independence of Australia. The *immigration* policy of the Australian government furnishes the Japanese imperialists a kind of justification in the opinion of the Japanese people. By its *general* policy the bourgeois government weakens the Australian people economically, politically, and militarily. Finally, in the case of a great social crisis the bourgeois government would inevitably be ready to compromise with the foreign imperialists, sacrificing the vital interests of the country, in order to have the opportunity to prevent the social revolution. All these reasons are more than sufficient to justify our irreconcilable policy toward the bourgeois ruling class in every capitalist country. But there is not the slightest reason to proclaim our indifference on the question of national independence.

I will add an important practical consideration already expressed in my other letters in the last period.

We cannot, as stated above, entrust the bourgeoisie with the necessary means for helping China. But our policy would differ in these cases depending on whether Australia intervened in the war on the side of Japan or on the side of China. We would naturally in both cases remain in the sharpest opposition to the government. But at the same time as we boycotted with every means material help to Japan, we would on the contrary accuse the government of not sufficiently supporting China, that is, of betraying her ally, and so on.

I must limit myself to these short remarks. In connection with the last articles and letters I wrote on this matter they can, I hope, sufficiently explain my point of view.

With my best comradely greetings,
Leon Trotsky

# THE SPANISH LESSON
# FOR THE FOURTH INTERNATIONAL[128]

## December 24, 1937

Dear Comrade Cannon:

I am sending you a big article on Spain which tries to cover the more important phases and conclusions of the Spanish revolution.[129] I attribute some importance to this article: first, in view of the importance of the Spanish lesson for the education of the Fourth International; and second, in view of the fact that Sneevliet, Vereecken, Victor Serge, and some other comrades[130] propagate on the Spanish matter absolutely Menshevist ideas. The Dutch party is profoundly contaminated by the spirit of Sneevliet. Vereecken does the same work in the Belgian section but without the brutality of Sneevliet, with the leaps to the left, extravaganzas, and caprices which characterize our friend Vereecken. We cannot save these two important sections without showing them that there are questions upon which we can make no concessions. It would be a childish job to create a new International as a party of world revolution and to make concessions to Sneevliet's and Vereecken's Menshevism on the most important question of our time. That is why I hope the American comrades will not only publish the article but will express in an editor's note their fundamental rejection of the conceptions of Sneevliet, Victor Serge, and Vereecken.

Now as to the question as to how and where you can publish this article. I personally would prefer that you publish it in two issues of the *Socialist Appeal* in the same make-up as "Stalinism and Bolshevism." You can then use the type either for a pamphlet or for a preface or supplement to the coming book by Felix Morrow,[131] if the author accepts this proposition.

If publication in the *Socialist Appeal* seems to you inadvisable you can use the article for the *New International,* or solely as a pamphlet. I leave to you the definite decision. Personally I prefer as mentioned the publication in the *Socialist Appeal.*

Leon Trotsky

# FOR A PERMANENT
# DEFENSE COMMITTEE[132]

## December 30, 1937

Dear Comrades:

When this letter arrives the conference should be over,[133] and this gives me the hope that you will pay sufficient attention to the matter. I mean the international committee of defense for revolutionaries against persecution, especially that of the GPU.

I don't know whether you realized your plan of dissolving the defense committee immediately after the announcement of the verdict. If the composition of the committee and its inner situation don't permit any other solution, a new committee should be organized immediately. I believe even that the proclamation of the dissolving of the committee and the creation of the new one should be issued simultaneously.

It would be fatal to believe that our first tremendous victory—now strengthened by the declarations of Barmin and Krivitsky—signifies the end of Stalinist criminal activity or the weakening of it. Theoretically it is not excluded. Practically it depends upon the degree of the disintegration of the Stalinist apparatus inside the USSR. The power of this apparatus is tremendous. Even its death agonies can last a long time. But we cannot say with assurance that this death agony has begun. From the other side it is almost sure that Stalin and his nearest collaborators are incapable of understanding immediately the international extent of their defeat: none of their agents dares to tell them the truth. Thus the old lines of frame-ups, kidnapings, assassinations, and so on can automatically follow in spite of the latest revelations. The wounded beast can give us the most terrible blows five minutes before its collapse. That is why the best utilization of our first victory is the creation of a serious defense machine.

The committee, in my opinion, should have different functions:

(a) An open political function in direct connection with the work of the first committee and the inquiry commission: the systematic popularization of the verdict; unmasking of new crimes, investigating through new commissions, especially the crimes in Spain; a systematic press service, and so on.

(b) A special permanent treasury for these aims as well as for direct support of the victims and their families.

(c) A secret service for investigation of the GPU activities in different workers' organizations as also in other spheres—so to speak, a counterespionage. This proposition can seem to some "skeptical" minds (often they imagine themselves to be realistic ones) fantastic, especially in view of our general weakness. But that is an absolutely false point of view. An objective necessity creates new, often unexpected possibilities. We have won new sympathies in different strata of society. It is necessary to utilize the new sympathies and possibilities through a centralized organization with concrete aims. A special, if not official, center is necessary with serious and experienced comrades at the head. This center should have its agents in all the workers' organizations with the purpose of observing the maneuvers of the Stalinists and [should] send timely reports to the center. The Stalinist press should be concentrated, classified, and studied in this center from the same point of view. (I spoke about this in my open letter ["It Is High Time to Launch a World Offensive Against Stalinism"] published by you.)

One example shows the urgency of such a committee from the financial point of view. Scores of Americans visit us here. Many of them could contribute for a committee but it is necessary to have a printed prospectus of the aims of the committee and a special contributors' list, stamps, and so on. It would be absolutely possible to create here a financial commission working under the auspices of New York.

Can we hope that the new National Committee will immediately take the matter in its hands, name responsible comrades, etc., so that at the beginning of February the new committee can officially appear on the scene? I hope that it is possible under the conditions of a strong division of labor. The efforts spent now will give in the next period greatly appreciable results.

L. Trotsky

# ON MODERN MONTHLY[134]

## December 31, 1937

Dear Comrades:

I believe that it is necessary to determine our attitude toward Calverton and his *Modern Monthly*. At the time you published my letter to him he finally wrote me an answer, a very equivocal one, in its essence totally hostile. You know that Max Eastman proposed to him that he strike out silently the name of Carleton Beals. But in a letter, a copy of which was sent to you, Diego Rivera protested against this proposition because in the actual situation it signified protecting Beals, sparing him a public condemnation. After a month of vacillation, Calverton agreed with Eastman's proposition, but in his letter to me he repeats three times that "they" don't suspect the honesty of Beals, and so on. At least three times Calverton repeats that "their" magazine is totally independent and will accept no command from groups and "individuals." This declaration is not very intelligent. No one of us has or has had the high pretension to "command" the *Modern Monthly*. It was Calverton who wished my collaboration and I answered him that I cannot collaborate with Beals or with people who tolerate Beals instead of condemning him openly.

But these formal things are not of importance. A long time ago Diego Rivera warned me against Calverton as a very dubious fellow. Now with the appearance of the *New International*, *Modern Monthly* comes into a very difficult position. The essence of its program is ambiguity. The essence of the *New International* is the fight against every ambiguity. It is not difficult to foresee that the *Modern Monthly* will look, is possibly already looking, for support from embarrassed Stalinists and semi-Stalinists and can become in this way a hindrance for rapprochement between us and many valuable radical elements. The effort to hold Beals so long as possible, the tender separation from him, and the hypocritical hostile letter to me are very clear symptoms and warnings. We haven't the slightest interest in protecting Calverton by silence or expectation. On the contrary we must unmask him as early and clearly as possible.

I haven't yet answered his last letter to me because I wish to see beforehand what he says in the *Monthly* about the whole thing and then I will coordinate my answer with your attitude toward the *Monthly*. Since the issue on Spain we have not received any new copies here. It is possible that Calverton cut off sending it. In any case I hope that you agree with the necessity of an open and sharp demarcation between us and the "independent" Calverton. We have naturally not the slightest interest in repulsing such valuable people as Anita Brenner,[135] for example, but I don't believe that she is connected with Calverton (?).

                                                    Leon Trotsky

# LETTER ON DEFEATISM[136]

## January 2, 1938

Dear Comrade Van:

I haven't even a copy of *The Case of Leon Trotsky* here. I cannot therefore analyze the text nor, above all, the context. But the question is very clear even without that—at least for those who do not deliberately want to get tangled up. The commission, as was its duty, manifested a deep interest toward the question of my attitude toward the USSR and especially during war. "If you don't want to support the governments allied to the USSR, you are practically a defeatist." Such was the meaning of the commissioners' arguments, particularly, if I do not deceive myself, Stolberg and, in part, the lawyer Finerty.[137] It is easy to see that they reproduce in this way the argumentation of our ultralefts, only with the opposite sign (one can see even in this that ultraleftism is bourgeois thought, only turned upside down and carried to an extreme).

I answered in the sense that we develop our policy not through governments, but through the masses and while remaining in irreconcilable opposition toward the bourgeois governments allied to the USSR, such as France; in the practical application of our general line we do all—all we possibly can—to protect the interests of the defense of the USSR (or China, etc.). Then I had to give in this connection some brief examples, along the line of those which served me in the discussion on the Chinese question (two ships, etc.). In sum, the question reduces itself to knowing whether we are obliged to defend the USSR or another more "authentic" workers' state, in case of war, without giving up revolutionary opposition—and if so, by what means. This question is dealt with in my article directed against Craipeau. For the moment I have nothing to add to it.

It is possible that there is some lack of precision in the

stenographic report. It is not a matter here either of a
programmatic text well thought out, or even of an article, but of a
stenographic report drawn up by the commission. You know that
I did not even have a chance to revise it myself. Some
misunderstandings, imprecisions, may have crept in. Enemies
can make use of them, but serious comrades must grasp the
question in its totality. I remain completely on the basis of the
theses of the Fourth International on war. There is a subject
precisely related to this theme and which from its inception had
aroused the opposition of Ver[eecken] and Craipeau. It is on this
that we must speak out: Has or has not the experience of the last
years confirmed our theses on this decisive point?

I saw by chance that the American Lovestoneites have also
tried to use the same isolated citation so as to present the matter
as if I had two opposing policies during war—one for the
democratic countries, the other for the fascist countries. Nothing
is more absurd. The war will not be the competition of political
regimes. It is a question of sharing the world, of definitively
subjugating China and winning back the USSR for capitalism.
Our policy during the war must therefore be adapted to the
character of the war. We are against the enslavement of China as
we are against the reestablishment of capitalism in the USSR.
We therefore help the USSR, likewise China, during war by all
the means at the disposal of an oppressed and nonruling class
which remains in irreconcilable opposition toward its government: by preparing to overthrow it and seize power. This is how
the question is posed. Whoever poses it otherwise seeks to evade
answering it or else, very simply, to tangle it all up.

As for Comrade Ver., who unfortunately moves further and
further away from Marxism, it is extremely characteristic that he
finds it possible to support Sneevliet in his totally opportunist
struggle, henceforth in the open, against the Fourth International
and at the same time direct against us his ultraleft intransigence.
So as not to deprive the NAS of governmental manna, Sneevliet
has a completely conciliatory, diplomatic, and equivocal attitude
toward his government in peacetime. Can one believe for an
instant that in case of war, with Holland's participation,
Sneevliet will be capable of a revolutionary attitude? Only a blind
man could believe it. The duty of every revolutionist in Holland,
as elsewhere, is to denounce pitilessly the policy of Sneevliet,
which can only compromise the Fourth International. Instead of
that, Ver. sets himself up as Sneevliet's guardian angel. He
protects him against faction work, that is, against Marxism, as

he already had protected those poor centrists of the POUM against "nuclei-work" on the part of the Fourth International.

The world appears to be upside down in Ver.'s head. On every occasion, he only makes new mistakes to cover up the preceding ones or to turn attention away from them. He is oscillating now between Sneevliet and the Bordigists[138] and his oscillations become more and more menacing, fortunately not for the Fourth International, but unfortunately for Ver. himself. I have already written in a preceding letter that we must save Ver. from himself. This task becomes more burning than ever. But Comrade Ver. can be saved neither by concessions nor by considerations. The firm bulwark of all the Fourth International sections, the Belgian included, must be opposed to him. In any case, the decisive question for Ver.'s future is not his factious distortion with regard to badly interpreted, isolated quotations, but his attitude toward the POUM and Sneevliet, that is, for Marxism or opportunism, for the Fourth International or for the London Bureau.[139]

This is all I can say for the moment and I really believe that after all the polemics of these last years, it completely suffices.

My best greetings,
L. Trotsky

# DOES THE SOVIET GOVERNMENT STILL FOLLOW THE PRINCIPLES ADOPTED TWENTY YEARS AGO?[140]

## January 13, 1938

In order to correctly answer the question raised in the title of this article, it is first of all necessary to establish the difference between the basic conquest of the October Revolution—nationalized property—and the policy pursued by the present government. There is a contradiction between the revolutionary form of property and the Thermidorean, i.e., reactionary, policy. But up to the present this policy has been unable or hasn't dared or hasn't succeeded as yet in overthrowing the revolutionary form of property. The incumbent government's tendencies are diametrically opposed to the program of Bolshevism. But inasmuch as the institutions erected by the revolution still continue to exist, the bureaucracy is compelled to externally adapt its tendencies to the old principles of Bolshevism: it continues to swear by the covenants of October; it invokes the interests of the proletariat and invariably refers to the Soviet system as socialist. One may say without risking a blunder that in the history of mankind there has never been a government so given to lies and hypocrisy as the Soviet bureaucracy of today.

In and of itself, the preservation of state ownership of the means of production is of enormous progressive significance, inasmuch as with the aid of planned economy this permits the attainment of a swift development of the productive forces. True, the economic statistics issued by the bureaucracy do not merit any confidence: they systematically exaggerate successes while concealing failures. It is nonetheless unthinkable to deny the fact that even today the Soviet Union's productive forces are still developing at a tempo that was not and is not known in any other country in the world. Whoever refuses to see this side of the case, identifying the Soviet regime with fascism—as, for example, Max Eastman does—throws out, as the Germans say, the baby with the bathwater. The development of the productive forces is the fundamental factor of human culture. Without increasing man's power over nature it is impossible even to think of destroying the rule of man over man. Socialism cannot be erected on backwardness and poverty. The technical premise of socialism has taken an enormous step forward in the Soviet Union in the course of these twenty years.

However, least of all is this the merit of the bureaucracy. On the contrary, the ruling caste has become transformed into the greatest brake upon the development of the productive forces. Socialist economy must by its very essence take as its guide the interests of the producers and the needs of the consumers. These interests and needs can find their expression only through the medium of a fully flowering democracy of producers and consumers. Democracy, in this particular case, is not some sort of abstract principle. It is the one and only conceivable mechanism for preparing the socialist system of economy and realizing it in life.

The incumbent ruling clique has replaced Soviet, party, trade union, and cooperative democracy by the domineering of functionaries. But a bureaucracy, even one composed entirely of geniuses, could not assure from its bureaus the necessary proportions between all branches of economy, that is, the necessary correspondence between production and consumption. What the lexicon of Stalin's justice designates as "sabotage" is in reality one of the evil consequences of bureaucratic methods of domineering. The manifestations of disproportion, wastefulness, and entanglement, constantly increasing, threaten to undermine the very foundations of planned economy. The bureaucracy invariably seeks "the guilty one." Such in the majority of cases is the secret meaning of the Soviet trials of saboteurs.

To find an explanation of the existing regime in Stalin's personal "lust for power" is far too superficial. Stalin is not an individual but a caste symbol. Power is not something incorporeal. Power enables one to dispose of and appropriate material values. Naturally, complete equality cannot be attained in a single leap. A certain differentiation in labor payments is dictated at the given stage in the interests of raising labor productivity. However, of decisive importance in evaluating the nature of society is the following question: is the society evolving in the direction of equality or in the direction of privileges? The answer to this question does not leave room for any doubts whatever. The differentiation of [Soviet] society has long exceeded the limits of economic necessity. The material privileges of the bureaucracy have grown like a glacier. Fearful of their isolation from the masses, the bureaucracy seeks to create a new labor and *kolkhoz* aristocracy under the banner of Stakhanovism.[141]

The division of national income in its turn determines the political regime. The ruling caste cannot permit a producers'-consumers' democracy for the simple reason that it ruthlessly despoils both the producers and the consumers. One may accept as an established fact that the bureaucracy devours not less than half of the national consumption fund, taking of course into account not only living quarters, food, clothing, means of transport and communication, but also educational institutions, press, literature, sports, cinema, radio, theaters, museums, and so on. We can therefore say with complete justification that although the bureaucracy is still compelled to adapt itself to the institutions and traditions of the October Revolution, its policy, which expresses its own interests, is directly opposed to the interests of the people and of socialism.

The same basic contradiction can be corroborated in all other spheres of social life, such as the state, the army, the family, the school, culture, science, art, and so on.

From the standpoint of *Marxism,* the state is a machine whereby one class rules over another. The dictatorship of the proletariat is only a temporary institution, indispensable to the toilers for coping with the resistance of the exploiters and for destroying exploitation. In a society without classes the state, as an apparatus of coercion, must gradually wither away and become replaced by the free self-administration of producers and consumers. But what do we observe in reality? Twenty years after the revolution the Soviet state has become the most centralized, despotic, and bloodthirsty apparatus of coercion and compulsion. The evolution of the Soviet state therefore proceeds in complete contradiction to the principles of the Bolshevik program. The reason for it is to be found in this, that society, as has already been said, is evolving not toward socialism but toward the regeneration of social contradictions. Should the process continue in this direction, it must inevitably lead to the rebirth of classes, the liquidation of planned economy, and the restoration of capitalist property. The state regime will in that case inevitably become fascist.

The October Revolution proclaimed as one of its tasks: to dissolve the *army* in the people. It was presumed that the armed forces would be built on the militia principle. Only this type of army organization, making the people the armed master of their own fate, corresponds to the nature of socialist society. In the course of the first decade systematic preparation was made for the transition from a barracks-army to a militia-army. But from the moment when the bureaucracy succeeded in crushing every manifestation of working class independence, it openly transformed the army into an instrument of its own domination. The militia system has been completely set aside. An army of two million is now a purely barracks-army in character. An officer caste with generals and marshals has been reinstituted. From an instrument of socialist defense the army has been turned into an instrument of defense of the bureaucracy's privileges. Things, however, did not stop there. The struggle between Stalin's narrow clique and the more authoritative and talented military leaders, genuinely devoted to the interests of defense, has led to the beheading of the Red Army.

The position of *woman* is the most graphic and telling indicator for evaluating a social regime and state policy. The October Revolution inscribed on its banner the emancipation of womankind and created the most progressive legislation in history on marriage and the family. This does not mean, of course, that a "happy life" was immediately in store for the Soviet woman. Genuine emancipation of women is inconceivable without a general rise of economy and culture, without the destruction of the petty-bourgeois economic family unit, without the introduction of socialized food preparation and education. Meanwhile, guided by its conservative instinct, the bureaucracy has taken alarm at the "disintegration" of the family. It began singing panegyrics to the family supper and the family laundry, that is, the household slavery of woman. To cap it all, the bureaucracy has restored criminal punishment for abortions, officially returning women to the status of pack animals. In complete contradiction with the ABC of communism the ruling caste has thus restored the most reactionary and benighted nucleus of the class regime, i.e., the petty-bourgeois family.

The situation is not much better in the field of *culture*. The growth of productive forces created the material premise for a new culture. But the development of culture is unthinkable without criticism, without faltering and error, without independent creative work, in a word, without the awakening of the human personality. The bureaucracy, however, refuses to tolerate independent thought in a single field of creative activity. And in its own way it is right: should criticism awaken in the sphere of art or pedagogy, it will inevitably become directed against the bureaucracy, against its privileges, against its ignorance and its arbitrary rule. Herein is to be found the explanation for the fact that the "purge," having started with the party, penetrated later into all spheres of social life without exception. With "Trotsky-ism" as the token, the GPU "purges" poets, astronomers, pedagogues, and musicians, and therewith the best heads come under the muzzle of revolvers. Is it conceivable under such conditions to talk of "socialist" culture?

In the sphere of ordinary *literacy* the successes are unquestionable. Tens of millions have learned how to read and write. Parallel with this, however, they have been deprived of the right to express their views and their interests through the medium of the printed word. The press serves only the bureaucracy. The so-called "socialist" poets have the right to write only hymns to Stalin. The same right is bequeathed to the prose writers. The population is duty-bound to read these hymns. The same thing takes place with regard to cinema, radio, theater, and so on. A new prize-winning textbook on Russian history has been recently introduced in the schools. One can say without exaggeration that this textbook consists solely of falsifications, the aim of which is to justify the despotism of the bureaucracy and the personal autocracy of Stalin. Even textbooks on the history of the Catholic Church, published with the approval of the Vatican, are models of scientific conscientiousness in comparison with the Stalinized textbooks in the USSR. Tens of millions of children's heads are infected and poisoned by this meretricious literature.

The October Revolution proclaimed the right of every *nation* not only to an independent cultural development but also to state separation. As a matter of fact, the bureaucracy has transformed the Soviet Union into a new prisonhouse of the peoples. True enough, the national language and the national school continue to exist: in this sphere the mightiest despotism can no longer turn back the wheel of evolution. But the language of the various nationalities is not an organ of their independent development, but the organ of bureaucratic domineering over them. The governments of the national republics are, naturally, appointed by Moscow, or to put it more precisely, by Stalin. But the astonishing thing is that thirty of these governments suddenly turn out to have consisted of "enemies of the people" and agents of a foreign government. Behind this accusation, which rings far too rudely and ludicrously even on the lips of Stalin and Vyshinsky, there lurks in reality the fact that, in the national republics, functionaries, even those appointed by the Kremlin, fall into dependence upon local conditions and moods and become gradually infected with an oppositional spirit against the stifling centralism of Moscow. They begin dreaming or talking about replacing the "beloved leader" and relaxing the steel tentacles. This is the real reason why all the national republics of the USSR were recently beheaded.

It is hard to find in history an example of reaction uncolored by *anti-Semitism*. This peculiar historical law is likewise completely corroborated nowadays in the Soviet Union. In his interesting, though not profound, book, *Assignment in Utopia,* Eugene Lyons, who spent many years in Moscow, relates how the bureaucracy exploited systematically, even if covertly, anti-Semitic prejudices in order to intrench its rule. And how can it be otherwise? Bureaucratic centralism is unthinkable without chauvinism, while anti-Semitism has always been the line of least resistance so far as chauvinism is concerned.

In the sphere of *foreign policy,* in the course of these twenty years there has occurred a turn no less drastic than in internal policies. Only from inertia, or with some hidden thought in mind, does bourgeois reaction continue to indict Stalin as the inspirer of world revolution. As a matter of fact, the Kremlin has become one of the pillars of conservative law and order. The period when the Moscow government used to tie up the fate of the Soviet Republic with the fate of the world proletariat and of the oppressed peoples of the East has been left far behind. Apart from the question of whether the policy of the "People's Front" is good or bad, it happens to be the traditional policy of Menshevism against which Lenin fought all his life. It signals the renunciation of proletarian revolution in favor of conservative bourgeois democracy. The ruling Moscow caste seeks today one thing and one thing only: to abide in peace with all the ruling classes.

The contradiction between the October Revolution and the Thermidorean bureaucracy found its most dramatic expression in the annihilation of *the old generation of Bolsheviks*. Vyshinsky, Yezhov, Troyanovsky, Maisky, agents of the Comintern and the GPU, journalists of the Duranty-Louis Fischer type, attorneys of the Pritt type, will not dupe world public opinion. Not a single serious person any longer believes that hundreds of old revolutionists, leaders of the Bolshevik Party under [czarist] illegality, leaders of the civil war, revolutionary Soviet diplomats, military heads of the Red Army, heads of thirty national Soviet Republics, became—all at once and as if by command—agents of fascism. The New York Commission of Inquiry, comprised of impeccable and impartial people, after nine months' work found the Moscow trials to be the most elaborate deception in human history.

Today the issue is not that of proving that Zinoviev, Kamenev, Smirnov, Pyatakov, Serebriakov, Sokolnikov, Radek, Rakovsky, Krestinsky, Tukhachevsky, and hundreds of others have fallen victims of a frame-up.[142] This has been proved. What is at issue is to explain how and why the Kremlin clique could have risked undertaking so monstrous a frame-up. The answer to this flows from everything that has preceded.

In its struggle for power and revenue the bureaucracy is compelled to lop off and batter down those groups who are connected with the past, who know and remember the program of the October Revolution, who are sincerely devoted to the tasks of socialism. The slaying of Old Bolsheviks and of socialist elements among the middle and younger generations is the necessary link in the chain of anti-October reaction. That is why the accuser-prosecutor at the trials came forward in the person of a former White Guardist—Vyshinsky. That is why the USSR is represented in Washington by a former White Guardist— Troyanovsky—and in London by a former minister of Kolchak[143]—Maisky. And so on and so forth. The necessary people turn up in the necessary places.

Hardly anyone will permit himself to be duped by the farce of the recent Moscow elections. Hitler and Goebbels[144] have more than once perpetrated exactly the same thing, in exactly the same way. One need only read what the Soviet press itself has written concerning Hitler's plebiscites in order to grasp the secret of Stalin's "success." Totalitarian parliamentary experiments testify only to this: that once all the parties have been crushed, including one's own; once the trade unions have been strangled; once the press, the radio, and the cinema have been subordinated to the Gestapo or the GPU; if bread and work are given only to the docile or the silent, while a revolver is placed at the temple of every voter—then it is possible to achieve "unanimous" elections. But this unanimity is neither eternal nor stable. The traditions of the October Revolution have disappeared from the official arena, but they continue to live in the memory of the masses. Under the cover of juridical and electoral frame-ups, the contradictions continue to deepen and cannot fail to lead to an explosion. The reactionary bureaucracy has to be overthrown and it will be overthrown. The political revolution in the USSR is inevitable. It will signify the liberation of the elements of the new society from the yoke of the usurping bureaucracy. Only if this condition is given will the USSR be able to develop in the direction of socialism.

# HUE AND CRY OVER KRONSTADT[145]

## January 15, 1938

### A "People's Front" of Denouncers

The campaign around Kronstadt is being carried on with undiminished vigor in certain circles. One would think that the Kronstadt revolt occurred not seventeen years ago, but only yesterday. Participating in the campaign with equal zeal and under one and the same slogan are Anarchists, Russian Mensheviks, left Social Democrats of the London Bureau, individual blunderers, Miliukov's paper,[146] and, on occasion, the big capitalist press. A "People's Front" of its own kind!

Only yesterday I happened across the following lines in a Mexican weekly which is both reactionary Catholic and "democratic": "Trotsky ordered the shooting of 1,500 (?) Kronstadt sailors, these purest of the pure. His policy when in power differed in no way from the present policy of Stalin." As is known, the left Anarchists draw the same conclusion. When for the first time in the press I briefly answered the questions of Wendelin Thomas, member of the New York Commission of Inquiry, the Russian Mensheviks' paper immediately came to the defense of the Kronstadt sailors and . . . of Wendelin Thomas.[147] Miliukov's paper came forward in the same spirit. The Anarchists attacked me with still greater vigor. All these authorities claim that my answer was completely worthless. This unanimity is all the more remarkable since the Anarchists defend, in the symbol of Kronstadt, genuine antistate communism; the Mensheviks, at the time of the Kronstadt uprising, stood openly for the restoration of capitalism; and Miliukov stands for capitalism even now.

How can the Kronstadt uprising cause such heartburn to Anarchists, Mensheviks, and "liberal" counterrevolutionists, all at the same time? The answer is simple: all these groupings are interested in compromising the only genuinely revolutionary current, which has never repudiated its banner, has not compromised with its enemies, and alone represents the future. It is because of this that among the belated denouncers of my Kronstadt "crime" there are so many *former* revolutionists or *semi*revolutionists, people who have lost their program and their principles and who find it necessary to divert attention from the degradation of the Second International or the perfidy of the Spanish Anarchists. As yet, the Stalinists cannot openly join this campaign around Kronstadt but even they, of course, rub their hands with pleasure; for the blows are directed against "Trotskyism," against revolutionary Marxism, against the Fourth International!

Why in particular has this variegated fraternity seized precisely upon Kronstadt? During the years of the revolution we clashed not a few times with the Cossacks, the peasants, even with certain layers of workers (certain groups of workers from the Urals organized a volunteer regiment in the army of Kolchak!). The antagonism between the workers as consumers and the peasants as producers and sellers of bread lay, in the main, at the root of these conflicts. Under the pressure of need and deprivation, the workers themselves were episodically divided into hostile camps, depending upon stronger or weaker ties with the village. The Red Army also found itself under the influence of the countryside. During the years of the civil war it was necessary more than once to disarm discontented regiments. The introduction of the "New Economic Policy" (NEP) attenuated the friction but far from eliminated it.[148] On the contrary, it paved the way for the rebirth of kulaks [wealthy peasants] and led, at the beginning of this decade, to the renewal of civil war in the village. The Kronstadt uprising was only an *episode* in the history of the relations between the proletarian city and the petty-bourgeois village. It is possible to understand this episode only in connection with the general course of the development of the class struggle during the revolution.

Kronstadt differed from a long series of other petty-bourgeois movements and uprisings only by its greater external effect. The problem here involved a maritime fortress under Petrograd itself. During the uprising proclamations were issued and radio broadcasts were made. The Social Revolutionaries[149] and the Anarchists, hurrying from Petrograd, adorned the uprising with "noble" phrases and gestures. All this left traces in print. With the aid of these "documentary" materials (i.e., false labels), it is not hard to construct a legend about Kronstadt, all the more exalted since in 1917 the name Kronstadt was surrounded by a revolutionary halo. Not idly does the Mexican magazine quoted above ironically call the Kronstadt sailors the "purest of the pure."

The play upon the revolutionary authority of Kronstadt is one of the distinguishing features of this truly charlatan campaign. Anarchists, Mensheviks, liberals, reactionaries try to present the matter as if at the beginning of 1921 the Bolsheviks turned their weapons on those very Kronstadt sailors who guaranteed the victory of the October insurrection. Here is the point of departure for all the subsequent falsehoods. Whoever wishes to unravel these lies should first of all read the article by Comrade J.G. Wright in the *New International* (February 1938).[150] My problem is another one: I wish to describe the character of the Kronstadt uprising from a more general point of view.

## Social and Political Groupings in Kronstadt

A revolution is "made" directly by a *minority*. The success of a revolution is possible, however, only where this minority finds more or less support, or at least friendly neutrality, on the part of the majority. The shift in different stages of the revolution, like the transition from revolution to counterrevolution, is directly determined by changing political relations between the minority and the majority, between the vanguard and the class.

Among the Kronstadt sailors there were three political layers: the proletarian revolutionists, some with a serious past and training; the intermediate majority, mainly peasant in origin; and finally, the reactionaries, sons of kulaks, shopkeepers, and priests. In czarist times, order on battleships and in the fortress could be maintained only so long as the officers, acting through the reactionary sections of the petty officers and sailors, subjected the broad intermediate layer to their influence or terror, thus isolating the revolutionists, mainly the machinists, the gunners, and the electricians, i.e., predominantly the city workers.

The course of the uprising on the battleship *Potemkin* in 1905 was based entirely on the relations among these three layers, i.e., on the struggle between proletarian and petty-bourgeois reactionary extremes for influence upon the more numerous middle peasant layer. Whoever has not understood this problem, which runs through the whole revolutionary movement in the fleet, had best be silent about the problems of the Russian revolution in general. For it was entirely, and to a great degree still is, a struggle between the proletariat and the bourgeoisie for influence upon the peasantry. During the Soviet period the bourgeoisie has appeared principally in the guise of kulaks (i.e., the top stratum of the petty bourgeoisie), the "socialist" intelligentsia, and now in the form of the "Communist" bureaucracy. Such is the basic mechanism of the revolution in all its stages. In the fleet it assumed a more centralized, and therefore more dramatic expression.

The political composition of the Kronstadt Soviet reflected the composition of the garrison and the crews. The leadership of the soviets as early as the summer of 1917 belonged to the Bolshevik Party, which rested on the better sections of the sailors and included in its ranks many revolutionists from the underground movement who had been liberated from the hard-labor prisons. But I seem to recall that even in the days of the October insurrection the Bolsheviks constituted less than one-half of the Kronstadt Soviet. The majority consisted of SRs and Anarchists. There were no Mensheviks at all in Kronstadt. The Menshevik Party hated Kronstadt. The official SRs, incidentally, had no better attitude toward it. The Kronstadt SRs quickly went over into opposition to Kerensky and formed one of the shock brigades of the so-called "left" SRs. They based themselves on the peasant part of the fleet and of the shore garrison. As for the Anarchists, they were the most motley group. Among them were real revolutionists, like Zhuk and Zhelezniakov, but these were the elements most closely linked to the Bolsheviks. Most of the Kronstadt "Anarchists" represented the city petty bourgeoisie and stood upon a lower revolutionary level than the SRs. The president of the soviet was a nonparty man, "sympathetic to the Anarchists," and in essence a peaceful petty clerk who had been formerly subservient to the czarist authorities and was now subservient . . . to the revolution. The complete absence of Mensheviks, the "left" character of the SRs, and the Anarchist hue of the petty bourgeois were due to the sharpness of the revolutionary struggle in the fleet and the dominating influence of the proletarian sections of the sailors.

## Changes During the Years of Civil War

This social and political characterization of Kronstadt which, if desired, could be substantiated and illustrated by many facts and documents, is already sufficient to illuminate the upheavals which occurred in Kronstadt during the years of the civil war and as a result of which its physiognomy changed beyond recognition. Precisely about this important aspect of the question, the belated accusers say not one word, partly out of ignorance, partly out of malevolence.

Yes, Kronstadt wrote a heroic page in the history of the revolution. But the civil war began a systematic depopulation of Kronstadt and of the whole Baltic fleet. As early as the days of the October uprising, detachments of Kronstadt sailors were being sent to help Moscow. Other detachments were then sent to the Don, to the Ukraine, to requisition bread and organize the local power. It seemed at first as if Kronstadt were inexhaustible. From different fronts I sent dozens of telegrams about the mobilization of new "reliable" detachments from among the Petersburg workers and the Baltic sailors. But beginning as early as 1918, and in any case not later than 1919, the fronts began to complain that the new contingents of "Kronstadters" were unsatisfactory, exacting, undisciplined, unreliable in battle, and doing more harm than good. After the liquidation of Yudenich (in the winter of 1919),[151] the Baltic fleet and the Kronstadt garrison were denuded of all revolutionary forces. All the elements among them that were of any use at all were thrown against Denikin in the south.[152] If in 1917-18 the Kronstadt sailor stood considerably higher than the average level of the Red Army and formed the framework of its first detachments as well as the framework of the Soviet regime in many districts, those sailors who remained in "peaceful" Kronstadt until the beginning of 1921, not fitting in on any of the fronts of the civil war, stood by this time on a level considerably lower, in general, than the average level of the Red Army, and included a great percentage of completely demoralized elements, wearing showy bell-bottom pants and sporty haircuts.

Demoralization based on hunger and speculation had in general greatly increased by the end of the civil war. The so-called "sack-carriers" (petty speculators) had become a social blight, threatening to stifle the revolution. Precisely in Kronstadt where the garrison did nothing and had everything it needed, the demoralization assumed particularly great dimensions. When conditions became very critical in hungry Petrograd the Political Bureau more than once discussed the possibility of securing an "internal loan" from Kronstadt, where a quantity of old provisions still remained. But delegates of the Petrograd workers answered: "You will get nothing from them by kindness. They speculate in cloth, coal, and bread. At present in Kronstadt every kind of riffraff has raised its head." That was the real situation. It was not like the sugar-sweet idealizations after the event.

It must further be added that former sailors from Latvia and Estonia who feared they would be sent to the front and were preparing to cross into their new bourgeois fatherlands, Latvia and Estonia, had joined the Baltic fleet as "volunteers." These elements were in essence hostile to the Soviet authority and displayed this hostility fully in the days of the Kronstadt uprising. . . . Besides these there were many thousands of Latvian workers, mainly former farm laborers, who showed unexampled heroism on all fronts of the civil war. We must not, therefore, tar the Latvian workers and the "Kronstadters" with the same brush. We must recognize social and political differences.

## The Social Roots of the Uprising

The problem of a serious student consists in defining, on the basis of the objective circumstances, the social and political character of the Kronstadt mutiny and its place in the development of the revolution. Without this, "criticism" is reduced to sentimental lamentation of the pacifist kind in the spirit of Alexander Berkman, Emma Goldman, and their latest imitators.[153] These gentlefolk do not have the slightest understanding of the criteria and methods of scientific research. They quote the proclamations of the insurgents like pious preachers quoting Holy Scriptures. They complain, moreover, that I do not take into consideration the "documents," i.e., the gospel of Makhno and the other apostles.[154] To take documents "into consideration" does not mean to take them at their face value. Marx has said that it is impossible to judge either parties or peoples by what they say about themselves. The characteristics of a party are determined considerably more by its social composition, its past, its relation to different classes and strata, than by its oral and written declarations, especially during a critical moment of civil war. If, for example, we began to take as pure gold the innumerable proclamations of Negrin, Companys, Garcia Oliver, and Company,[155] we would have to recognize these gentlemen as fervent friends of socialism. But in reality they are its perfidious enemies.

In 1917-18 the revolutionary workers led the peasant masses, not only of the fleet but of the entire country. The peasants seized and divided the land most often under the leadership of the soldiers and sailors arriving in their home districts. Requisitions of bread had only begun and were mainly from the landlords and kulaks at that. The peasants reconciled themselves to requisitions as a temporary evil. But the civil war dragged on for three years. The city gave practically nothing to the village and took almost everything from it, chiefly for the needs of war. The peasants approved of the "Bolsheviks" but became increasingly hostile to the "Communists." If in the preceding period the workers had led the peasants forward, the peasants now dragged the workers back. Only because of this change in mood could the Whites partially attract the peasants, and even the half-peasants–half-workers, of the Urals to their side. This mood, i.e., hostility to the city, nourished the movement of Makhno, who seized and looted trains marked for the factories, the plants, and the Red Army, tore up railroad tracks, shot Communists, etc. Of course, Makhno called this the Anarchist struggle with the "state." In reality, this was a struggle of the infuriated petty property owner against the proletarian dictatorship. A similar movement arose in a number of other districts, especially in Tambovsky, under the banner of "Social Revolutionaries." Finally, in different parts of the country so-called "Green" peasant detachments were active. They did not want to recognize either the Reds or the Whites and shunned the city parties. The "Greens" sometimes met the Whites and received severe blows from them, but they did not, of course, get any mercy from the Reds. Just as the petty bourgeoisie is ground economically between the millstones of big capital and the proletariat, so the peasant partisan detachments were pulverized between the Red Army and the White.

Only an entirely superficial person can see in Makhno's bands or in the Kronstadt revolt a struggle between the abstract principles of Anarchism and "state socialism." Actually these movements were convulsions of the peasant petty bourgeoisie which desired, of course, to liberate itself from capital but which at the same time did not consent to subordinate itself to the dictatorship of the proletariat. The petty bourgeoisie does not know concretely what it wants, and by virtue of its position cannot know. That is why it so readily covered the confusion of its demands and hopes, now with the Anarchist banner, now with the populist, now simply with the "Green." Counterposing itself to the proletariat, it tried, flying all these banners, to turn the wheel of the revolution backwards.

## The Counterrevolutionary Character of the Kronstadt Mutiny

There were, of course, no impassable bulkheads dividing the different social and political layers of Kronstadt. There were still at Kronstadt a certain number of qualified workers and technicians to take care of the machinery. But even they were identified by a method of negative selection as politically unreliable and of little use for the civil war. Some "leaders" of the uprising came from among these elements. However, this completely natural and inevitable circumstance, to which some accusers triumphantly point, does not change by one iota the anti-proletarian character of the revolt. Unless we are to deceive ourselves with pretentious slogans, false labels, etc., we shall see that the Kronstadt uprising was nothing but an armed reaction of the petty bourgeoisie against the hardships of social revolution and the severity of the proletarian dictatorship.

That was exactly the significance of the Kronstadt slogan, "Soviets without Communists," which was immediately seized upon, not only by the SRs but by the bourgeois liberals as well. As a rather farsighted representative of capital, Professor Miliukov understood that to free the soviets from the leadership of the Bolsheviks would have meant within a short time to demolish the soviets themselves. The experience of the Russian soviets during the period of Menshevik and SR domination and, even more clearly, the experience of the German and Austrian soviets under the domination of the Social Democrats, proved this. Social Revolutionary-Anarchist soviets could serve only as a bridge from the proletarian dictatorship to capitalist restoration. They could play no other role, regardless of the "ideas" of their participants. The Kronstadt uprising thus had a counterrevolutionary character.

From the class point of view, which—without offense to the honorable eclectics—remains the basic criterion not only for politics but for history, it is extremely important to contrast the behavior of Kronstadt to that of Petrograd in those critical days. The whole leading stratum of the workers had also been drawn out of Petrograd. Hunger and cold reigned in the deserted capital, perhaps even more fiercely than in Moscow. A heroic and tragic period! All were hungry and irritable. All were dissatisfied. In the factories there was dull discontent. Underground organizers sent by the SRs and the White officers tried to link the military uprising with the movement of the discontented workers.

The Kronstadt paper wrote about barricades in Petrograd, about thousands being killed. The press of the whole world proclaimed the same thing. Actually the precise opposite occurred. The Kronstadt uprising did not attract the Petrograd workers. It repelled them. The stratification proceeded along class lines. The workers immediately felt that the Kronstadt mutineers stood on the opposite side of the barricades—and they supported the Soviet power. The political isolation of Kronstadt was the cause of its internal uncertainty and its military defeat.

## The NEP and the Kronstadt Uprising

Victor Serge, who, it would seem, is trying to manufacture a sort of synthesis of anarchism, POUMism, and Marxism, has intervened very unfortunately in the polemic about Kronstadt. In his opinion, the introduction of the NEP one year earlier could have averted the Kronstadt uprising. Let us admit that. But advice like this is very easy to give after the event. It is true, as Victor Serge remembers, that I had proposed the transition to the NEP as early as 1920. But I was not at all sure in advance of its success. It was no secret to me that the remedy could prove to be more dangerous than the malady itself. When I met opposition from the leaders of the party, I did not appeal to the ranks, in order to avoid mobilizing the petty bourgeoisie against the workers. The experience of the ensuing twelve months was required to convince the party of the need for the new course. But the remarkable thing is that it was precisely the Anarchists all over the world who looked upon the NEP as . . . a betrayal of communism. But now the advocates of the Anarchists denounce us for not having introduced the NEP a year earlier.

In 1921 Lenin more than once openly acknowledged that the party's obstinate defense of the methods of Military Communism had become a great mistake.[156] But does this change matters? Whatever the immediate or remote causes of the Kronstadt rebellion, it was in its very essence a mortal danger to the dictatorship of the proletariat. Simply because it had been guilty of a political error, should the proletarian revolution really have committed suicide to punish itself?

Or perhaps it would have been sufficient to inform the Kronstadt sailors of the NEP decrees to pacify them? Illusion! The insurgents did not have a conscious program and they could not have had one because of the very nature of the petty bourgeoisie. They themselves did not clearly understand that what their fathers and brothers needed first of all was free trade. They were discontented and confused but they saw no way out. The more conscious, i.e., the rightist elements, acting behind the scenes, wanted the restoration of the bourgeois regime. But they did not say so out loud. The "left" wing wanted the liquidation of discipline, "free soviets," and better rations. The regime of the NEP could only gradually pacify the peasant, and, after him, the discontented sections of the army and the fleet. But for this time and experience were needed.

Most puerile of all is the argument that there was no uprising, that the sailors had made no threats, that they "only" seized the fortress and the battleships. It would seem that the Bolsheviks marched with bared chests across the ice against the fortress only because of their evil characters, their inclination to provoke conflicts artificially, their hatred of the Kronstadt sailors, or their hatred of the Anarchist doctrine (about which absolutely no one, we may say in passing, bothered in those days). Is this not childish prattle? Bound neither to time nor place, the dilettante critics try (seventeen years later!) to suggest that everything would have ended in general satisfaction if only the revolution had left the insurgent sailors alone. Unfortunately, the world counterrevolution would in no case have left them alone. The logic of the struggle would have given predominance in the fortress to the extremists, that is, to the most counterrevolutionary elements. The need for supplies would have made the fortress directly dependent upon the foreign bourgeoisie and their agents, the White emigres. All the necessary preparations toward this end were already being made. Under similar circumstances only people like the Spanish Anarchists or POUMists would have waited passively, hoping for a happy outcome. The Bolsheviks, fortunately, belonged to a different school. They considered it their duty to extinguish the fire as soon as it started, thereby reducing to a minimum the number of victims.

## The "Kronstadters" without a Fortress

In essence, the venerable critics are opponents of the dictatorship of the proletariat and by that token are opponents of the revolution. In this lies the whole secret. It is true that some of them recognize the revolution and the dictatorship—in words. But this does not help matters. They wish for a revolution which will not lead to dictatorship or for a dictatorship which will get along without the use of force. Of course, this would be a very "pleasant" dictatorship. It requires, however, a few trifles: an equal and, moreover, an extremely high, development of the toiling masses. But in such conditions the dictatorship would in general be unnecessary. Some Anarchists, who are really liberal pedagogues, hope that in a hundred or a thousand years the toilers will have attained so high a level of development that coercion will prove unnecessary. Naturally, if capitalism could lead to such a development, there would be no reason for overthrowing capitalism. There would be no need either for violent revolution or for the dictatorship which is an inevitable consequence of revolutionary victory. However, the decaying capitalism of our day leaves little room for humanitarian-pacifist illusions.

The working class, not to speak of the semiproletarian masses, is not homogeneous, either socially or politically. The class struggle produces a vanguard that absorbs the best elements of the class. A revolution is possible when the vanguard is able to lead the majority of the proletariat. But this does not at all mean that the internal contradictions among the toilers disappear. At the moment of the highest peak of the revolution they are of course attenuated, but only to appear later at a new stage in all their sharpness. Such is the course of the revolution as a whole. Such was the course of Kronstadt. When parlor pinks try to mark out a different route for the October Revolution, after the event, we can only respectfully ask them to show us exactly where and when their great principles were confirmed in practice, at least partially, at least in tendency? Where are the signs that lead us to expect the triumph of these principles in the future? We shall of course never get an answer.

A revolution has its own laws. Long ago we formulated those "lessons of October" which have not only a Russian but an international significance. No one else has even tried to suggest any other "lessons." The Spanish revolution is negative confirmation of the "lessons of October." And the severe critics are silent or equivocal. The Spanish government of the "People's Front" stifles the socialist revolution and shoots revolutionists. The Anarchists participate in this government, or, when they are driven out, continue to support the executioners. And their foreign allies and lawyers occupy themselves meanwhile with a defense . . . of the Kronstadt mutiny against the harsh Bolsheviks. A shameful travesty!

The present disputes around Kronstadt revolve around the same class axis as the Kronstadt uprising itself, in which the reactionary sections of the sailors tried to overthrow the proletarian dictatorship. Conscious of their impotence on the arena of present-day revolutionary politics, the petty-bourgeois blunderers and eclectics try to use the old Kronstadt episode for the struggle against the Fourth International, that is, against the party of the proletarian revolution. These latter-day "Kronstadters" will also be crushed—true, without the use of arms since, fortunately, they do not have a fortress.

# SNEEVLIET'S ROLE[157]

## January 21, 1938

Dear Comrade Cannon:

The situation with Sneevliet, as I have already written you many times, is not only bad but hopeless. Sneevliet is a conservative philistine without any revolutionary perspective. In '33 or '34, when he got his parliamentary mandate, he said to me: "I will try to extract from the NAS a thousand more party members and will abandon this hopeless organization." But it was just talk. When he lost his mandate he again seized with both hands his post as secretary of the NAS. It is a question of jobs for a Lilliputian bureaucracy. The politics of Sneevliet are totally subordinate to the task of preserving these jobs for himself and his closest collaborators. His open rupture with us will be naturally an indisputable blow to the Fourth International (a mortal blow to his own party). But nothing can be done.

I am sending you documents on the case. It is necessary to prepare the American party. The documents in my opinion should be published in the *Internal Bulletin*. It is possible that some American comrades who could not follow the developments during the last two years would be suspicious that the rupture was provoked by some precipitous or tactless actions from the International Secretariat or from me. By God, that is not the case. I can say that the International Secretariat had a very Christian attitude: when Sneevliet struck one cheek they turned the other. More or less all of us tolerated this situation.

I wrote you about Sneevliet's attitude in the Reiss case. This attitude was the most important cause for the loss of Reiss. Thanks to the fact that we withdrew this matter from the hands of Sneevliet we have an incomparably more favorable situation with Barmin and Walter Krivitsky and even the widow of Reiss. But from the moment the unhappy woman entered into direct relations with our comrades in Paris Sneevliet has spread a terrible scandal so that Mrs. Reiss, who had great esteem for Sneevliet, asked one of our comrades if Sneevliet was not drunk.

The man is not only politically opportunistic but in his anthill he is accustomed to be an absolute dictator. He intervenes in the life of all other sections (which is his good right) with extreme brutality (which is superfluous), but he doesn't tolerate the slightest criticism from the other sections or from the members of his own party. During the last few years the reactionary trend of European politics approached Sneevliet totally not only with the POUM but with the London Bureau. His aim is to dock in the harbor of Fenner Brockway. Nothing can be done.

If your National Committee or you personally find it necessary to verify our long experience by your own intervention, you could write an official or personal letter to Sneevliet asking him for explanations and so on. I would for my part only welcome such a step because it will have a good educational influence not only upon the American but also upon other sections. Practically your intervention, as I wrote you a couple months ago, can change nothing.

I must repeat again that it is absolutely necessary to give moral and at least a small financial support to the IS.

Yours, as ever,
Old Man [Trotsky]

# AN OPEN LETTER
## TO DE NIEUWE FAKKEL[158]

## January 21, 1938

To the editors of *De Nieuwe Fakkel* and *De Internationale*

Dear Comrades:

You have more than once given me the honor of publishing my articles. I do not doubt, therefore, that you will not refuse to publish the following brief letter.

From the very beginning of the existence of your party I have disagreed with its leaders, and first of all with Comrade Sneevliet, upon all basic questions. Actually the leadership of the RSAP has always been in irreconcilable opposition to all the other sections of the Fourth International and during the last two years the differences have become increasingly aggravated.[159]

In full agreement with the overwhelming majority of our international organization I have considered and still consider the politics of Sneevliet to be ruinous in the sphere of the trade union movement.

I have considered and still consider the RSAP's lack of a revolutionary program of action and the resultant unprincipled character of its agitation to be completely impermissible.

I have considered and still consider that the attitude of the leadership of the RSAP toward the politics of the "People's Front" has at all times remained equivocal, i.e., covertly and at times openly opportunistic.

The policy of Comrade Sneevliet on the question of the POUM is in full contradiction with the alphabet of the class struggle and has caused an indubitable injury to the Spanish revolution and the Fourth International.

The policy of Comrade Sneevliet on the Russian question was and still is false in essence and disloyal in attitude toward the Russian Bolshevik-Leninists.

I have considered and still consider the parliamentary activity of Comrade Sneevliet to be opportunistic.

I have considered and still consider the completely uncomradely attitude of the leadership of the RSAP toward all other sections and to the International Secretariat to be impermissible.

I have considered and still consider that political correctness in all basic conflicts between Comrade Sneevliet and the International Secretariat has been on the side of the IS.

Dozens of times the International Secretariat has proposed to your Central Committee to open a frank discussion upon all disputed questions. You have stubbornly refused to fulfill this elementary duty in relation to your own party. Instead of opening a discussion your Central Committee resorted to the expulsion of genuine partisans of the Fourth International from your organization. This measure could signify nothing less than the preparation for a split with the Fourth International and a shift into the camp of the "left" Social Democrats united around the London Bureau.

My last letter to Comrade Sneevliet, dated December 2, 1937, in which I asked whether your party intended to participate in the International Conference, has been unanswered. More important is the fact that the official inquiry of the International Secretariat has also remained unanswered.

The present letter, summing up the five-year attempt at collaboration, comradely criticism, mutual clarification, and rapprochement, has as its aim to say frankly what is. Each one has to bear responsibility for his political line. The members of your party and of all the sections of the Fourth International will judge.

With revolutionary greetings,
Leon Trotsky

# CONCLUSION OF
# A LONG EXPERIENCE[160]

## January 21, 1938

Dear Comrades:

It is quite possible that my last letter was not sufficiently explicit, since you have suggested the idea that I retain some illusions on the attitude and on the plans of Comrade Sneevliet. No, unfortunately, after five years of uninterrupted experience, I am not able to permit myself the least illusion. The sole reproach that we can make against ourselves, and I am not excluded in this, is the same as that in the case of Nin: we have been too patient, too indulgent, too tolerant toward the attitude of Comrade Sneevliet. It is always difficult in cases of this nature to ascertain the moment when it is necessary to pass to open struggle. I believe that this moment was determined by the intervention of Sneevliet on the Spanish question. His attitude in this question was an open betrayal of the most elementary principles of revolutionary Marxism and of all our decisions. It is he and his kind who have prompted added confidence on the part of the POUM in their own confusion and added distrust toward revolutionary Marxism. We know the result.

Unfortunately, it was precisely at this time that the Moscow trials supervened, the internment, etc. All our sections were absorbed over these new questions and the Dutch problem continued to drag on. The IS has done its duty. All that the IS has written about and against Sneevliet was and still is absolutely correct. That is precisely the reason why Sneevliet has never dared to respond with political arguments, utilizing instead—and that is his manner—abusive language that is absolutely intolerable and not at all justified. Sneevliet does not take the least interest in Marxism, in theories, in a general orientation. What interests him is the NAS, a tiny bureaucratic machine, a parliamentary post. Sneevliet utilizes the banner of the Fourth International above all in order to protect his opportunistic work in Holland. Since the NAS depends financially entirely upon the government, Sneevliet has evaded all precise politics, that is to say, Marxist politics, in order not to provoke the thunder of the government against the NAS. The RSAP has not been and still is nothing more than a political appendage of the NAS, which itself is not viable and which has fallen in the last years from 25,000 to 12,000 members and very likely still lower.

On the Spanish question, on the question of the People's Front, not to speak of internal Dutch politics, Sneevliet occupies a position that is not in any way superior to that of the parties adhering to the London Bureau. Moreover, he has never concealed having a double connection: with the IS and with the London Bureau. Practically, he broke connections with the IS, it is my belief, a year ago or more. He has utilized this time in order to prepare his organization for the definitive rupture. He has always refused to engage in an honest discussion of the differences. On the question of Reiss he behaved in an absolutely disloyal manner toward the Russian section, greatly contributing to the tragic denouement.

The IS in my opinion has done all that it could in order to facilitate collaboration, and we cannot reproach it with not having succeeded in changing the nature of the leadership of the RSAP, thoroughly opportunistic, syndicalist, and anti-Marxist. That is the incontrovertible conclusion of a long experience. If I proposed that you write a letter once more to Sneevliet, inviting him to participate in the International Conference and demanding the participation of his party in the international discussion, this was not because I personally have the slightest illusions but because I am under the impression that the other sections, particularly those of the New World, have not sufficiently followed the involved development of this problem and that someone might entertain the impression that it could possibly be the incorrect "methods" of the IS and not organic opportunism on the part of the RSAP leadership which has pushed Sneevliet into preparing a break from the Fourth International and eventual adherence to the London Bureau. (No one has forgotten, I hope, that Sneevliet obstinately fought the resolution of our last International Conference on the London Bureau.[161] This is not astonishing; he felt that he was affected by this resolution.) On December 2, 1937, I sent Sneevliet a personal letter where I made a final endeavor to extract his reply. *He has not responded to this letter.* Hence I send a copy of this letter to all sections.

It is necessary that the Dutch question take its place in the international discussion preceding the conference. It is a question in the first place of analyzing the trade union experience of Sneevliet in order to exclude once and for all the possibility of analogous policies in other sections. We see that they toy here and there with the idea of "their own" trade unions. This policy signifies inevitable ruin. The Fourth International cannot tolerate such a policy in its ranks without inviting death. On this question as on others, the Dutch experience teaches us what must not be done.

I am simultaneously sending an open letter to the press of the RSAP and I enclose a copy for you.

Leon Trotsky

# AN EXCELLENT ARTICLE
## ON DEFEATISM[162]

### January 26, 1938

In my letter to Comrade Van (January 2, 1938), I had admitted the possibility that in the stenographic report (*The Case of Leon Trotsky*) some unfortunate expressions might have slipped in (at the moment I did not have the book at hand). No man who thinks sanely and honestly, besides, will start to find the reply to the fundamental problems of our policy during war in a brief, verbal remark made during discussions which lasted one week. However, I now see with satisfaction that my reply to Stolberg is transcribed in the report with sufficient exactitude and is in full accord with our programmatic theses (*War and the Fourth International*).

There is however no need for me to return to this question. Comrade W. St. has written on this subject an article in German ("Zu den Aufgaben des Proletariats im Kriege"—On the Tasks of the Proletariat in War).[163] I most warmly recommend this article to the attention of all comrades. As the article is not confined to any "internal" polemic, it can and must, in my opinion, be reproduced in all our publications. The excellent article of Comrade W. St. shows anew that new, very serious Marxist cadres have grown up amongst us. This article has completely done away with any necessity of my personally polemicizing against Comrade Ver.'s recent writings, where there is nothing but scholasticism and casuistry.

On the subject of Comrade W. St.'s article, I allow myself to make one particular remark. W. St. draws an absolutely correct principled difference between revolutionary "defeatism" with respect to one's own imperialist government and acts of direct military sabotage in favor of another country (workers' state, colonial country, etc.). However, it would hardly be correct to include among acts of this type "mass desertion." Desertion of a revolutionary character can only become a mass one under conditions of an enormous influence of the revolutionary party. But such a condition in the army and country in itself already signifies the approach or the beginning of the revolution. Under these conditions, it would hardly be admissible to cut off the revolutionary vanguard from its mass army in the name of episodic military aid to a workers' state or an oppressed country. Concerning "mass desertion," one can say in this case the same thing as in many others: it is either impossible or superfluous and harmful.[164]

I hope that the German text of W. St.'s article has been sent to all sections and will be translated into the different languages.

T.

# FACTORY PAPERS
## AND A THEORETICAL JOURNAL[165]

### January 27, 1938

I received your large packet of factory newspapers and leaflets, etc. Indeed, this is the only suitable way for a weak organization with a small paper to approach the least educated masses while not only maintaining but continually deepening its theoretical understanding. A certain type of "democratic centralism" is necessary in the organization of written propaganda and agitation as well. You approach the workers with the simplest demands and slogans, which flow directly from life in the factory. You are not obliged to draw all the conclusions on every occasion, that is to say, in every article. Every day has its task.

But in order to do this loose, uncoordinated mass work, the party's thinking must be sufficiently centralized and it must find its daily inspiration in a laboratory where all questions, even the most complex, are analyzed and sharply focused. The Bank of France is obliged at certain times to renew its gold reserves so that the money in circulation is not debased by inflation.

I don't know what the current circulation of *Lutte* is, but there are tens of thousands of workers in France who are not only capable of understanding an article that takes a broader view, but who are demanding from the workers' press in-depth answers to the complex questions posed by the world situation.

Let us recall the discussion with the Molinier group on "a mass paper." The pamphlet by our poor N. Braun makes a number of excellent points on this subject.[166] *By transforming the central organ of the party into a kind of factory paper, you will never reach the masses, but you will lose your distinguishing political character, and with it your own members.*

The fact that Craipeau was able to get about one-third (he himself claims 40 percent) of the party membership [at the POI's

155

second congress in the autumn of 1937] is a disquieting symptom of political degeneration. Personally Craipeau is an excellent comrade, sincere, devoted; but I fear that he is moving more and more in the direction of Vereecken, i.e., into an impasse.

I am following the discussion in the Belgian Central Committee with great concern. As the apostle says, they strain at gnats and swallow camels. I believe that the difficulties of the Belgian section can be explained to a great extent *by the lack of a French-language theoretical journal.* The importance of this question cannot be overestimated. These are stormy times; the masses are restless; the most intelligent workers are seeking above all to understand what is going on. They will not be satisfied with the mere repetition of the current slogans. They must be given a complete answer. A dozen or a hundred workers of this caliber won to our general ideas can lead tens of thousands of rank-and-file workers to our movement.

None of this is in any way directed against mass work. Our work in the unions is absolutely decisive. The worst mistake committed by the Borinage comrades was in wasting their time, energy, and prestige by creating "unions" for their own satisfaction. They took their inspiration not from the experience of decades, not from the lessons of the first four congresses of the [Third] International, but from the example of a bureaucrat without program or principles, that is, Sneevliet.

Work in the reformist unions, I repeat, should come first. But in order for this work to be carried out in a truly revolutionary fashion, *the party must have a good central paper and a theoretical journal.* Don't you think that it would be possible for the French section together with the Belgian section (and possibly the Geneva group) to maintain a monthly theoretical journal? Is the "internationalism," which is proclaimed verbally, insufficient for such an undertaking? Moreover, it is a question of the very existence of both the French and the Belgian sections.

I do not know whether the French comrades have sufficient opportunity to follow the life of our section in the United States. They have made very remarkable progress. The level of discussion was very high and the convention ended with nearly complete agreement and with heightened authority of the leadership. I remember the hue and cry that Sneevliet raised over the entry of the Americans into the Socialist Party. He fulminated against the "Second International," opportunism, etc. Naturally, Vereecken repeated all these accusations. However, the American section is the only one that has made appreciable progress and has shown real political maturity.

Crux [Trotsky]

I just received number 4 of *Quatrieme Internationale.* It is very cheering. But despite all the solemn promises, there is not the least hope that number 5 will appear soon. In my opinion the only way to assure its regular publication is through collaboration with the Belgians.

# THE LUDLOW AMENDMENT[167]

## February 1, 1938

### I

Dear Comrade Cannon:

I am sending you a personal letter about the referendum case. You can judge yourself whether it is advisable to show it now to the Political Bureau. You understand that I am not interested in provoking internal discussions. The matter itself is practically over. You can thus view the letter as a purely personal matter, or even burn it. But if you consider that by showing the letter to Burnham you can create a better atmosphere of mutual understanding I am naturally not opposed. For my part I will not now make any supplementary step in this connection.

My best wishes and greetings,
Hansen [Trotsky]

### II

Dear Comrade Cannon:

In the Ludlow referendum case I am with Burnham, not with the majority of the Central Committee. This letter is not an attempt to provoke a reconsideration of the question, which has been decided and practically liquidated, but methodologically the question is of importance. The government position in the question represents the conceptions and the interests of the imperialists, that is, of big business. The capitalists want free hands for international maneuvering, including a declaration of war.

What is the Ludlow initiative? It represents the apprehension of the man in the street, of the average citizen, the middle

158

bourgeois, the petty bourgeois, and even the farmer and the worker. They are all looking for a brake upon the bad will of big business. In this case they name the brake the referendum. We know that the brake is not sufficient and even not efficient and we openly proclaim this opinion, but at the same time we are ready to help the little man go through his experience against the dictatorial pretensions of big business. The referendum is an illusion? Not more and not less an illusion than universal suffrage and other means of democracy. Why can we not use the referendum as we use the presidential elections?

When the Belgian Socialists elaborated their "Plan," Vereecken named the plan illusion and turned away from the Socialist Party. We demanded: that the Socialist Party hold office in order to put its plan into practice. This tactic had as its objective the utilization of the progressive tendencies of the illusion for the revolutionary education of the workers. The referendum illusion of the American little man has also its progressive features. Our task is not to turn away from it, but to utilize these progressive features without taking the responsibility for the illusion. If the referendum motion should be adopted, it would give us in case of a war crisis tremendous possibilities for agitation. That is precisely why big business stifled the referendum illusion.

Fraternally,
Hansen [Trotsky]

# LETTER TO
# AN AMERICAN YOUTH[168]

## February 4, 1938

Dear Friend:

Your difficulty in understanding the great controversy over the Moscow trials comes from a lack of necessary historical study and life experience. For anyone who knows history and its laws, especially the history of revolutions and counterrevolutions, the Moscow trials do not present the slightest mystery. You can say, however, that there are many ladies and gentlemen who in spite of their very mature age and scholarship believe or pretend to believe the Moscow accusations. Yes. But there are people who believe that Eve was made from Adam's rib and that Christ fed multitudes of people with five loaves of bread and two fish, transformed water into wine, and so on. It was mainly for this kind of people that the Moscow trials were devised.

People with an open mind and logical sense are now in the minority, it is true, but this progressive minority will have the privilege of convincing the majority. All genuine progress is made in this way. If you would belong to this progressive minority you must study Marxism and the history of revolutions. You will learn, for example, that the bourgeois, bureaucratic, Thermidorean reaction accused Robespierre, Saint-Just, Couthon, and their friends[169]—all of them unshakable revolutionaries—of being royalists, traitors, and agents of the British monarchy. All of them were guillotined and the majority of people at that time believed the accusations to be correct. Who believes it now?

My best greetings,
Leon Trotsky

# OPTIMISTIC OVER THE FUTURE[170]

## February 4, 1938

My Dear Friend:

I just this moment received your letter concerning the general situation of the party. I find myself in absolute solidarity with all your considerations and appreciations, and I am ready to subscribe to every word of your letter. I am with you very optimistic over the future of our party.

Natalia and I wish you personally good health; it is not necessary to wish you energy. Best greetings to Rose.

Yours,

L.D. [Trotsky]

P.S.—It is very, very good that you are sending a bit of money to the IS. They were boycotted all the time by the Dutch organization and half the time by the Belgian. Your support will have the greatest influence materially as well as morally upon their activity. In all the fundamental questions they were right against the Dutch and the Belgians.

# A NEW GPU ATTEMPT[171]

## February 15, 1938

Dear Friend:

Through my French attorney, Gerard Rosenthal,[172] who is also the attorney of Mrs. Reiss and has the opportunity to see part of the documents, we are in possession of very precious information concerning the preparation of a terrorist attempt by the GPU here in Mexico.

The first practical step has already been made. A man came to our house with big packages, declaring that he was sent by General Mujica, minister of communications,[173] and that the packages contained fertilizer for the garden of Diego Rivera. It was during our absence The packages were refused. The man promised to come back the next day with credentials from General Mujica. Immediately after the departure of the man we learned of the incident and we telephoned General Mujica, who told us that he had not sent anyone.

This occurrence is so significant that we have taken exceptional measures of prudence. I have even left the house for an indefinite time, disorganizing my work. We must say that the Mexican authorities are not only loyal but extremely obliging and did abolutely everything in their power. But on the other hand the resources of the enemy are too powerful not to take the exceptional measures indicated above. In spite of my involuntary displacement, I hope in eight or ten days to be able to send you a big article on "Their Morals and Ours," where I take the measure of the *Nation*, the *New Republic, Common Sense,* and similar elements in Europe concerning our "amoralism."[174] I think that you can publish this article as a pamphlet and that it will not remain without effect. In the worst case you could publish it in the *New International* although it is too big for the review (at least thirty pages typewritten).

L. Trotsky

# THE POSSIBILITY
# OF FOUL PLAY[175]

## February 18, 1938

The wound is still too fresh for me to be able to talk yet about Leon Sedov as of someone dead. He was not only my son but my best friend. But there is one question upon which I am duty-bound to make myself heard immediately: this question deals with the causes of his death. I must say from the very beginning that I do not have direct data at my command which would allow me to assert that the death of L. Sedov is the handiwork of the GPU.

In the telegrams that my wife and I have received from friends in Paris there is no more information than that included in the news over the press wires. But I should like to give some indirect information which may, however, have great significance for the judicial investigation in Paris.

1. It is not true that my son suffered from a chronic intestinal disease. The announcement about this sickness came as a complete surprise to his mother and me.

2. It it not true that he supposedly suffered heavily during the past few weeks. I have at hand the letter received by me from him, dated February 4. There is not a word in this letter, which is very optimistic in tone, about any illness. On the contrary, the letter shows that at that time he had become very active, especially in connection with the imminent trial of Reiss's murderers in Switzerland, and was intending to continue his activity.

3. The death of L. Sedov occurred evidently in the night of February 15-16. Thus between the letter and the death only eleven days passed. In other words, the sickness fully had the character of suddenness.

4. There is, of course, no basis for doubting the impartiality of the medico-judicial examination, no matter what its conclusions

were. Not being a specialist, I permit myself, nevertheless, to point to one important circumstance. If we are to admit the possibility of poisoning, then we must remember that the question is not one of ordinary poisoning. At the disposal of the GPU there are very exceptional scientists and technical means which would make the problem of medical examination more than difficult.

5. How could the GPU gain access to my son? Here too I can reply only hypothetically. During the past period there have been several cases of GPU agents breaking with Moscow. Naturally all those who broke sought connection with my son and he—with that courage which characterized him in all his actions—always accepted such appointments. In connection with these breaks, was there not some kind of trap? I can only advance this postulate. Others must verify this.

6. The French Communist press paid a great deal of attention, hostile of course, to Leon Sedov. However, not a single one of the Communist papers has so much as printed a line about his death (see the dispatches from Paris). It was exactly like this after the murder of Ignace Reiss in Lausanne. Such "caution" becomes of especially great significance if we take into consideration that in questions that are acute for Moscow the French press of the Comintern receives direct instructions from the GPU through the old agent of the GPU, Jacques Duclos, and others.

I do not affirm anything, I only announce the fact and pose the question.

Leon Sedov.

# LEON SEDOV—
## SON, FRIEND, FIGHTER[176]

### February 20, 1938

As I write these lines, with Leon Sedov's mother by my side, telegrams of condolence keep coming from different countries. And for us each telegram evokes the same appalling question: "Can it really be that our friends in France, Holland, England, the United States, Canada, South Africa and here in Mexico accept it as definitely established that Sedov is no more?" Each telegram is a new token of his death, but we are unable to believe it as yet. And this, not only because he was our son, truthful, devoted, loving, but above all because he had, as no one else on earth, become part of our life, entwined in all its roots, our cothinker, our co-worker, our guard, our counselor, our friend.

Of that older generation whose ranks we joined at the end of the last century on the road to revolution, all, without exception, have been swept from the scene. That which czarist hard-labor prisons and harsh exiles, the hardships of emigration, the civil war, and disease had failed to accomplish has in recent years been achieved by Stalin, the worst scourge of the revolution. Following the destruction of the older generation, the best section of the next, that is, the generation which awakened in 1917 and which received its training in the twenty-four armies of the revolutionary front, was likewise destroyed. Also crushed underfoot and completely obliterated was the best part of the youth, Leon's contemporaries. He himself survived only by a miracle, owing to the fact that he accompanied us into exile and then to Turkey. During the years of our last emigration we made many new friends, some of whom have entered intimately into our lives, becoming, as it were, members of our family. But we met all of them for the first time in these last few years when we had already neared old age. Leon was the only one who knew us

when we were young; he became part of our lives from the very
first moment of his self-awakening. While young in years, he still
seemed our contemporary. Together with us, he went through our
second emigration: Vienna, Zurich, Paris, Barcelona, New York,
Amherst (concentration camp in Canada), and finally Petrograd.

While but a child—he was going on twelve—he had, in his own
way, consciously made the transition from the February
revolution to that of October.[177] His boyhood passed under high
pressure. He added a year to his age so that he might more
quickly join the Young Communist League, seething at that time
with all the passion of awakened youth. The young bakers,
among whom he carried on propaganda, would award him a
fresh loaf of white bread which he happily brought home under
his arm, protuding from the torn sleeve of his jacket. Those were
fiery and cold, great and hungry years. Of his own volition Leon
left the Kremlin for a proletarian student dormitory, in order not
to be any different from the others. He would not ride with us in
an automobile, refusing to make use of this privilege of the
bureaucrats. But he did participate ardently in all Red Saturdays
and other "labor mobilizations," cleaning snow from the Moscow
streets, "liquidating" illiteracy, unloading bread and firewood
from freight cars, and later, as a polytechnic student, repairing
locomotives. If he did not get to the war front, it was only because
even adding two or as much as three years to his age could not
have helped him; for he was not yet fifteen when the civil war
ended. However, he did accompany me several times to the front,
absorbing its stark impressions, and firmly understanding why
this bloody struggle was being waged.

The latest press reports speak of Leon Sedov's life in Paris
under "the most modest conditions"—much more modest, let me
add, than those of a skilled worker. Even in Moscow, during those
years when his father and mother held high posts, he lived not
better but worse than for the past few years in Paris. Was this
perhaps the rule among the youth of the bureaucracy? By no
means. Even then he was an exception. In this child, growing to
boyhood and adolescence, a sense of duty and achievement
awakened early.

In 1923 Leon threw himself headlong into the work of the
Opposition. It would be entirely wrong to see in this nothing more
than parental influence. After all, when he left a comfortable
apartment in the Kremlin for his hungry, cold, and dingy
dormitory, he did so against our will, even though we did not
resist this move on his part. His political orientation was

determined by the same instinct which impelled him to choose crowded streetcars rather than Kremlin limousines. The platform of the Opposition simply gave political expression to traits inherent in his nature. Leon broke uncompromisingly with those of his student friends who were violently torn from "Trotskyism" by their bureaucratic fathers and found a way to his baker friends. Thus, at seventeen he began the life of a fully conscious revolutionist. He quickly grasped the art of conspiratorial work, illegal meetings, and the secret issuing and distribution of Opposition documents. The Young Communist League rapidly developed its own cadres of Opposition leaders.

Leon had exceptional mathematical ability. He never tired of assisting many worker-students who had not gone through grammar school. He engaged in this work with all his energy; encouraging, leading, chiding the lazy ones—the youthful teacher saw in this work a service to his class. His own studies in the Superior Technical Academy progressed very favorably. But they took up only a part of his working day. Most of his time, strength, and spirit were devoted to the cause of the revolution.

In the winter of 1927, when the police massacre of the Opposition began, Leon had passed his twenty-second year. By that time a child was born to him and he would proudly bring his son to the Kremlin to show him to us. Without a moment's hesitation, however, Leon decided to tear himself away from his school and his young family in order to share our fate in Central Asia. In this he acted not only as a son but above all as a cothinker. It was essential, whatever the cost, to guarantee our connection with Moscow. His work in Alma Ata, during that year, was truly peerless. We called him our minister of foreign affairs, minister of police, and minister of communications. And in fulfilling all these functions he had to rely on an illegal apparatus. Commissioned by the Moscow Opposition center, Comrade X, very devoted and reliable, acquired a carriage and three horses and worked as an independent coachman between Alma Ata and the city of Frunze (Pishpek), at that time the terminus of the railroad. It was his task to convey the secret Moscow mail to us every two weeks and to carry our letters and manuscripts back to Frunze, where a Moscow messenger awaited him. Sometimes special couriers also arrived from Moscow. To meet with them was no simple matter. We were lodged in a house surrounded on all sides by the institutions of the GPU and the quarters of its agents. Outside connections were handled entirely by Leon. He would leave the house late on a rainy night or when the snow fell heavily, or, evading the vigilance of the spies, he would hide himself during the day in the library to meet the courier in a public bath or among the thick weeds on the outskirts of the town, or in the oriental market place where the Kirghiz crowded with their horses, donkeys, and wares. Each time he returned excited and happy, with a conquering gleam in his eyes and the precious booty under his clothing. And so for a year's time he eluded all enemies. What is more, he maintained the most "correct," almost "friendly," relations with these enemies who were "comrades" of yesterday, displaying uncommon tact and restraint, carefully guarding us from outside disturbances.

The ideological life of the Opposition seethed like a cauldron at the time. It was the year of the Sixth World Congress of the Communist International. The Moscow packets arrived with scores of letters, articles, theses, from comrades known and unknown. During the first few months, before the sharp change in the conduct of the GPU, we even received a great many letters by the official mail services from different places of exile. It was necessary to sift this diversified material carefully. And it was in this work that I had the occasion to realize, not without surprise, how this little boy had imperceptibly grown up, how well he could judge people—he knew a great many more Oppositionists than I did—how reliable was his revolutionary instinct, which enabled him, without any hesitation, to distinguish the genuine from the false, the substance from the veneer. The eyes of his mother, who knew our son best, glowed with pride during our conversations.

Between April and October we received approximately 1,000 political letters and documents and about 700 telegrams. In this same period we sent out 550 telegrams and not fewer than 800 political letters, including a number of substantial works, such as the *Criticism of the Draft Program of the Communist International* and others.[178] Without my son I could not have accomplished even one-half of the work.

So intimate a collaboration did not, however, mean that no disputes or occasionally even very sharp clashes arose between us. Neither at that time, nor later in emigration—and this must be said candidly—were my relations with Leon by any means of an even and placid character. To his categorical judgments, which were often disrespectful to some of the "old men" of the Opposition, I not only counterposed equally categoric corrections and reservations, but I also displayed toward him the pedantic

and exacting attitude which I had acquired in practical
questions. Because of these traits, which are perhaps useful and
even indispensable for work on a large scale but quite insuffer-
able in personal relationships, people closest to me often had a
very hard time. And inasmuch as the closest to me of all the
youth was my son, he usually had the hardest time of all. To a
superficial eye it might even have seemed that our relationship
was permeated with severity and aloofness. But beneath the
surface there glowed a deep mutual attachment based on
something immeasurably greater than bonds of blood—a solidarity of views and appraisals, of sympathies and antipathies, of joys
and sorrows experienced together, of great hopes we had in
common. And this mutual attachment blazed up from time to
time so warmly as to reward us three hundredfold for the petty
friction in daily work.

Thus four thousand kilometers from Moscow, two hundred and
fifty kilometers from the nearest railway, we spent a difficult and
never-to-be-forgotten year which remains in our memory under
the sign Leon, or rather Levik or Levusyatka as we called him.

In January 1929, the Political Bureau decided to deport me
"beyond the borders of the USSR"—to Turkey, as it turned out.
Members of the family were granted the right to accompany me.
Again without any hesitation Leon decided to accompany us into
exile, tearing himself forever from his wife and child whom he
dearly loved.

A new chapter, with its first pages almost blank, opened in our
life. Connections, acquaintances, and friendships had to be built
anew. And once again our son became all things for us: our go-
between in relations with the outside world, our guard, collaborator and secretary as in Alma Ata, but on an incomparably
broader scale. Foreign languages, with which he had been more
familiar in his childhood than he was with Russian, had been
almost completely forgotten in the tumult of the revolutionary
years. It became necessary to learn them all over again. Our joint
literary work began. My archives and library were wholly in
Leon's hands. He had a thorough knowledge of the works of
Marx, Engels, and Lenin, was very well acquainted with my
books and manuscripts, with the history of the party and the
revolution, and the history of the Thermidorean falsification. In
the chaos of the Alma Ata public library he had already studied
the files of *Pravda* for the Soviet years and gathered the
necessary quotations and references with unfailing resourceful-

ness. Lacking this precious material and without Leon's subsequent researches in archives and libraries, first in Turkey, later
in Berlin, and finally in Paris, not one of my works during the
past ten years would have been possible. This applies especially
to the *History of the Russian Revolution.* Vast in point of
quantity, his collaboration was by no means of a "technical"
nature. His independent selection of facts, quotations, characteri-
zations, frequently determined the method of my presentation as well as the conclusions. *The Revolution Betrayed* contains
not a few pages which I wrote on the basis of several lines from
my son's letters and the quotations which he sent from Soviet
newspapers inaccessible to me. He supplied me with even more
material for the biography of Lenin. Such collaboration was
made possible only because our ideological solidarity had
penetrated our very flesh and blood. My son's name should
rightfully be placed next to mine on almost all my books written
since 1928.

In Moscow, Leon had lacked a year and a half to complete his
engineering course. His mother and I insisted that while abroad
he return to his abandoned science. In Prinkipo a new group of
young co-workers from different countries had meanwhile been
successfully formed, in intimate collaboration with my son. Leon
consented to leave only because of the weighty argument that in
Germany he would be able to render invaluable services to the
International Left Opposition. Resuming his scientific studies in
Berlin (he had to start from the beginning), Leon simultaneously
threw himself headlong into revolutionary activity. In the
International Secretariat he soon became the representative of
the Russian section. His letters for that period to his mother and
myself show how quickly he acclimated himself to the political
atmosphere of Germany and Western Europe, how well he judged
people and gauged the differences and countless conflicts of that
early period of our movement. His revolutionary instinct, already
enriched by serious experience, enabled him in almost all cases to
find the right road independently. How many times were we
gladdened when, upon opening a letter just arrived, we discovered
in it the very ideas and conclusions which I had just recommended to his attention. And how deeply and quietly happy he
was over such coincidences of our ideas! The collection of Leon's
letters will undoubtedly constitute one of the most valuable
sources for the study of the inner prehistory of the Fourth
International.

But the Russian question continued to occupy the center of his attention. While still in Prinkipo he became the actual editor of the *Biulleten Oppozitsii* from its inception (the middle of 1929), and took complete charge of this work upon his arrival in Berlin (the beginning of 1931), where the *Biulleten* was immediately transferred from Paris. The last letter we received from Leon, written on February 4, 1938, twelve days before his death, begins with the following words: "I am sending you page-proofs of the *Biulleten*, for the next ship will not leave for some time, while the *Biulleten* will come off the press only tomorrow morning." The appearance of each issue was a minor event in his life, a minor event which demanded great exertions; making up the issue, polishing the raw material, writing articles, meticulous proof-reading, prompt correspondence with friends and collaborators, and, not the least, gathering funds. But how proud he was over each "successful" number!

During the first years of emigration he engaged in a vast correspondence with Oppositionists in the USSR. But by 1932 the GPU destroyed virtually all our connections. It became necessary to seek fresh information through devious channels. Leon was always on the lookout, avidly searching for connecting threads with Russia, hunting up returning tourists, Soviet students assigned abroad, or sympathetic functionaries in the foreign representations. To avoid compromising his informant, he chased for hours through the streets of Berlin and later of Paris to evade the GPU spies who trailed him. In all these years there was not a single instance of anyone suffering as a consequence of indiscretion, carelessness, or imprudence on his part.

In the files of the GPU he was referred to by the nickname of "synok" or "Little Son." According to the late Ignace Reiss, in the Lubyanka [Prison] they said on more than one occasion: "The Little Son does his work cleverly. The Old Man wouldn't find it so easy without him." This was the actual truth. Without him it would not have been easy. Without him it will be hard. It was just for this reason that agents of the GPU, worming their way even into the organizations of the Opposition, surrounded Leon with a thick web of surveillance, intrigues, and plots. In the Moscow trials his name invariably figured next to mine. Moscow was seeking an opportunity to get rid of him at all costs!

After Hitler assumed power, the *Biulleten Oppozitsii* was immediately banned. Leon remained in Germany for several weeks, carrying on illegal work, hiding from the Gestapo in different apartments. His mother and I sounded the alarm, insisting on his immediate departure from Germany. In the spring of 1933 Leon finally decided to leave the country which he had learned to know and to love, and moved to Paris, where the *Biulleten* followed him. Here Leon again resumed his studies. He had to pass an examination for the French intermediate school and then for the third time to begin with the first term in the Faculty of Physics and Mathematics at the Sorbonne. In Paris he lived under very difficult conditions, in constant want, occupying himself with scientific studies at the university at off moments; but thanks to his exceptional ability he completed his studies, i.e., obtained his diploma.

His main efforts in Paris, even to a greater extent than in Berlin, were devoted to the revolution and the literary collaboration with me. During recent years Leon himself began to write more systematically for the press of the Fourth International. Isolated indications, especially the notes on his reminiscences for my autobiography, made me suspect while still in Prinkipo that he had literary gifts. But he was loaded down with all sorts of other work, and inasmuch as we held our ideas and subject matter in common, he left the literary work to me. As I recall, in Turkey he wrote only one major article: "Stalin and the Red Army—or How History is Written," under the pseudonym of N. Markin, a sailor-revolutionist to whom in his childhood he was bound by a friendship deepened by profound admiration. This article was included in my book *The Stalin School of Falsification*. Subsequently his articles began to appear more and more frequently in the pages of the *Biulleten* and in other publications of the Fourth International, written each time under the pressure of necessity. Leon wrote only when he had something to say and when he knew that no one else could say it better. During the period of our life in Norway I received requests from various places for an analysis of the Stakhanovist movements which to some extent caught our organizations by surprise. When it became clear that my prolonged illness would prevent me from fulfilling this task, Leon sent me a draft of an article by him on Stakhanovism, with a very modest accompanying letter. The work appeared to me excellent both in its serious and thorough analysis and in the terseness and clarity of its presentation. I remember how pleased Leon was by my warm praise! This article was published in several languages[179] and immediately provided a correct point of view upon this "socialist" piecework under the whip of the bureaucracy. Scores of subsequent articles have not added anything essential to this analysis.

Leon's chief literary work was his *Red Book on the Moscow*

*Trial,* devoted to the trial of the sixteen (Zinoviev, Kamenev, Smirnov, et al.). It was published in French, Russian, and German. At that time my wife and I were captives in Norway, bound hand and foot, targets of the most monstrous slander. There are certain forms of paralysis, in which people see, hear, and understand everything but are unable to move a finger to ward off mortal danger. It was to such political paralysis that the Norwegian "socialist" government subjected us. What a priceless gift to us, under these conditions, was Leon's book, the first crushing reply to the Kremlin falsifiers. The first few pages, I recall, seemed to me pale. That was because they only restated a political appraisal, which had already been made, of the general condition of the USSR. But from the moment the author undertook an independent analysis of the trial, I became completely engrossed. Each succeeding chapter seemed to me better than the last. "Good boy, Levusyatka!" my wife and I said. "We have a defender!" How his eyes must have glowed with pleasure as he read our warm praise! Several newspapers, in particular the central organ of the Danish Social Democracy, said with assurance that I apparently had, despite the strict conditions of internment, found the means of participating in the work which appeared under Sedov's name. "One feels the pen of Trotsky. . . ." All this is—fiction. In the book there is not a line of my own. Many comrades who were inclined to regard Sedov merely as "Trotsky's son"—just as Karl Liebknecht was long regarded only as the son of Wilhelm Liebknecht[180]—were able to convince themselves, if only from this little book, that he was not only an independent but an outstanding figure.

Leon wrote as he did everything else, that is, conscientiously, studying, reflecting, checking. The vanity of authorship was alien to him. Agitational declamation had no lures for him. At the same time every line he wrote glows with a living flame, whose source was his unfeigned revolutionary temperament.

This temperament was formed and hardened by events of a personal and family life indissolubly linked to the great political events of our epoch. In 1905, his mother sat in a Petersburg jail expecting a child. A gust of liberalism set her free in the autumn. In February of the next year, the boy was born. By that time I was already confined in prison. I was able to see my son for the first time only thirteen months later, when I escaped from Siberia. His earliest impressions bore the breath of the first Russian revolution whose defeat drove us into Austria. The war, which drove us into Switzerland, hammered into the conscious-

ness of the eight-year-old boy. The next big lesson for him was
my deportation from France. On board ship he conversed, in sign
language, about the revolution with a Catalan stoker. The
revolution signified for him all possible boons, above all a return
to Russia. En route from America, near Halifax, the eleven-year-
old Levik struck a British officer with his fist. He knew whom to
hit; not the sailors who carried me off the ship, but the officer
who issued the orders. In Canada, during my incarceration in the
concentration camp, Leon learned how to conceal letters not read
by the police and how to place them unobserved in the mail box.
In Petrograd he found himself immediately plunged into the
atmosphere of Bolshevik-baiting. In the bourgeois school where
he happened to be enrolled at the beginning, sons of liberals and
Social Revolutionaries beat him up because he was Trotsky's son.
Once he came to the Woodworkers' Trade Union, where his
mother worked, with his hand all bloody. He had had a political
discussion in school with Kerensky's son.[181] In the streets he
joined all the Bolshevik demonstrations, took refuge behind gates
from the armed forces of the then People's Front (the coalition of
Cadets, SRs, and Mensheviks). After the July days,[182] grown pale
and thin, he came to visit me in the jail of Kerensky-Tseretelli.[183]
In the home of a colonel they knew, at the dinner table, Leon and
Sergei[184] threw themselves, knives in hand, at an offi ;er who had
declared that the Bolsheviks were agents of the Kaiser. They
made approximately the same reply to the engineer Serebrovsky,
now a member of the Stalinist Central Committee, when he tried
to assure them that Lenin was—a German spy. Levik learned
early to grind his young teeth when reading slanders in the
newspapers. He passed the October days in the company of the
sailor Markin who, in leisure moments, instructed him in the
cellar in the art of shooting.

Thus the future fighter took shape. For him, the revolution was
not an abstraction. Oh, no! It seeped into his very pores. Hence
derived his serious attitude toward revolutionary duty, beginning
with the Red Saturdays and tutoring of the backward ones. That
is why he later joined so ardently in the struggle against the
bureaucracy. In the autumn of 1927 Leon made an "Oppositional" tour to the Urals in the company of Mrachkovsky and
Beloborodov.[185] On their return, both of them spoke with genuine
enthusiasm about Leon's conduct during the sharp and hopeless
struggle, his intransigent speeches at the meetings of the youth,
his physical fearlessness in the face of the hooligan detachments
of the bureaucracy, his moral courage which enabled him to face

defeat with his young head held high. When he returned from the Urals, having matured in those six weeks, I was already expelled from the party. It was necessary to prepare for exile. He was not given to imprudence, nor did he make a show of courage. He was wise, cautious, and calculating. But he knew that danger constitutes an element in revolution as well as war. Whenever the need arose, and it frequently did, he knew how to face danger. His life in France, where the GPU has friends on every floor of the governmental edifice, was an almost unbroken chain of dangers. Professional killers dogged his steps. They lived in apartments next to his. They stole his letters and archives and listened in on his phone conversations. When, after an illness, he spent two weeks on the shores of the Mediterranean—his only vacation for a period of years—the agents of the GPU took quarters in the same pension. When he arranged to go to Mulhouse for a conference with a Swiss lawyer in connection with a legal action against the slanders of the Stalinist press, a whole gang of GPU agents was waiting for him at the station. They were the same ones who later murdered Ignace Reiss. Leon escaped certain death only because he fell ill on the eve of his departure, suffered from a high fever, and could not leave Paris. All these facts have been established by the judicial authorities of France and Switzerland. And how many secrets still remain unrevealed? His closest friends wrote us three months ago that he was subject to a danger too direct in Paris and insisted on his going to Mexico. Leon replied: The danger is undeniable, but Paris today is too important a battle post; to leave it now would be a crime. Nothing remained except to bow to this argument.

When in the autumn of last year a number of foreign Soviet agents began to break with the Kremlin and the GPU, Leon naturally was to be found in the center of these events. Certain friends protested against his consorting with "untested" new allies: there might possibly be a provocation. Leon replied that there was undoubtedly an element of risk but that it was impossible to develop this important movement if we stood aside. This time as well we had to accept Leon as nature and the political situation made him. As a genuine revolutionist he placed value on life only to the extent that it served the struggle of the proletariat for liberation.

On February 16, the Mexican evening papers carried a brief dispatch on the death of Leon Sedov following a surgical operation. Absorbed in urgent work I did not see these papers.

Diego Rivera on his own initiative checked this dispatch by radio and came to me with the terrible news. An hour later I told Natalia of the death of our son—in the same month of February in which thirty-two years ago she brought to me in jail the news of his birth. Thus ended for us the day of February 16, the blackest day in our personal lives.

We had expected many things, almost anything, but not this. For only recently Leon had written us concerning his intention to secure a job as a worker in a factory. At the same time he expressed the hope of writing the history of the Russian Opposition for a scientific institute. He was full of plans. Only two days prior to the news of his death we received a letter from him dated February 4, brimming with courage and vitality. Here it is before me. "We are making preparations," he wrote, "for the trial in Switzerland where the situation is very favorable as regards both so-called 'public opinion' and the authorities." And he went on to list a number of favorable facts and symptoms. *"En somme, nous marquons des points"* [All in all, we're making progress]. The letter breathes with assurance concerning the future. Whence then this malignant disease and lightning death? In twelve days? For us, the question is shrouded in deep mystery. Will it ever be cleared up? The first and natural supposition is that he was poisoned. It presented no serious difficulty for the agents of Stalin to gain access to Leon, his clothing, his food. Are judicial experts, even if untrammeled by "diplomatic" considerations, capable of arriving at a definitive conclusion on this point? In connection with war chemistry the art of poisoning has nowadays attained an extraordinary development. To be sure the secrets of this art are inaccessible to common mortals. But the poisoners of the GPU have access to everything. It is entirely feasible to conceive of a poison which cannot be detected after death, even with the most careful analysis. And who will guarantee such care?

Or did they kill him without resorting to the aid of chemistry? This young and profoundly sensitive and tender being had had far too much to bear. The long years of the campaign of lies against his father and the best of the older comrades, whom Leon from his childhood had become accustomed to revere and love, had already deeply shaken his moral organism. The long series of capitulations by members of the Opposition dealt him blows that were no less heavy. Then followed in Berlin the suicide of Zina, my older daughter, whom Stalin had perfidiously, out of the sheerest vindictiveness, torn from her children, her family, her own milieu. Leon found himself with his older sister's corpse and her six-year-old boy on his hands. He decided to try to reach his younger brother Sergei in Moscow by phone. Either because the GPU was momentarily disconcerted by Zina's suicide or because it hoped to listen in to some secrets, a phone connection, contrary to all expectations, was made, and Leon was able to transmit the tragic news to Moscow by his own voice. Such was the last conversation between our two boys, doomed brothers, over the still-warm body of their sister.

Leon's letters to us in Prinkipo were terse, meager, and restrained when they described his ordeal. He spared us far too much. But in every line one could feel an unbearable moral strain.

Material difficulties and privations Leon bore lightly, jokingly, like a true proletarian; but of course they too left their mark. Infinitely more harrowing were the effects of subsequent moral tortures. The Moscow trial of the sixteen, the monstrous nature of the accusations, the nightmarish testimony of the defendants, among them Smirnov and Mrachkovsky, whom Leon so intimately knew and loved; the unexpected internment of his father and mother in Norway, the period of four months without any news; the theft of the archives; the mysterious removal of my wife and myself to Mexico; the second Moscow trial and its even more delirious accusations and confessions; the disappearance of his brother Sergei, accused of "poisoning workers"; the shooting of countless people who had either been close friends or remained friends to the end; the persecutions and the attempts of the GPU in France, the murder of Reiss in Switzerland, the lies, the baseness, the perfidy, the frame-ups—no, "Stalinism" was for Leon not an abstract political concept but an endless series of moral blows and spiritual wounds. Whether the Moscow masters resorted to chemistry, or whether everything they had previously done proved sufficient, the conclusion remains one and the same: *it was they who killed him.* The day of his death they marked on the Thermidorean calendar as a major celebration.

Before they killed him they did everything in their power to slander and blacken our son in the eyes of contemporaries and of posterity. Cain Dzhugashvili [Stalin] and his henchmen tried to depict Leon as an agent of fascism, a secret partisan of capitalist restoration in the USSR, the organizer of railway wrecks and murders of workers. The efforts of the scoundrels are in vain. Tons of Thermidorean filth rebound from his young figure, leaving not a stain on him. Leon was a thoroughly clean, honest, pure human being. He could before any working class gathering tell the story of his life—alas, so brief—day by day, as I have briefly told it here. He had nothing to be ashamed of or to hide. Moral nobility was the basic warp of his character. He unwaveringly served the cause of the oppressed, because he remained true to himself. From the hands of nature and history he emerged a man of *heroic* mold. The great awe-inspiring events which hover over us will need such people. Had Leon lived to participate in these events he would have shown his true stature. But he did not live. Our Leon, boy, son, heroic fighter, is no more!

His mother—who was closer to him than any other person in the world—and I are living through these terrible hours recalling his image, feature by feature, unable to believe that he is no more and weeping because it is impossible not to believe. How can we accustom ourselves to the idea that upon this earth there no longer exists the warm, human entity bound to us by such indissoluble threads of common memories, mutual understanding, and tender attachment? No one knew us and no one knows us, our strong and our weak sides, so well as he did. He was part of both of us, our young part. By hundreds of channels our thoughts and feelings daily reach out to him in Paris. Together with our boy has died everything that still remained young within us.

Goodbye, Leon, goodbye, dear and incomparable friend. Your mother and I never thought, never expected that destiny would impose on us this terrible task of writing your obituary. We lived in firm conviction that long after we were gone you would be the continuator of our common cause. But we were not able to protect you. Goodbye, Leon! We bequeath your irreproachable memory to the younger generation of the workers of the world. You will rightly live in the hearts of all those who work, suffer, and struggle for a better world. Revolutionary youth of all countries! Accept from us the memory of our Leon, adopt him as your son— he is worthy of it—and let him henceforth participate invisibly in your battles, since destiny has denied him the happiness of participating in your final victory.

# AFTER SEDOV'S DEATH[186]

## February 22, 1938

Dear Friends:

We received your cables and letters. You understand without further words that they were of high moral value for us in these terrible days, I can say the most terrible in our life.

Together with Natalia I wrote an article during these days on Leon. It was not only a political duty but was the only one means not to lose one's reason. I dedicated the article to our youth. It would be of great moral support to Natalia and me if this writing could be published as early as possible by our youth organization in the form of a small pamphlet. It is possible that some things would not be clear enough for the young generation. Some comrade, if possible Shachtman, could write an annotation at the end as an appendix; not more, I believe, than one or two pages in order not to change the general character of this writing. I avoided subtitles. They seem to me superfluous in this case.

Eleven pages are being translated here and will be sent tomorrow by airmail, and the last eleven pages should be immediately translated in New York. We are sending one copy of the Russian text to Comrade Wright, and in case that he is absent, a second copy to Comrade Glenner.[187] We leave to them, Shachtman, or one of you the last editing. It is not necessary to return the manuscript for revision. I am sure the work will be done with all the necessary carefulness.

I promised you in my last letter to send you another manuscript, that of a pamphlet, *Their Morals and Ours*. But at that time I didn't know that I would have to write in the next few days a necrology for Leon. The promised pamphlet is almost ready. I shall dedicate it to Leon's memory because he was an authentic representative of *our* morals.

The cable concerning the trip of Comrade Hank Stone was sent last night. He will be welcomed in our home as a new member of our family.

From the last letters I see two propositions or plans, one concerning your arrival with Minnesota friends, the second concerning a more immediate trip of Glenner and yourself. It is not necessary to say that Natalia and myself will await you with friendship and love, but the urgent trip of Glenner and yourself is not necessary especially in view of the trip of Hank Stone. I am writing about the matter separately to Van.

Warmest greeting to you and all our friends and hearty thanks for everything you have done and are doing.

> From Natalia and myself,
> Yours fraternally,
> Leon Trotsky

P.S.—We now have a little supplementary house in the next yard. It is more than modest and not furnished. It can be put at your disposal if you will stay here for more than a week; then it would be reasonable from a financial point of view to buy some beds and to arrange the kitchen in this little house. In this case it would be advisable for you to take with you some sheets and blankets. There are four little rooms and a kitchen in the "house." If you accept this suggestion cable "Accept housing." We will try in this case to clean the rooms.

> L.T.

# A FRESH ATTACK ON ASYLUM[188]

## February 24, 1938

Mr. Lombardo Toledano and his clique, after lengthy and assiduous preparation, have made a malicious attempt to deceive public opinion in this country. The "material" on which they based themselves at the February convention of the Confederation of Mexican Workers (CTM) does not represent anything new: it is the material of Yagoda,[189] Yezhov, Vyshinsky. It is the material of Stalin. On the basis of this material thousands of people have been shot. Their only guilt was that they detested the dictatorship of the Kremlin clique and felt contempt for its lawyers and lackeys.

The "material" which Lombardo Toledano uses in order to deceive Mexican public opinion received the necessary evaluation in the findings of the International Commission of Inquiry at New York. In moral height, past, irreproachability of reputation, personal disinterestedness, each member of this commission, beginning with its president, Dr. John Dewey, surpasses Lombardo Toledano and his kind by several heads.

The commission, point by point, refuted all the accusations of Yagoda, Yezhov, Vyshinsky, Stalin, and their international lackeys. The twenty-first paragraph of the verdict states: "We find the prosecutor fantastically falsified Trotsky's role before, during, and after the October Revolution." It is exactly this "fantastic falsification" which lies at the root of the slanders of Mr. Toledano and his helpers.

My real politics are accessible to all. They are set forth in my books and articles. As in October 1917, I defend the interests and rights of the workers and peasants in the USSR—against the new, insatiable, and tyrannical aristocracy. In Spain I defend those methods of struggle against fascism that guaranteed the victory of the soviets in the civil war (1917-20), and I oppose the ruinous methods of the Comintern that guaranteed the victory of fascism in Germany, Austria, and other countries, and are laying the basis for the victory of General Franco. Throughout the world I defend those irreconcilable methods of struggle against imperialism that Lenin, Rosa Luxemburg, and Karl Lieb-knecht,[190] my old friends and companions-in-arms, applied; opposing the methods of the now thoroughly putrid Comintern, which crawls on all fours before "democratic" imperialism, betraying the interests of the colonial and semicolonial peoples for the sake of caste privileges for the Soviet bureacracy. Such are my views. I do not intend to change them. I carry full responsibility for them.

After the decision of the International Commission of Inquiry I have no reason to enter into political or juridical altercations with Mr. Lombardo Toledano. But I will be able to explain the truth to the people who have been deceived by him. It is this that Mr. Lombardo Toledano and his clique fear. Their whole machination at the convention, as the authors themselves have quite clearly revealed, follows but one single aim: *to seal my mouth.*

They act, of course, not upon their own initiative. Their inspirer lives in Moscow. The verdict of the International Commission, the published stenographic report of the inquiry at Coyoacan, the disclosures of the former responsible agents of the Kremlin (Reiss, Barmin, and Walter Krivitsky), as well as many other facts during the past year, delivered an irreparable blow to the Kremlin clique. My latest book, *Les Crimes de Staline,* has already appeared in several languages. I hope that it will also appear in Spanish. Progressive public opinion throughout the world, with ever greater disgust, is turning away from Stalin. This explains the furious attempt of the GPU to force me into silence.

Mr. Lombardo Toledano and his clique are mistaken, however, if they think that they will succeed in executing the mission entrusted to them. Many much stronger than they have tried to accomplish this task before without success. The czar taught me silence for four years in prison and twice exiled me to Siberia. Kaiser Wilhelm sentenced me to prison because I did not wish to keep quiet in Switzerland during the war. The French allies of the czar expelled me in 1916 from France for the same crime. King Alfonso XIII threw me into a Madrid prison in order to force me into silence. With the same objective, the British imperialists threw me into a Canadian concentration camp. The lawyer Kerensky, who was successful during a certain period of time in deceiving a considerable part of public opinion, tried to seal my mouth in the Petrograd Kresty Prison. But it is written on the pages of history that I have not learned to be silent on command. On the other hand, during the forty years of revolutionary struggle I have seen in the ranks of the workers' movement not a few careerists who can be not only silent but also slanderous on command.

If I had wished to remain silent about the crimes of the Stalin bureaucracy against the workers and peasants, they would have raised me high on their shield and the Lombardo Toledanos of the whole world would have crawled before me as they now crawl before the Kremlin clique. The Norwegian Social Democrats, older brothers in spirit to Toledano, discovered only one means with which to force me into silence about the GPU: to throw me into prison. But through a book my son, whom only death has now brought to silence, answered for me. Stalin, who understands this better than his agents, does not doubt that Toledano will be unsuccessful in forcing me into silence by some ancient warmed-up slanders. It is exactly because of this that Stalin is preparing *other measures,* considerably more realistic. But for these plans, about which we will speak in due time, Stalin as a preliminary needs to poison public opinion. For this work he requires Lombardo Toledano.

Several months ago this man asserted at a public meeting that I was plotting a general strike against the Mexican government in the interests of fascism. In his turn, Mr. Laborde—partly a helper of Toledano in slander, partly his master—asserted after this at a public demonstration that I was conspiring with "fascist generals." The answer to this "accusation" was a general contemptuous laugh. But it is impossible to embarrass these gentlemen. They cast these accusations aside only in order to present others immediately. If you throw enough mud, as the saying goes, some of it is bound to stick!

Messrs. Slanderers continue to build their game on the accusation that I am breaking my obligation about "noninterference in the internal politics of Mexico." The importation of odious slanders from Moscow and their translation into Spanish these gentlemen identify . . . with the internal politics of Mexico. I announce: no one has ever demanded of me and I at no time promised anyone that I would renounce the right to defend my political honor from slanderers, and my ideas—from their opponents. I pledged the government of General Cardenas that I would not interfere in the internal politics of this country according to the *general understanding of the word "politics."*[191] This pledge I am fulfilling with absolute conscientiousness. But if on the streets of the capital someone should shove his hand into my pocket in order to steal my documents and letters, I would consider myself completely in the right to seize the criminal's hand. And let the owner of the hand not scream after this that I am interfering in the internal politics of Mexico! Lombardo Toledano tries to despoil something bigger, my political honor, and demands at that—O democrat, O revolutionist!—that I be hindered by force from designating his actions and himself by the names they deserve.

I have never concerned myself with the political program and public actions of Mr. Toledano, nor with his references to Lenin, which belong in the sphere of unintentional humor. Likewise I now leave aside the question concerning the kind of machinations that made it possible for Toledano to palm off on the trade union convention a decision upon a question about which the overwhelming majority had not the least conception. But it is completely clear that when Mr. Toledano with the help of forged material mobilizes the whole convention against me, a private individual, a political exile who has no relations whatever with the trade unions of Mexico, and does this with but a single aim— to force me into silence or to deprive me of the right of asylum— *then Mr. Toledano acts not as a representative of the internal politics of Mexico but as an agent of the foreign politics of the GPU.* Let him then carry the responsibility of this unworthy function!

The readers of these lines will understand without difficulty that neither the present circumstances of my personal life nor the general character of my work afford me time to occupy myself over Mr. Toledano. But this question is something altogether different. It is a question concerning public opinion in the country which has shown me and my wife hospitality and which during the past year I have learned to value and to love. It is because of this, and only this, that I consider myself compelled to answer with this declaration the carefully prepared slander of the Mexican agents of Stalin.

# THE TRIAL OF THE TWENTY-ONE[192]

## February 28, 1938

During February of last year, at the time of the second Moscow trial (Pyatakov-Radek), which was supposed to correct the bad impression of the first trial (Zinoviev-Kamenev), I stated in the press: "Stalin resembles a man who tries to satisfy his thirst with salt water. He will be forced to stage further judicial frame-ups one after the other."

The third Moscow trial has been prepared during a more protracted period and, one must think, more elaborately than the previous ones. The international preparation has been going on during the past few weeks before the eyes of the whole world. The notorious article of Stalin (February 14) about international revolution, striking many with its suddenness, has as its objective the creation of a more favorable atmosphere within the ranks of the working class for the future trial. Stalin wished to tell the workers that if he is shooting the whole revolutionary generation, it is exclusively in the interests of the international revolution. His article does not have any other purpose.

The death of my son, Leon Sedov, which remains shrouded in mystery, should, until proved to the contrary, be considered as the second act of preparation for the trial: it was necessary at no matter what cost to force into silence an informed and courageous accuser.

The third act in the preparation was the attempt of Mr. Lombardo Toledano, Laborde, and other Mexican agents of Stalin to force me into silence on the eve of the third trial just as the Norwegian government forced me into silence after the first trial (August 1936). Such are the main ingredients of the preparation!

The accusation against the twenty-one defendants is once again published only four days before the trial in order to take public opinion unawares and to hinder the timely delivery of refutations from abroad.

The present trial far surpasses the trial of Radek-Pyatakov in the importance of the accused and approaches the Zinoviev-Kamenev trial. In the list of the accused there are no fewer than seven former members of the Central Committee of the party, including Krestinsky, Bukharin, Rykov,[193] former members of the *Political Bureau*, i.e., the institution which actually constitutes the highest power of the Soviet government.

After the death of Lenin, Rykov was the official head of the government for more than five years. From 1918 Bukharin was the editor of the central organ of the party, *Pravda*, and from 1926 the official head of the Communist International. Later, after his fall into disfavor, he became the editor of *Izvestia*. Rakovsky was the head of the Ukrainian government and later ambassador to London and Paris. Krestinsky, the predecessor of Stalin as secretary of the Central Committee of the party, was afterward ambassador to Berlin for several years. For almost all of the last ten years Yagoda stood at the head of the GPU as Stalin's most trusted henchman and cooked up the Zinoviev-Kamenev trial in its entirety. In the list of the accused there are no fewer than six former members of the central government.

Of the nine people who were members of the Political Bureau during Lenin's lifetime, i.e., actual rulers of the fate of the USSR, there remains only one unaccused, Stalin. All the others have been declared agents of foreign states, and in addition the accusations revert back to 1928 and even to 1918. The Russian White emigres have more than once accused Lenin, myself, and all the other Bolshevik leaders of having achieved the October Revolution at the orders of the German general staff. At the present time Stalin is trying to confirm this accusation.

According to their political tendencies, those of the accused who are known to me fall into three groups. (a) Bukharin and Rykov, former leaders of the *Right* Opposition. The third leader of this group, Tomsky, former president of the Soviet trade unions, was last year harrassed to suicide. From 1923 the Right Opposition found itself in irreconcilable struggle against the Left Opposition, the so-called Trotskyists. Rykov, Bukharin, and Tomsky, shoulder to shoulder with Stalin, carried on the whole campaign of destroying the Left Opposition. (b) The second group is composed of those accused who during a certain time actually belonged to the Left Opposition. Such were Krestinsky, Rosengolts—who, however, had already gone over to Stalin by

1927[194]—and Rakovsky, who returned to the government camp four years ago. (c) The third group insofar as I know it consists either of active Stalinists or nonpolitical specialists.

The name of Professor Pletnev sheds a singular light upon the whole trial.[195] Last year he was arrested on a charge of *sexual delinquency*. The whole Soviet press wrote about this openly. Now Pletnev has been thrown into a trial of . . . the political opposition. One of the following hypotheses may account for this: either the accusations of sexual delinquency were advanced against him only in order to extort the necessary "confessions" from him; or Pletnev is actually guilty of sadism but hopes to earn mercy through "confessions" directed against the opposition. We shall, perhaps, have the opportunity to verify this hypothesis during the trial.

How could Stalin come to this provocation against world public opinion? The answer to this natural question is composed of four elements: (1) Stalin is contemptuous of public opinion; (2) he does not read the foreign press; (3) the agents of the Comintern in all countries report to him only his "victories" over public opinion; (4) informed people do not dare to reveal the truth to Stalin. Thus he has unconsciously become a victim of his own politics. He is forced to drink salt water in order to quench his thirst.

# EIGHT MINISTERS[196]

## March 1, 1938

Yesterday I stated that there were no fewer than seven former members of the central Soviet government sitting on the defendants' bench. Today after more precise study of the names I see that among the accused, not counting the author of these lines, there are eight former Soviet ministers including the former head of the government, Rykov.

Bukharin, devoid of administrative capacity, never became a staff member of the government, but as a member of the Political Bureau and as the head of the Communist International from the time of Zinoviev's fall into disfavor (1926), he occupied a position considerably higher than that of a minister. All these people, it seems, strived for nothing except the humiliation and the dismemberment of the USSR!

Apart from the other crimes, about which we will speak in the future, the new defendants are also accused of the murder of Kirov. I recall that Kirov, a Leningrad agent of Stalin, was killed on December 1, 1934, by Nikolaev,[197] a young Communist unknown to anyone, apparently on personal grounds, and in any case, as was evident even from the Soviet accounts, with the direct participation of GPU agents. Immediately after the murder of Kirov, 104 "White Guards," who had supposedly come from abroad in order to commit terrorist acts, were shot without trial.

Although the names of the 104 were not published, it is known that among them were Bulgarian, Hungarian, and Polish Oppositionist members of the Communist International. Later the Leningrad "Center" of the Zinoviev group was accused of the murder of Kirov and thirteen men were shot. After this, the "Zinoviev-Trotskyist Center" was accused of the same crime and sixteen people were shot, not counting those shot during the GPU investigation. In January of last year the "Parallel Trotskyist

Center" (Radek, Pyatakov, and others) was accused of the murder of Kirov, and thirteen of the accused were shot. Finally, we now learn that the Right Opposition (Rykov, Bukharin) was likewise occupied with plotting the murder of this same Kirov. Thus all the leaders of the Bolshevik Party, people of great political and revolutionary experience, with names known to the whole world, during a number of years constructed "main," "united," and "parallel" terroristic centers and each of these centers plotted the murder of one and the same secondary Stalinist agent, Kirov, whose name became known only thanks to the trials.

According to the new charges, the terrorist plans of Bukharin and Trotsky began in 1918. In 1921 Trotsky was already secretly plotting with a foreign power (Germany?). The most important of the new defendants were members of the Central Committee of the party and government and daily met the "victims" marked by them. Moreover, Trotsky held in his hands the unlimited means provided by a military apparatus. And the result? The victim of this infernal conspiratorial activity beginning with 1918 proves to be no more than the same Kirov who was killed in turn by the White Guards, Leningrad Zinovievists, the United Center, the Trotskyists, and finally the Bukharinists.

Having cut themselves loose from every responsibility, the totalitarian leaders have cut themselves loose from the elementary laws of common sense. The Moscow trials strike one as elaborate nonsense, as the delirium of a lunatic armed with enormous power. It would be no exaggeration to say that this part of the accusation is saturated with the spirit of *totalitarian idiocy*. We will show in the future that the accusation is no more meritorious in all its other parts.

# TRIAL SEEN AS REPLY
# TO DEWEY COMMISSION[198]

## March 2, 1938

The new Moscow trial is designed to bolster with more impressive arguments shaken world confidence in Stalin's "justice." One cannot doubt that to a significant degree the trial is Joseph Stalin's dramatized answer to the verdict of the inquiry commission headed by John Dewey. We shall speak of this in future articles. At the moment we are concerned with the prehistory of the trial.

The investigation was of course conducted in impenetrable secrecy. However, some very important episodes in this investigation have become known, partly from the Soviet press, partly from the revelations of Soviet representatives who have broken with the Kremlin (Reiss, Barmin, Krivitsky, and others), and partly from other sources.

In his testimony at the January 24, 1937, session of the Moscow court, Karl Radek designated Nikolai Bukharin as a "conspirator." Bukharin has been in prison ever since. The GPU arranged a meeting between Bukharin and Radek, who has played the role of agent for Attorney General Andrei Vyshinsky. Radek appealed to Bukharin, with whom he had once been on friendly terms: "Confess everything they demand of you, and your life will be spared. I am living tranquilly in a villa, I have my library, I am only forbidden to meet other people." These arguments had no effect upon Bukharin.

At one of the sessions of the February 1937 plenum of the Central Committee, Bukharin, former head of the Communist International, and Alexei Rykov, former head of the Soviet government, were brought from prison—an unprecedented occurrence in the history of the Bolshevik Party! They were ordered to make "voluntary confessions" and thus help to crush the enemies of the party (Trotsky and his partisans).

191

Rykov wept at the session of the Central Committee. Gentle Bukharin, on the contrary, behaved aggressively, accusing Stalin of judicial frame-ups. Both of them refused to assume the shameful role. Stalin shouted: "Take them back to jail. Let them defend themselves from there!!!" Bukharin and Rykov were taken back to the prison by agents of the GPU waiting at the door. Thanks to the great number of members at the plenum, Moscow bureaucratic circles learned of this scene the very same day.

The accused Rakovsky, former head of the Ukrainian government, later ambassador to London and Paris, was arrested in February 1937. The first questioning in his apartment lasted eighteen hours without interruption. His inquisitors worked in relays, but the sixty-four-year-old Rakovsky was held for eighteen hours without food or water. Rakovsky's wife wished to give him tea, but they forbade her, stating that she might poison her husband!

Hour after hour of incessant questioning under the hypnotic glare of special spotlights constitutes the GPU's ordinary system of weakening resistance. Mrachkovsky, who was shot in the Zinoviev-Kamenev trial, was questioned for ninety hours at one stretch, with but short interruptions. This seems incredible, but the methods of the GPU in general are "incredible." Among others, Reiss revealed the above-mentioned fact, based on information received from Slutsky, one of the central figures of the GPU.[199] The fact is also known to some American journalists.

Meanwhile, the so-called "purge" continued, its main objective during the past year the preparation of the principals for the third trial. Dozens and hundreds of relatives, friends, collaborators, and colleagues of the defendants were arrested. With these arrests the GPU aimed to enclose every one of the accused within a ring of false depositions made by people closest to him.

Those candidates for the defendants' bench not broken by ceaseless inquisitions and by dozens of false depositions were executed during the investigation itself, without any trial, simply by decision of the GPU, which means, plainly, on the personal order of Stalin.

Last December 19, Moscow dispatches revealed that the eminent Soviet diplomat, Karakhan, and the former secretary of the Central Executive Committee of the Soviets, Abel S. Yenukidze, had been executed as "spies."[200] In all their political activity, Karakhan and Yenukidze were closely connected with the defendants in this new trial. They were denounced as perpetrators of the same crimes.

Why are they not on the defendants' bench? Only because the GPU did not succeed in breaking them during the preparation of the case. They were executed in order to give a last and definitive warning to the others.

We must add that those who have been arrested not only are without benefit of defense attorneys, but also are denied interviews with close friends and relatives. The exceptions to this ironclad rule are individuals like Radek, who are used exclusively to cajole the prisoners into making the demanded confessions. It is in this manner that the accused were "educated" during the past twelve months, some of them after undergoing years of preparatory persecutions and repressions.

Last January 19, the world press announced that the January plenum of the Central Committee in Moscow had ordered a letup on the mass purge. World public opinion hastened to conclude that a new, more moderate course was beginning. In reality, the mass purge was halted only because its immediate purpose had already been gained; that is to say, the will of the important defendants had been broken and the possibility of a trial assured. Such was the course of the investigation.

Moscow's foreign agents have hastened to call the new mockery a "public" trial. As if the legal machinery becomes "public" just because the inquisition at a chosen moment raises the curtain over a small part of its work! The trial opens on March 2. However, *Pravda* had already declared on February 28 that the accused would not escape execution.

*Pravda* is Stalin's personal newspaper. What significance does the trial bear if Stalin, through his newspaper, dictates the verdict before the opening of the trial? Only such lackeys as have recently declared Stalin's constitution to be "the most democratic in the world" can call this trial "public."

In this new trial we can expect some improvement over those preceding it. The monotony of the breast-beating confessions of the accused in the first two trials produced a suffocating impression even among the rubber-stamped "friends of the USSR." That is why it is possible that this time we may see some of the defendants, in obedience to their assigned roles, deny their culpability, in order to confess their guilt later under cross-examination. We can predict, however, that not one of the accused will raise difficulties for Prosecutor Vyshinsky by obdurate recalcitrance.

Another innovation is also possible. In the preceding trials we were astounded by the complete absence of all material proofs—

documents, letters, conspiratorial addresses, guns, bombs. All letters mentioned in those trials invariably had been "burned." It is very likely that this time the GPU has decided to fabricate a few false documents in order to give at least a semblance of support to the friendly foreign lawyers and journalists. The risk is not great—who in Moscow can check up on the work of the GPU?

Is it possible during the coming trial, despite everything, to expect from the defendants some surprise disagreeable to Stalin and the GPU? Will an indignant outcry break in upon the rushing torrent of confessions: "All this is a frame-up from beginning to end!"?

Such a surprise is not excluded. But at the same time it is scarcely probable. The courtroom will be crowded with well-drilled agents of the GPU capable of creating the proper atmosphere, both for the accused, already morally broken, as well as for the journalists, judiciously selected.

Moreover, each of the defendants has been secretly promised his life. The image of Radek and his comfortable villa will continually flash before the eyes of these tortured victims. An even stronger brake unquestionably is the thought of their families and people near to them who will inevitably perish in case of an open protest. But no matter how smoothly the trial proceeds in its outward aspects, it will explode in mid-air as political, moral, and psychological nonsense. We will speak of this in due time.

# TO THE ATTENTION
# OF THINKING PEOPLE[201]

## March 3, 1938

On March 2, through the press, I warned public opinion in the United States as follows: "In this new trial we can expect some improvement over those preceding it. The monotony of the breast-beating confessions of the accused in the first two trials produced a suffocating impression even among the rubber-stamped 'friends of the USSR.' That is why it is possible that this time we may see some of the defendants, in obedience to their assigned roles, deny their culpability, in order to confess their guilt later under cross-examination. We can predict, however, that not one of the accused will raise difficulties for Prosecutor Vyshinsky by obdurate recalcitrance."

At the first session of the trial the defendant Krestinsky categorically repudiated the testimony which he had given during the preliminary investigation and denied his guilt. In response to this I announced in the Mexican press: "It is necessary to be very cautious in our predictions. . . . What will Krestinsky say tomorrow if he discovers that his wife and daughter can become the first victims of his boldness?" The latest Moscow dispatches state that at the following session Krestinsky hastened to reaffirm his "guilt." Yesterday I *conditionally* made allowance for the possibility that Krestinsky's rebellion was genuine. Until proved wrong I did not consider that I had the right to assert that in my opinion this unfortunate prisoner of the GPU was merely playing out a comedy upon command. Today there can be no doubt of this. Krestinsky belongs precisely among those defendants about whom I wrote three days before the trial started: *"In obedience to their assigned roles* they will deny their culpability, in order to confess their guilt later under cross-examination. We can predict, however, that not one of the accused will raise difficulties for Prosecutor Vyshinsky by obdurate recalcitrance." Permit me to add that the sedative medicine was prepared in advance by the GPU.

The prosecutor asserts that I am in secret agreement with the general staffs of various imperialist countries. No one, however, will say that I am in secret agreement with Vyshinsky himself. Then how do I know these secrets? Though thinking people can find the solution without aid, I nevertheless hasten to explain: the structure of the Moscow frame-up is so crude, the creative imagination of Stalin, Vyshinsky, and Yezhov so barren, that with the very faintest effort of the mind one can almost always foresee the type of falsification they will resort to tomorrow.

# BEHIND THE MOSCOW TRIALS[202]

## March 3, 1938

Three men, Bukharin, Rykov, and Rakovsky, are the chief figures in the present treason trial in Moscow. Through their attitude one can measure the depth of the reaction in the USSR for the first time.

In 1910, in Paris, Dubrovinsky, a Bolshevik long since dead, whispered to me, pointing to Rykov, "Alexei would have been prime minister in any other country." *Fourteen years later, upon my recommendation, Rykov was chosen for the post that became vacant by Lenin's death—president of the Council of People's Commissars.*

Devoid of interests of a purely theoretical nature, Rykov possesses a clear political mind and exceptional ability as an administrator. In spite of the fact that he stammers, he is an orator of great force. Rykov has devoted his entire conscious life to one ideal.

Bukharin, in contrast to Rykov, is a pure theoretician, lecturer, and writer. One of the new Bolsheviks, devoid of organizing capacity, it is precisely because of this that he never became part of the government staff; but he was editor of the central organ *Pravda,* a post of exceptional significance. After Zinoviev's fall into disfavor he became leader of the Communist International (1926-27). There was always an appealing, childish quality about Bukharin's character which made him, as Lenin expressed it, "the favorite of the party."

Bukharin's theoretical thinking is distinguished by capriciousness and a tendency toward posing paradoxes. Often he argued very heatedly against Lenin, who answered him in the tones of a teacher. This polemical sharpness, however, never spoiled their friendly relations. Bukharin loved Lenin and was as attached to him as a child to its mother. *If someone had told us during those years that Bukharin would be accused of attempting to assassinate Lenin, every one of us would have come forward to throw the prophet into an insane asylum.*

I have known Rakovsky since 1903. Our intimate friendship lasted until 1934, when he repented of his "Oppositional" sins and returned to the government camp. An international revolutionist in the fullest sense of the word, Rakovsky speaks fluently, in addition to Bulgarian (his native tongue), French, Russian, Rumanian, English, and German. He has a reading acquaintance with Italian and other languages. Deported from nine European countries, Rakovsky tied his fate to the October Revolution, which he served in the most responsible posts. A physician by profession, a brilliant orator and writer, he won everyone's heart through his qualities of frankness, humane kindliness, and the richness of his mental equipment.

*Bukharin has thirty years of revolutionary work to his credit, Rykov almost forty, Rakovsky nearly fifty.* These three men are now accused of having suddenly become "spies" and "agents" of foreign powers, aiming to destroy and dismember the USSR and establish capitalism. All three, after long periods of inquisitorial treatment in a GPU prison, have confessed their guilt.

Next of the accused men in importance is Krestinsky, a lawyer by profession, and one of the Old Bolsheviks. He was Stalin's predecessor as general secretary of the party before he became people's commissar of finance, and later ambassador to Berlin.

Yagoda, first as chief power in the GPU, and later also as its official head, occupies a special place on the defendants' bench. He was Stalin's closest confidant for ten years in the struggle against the Opposition. Essentially an insignificant person, without any special distinctive characteristics, he personifies the spirit of the secret police.

After preparing the trial of Zinoviev and Kamenev in August 1936, Yagoda grew frightened at the prospect of further extermination of the Old Bolsheviks, within whose ranks were not a few of his personal friends. This sealed his fate. Only yesterday exalted to the order of police "marshal," he was dethroned, arrested, and declared the betrayer and enemy of the people. *Yezhov, the new chief of the GPU, applied to Yagoda the very methods of investigation invented by Yagoda himself and thereby obtained the same results.*

Among the other defendants, Rosengolts and Zelensky[203] have a certain political interest because both are Old Bolsheviks and former members of the Central Committee. Rosengolts is first and foremost an organizer. He played an important role in the civil war, to a large extent under my personal supervision.

Zelensky was for many years the head of the most important party section—the Moscow section.

Ivanov, Grinko, and Chernov are purely administrative figures who have only become prominent in recent years.[204]

I recognize three of the remaining names—Ikramov, Khodzhaev, and Sharangovich—as those of people who played a progressive role in the party movement in the provinces.[205]

Five other names—Kryuchkov, Bessonov, Zubarev, Maximov-Dikovsky, and Bulanov—call forth no particular associations for me.[206] In all cases, these people are stars of the third or fourth magnitude.

The four doctors of the Kremlin hospital deserve particular attention. On more than one occasion I took advantage of the medical care two of these physicians had to offer me—namely, Levin and Pletnev.[207] The other two, Kazakov and Vinogradov, I remember only by their names.[208]

The doctors are accused of having poisoned People's Commissar of Heavy Industry Kuibyshev, the head of the GPU, Menzhinsky, and the author, Maxim Gorky.[209] Only this incredible accusation was lacking to make the others stand out in clear relief.

Let us check briefly the present status of the Bolshevik Party and the Soviet power as now characterized by Stalin's series of judicial frame-ups of people who, during Lenin's lifetime, were members of the Political Bureau—that is to say, the highest institutions of the party and government. All, with the sole exception of Lenin (who died opportunely) and Stalin, have turned out to be "agents of foreign powers."

Each and every head of the Red Army and Navy, without exception, were "betrayers"—Trotsky, Tukhachevsky, Yakir, Uborevich, and others—all the Soviet ambassadors—Sokolnikov, Rakovsky, Krestinsky, Karakhan, Yurenev, and others[210]—have turned out to be "enemies of the people." All the heads of industry and railroads now appear to be "organizers of sabotage."

Pyatakov, Serebriakov, Smirnov, and others in the leadership of the Communist International were "agents of fascism." The head of the Soviet press and leaders of thirty national Soviet republics turned out to be "agents of imperialism." *Finally, the lives and health of the leaders of the party and government were entrusted to poisoners.*

To complete this picture we need only to place on it the signature of its artist, Joseph Stalin.

The defendants in the present trial, as well as in the former trials, belong politically to various and moreover hostile groups. Bukharin and Rykov were leaders of the party's right wing along with the president of the trade unions, Tomsky, who was driven to suicide. Their struggle against Trotskyism was implacable and thoroughly principled. Working closely with them, Stalin, who played a centrist role, prepared the destruction of the Left Opposition in 1928. I first learned of the existence of a Trotskyist-Rightist "bloc" from the Moscow dispatches. The real bloc that the party right wing participated in for many years was a bloc with Stalin against me.

My friends Rakovsky, Krestinsky, and Rosengolts were for a time sincere adherents to my position. But Rakovsky was the only one who played any active role in the Left Opposition. From his pen came the most sterling analyses of the political and moral degeneration process within the Soviet bureaucracy. Rosengolts and Krestinsky could be characterized more as sympathizers of the Opposition than as active members. In 1927 both of them went over to Stalin's camp and became his faithful functionaries. Rakovsky held out longer than the others. I received a report, unfortunately unconfirmed, that Rakovsky tried to flee abroad by way of Barnaul (in Altai) in 1934, that he was wounded in the escape attempt and taken to the Kremlin hospital. It was only after this bitter experience that he capitulated to the ruling clique, sick and tortured as he was.

Former rightists, former leftists, bureaucrats of the Stalin school, and apolitical doctors could not have taken part in a common political conspiracy. They were brought together only to serve the malicious ends of the prosecutor.

The present elaborate trial, like the first two, revolves as if on an unseen axis, upon the author of these lines. *Invariably all the crimes were committed at my request. People who have been my irreconcilable opponents and who conducted daily campaigns against me in the press and at mass meetings—like Bukharin and Rykov—suddenly prove to be ready, no one knows why, to undertake any kind of crime upon my signal from abroad.* Leaders of the Soviet government, at my command, became agents of foreign powers, "provoked" wars, prepared the destruction of the USSR, ruined industry, wrecked trains, poisoned workers with lethal gases. My younger son, Sergei

Sedov, a professor in the engineering school, in particular, was accused of this crime.

And to top things off, Kremlin physicians poisoned a good percentage of their patients simply out of dedication to me!

I know the circumstances and the people intimately, including the organizer of the trials, Stalin. I have carefully followed the inner evolution of the Soviet system in my time. I have made a diligent study of the history of the revolutions and counterrevolutions in other countries, where they likewise did not occur without "frame-ups" and amalgams.

During the past year and a half I have lived almost incessantly in the atmosphere of the Moscow trials. But when one reads dispatch after dispatch about how Bukharin wanted to murder Lenin, about Rakovsky's ties to the Japanese general staff, and how the Kremlin doctors murdered the elderly Gorky, it all seems like a delirious dream.

*It is with almost a physical effort that I tear my own thoughts away from the nightmarish combinations of the GPU and direct them upon the question, "How and why could all this be possible?"*

Whoever tries to judge the events unfolding in Russia finds himself faced with the following alternatives: (1) either all the old revolutionists—who led the struggle against czarism, built the Bolshevik Party, achieved the October Revolution, led the three years of civil war, established the Soviet state and created the Communist International—either all these figures, almost to a man, were at the very moment of these achievements, or in the years immediately following, agents of capitalist states; or (2) the present Soviet government, headed by Stalin, has perpetrated the most heinous crimes in world history.

Many attempt to come to a decision on this question by a purely psychological method. "Who earned for himself the greater confidence," they ask themselves, "Stalin or Trotsky?" Speculation on such a level in the majority of instances remains sterile. Using the "golden mean," some people are inclined to employ a compromise. Probably, they say, Trotsky did carry on some sort of conspiracy, but Stalin has exaggerated it colossally.

*I propose to ask the reader to thrash out this question for himself, not by the subjective or psychological method, or by moral speculation, but upon the plane of objective analysis of historical factors.* This is the more reliable method. The question of personal psychology still retains its significance, but the individual, by this method, ceases to be or seem to be the master of the nation's fate. He becomes himself, the product of certain historical conditions, the agent of certain social forces.

It is necessary to examine the program of the most powerful personality, including the program which led to his "frame-ups," in the light of those historical forces which he represents.

Stalin indubitably belongs to the category of the old revolutionists. He has been a member of the Bolshevik Party since the 1905 revolution. But one cannot depict all Bolsheviks in one and the same light. Stalin represents the type directly contrary to that of Lenin or, to measure greatness by something more commensurable, Zinoviev and Kamenev, who long labored in exile under the direct leadership of Lenin. Stalin went abroad only by chance in connection with party matters. He does not command a single foreign language. On the theoretical plane he possesses all the traits common to a self-taught person. *At every step one comes across yawning gaps in his knowledge.* At the same time, his is a strongly practical mind, both careful and suspicious.

Unquestionably, his character is superior to his mind. He is a man of indisputable personal courage, thoroughly unpossessed of any kind of distinctive talents, flights of thought, creative imagination, oratorical or literary ability. *His ambition has always been colored by suspicion and vengefulness.* All these qualities, however, positive as well as negative, remained locked up in him for many years, unexpressed and therefore all the more strained.

Stalin creates the impression of being an outstanding mediocrity, but no more. Only by dint of peculiar historical circumstances were his underlying traits of character given the opportunity to flower extraordinarily. The year 1917 found Stalin, in the political sense, a "thoroughgoing provincial." He did not even dare to think about the dictatorship of the proletariat and the socialist reorganization of society. *From beginning to end his program was that of the formation of a bourgeois republic.*

After the February revolution he favored unity with the Mensheviks and supported the first Provisional Government, whose president was Prince Lvov.[211] Lenin's socialist program caught Stalin unawares. He played no role at all in the great mass movements of the early years, but, bowing before Lenin, he stepped into the gloom, retired to the editorial offices of *Pravda,* and wrote articles.

Lenin valued Stalin for his sturdiness, firmness of character, and cautiousness. Concerning Stalin's theoretical preparation and the limits of his political horizon, Lenin entertained no illusions. At the same time he, more aptly than anyone else, understood and summed up the moral character of this "remarkable Georgian," as he referred to him in a letter written in 1913.

Lenin did not trust Stalin in 1921, when Zinoviev recommended him for the post of general secretary. Lenin gave the following warning: *"I don't advise this. This cook will prepare only peppery dishes."*

In his testament of January 1923 Lenin flatly urged the party to remove Stalin from the post of general secretary, referring to his rudeness, his disloyalty, his tendency to abuse power.[212] Let us steadfastly keep these traits in mind in the course of discussions over the problems of the Communist International.

During Lenin's lifetime Stalin was never heard from. Just as previously on the question of a socialist revolution in Russia, so later on the question of international revolution, he remained always a skeptic and an unbeliever.

The restrictions in his historical outlook and his conservative social instincts, carried over from his petty-bourgeois Georgian circle, inspired in him an extreme distrust of the masses. On the other hand, he placed high value on the operations of committee "cadres." In this sphere of activity he was in complete harmony with his qualifications as a surreptitious conspirator.

*In the first period of the revolution—that is, until 1923, when the participation and the initiative of the masses still played a decisive role—Stalin remained in the background as a secondary figure.*

His name signified nothing to anyone. The masses did not know him at all. He was a quasi-authority only for those party bureaucrats who came to depend on him. But the more the masses came under the whip of historical necessities, the less sanguine they became; the more they tired, the more the bureaucratic apparatus was able to elevate itself on their necks.

Meanwhile the bureaucracy had completely changed its international character. Revolution, by the very essence of the term, implies the use of violence by the masses. But the bureaucracy, which, thanks to revolution, had come to power, decided that violence was the prime factor in history. As early as 1923-24, I struck out against this common aphorism in the Kremlin, which said, in effect, "If political regimes in the past fell, it was only because the leaders had not decided to employ the necessary violence which would have maintained them." At the same time, the bureaucracy was coming more and more to the conviction that, having swept it into power, the masses had achieved their mission. *The Marxist philosophy of history was transformed into a kind of police philosophy.*

The most complete and consistent expression of the new tendencies of bureaucracy was given by one man, Stalin. His secret impulsions, his self-willed character, had finally found a convenient application. *In the course of a few years Stalin became, in the full and complete sense of the word, "czar" of the new bureaucracy, the caste of rapacious parvenus.*

Mussolini, Pilsudski,[213] Hitler, each in his own way, was the initiator of a mass movement, albeit reactionary. One and all rose to power together with this movement; but Stalin, in this sense, was never the initiator, and, according to the outlines of his character, could not have been so. He was the skulking conspirator, the man working always in the shadow.

When the bureaucracy placed itself at the head of the revolution in an isolated, backward country, it almost automatically placed Stalin on its shoulders—Stalin, who was in complete accord with its brutal police philosophy and was better equipped—that is to say, more pitiless—than any others to defend the bureaucracy's power and privileges.

"Socialism," "proletariat," "people," "international revolution" are today but pseudonyms for the bureaucratic caste. The more acute its internal uneasiness, the more often it makes use of them. Its entire embodiment in postrevolutionary society is based on deceptions, falsifications, lies. *It cannot permit the slightest opposition, because it is not able to defend its covetous policy by one convincing argument.* It is constrained to strangle at birth any criticism directed against its despotism and privileges, to proclaim that any disagreement is treason and perfidy. At the beginning these attacks on the Oppositionists consisted of journalistic slanders, of falsifications of quotations and statistics. The bureaucracy thereby concealed its revenues. But the more the new caste straddled Soviet society, the more necessary it became to use more powerful means for crushing adversaries and intimidating the masses.

It was precisely at this point that Stalin brought into complete view the dangerous qualities which Lenin had warned against— rudeness, disloyalty, propensity to abuse power. *The "cook of the Kremlin" had indeed prepared the most peppery of dishes.*

The living traditions of the revolution impinged upon Stalin's consciousness to show him that his power was that of a usurper. The generation of the revolution, though debased and crushed, remained, in his eyes, a menace. His fear of the masses was greater than anything and he mobilized the whole bureaucratic apparatus to hold them in check. But this bureaucracy itself has never achieved the necessary unity. Old traditions and newly aroused social apprehensions have created friction and criticism even within the narrow ranks of the bureaucracy. And for this very reason, it became necessary to undertake "purges."

The journalistic persecution of the Opposition had to give way to juridical theatrical productions—show trials with witnesses, judges, and defendants. And since the Old Bolsheviks were the most dangerous, the GPU must therefore debase these Old Bolsheviks by proving them spies and traitors.

The method of the GPU is the method of a modernized Inquisition—complete isolation, arrest of relatives, of children, of friends, the execution of "some" of the accused during the preparation of the case (Karakhan, Yenukidze, and many another), the threat of executing relatives, and the uniform clamor from the totalitarian press. *All this is sufficient to destroy the nerves and crush the will of the imprisoned men. This, without the use of the branding iron or boiling water, is all that is necessary, and "voluntary confessions" are obtained.*

Until recently Stalin was absolutely convinced of the omnipotence of this system. However, it is doubtful if he still maintains this conviction. Each trial has given birth to a growing discontent, an alarm, not only among the masses but among the bureaucrats themselves. In order to beat down this discontent it was necessary to concoct a new trial. Behind this diabolical play we can perceive the pressure, still compressed but ever growing, of a new society which asks for freer cultural conditions and a more dignified existence.

*The struggle between the bureaucracy and society becomes more and more intense. In this struggle victory will inevitably go to the people.* The Moscow trials are but episodes of the death agony of the bureaucracy. Stalin's regime will be swept away by history.

# FOUR DOCTORS KNEW TOO MUCH[214]

## March 3, 1938

Four physicians are accused of having assassinated two Soviet functionaries, Valerian V. Kuibyshev and Vyacheslav Menzhinsky, and the writer Maxim Gorky.

Until now it was believed that these three persons had died of natural causes; Menzhinsky and Gorky had been ill for many years. Their death certificates were signed by half a dozen luminaries of Soviet medicine and also by the people's commissar of public health.

The corpses were cremated. Consequently, there cannot now be raised the possibility of exhumation and public examination. On what hook, then, can the accusations be hung? It is readily apparent that they again depend on "voluntary confessions."

I personally remember well two of the "physician terrorists," L.G. Levin and D.D. Pletnev. They were the official physicians of the government since the first years of the revolution. The two others, I. N. Kazakov and Dr. Vinogradov, I recall only by their names.

All four, as physicians, could not conceivably dream of attaining posts higher than they held. None of them ever attempted to take any part in political activity. Then what could have been their motive in committing the most reprehensible of all crimes—the murder of a patient by his physician?

The accusations become even more inexplicable if we consider the three supposed victims of terror.

Kuibyshev, though he dwelt upon the Soviet Olympus, was never considered by anyone a personage in his own right. He was transferred from pillar to post as a bureaucratic jack of all trades. He enjoyed no authority in the party; he had no political ideas. To benefit whom and to advance what was it necessary to do away with him?

Menzhinsky, already then gravely ill, became the head of the GPU in 1927, following the death of Felix Dzerzhinsky.[215] The individual in the GPU who enjoyed Stalin's confidence for carrying out the more secret of missions was in reality Henry G. Yagoda. But since Yagoda, also one of the present accused, was held in general and merited contempt, the sick Menzhinsky was appointed as a blind for Yagoda's activities.

Often at government sessions Menzhinsky would lie prostrated, with a countenance contracted in pain. His death occurred not sooner but later than was expected. Why, in the name of reason, was it necessary to poison him?

The most astonishing fact of all, however, is the inclusion of Maxim Gorky's name in the list of those "assassinated." As a writer and a man he enjoyed the widest possible sympathy. At no time was he a political figure.

A victim of tuberculosis from youth, he was forced to live in the Crimea. Afterward, in fascist Italy, precisely because of the purely literary character of his activity, he met with no difficulties from Mussolini's police. In his last years Gorky again lived in the Crimea.

Since he was compassionate over the troubles of others and easily influenced, the GPU surrounded him with a veritable ring of agents under the guise of secretaries, whose task it was not to permit undesirable visitors near him. What sense was there in the assassination of this sick writer, at a time when he was sixty-seven years old?

The GPU's incredible choice of executioners and victims is explained by the fact that even the most fantastic frame-up must nevertheless be concocted out of some elements of reality. It must be remembered the GPU was finding itself in difficulties.

In spite of the fact that the "plot," as now explained, had already begun in 1918, in spite of the great number of terrorist "centers," the members of which were once the traditional leaders of the Bolshevik Party, members of the Central Committee and of the government, and finally, in spite of the participation in the plot of the generals of the Red Army (Marshal Mikhail N. Tukhachevsky, General I. E. Yakir, and others), in reality—that is to say, in the realm of the three dimensions—the world did not see a coup d'etat, an insurrection, or terroristic acts, but merely arrests, deportations, and executions.

Actually, the GPU could invoke only one real terroristic act— the assassination of Sergei Kirov. This was done by a Young Communist, Leonid V. Nikolaev, in December 1934, for unknown reasons, probably personal ones. The corpse of Kirov has invariably appeared at all the political trials of the past three years. In turn, all the following assassinated Kirov—the White Guards, the Zinovievites, the Trotskyites, and the Rightists.

But in time this unique resource was exhausted. In order for the GPU to keep aloft the vast edifice of the "plot," new victims of "terror" had to be discovered. It was necessary to seek them from among more recently deceased dignitaries. But since the dignitaries had, indeed, died in the Kremlin—that is to say, under conditions excluding the intervention of outside "terrorists"—it was imperative to resort to the charge that the physicians of the Kremlin had poisoned their patients, in accordance, of course, with the instructions of Nikolai Bukharin, Alexei Rykov, or, even worse, Leon Trotsky.

On first glance it is surprising not to find Gregory K. Ordzhonikidze, late head of heavy industry, included among the "victims"—Ordzhonikidze, who, in contrast to the three afore-mentioned personages, played an enormous political role as one of the more eminent members of the Political Bureau.[216]

Here we come to the most perfidious knot in the juridical "amalgam." According to the information from Moscow, Ord-zhonikidze strenuously opposed the extermination of the Old Bolsheviks. In taking such a stand he was completely in character, for Ordzhonikidze, more than anybody else in Stalin's entourage, retained a sense of moral responsibility and personal dignity.

His opposition, in regard to a question of such acute impor-tance, represented a source of enormous danger for Stalin. Gorky was able only to lament and deplore; Ordzhonikidze was able to act. From this single fact stem the rumors of the poisoning of Ordzhonikidze. True or false, these rumors have an extremely persistent character.

Immediately following the arrest of Dr. Levin, chief of the Kremlin Hospital, information appeared in the foreign press to the effect that Dr. Levin himself had been the first to state that the death of Ordzhonikidze might have been due to poisoning. An extremely remarkable fact! Dr. Levin suspected the GPU of having poisoned Ordzhonikidze some months before the GPU accused him of having poisoned Kuibyshev, Menzhinsky, and Gorky.

Previously, none of the names of the other three physicians was connected with this affair. But it is very plausible that conversations on the cause of Ordzhonikidze's death should take place precisely among the physicians of the Kremlin. This was more than sufficient cause for arrests. The arrests, in turn, became the point of departure for the "amalgam" created.

The reply of the GPU was simple: "So you suspect that Ordzhonikidze was poisoned? We suspect you of having poisoned Kuibyshev, Menzhinsky, and Gorky. Confess! You will not? Then we will execute you immediately. But if you should confess that the poisoning was accomplished on orders from Bukharin, Rykov, or Trotsky—why, then, you may hope for leniency."

All this may seem incredible, but incredibility is the very essence of the Moscow trials. Such trials are possible only in the completely poisoned atmosphere under the heavy, tightly screwed-down lid of the totalitarian regime.

# THE SECRET ALLIANCE
# WITH GERMANY[217]

## March 3, 1938

When the young diplomat Butenko fled from Rumania into Italy and there issued a statement of a semifascist character, the people's commissar of foreign affairs, Mr. Litvinov, hastened to reassure the world (February 17, 1938) that such sentiments could not have come from a Soviet diplomat but only from an impostor belonging to the White Guards. But, Litvinov added, if the declaration had actually come from Butenko's lips, then he, the people's commissar, did not doubt for a minute but that such a statement could not have been extorted save through torture. Let us attempt in all calmness to apply this authoritative dictum as a rule in judging the unfolding events in the present Moscow trial.

The question this time concerns not some completely unknown individual like Butenko but the former head of the government, Rykov; the former head of the Comintern, Bukharin; a host of Soviet ambassadors and ministers, all of whose names have become indissolubly fused with the history of the USSR. These men did not merely escape into fascist Italy at the moment of personal danger; they collectively placed themselves at the disposal of foreign powers for the purpose of dismembering the Soviet Union and reestablishing capitalism.

If Mr. Litvinov thought the fascist-like utterances of a single young diplomat incredible, are we not correct in saying that it is a thousand times harder to believe that the entire older generation of the Bolshevik Party has gone over to the fascist camp?

It is true that the defendants confessed their guilt. But these confessions are capable of convincing us immeasurably less even than the declaration of Butenko convinced Litvinov. We reserve the right, moreover, to repeat the words of the Moscow diplomat with tenfold force: "Such confessions could have been torn from the lips of the accused only by torture."

It might be possible for one man, or for several men, to accomplish a series of horrible crimes, if these crimes would in some way benefit the criminals. An individual might perform an absurd crime. But it is impossible to allow that a large group of men, not merely mentally normal but of superior intelligence, over the course of several years, accomplished a whole series of crimes as monstrous as they are senseless. The feature which distinguishes the present trial is the exaggeration of the old accusations to the point where they relapse into a complete and definitive absurdity.

The formula of accusation in the case of Zinoviev, Kamenev, and others (August 1936) stated that the conspirators out of mere "thirst for power" resorted to terroristic acts and even to an alliance with the Gestapo. In the Radek-Pyatakov trial (January 1937) the charge was that the plotters aimed for power in order to establish fascism in the USSR. Let us accept both these versions at their face value. But in the present trial it is charged that the writer of these lines became an agent of Germany as far back as 1921 when he was a member of the Politburo and chief of the Red Army and when Germany was not yet fascist. At this point we are entering the realm of psychopathology.

In 1921 we had just finished the civil war triumphantly. The international position of the Soviet Union had become stabilized. The introduction of the New Economic Policy (NEP) gave life to frozen economic forces. We had the right to contemplate the future with real optimism. An expression of this optimism in particular was my report to the Third Congress of the Comintern (June 1921).[218]

On the other hand, Germany at that time was groping in the Versailles blind alley.[219] Its economic strength had been sapped; its military power was practically nonexistent. Thousands of German officers became free lancers, offering their services to many farflung countries. Even if we were to allow—and in the interests of a thorough analysis I am prepared to make any allowance—that I aimed not merely for power but for personal dictatorship—be it at the price of betrayal and secret agreements with capitalist governments—I would not in any case have chosen disarmed and humiliated Germany, which itself needed help and was incapable of offering it to others.

Moscow dispatches link my name, in some sort of tie-up, with that of General Von Seeckt, at that time head of the Reichs-

wehr.[220] This gives an inkling of justification for the hypothesis
which, I presume, will be indirectly affirmed later on in the trial.
It is obvious that even a delirious dream is made up of some
elements of reality. At the same time, a lie can be given the
appearance of veracity only if some particles of truth are kneaded
into it. From this perspective we will attempt to discover the sort
of materials used by the prosecution as a base on which to rear
their superstructure.

From the moment of the overthrow of the Hohenzollerns,[221] the
Soviet government aimed for a defensive alliance with Germany
against the Entente and the peace of Versailles. But at that time,
the Social Democracy, playing first fiddle in Germany, feared
Moscow and placed all its hopes on London and especially on
Washington. From its side, the officer caste of the Reichswehr,
despite its political enmity against communism, considered a
diplomatic and military collaboration with the Soviet Republic
necessary. Since the Entente countries were in no hurry to put
themselves out to satisfy the Social Democrats' hopes, the
"Moscow" orientation of the Reichswehr proved to have an
influence upon government circles as well. The highlight of this
period was the conclusion of the Rapallo agreement, establishing
friendly relations between Soviet Russia and Germany (April 17,
1922).[222]

The military commissariat, which I headed, was planning in
1921 the reorganization and rearmament of the Red Army in line
with its passing from a state of war to one of peace. Vitally
concerned to improve military technology, we could then expect
cooperation only from Germany. At the same time the Reichswehr, deprived by the Versailles treaty of opportunities for
development, especially in the fields of heavy artillery, aviation,
and chemical warfare, naturally aimed to make use of the Soviet
military industry as a test field. The beginnings of German
concessions in Soviet Russia took place at a time when I was still
immersed in the civil war. The most important of these in its
potential—or more accurately, in its expectations—was the
concession granted to the Junker aircraft concern. This concession involved a certain number of German officers coming to
Soviet Russia. In turn, several representatives of the Red Army
visited Germany where they became acquainted with the
Reichswehr and with those German military "secrets" which
were graciously shown them. All this work, of course, was
conducted under the cover of secrecy, since the Damocles sword of
the Versailles obligations hung over the head of Germany.

Officially, the Berlin government took no part in these negotiations and acted as if it knew nothing about it: formal responsibility rested with the Reichswehr. The secret naturally could not long continue. Agents of the Entente, particularly of France, established without difficulty that a Junkers aircraft factory and a few other enterprises were operating near Moscow. Paris undoubtedly attributed exaggerated significance to our collaboration with Germany. The collaboration did not achieve a high stage of fruition, inasmuch as neither the Germans nor we had sufficient capital. In addition, mutual distrust was too great. Nevertheless, the semifriendly ties with the Reichswehr were maintained even after 1923 when the present defendant Krestinsky became ambassador to Germany.

On behalf of Moscow this work was conducted self-evidently not by me as an individual but by the Soviet government as a whole; more correctly, by its leading center, the Politburo. Throughout this period, Stalin was a member of the Politburo, and, as illustrated by his future conduct, up to 1934, when Hitler rejected the proffered hand of Moscow, Stalin was a most dogged partisan of collaboration with the Reichswehr and Germany in general.

The management of the German military concessions was in the hands of the present defendant, Rosengolts, as the representative of the head of the military commissariat. In view of the danger of the infiltration of military spies, Dzerzhinsky, head of the GPU, in collaboration with the same Rosengolts, kept the concessions under constant surveillance.

In the secret archives of the military commissariat and the GPU there should undoubtedly be documents in which collaboration with the Reichswehr is referred to in most guarded and conspiratorial terms. Save for people like Stalin, Molotov,[223] Bukharin, Rykov, Rakovsky, Rosengolts, Yagoda, and another dozen or so individuals, the contents of these documents may well appear to be "enigmatic," not only to Prosecutor Vyshinsky, who in that period was in the camp of the Whites, but likewise to several members of the present Politburo.

Will not the prosecutor offer these documents as material evidence in order to astound the friendly foreign journalists? It is fully possible that our hypothesis will have been given substantiation before these lines reach the reader.

# CORRECTIONS AND OBSERVATIONS ON THE TESTIMONY OF THE ACCUSED[224]

## March 4, 1938

1. In 1927, Krestinsky wrote me a letter from Berlin to Moscow, in which he informed me of his intention to capitulate to Stalin and advised me to do the same. I replied with an open letter, breaking off relations with Krestinsky, as with all other capitulators. A great amount of material about the irreconcilable struggle between the Oppositionists ("Trotskyists") and the capitulators was revealed by me in April 1937 to Dr. John Dewey's investigative commission. But the GPU continues to base its fake trials exclusively on capitulators who have been toys in their hands for years already. That is why it is necessary for Prosecutor Vyshinsky to show that my break with Krestinsky had a "fictitious character."

Showing this was entrusted to another capitulator, the sixty-five-year-old Rakovsky, who declared that the capitulation was a "maneuver," and that this maneuver had somehow taken place with my approval. Rakovsky did not explain, however, and the prosecutor of course did not ask him, why he himself, Rakovsky, had not carried out this "maneuver" for a period of seven years, but had preferred to stay in the difficult conditions of exile in Barnaul (Altai), isolated from the whole world. Or why, in autumn 1930, Rakovsky wrote from Barnaul, in an indignant letter against the capitulators, his famous phrase, "the worst thing is not exile and not solitary, but capitulation." Why, finally, he himself capitulated only in 1934, when his physical and moral forces were completely exhausted.

2. After denying his guilt (in complete accordance with the GPU script), Krestinsky admitted the correctness of all the accusations brought against him and told of a mythical meeting

with me in Merano, in October 1933. I declare that after 1926 I never met Krestinsky and never had any connections with him. I was never in Merano in my life. I spent October 1933 as a patient in France, under the eyes of friends and the doctor and under the observation of the French police. The facts concerning this were completely established by Dr. Dewey's investigative commission in New York. If Prosecutor Vyshinsky had consulted the French authorities, they would have given him exact information about where I was in October 1933. But that is precisely why Vyshinsky did not consult the French authorities!

3. The accused Rosengolts testified that he met my son Leon Sedov in Carlsbad and received through him from me all sorts of criminal instructions. The desertion of Mr. Rosengolts from the ranks of the Opposition twelve years ago had such a shameful character that there could be no possibility of any further relations between me and him. Leon Sedov was not in Carlsbad in 1934 or any other year, and this can be proved on the basis of letters and documents in the daily dossier of his short life, just as it was shown by Dr. Dewey's commission that in November 1932 Sedov was not in Copenhagen. Leon Sedov's calendar, as we see, did not coincide with the GPU's calendar. And that is why the GPU brought Leon Sedov to an untimely death.

4. Krestinsky and Rosengolts both testified that I had given them instructions on the necessity of forming an alliance with Tukhachevsky and other generals, with the aim of "overthrowing Soviet power." The phantom of the executed marshal Tukhachevsky is evidently, in general, hovering over the proceedings. Fearing the dissatisfaction of the best generals, Stalin beheaded the Red Army and thus evoked deep resentment in the whole world. Now he is trying, retrospectively, to show the public opinion of the USSR and of the whole world that the generals who were shot really were traitors.

I declare that in the testimony of Krestinsky and Rosengolts there is not a word of truth. I had neither personal meetings, nor correspondence, nor any kind of indirect link with Tukhachevsky since spring 1925, i.e., from the time I left the leadership of the Red Army. Tukhachevsky, and the other executed generals, despite close military connections with me, never were Trotskyists politically. They were soldiers. If, in the last period, Tukhachevsky rose in opposition to Stalin, he was led exclusively by feelings of patriotism. Tukhachevsky and the other generals could not fail to see that Stalin's policy was striking irreparable blows at the defense interests of the USSR.

# THE 'MILLION DOLLARS'[225]

## March 5, 1938

Defendant Rosengolts, ex-people's commissar of foreign trade, states that particularly through the agency of his commissariat, "during the last years Trotsky received nearly a million dollars for his activities directed toward overthrowing the Soviet state." According to Moscow dispatches, Rosengolts further described the machinations carried on in the Commissariat of Foreign Trade for the purpose of concealing embezzlements from the state.

I make complete allowance for the possibility that such machinations were and are being carried on now in the Commissariat of Foreign Trade, as well as in other commissariats. In all likelihood, Rosengolts was primarily removed precisely because of the revelation of some kind of serious misuse of funds—I hope without his personal complicity. The lack of control over the regime is the nourishment on which thieves and thievery thrive. I had occasion to write about this dozens of times in the course of the past few years in various publications, especially in the Russian *Biulleten Oppozitsii,* edited by Leon Sedov in Paris. In all likelihood Rosengolts spoke the truth in *this* part of his testimony. Upon an entirely different plane stands the second part of his testimony concerning the transmitting to me of a "million dollars."

In order to bring a note of clarity from the very beginning of this whole affair, *I state categorically:* the only sum which I have received from the Soviet treasury since my banishment from Russia was $2,500 given to me by a GPU agent in Constantinople for the livelihood of myself and my family. This sum of course was given with complete legality and the agent secured a receipt from me. I have received no other sums from the Soviet treasury during the years of my present exile (1929-38) either legally or illegally, directly or indirectly, in dollars, sterling, marks, or in any other national currency.

Testifying further, Rosengolts stated the matter more precisely when he said that during each of the last three years, "Trotsky

216

received more or less regularly nearly $110,000 a year." This addition of $10,000 to $100,000 is specified here of course in the interests of accurate bookkeeping. Precision is advisable also in falsehoods. *I state categorically:* I have received neither $100,000 nor $10,000; not even a single dollar from Soviet sources during the past three years, or during the six preceding.

It is not evident from the Moscow dispatches whether Mr. Rosengolts described how he transmitted such enormous sums to me: Through a bank? Through what kind of bank exactly? Who deposited the money in the bank and when? In whose name was the current account started? An immediate verification on this score is possible and imperative.

I have been in Mexico for more than a year. This means that the last $110,000 should already have reached me during my stay in Mexico. I repeat my questions: Through which bank? When? In whose name?

Or perhaps the money was handed to me by messenger in the form of a bank draft or in bags of gold. Who delivered these sums? When and where did this person reach me? Did he receive any kind of receipt from me? Where are these receipts?

One of the dispatches states that part of the sum was transmitted through some kind of "German firm." Thus the GPU evidently wishes to evade an investigation: Soviet justice cannot hope for help from fascist justice. For myself, I trust fascist justice as little as Stalin's. It is clear, however, that reference to a "German firm" represents merely a crude and miserable ruse. Rosengolts could not abandon this "secret" money to arbitrary disposition by the "firm." He could not have avoided making sure of a personal tie between this firm and me. His anxieties over the safe transmission of the money could have been satisfied only if the firm really handed over to me the amounts involved. Consequently, it must be known to Rosengolts exactly how this financial operation was accomplished, and he is obliged to relate everything he knows about it . . . if he knows anything.

From the latest dispatches it appears that Rosengolts has testified that $630,000 of the million were remitted to my son Sedov. All the questions asked above retain their full force in this instance, too: Who? When? Through what bank?

In reality the world press has already refuted these lies before they were published. Upon the death of Sedov, all foreign correspondents in Paris commented, not without astonishment, upon the more than modest circumstances in which my son lived. I have at hand all the letters of Sedov written during the years of our exile. From these letters it is clear what great efforts he exerted to collect the amount necessary for the regular appearance of each issue of the Russian *Biulleten,* once a month or once in two months. Moreover, the question was not one of hundreds of thousands of dollars, but of about 2,000 francs, that is, at most $100. Sedov lived and died a proletarian.

Investigation of all the foregoing facts, as well as investigation of all my expenditures, starting with the fourteen months of my residence in Mexico, should represent no difficulties. It is true that no diplomatic relations exist between the USSR and Mexico. But through the League of Nations[226] or through a third power, Soviet justice could easily find a means of approaching Mexican justice. There can be no doubt that the authorities of this magnanimous country will not refuse to cooperate with the investigation. But the question is not limited to Mexico. After my residence in Turkey, I lived in France and Norway. With both of these countries the USSR has not only normal but friendly relations. The people who surrounded me, the political organizations with which I am connected, are known by the entire world. Their income and expenditures can easily be checked. A million dollars in my modest budget could not remain unnoticed. So large a sum must leave some material trace. My alleged accomplices, the former "conspirators," the present defendants, and most of all Rosengolts, must know: (a) *how I received the money;* (b) *how I spent it.* Let them give some concrete facts which can be submitted to objective investigation in all the countries where I lived and worked. Verifications of this sort will inevitably reveal that upon the orders of the GPU, Rosengolts heaped slander not only upon me but also upon himself.

I challenge Mr. Troyanovsky, Soviet ambassador in Washington, and through him the Soviet government: *before Rosengolts is executed or reported executed, institute an immediate investigation of the mythical million dollars.* I pledge to present all my letters, documents, and financial accounts as I presented them to the New York Commission of Inquiry, headed by Dr. John Dewey.

I have no doubt that my challenge will not be accepted. The defendants will be executed or their execution announced. But some months later, perhaps a new trial will take place where new breast-beating "conspirators" will demonstrate the guilt of Rosengolts as Rosengolts has "bared" the guilt of the executed Marshal Tukhachevsky. Thus runs the course of the degrading and monstrous mechanics of Stalin's justice!

# ARMY OPPOSED TO STALIN[227]

## March 6, 1938

In the proceedings at Moscow they are trying not only shattered and broken people, morally semi-corpses, but also actually deceased ones. The specters of Marshal Mikhail N. Tukhachevsky, Generals I.E. Yakir, I.P. Uborevich, A.I. Kork, and other assassinated generals share the prisoners' dock.[228]

After their arrest and the executions which quickly followed, the Soviet press spoke of these men as "foreign agents" and "spies." About a military conspiracy, a plan to seize the Kremlin and assassinate Stalin, not a single mention was made. It would seem plausible, however, that the government by that time should have known exactly why it had executed the best of the Soviet military captains. But, in the grip of last summer's acute political panic, Stalin acted faster than he thought.

Fearing the army's reaction, he felt it impermissible to waste time on an inquisitorial "education" of the generals for a trial. Furthermore, these men belonged to the younger generation, had stronger nerves, and were inured to facing death. They were unfit for a public spectacle. There remained but one way out, to shoot first and explain later. But even after the echoes of the Mauser had died down Stalin still could not decide upon a convenient version of the indictment.

Today one can say with complete assurance that the deceased Ignace Reiss was correct when he asserted that there was no military trial "behind closed doors." Indeed, why would it have been necessary to have closed the doors, if the matter actually had involved a conspiracy? In plain language, the generals were assassinated in the same way that Hitler avenged himself upon Roehm and others in June 1934.[229]

Evidently, after the bloody retribution, eight other generals (Marshal T.I. Alksnis, Marshal S.M. Budenny, Marshal V.I.

Bluecher, General Boris M. Shaposhnikov, and others)[230] received the prepared text of the sentence which they were ordered to sign. The aim was to do away with several and at the same time check on the loyalty of others and kill their popularity. This was completely in harmony with Stalin's usual style.

Unquestionably, some of the alleged "judges," if not all, refused to appear before public opinion as executioners of their closest comrades-in-arms, especially after the executioner's work had already been accomplished by others. The signatures of the recalcitrant ones were nevertheless added to the sentence, and they themselves shortly afterward were removed, arrested, and shot. The task appeared to be completed.

But public opinion, including that of the Red Army itself, did not want and could not bring itself to believe that the heroes of the civil war, the pride of the country, had turned out to be, no one knows why, German or Japanese spies. A new version became necessary. In the course of preparing the present trial it was decided to impute retrospectively to the deceased generals a plot for a military coup d'etat.

Thus, the matter revolved not about miserable trafficking in espionage but about a grandiose scheme for a military dictatorship. Tukhachevsky was to have conquered the Kremlin, Marshal Ian B. Gamarnik[231] the Lubyanka (headquarters of the GPU), and Stalin was to have been killed for the hundred and first time.

As always, the new version was given retroactive force. The past was reconstructed according to the exigencies of the present. According to the testimony of A.P. Rosengolts, Leon Sedov, my deceased son, recommended to him as far back as 1934 in Carlsbad (where Sedov never was in his life) that a close watch be kept over the "ally," Tukhachevsky, because of his propensity for a "Napoleonic dictatorship." Thus the scheme of the plot is gradually expanding in time and space. The decapitation of the Red Army is but an episode in the campaign of extermination of the ubiquitous and all-penetrating "Trotskyists."

In the interests of clarity, I must say something here concerning the relations between Tukhachevsky and me. I aided him in the early days of his rise in the Red Army. I was appreciative of his military talents, as well as of the independence of his character, but I never took too seriously the communist convictions of this former officer of the Guard.[232]

Tukhachevsky was cognizant of both sides of my estimate. He bore himself toward me, so far as I can judge, with a sincere respect, but our conversations never went beyond the limits of official relations. I think he accepted my departure from the army partially with regret, partially with a sigh of relief. He could expect, not without foundation, that for his ambition and independence a larger arena was opened with my departure. Since the moment of my retirement, that is to say, the spring of 1925, Tukhachevsky and I never met and had no correspondence.

He followed a strictly official line. In the army political meetings, he was one of the foremost speakers against Trotsky-ism. I believed that he performed this task from obligation, without any enthusiasm. But his active participation in the venomous campaign against me was fully sufficient to exclude the possibility of any kind of personal relations between us. This was clear enough to all, so that it should be impossible to enter the mind of anyone to establish a political liaison between Tukhachevsky and me.

This explains why the GPU did not decide in May and June of last year to link up the case of the generals with the plot of the Trotskyist "centers." The passage of some months of oblivion and the addition of some complementary strata of falsifications were necessary before risking such an experiment.

The sentence of the so-called Supreme Court (*Pravda,* June 12, 1937) accuses the generals of having "systematically supplied . . . espionage information" to an enemy state and having "prepared in case of military attack on the USSR the defeat of the Red Army." This crime has nothing in common with the plan for the military coup d'etat.

In May 1937, when, according to the testimony of Nikolai N. Krestinsky, the seizure of the Kremlin, Lubyanka, etc., was to have been accomplished, there was no "military attack upon the USSR." The conspiring generals, consequently, were not at all expecting war. They had designated a definite date for their military blow in advance. However, the "crime" for which the generals were executed was that of espionage with the purpose of assuring, "in case" of war, the defeat of the Red Army.

Between the two versions there is nothing in common. They exclude one another. What can there be in common between a spy who hopes to be awarded in the uncertain future by a foreign power and a courageous conspirator who aspires to seize power by force of his own arms? But, of course, neither Prosecutor Andrei Y. Vyshinsky nor the president of the court, Vassily V. Ulrich, took the trouble of counterposing the testimony of the present defendants with the text of the death sentence imposed by the Supreme Court, June 11, 1937.

The new version is given currency as if there had never been a "Supreme Court," a sentence, and an execution. With almost maniacal insistence, Krestinsky and Rosengolts, chief assistants to the prosecutor in this matter, revert to the question involving the conspiracy of Tukhachevsky and my alleged connections with him.

Krestinsky states that he received a letter from me dated December 19, 1936—that is, ten years after I had broken off all relations with him—and in the letter I had recommended the creation of a "broad military organization." This alleged letter, obligingly underlining the "broad" scale of the plot, evidently aims at justifying the extermination of the best officers, which began last year but is still a long way from completion even today. Krestinsky, of course, "burned" my letter, following the example of Karl Radek, and presented nothing to the court beyond his confused reminiscences.

This same Krestinsky stated that he, together with Rosengolts, received a letter from me, written from far-away Mexico a short time before the execution of the generals, demanding that the coup d'etat be "accelerated." One must suppose that this letter likewise was "burned," like all other letters which have figured in the trials of the past few years.

In any case, after months of internment and a forced journey on a tanker, separated from the sphere of action by an ocean and a continent, I managed to be so precisely informed on the practical course of the latest "conspiracy" that I even gave instructions regarding the date of the coup d'etat.

But how did my letter from Mexico reach Moscow? American friends offer the supposition that the mysterious Adolph A. Rubens will figure in this trial as the courier designated to link me with the specters of the Moscow generals.[233] Inasmuch as I know nothing about Rubens or his orbit, I am constrained to suspend judgment. I presume that Messrs. Earl Browder and William Z. Foster could expand themselves with considerably more authority on this question.[234]

The chief witness against the defendants in the case of Tukhachevsky and the others, Nikolai Krestinsky, was arrested in May 1937 and, in his own words, gave a frank "confession" within a week of his arrest. The generals were shot on June 11. The judges supposedly should have had Krestinsky's testimony before them at that time. He himself should have been called as a witness to the trial (if a trial actually took place).

In any event, the government's announcement of the execution of the generals could not have mentioned espionage and been silent about a military coup d'etat, if Krestinsky's present testimony had not been invented after the execution.

The essence of the matter lies in the fact that the Kremlin could not proclaim aloud the real reason for the execution of Tukhachevsky and the others. The generals rushed to defend the Red Army from the demoralizing intrigues of the GPU. They defended the best officers from false accusations. They resisted the establishment of the GPU's dictatorship over the Red Army under the guise of "military soviets" and "commissars."

The generals fought for the interests of the security of the Soviet Union against the interests of Stalin's security. That is why they died. Thus, from the gaping contradictions and the heap of lies in the new trial, the shade of Marshal Tukhachevsky steps forth with a thunderous appeal to world public opinion.

# WHY SO MANY CENTERS?
# WHY DO THEY ALL
# SUBMIT TO TROTSKY?[235]

## March 6, 1938

In August 1936 the world learned of the existence of the "United Center" of Zinovievists-Trotskyists, which directed possible and impossible crimes. In January 1937, the "Parallel Center," or purely "Trotskyist Center" (Pyatakov-Radek) entered on the scene. To explain the appearance of this center, Radek, the chief herald of Prosecutor Vyshinsky, explained that Trotsky did not sufficiently trust the Zinovievists and therefore wished to have "his own" center.

This explanation was shot full of holes. First, ex-Trotskyists of more serious proportions than Pyatakov and Radek belonged to the Zinoviev-Kamenev Center. Secondly, Sokolnikov, former ambassador to England, a man who had never been connected with the Trotskyists, belonged to the so-called "Trotskyist" Center. But we will not carp at such "details." Let us concede that the parallel "Trotskyist Center" was really created for the more important and conspiratorial matters and that Sokolnikov wound up in this center by pure accident. But in March 1938 not only has the world learned of the existence of a third "Trotskyist-Right Center," but we are unexpectedly told that it is precisely this center, entirely unknown to the preceding two centers, which is the most powerful and conspiratorial organization. To this we must add that the members of these three independent centers had known each other for twenty or thirty years, lived in the same city of Moscow, and in general executed one and the same "work": terrorism, espionage, sabotage, defeatism, and the dismemberment of Russia. In particular, all these centers in turn assassinated Kirov.

But a difficulty arises here. If I created a Trotskyist Center

(Radek-Pyatakov) because I did not sufficiently trust Zinoviev-Kamenev, then how could I have trusted Rykov and Bukharin, who until the very day of my expulsion from the USSR were in close alliance with Stalin and led the whole struggle against Trotskyism, including my arrest and exile? Apparently during the period when I lived in Moscow and was a member of the Political Bureau and the government I was powerless to convince Bukharin and Rykov of the correctness of my views. They voted against me, they made hostile speeches against me at mass meetings, Bukharin wrote several hundred rabid articles against me. Both leaders of the Right voted for my expulsion from the party, for my banishment to Asia, and later for my expulsion from the USSR. But when I reached Turkey, and later France, Norway, and Mexico, and found myself separated from Moscow by thousands of kilometers, then Rykov and Bukharin, as in general all the defendants in the last trials, not only began definitely to agree with me, but also decided to carry out my "instructions" without reservation. Members of the government, ambassadors, generals of the Red Army, became foreign spies "upon the instructions of Trotsky." In this manner exactly acted Rykov, the former head of the government, and Bukharin, the former head of the Communist International. No other explanation of their monstrous and absurd "crimes" are proffered by the defendants.

During this trial Rykov and Bukharin tried to deny direct responsibility for the assassination of Kirov, who, as has been stated before, was killed in turn by all oppositionist groupings in the USSR. But Henry Yagoda, the former head of the GPU—who, before he sat on the defendants' bench, shot several hundred men for the assassination of Kirov—immediately declared Rykov and Bukharin to be lying. "They, as I," Yagoda stated, "really opposed the assassination of Kirov in the beginning. But instructions came from Trotsky and we submitted."

One becomes literally numb with amazement upon reading these words of yesterday's inquisitor. Assertions as to the omnipotence of "instructions" sounded sufficiently absurd on the lips of Pyatakov and Radek. But these men, at least, had been my partisans eleven years ago. It is true that they repudiated me and became my bitter enemies. But Prosecutor Vyshinsky asserts that this enmity was "fictitious," that actually a fervent personal devotion to Trotsky guided these ex-Trotskyists. Of course, it is incomprehensible how and why this fervent devotion so quickly cooled off in prison and permitted Pyatakov and Radek to paint me in the darkest colors. But we will push all this aside. Let us grant that the old ties actually assured me a hypnotic influence across continents and oceans upon my former partisans. But how explain the relation with Rykov and Bukharin? How and by what means can the fact be explained that they became obedient students of Trotsky only after they had expelled me from the USSR?

Especially mysterious, however, is the case of Yagoda. This man was, you see, against the assassination of Kirov but immediately capitulated to my "instructions." Since when has Yagoda learned to carry out my instructions? As the head of the GPU he directly supervised all repressions against the Opposition; destroyed my secretariat; harassed two of my secretaries to suicide; shot my pupils and young friends, Blumkin, Silov, Rabinovich;[236] hounded several members of my family to an untimely death; arrested and expelled me; prepared the Zinoviev-Kamenev trial; supervised frame-ups and crimes against the Opposition. Now it appears that he performed all these deeds as "camouflage." In reality he was a secret Trotskyist and carried out my "instructions."

No, this is too much! Not even the omnivorous "friends of the USSR" will swallow that. They swallowed the Zinoviev-Kamenev proceedings; they swallowed the Pyatakov-Radek proceedings; but I very much fear that they will choke on the testimony of Yagoda.

# THE ROLE OF YAGODA[237]

## March 7, 1938

Perhaps the most fantastic element in the entire series of Moscow judicial phantasmagoria is the inclusion of Henry G. Yagoda, for many years head of the GPU, as a "conspirator" in the Trotskyist-Bukharinist center. Anything could have been expected, but not this.

Stalin had to maneuver the Political Bureau for a long time before he succeeded in making the hated Yagoda, his most trusted henchman, head of the GPU. The struggle against all factions of the Opposition had been concentrated in Yagoda's hands since 1923. He was not only the privy executor of all the falsifications and frame-ups, but also the organizer of the first executions of the Oppositionists back in 1929: Blumkin, Silov, and Rabinovich.

In the pages of the *Biulleten Oppozitsii,* edited by the late Leon Sedov in Paris, the name of Yagoda is recorded again and again with approximately the same bitter indignation as once in revolutionary publications the name of the chief of the czarist Okhrana, Zubarev, was.[238]

Yagoda himself, hand in hand with Prosecutor Andrei Vyshinsky, prepared all the sensational trials since the assassination of Sergei M. Kirov, including the trial of Gregory Zinoviev and Leon Kamenev in August 1936. Systematized, breast-beating confessions will go down in history as the invention of Henry Yagoda. If someone were to say that Joseph Goebbels was an agent of Pope Pius, it would sound considerably less absurd than the assertion that Yagoda is the agent of Trotsky.

But the fact is that for the new judicial structure Yagoda was needed not as architect, but as material. The fate of the all-powerful chief of the secret police was weighed and disposed where all such questions are decided: Stalin's private study. Yagoda was tabbed to occupy a certain place in the trial, as is a pawn in a chess strategy. One problem remained, to force upon him acceptance of the role assigned. But this was the smallest difficulty.

In the first months following Yagoda's arrest there was heard

not even a whisper of his complicity in the conspiracy of Marshal
Mikhail N. Tukhachevsky, the Trotskyists, and the Rightists.
Neither Yagoda nor public opinion had yet matured for this
development, nor was there yet any certainty that Vyshinsky
would be able to exhibit his new client to the public.

The first accusations given currency by the Soviet and world
press against Yagoda listed: licentious manner of living;
embezzlement of funds; wild orgies. Were these accusations true?
Concerning Yagoda, one is justified in making full allowance for
such possibilities. Careerist, cynic, petty despot—he was surely
not a model of virtue in his personal life. This picture is
completed by adding that, if he permitted vicious instincts to rule
his life to criminal limits, it was only because he was convinced
of his complete impunity. What is more to the point, his mode of
life was known for a long time to everyone in Moscow, including
Stalin.

Indeed, all information impugning the private lives of high
Soviet functionaries is gathered by Stalin with scientific
meticulousness, and is the basis for a special archive brought to
light piecemeal, as dictated by the degree of political necessity.
The hour struck when it became necessary to break Yagoda's
moral fiber. This was done by scandalous disclosures regarding
his private life.

Following these body blows, the former head of the GPU for
several months was faced with this alternative—to be shot as an
embezzler of government funds, or possibly save his life as an
alleged conspirator. Yagoda made his choice and was included
among the twenty-one on trial. And at last the world learned that
Yagoda shot Trotskyists only to "camouflage" his real feelings;
actually, he was their ally and agent.

But to whom and why was it necessary to add so improbable
and compromising a complication to the juridical amalgam,
already so confused without it? Yagoda's name among the
defendants is too fantastic a phenomenon to be explained away
by generalities. There must have been a reason so all-
encompassing, direct, and acute as to force Stalin not to be
stopped even before the prospect of transforming his number one
agent into an agent of Trotsky. This reason is now disclosed by
Yagoda himself.

According to his own words (at the session of March 5), he had
ordered his subordinates in Leningrad, of course "under the
instructions of Trotsky," not to hinder the terrorist act against
Kirov. Deriving from the chief of the GPU such orders were

tantamount to saying that the assassination of Kirov be organized.

The most natural supposition: Yagoda assumed the onus for a crime with which he had no connection. Then why and for whom was the sincere or false confession of the former head of the GPU necessary?

Let us recall briefly the most important facts. Kirov was killed December 1, 1934, by the then unknown Leonid Nikolaev. The trial of the assassin and his alleged accomplices was held behind closed doors. All the fourteen defendants were shot. From the text of the sentence, partially published in the Soviet press, it was learned that a Latvian consul, George Bissenieks,[239] gave Nikolaev 5,000 rubles in payment for the terrorist act, demanding from him in exchange some sort of "letter from Trotsky."

On December 30, 1934, I stated with assurance in the press that Bissenieks was an agent of Yagoda (*Biulleten Oppozitsii*, January 19, 1935). I did not then, nor do I now, offer the explanation that the GPU actually meant to assassinate Kirov. What was intended was the preparation of a "conspiracy" involving the Opposition and especially myself, and at the last moment the disclosure of an attempt at assassination. Within less than a month, this hypothesis proved to be officially confirmed.

The military tribunal, on January 23, 1935, sentenced twelve responsible Leningrad officials of the GPU, headed by their chief, Medved,[240] to prison terms ranging from two to ten years. The exact wording of the published sentence was as follows: "They possessed information concerning the preparations for the attempt on Kirov . . . but they displayed . . . criminal carelessness (!) . . . and failed to take the necessary measures."

Greater candor could not be asked. "Criminal carelessness" signifies nothing less than the direct participation of the GPU in the assassination of Kirov. And with the role of Bissenieks in mind, it becomes even clearer that Nikolaev was but an instrument in the hands of official agents provocateurs. But this instrument turned out to be self-willed. For personal reasons, Nikolaev took his job seriously, made use of the auspicious moment, and shot Kirov before Yagoda succeeded in getting a "letter from Trotsky."

The driving necessity to publish the information for worldwide attention that the twelve responsible agents of the GPU knew in advance about the plot hatching for the assassination of Kirov can be explained only by the fact that it was necessary at any cost for certain very high officials to establish their alibis.

The circumstances that surrounded the assassination of Kirov could not help calling forth whispering among the gentry in the top government circles to the effect that, in the struggle against the Opposition, "the leader" was beginning to toy with the heads of his closest collaborators. Not a single informed person doubted that Medved, chief of the Leningrad GPU, had daily reported to Yagoda on the progress of operations as Yagoda had reported to Stalin, and received from him instructions.

To lay these extremely dangerous rumors to rest, there was nothing to do but sacrifice the Leningrad executors of the Moscow-hatched plan.

On January 26, 1935, I wrote: *"Without the direct agreement of Stalin*—more precisely, without his initiative—*neither Yagoda nor Medved would have decided to mount such a risky enterprise"* ["Everything Gradually Falls into Place," in *Writings 34-35*].

Kirov's death became the point of departure for the systematic extermination of the Old Bolshevik generation. But the more trials the GPU staged around Kirov's corpse, the more insistently clamored in all minds the question: Who benefits from all this? The extermination of the old guard is a manifest and conspicuous political aim of Stalin. The Moscow leaders thus did not doubt for a moment that Yagoda couldn't act without instructions from Stalin.

The suspicion spread in even broader circles, resolving into certainty. It became absolutely necessary for Stalin to disown Yagoda, to dig between himself and Yagoda a deep ditch, and, if possible, throw the corpse of Yagoda into this ditch.

It would be possible to furnish dozens of supplementary facts, quotations, and considerations (now in the archives of the John Dewey commission) irrefutably confirming our conclusion. The assassination of Kirov was nothing more than a by-product of a police amalgam concocted by Stalin and Yagoda in order to accuse the Opposition leaders of terrorism.

To camouflage this collaboration, Stalin tried first to abandon to public opinion only his secondary agents (Medved and others), but the piling up of revelations and the inner logic of the facts themselves forced Stalin finally to sacrifice his ace collaborator.

Thus can the deepest riddle in the present trial be comprehended: the testimony of the former head of the GPU that he participated in the assassination of Kirov "on instructions from Trotsky." Whoever understands this, the most hidden of all springs in the trial, can understand all the rest without difficulty.

# STRANGE NEW DEVELOPMENTS[241]

## March 7, 1938

On February 28, I put forward the supposition that after the experience of the preceding trials, the present trial would be better prepared and stage-managed. This supposition proved to be unfounded. Already brief dispatches testify to the fact that the present trial is no less abundant in contradictions and absurdities than the previous ones. To a great degree this is explained by the fact that the organizers of the frame-up could not begin their creative work upon a clean page; they were compelled to patch up gaps in the previous trials, sew up tears in the fabric, reconcile contradictions, and at the same time busy themselves with inventing ever-greater sensations by increasing the number of victims and the spatial dimensions of the crime.

1. Krestinsky states that he received a letter from me dated December 19, 1936—that is, ten years after I had broken off all relations with him—and in this letter I had recommended the creation of a "broad military organization." This alleged letter, obligingly underlining the "broad" scale of the plot, evidently aimed at justifying the extermination of the Red Army's best officers, which began last year but is still a long way from completion even today. Krestinsky, of course, "burned" my letter, following the example of Radek, and presented nothing to the court beyond his confused reminiscences.

Meanwhile, in December 1936 my wife and I were interned by the Norwegian government at the demand of Moscow and all my correspondence passed through the hands of the Norwegian police. If we allow for the possibility that I wrote my "instructions" with invisible ink there still remains the question of the envelope and the address to which it was sent. All incoming and outgoing mail was registered at the so-called "passport office" in Oslo: judicial verification therefore would not present any difficulties.

I wish to add that I wrote a formal letter at that time to my Norwegian lawyer, Puntervold, and asked him to observe the greatest caution with unknown visitors who might in the future figure in new trials as intermediaries between myself, my lawyer, and the Moscow "terrorists." All necessary documents on this matter are in the hands of Miss Suzanne La Follette, secretary of the Commission of Inquiry in New York.[242]

2. This same Krestinsky stated that I had allegedly written him another letter, already from Mexico, in which I expressed "indignation" over the revealing testimony of Pyatakov from the witness stand. The aim of this alleged letter is clear: to buttress by my "indignation" the testimony of Pyatakov, which is hopelessly discredited by his notorious flight from Berlin to Oslo in December 1935, when according to the testimony of the official authorities at Oslo not a single plane landed in that city that month.[243]

Such a letter might be helpful to Vyshinsky but why would it be helpful to me? The trial of Pyatakov had already ended and Pyatakov had already been executed. To express merely platonic indignation in a conspiratorial letter which had to pass several borders would have been the height of folly, especially if we take into consideration the personality of the individual addressed. The conduct of Krestinsky on trial stamps him as an accomplished hysteric. If my alleged friend, Pyatakov, "betrayed" me, one could presume with greater probability that Krestinsky would also betray me. What sense was there, then, in sending a letter to Krestinsky, profitless to me, which, if it fell into the hands of the GPU, would prove a more powerful weapon against me than all the confessions of the defendants taken together? But the letter did not fall into anyone's hands. It was, of course, "burned"; as much, that is, as an unwritten letter can be burned.

3. The accusation ascribes to Bukharin the plan of assassinating Lenin, Stalin, and Sverdlov in 1918, when Bukharin and his group fought against signing the Brest-Litovsk treaty.[244] Whoever knows these people and their relations will understand without difficulty the whole absurdity of this accusation. Bukharin was as attached to Lenin as a child to its mother. As far as Stalin is concerned, in 1918 he was such a second-rate figure that it would not have entered the mind of the most terrible "terrorist" to select him as a victim. It was the task of this part of the trial to extend the present bureaucratic "greatness" of Stalin to the past.

4. In connection with this accusation against Bukharin,

several participants of his group in 1918, Osinsky, Yakovleva, Mantsev, figured in the proceedings as witnesses, i.e., defendants of tomorrow.[245] But the names of two persons who played an important role in the group of opponents to the Brest-Litovsk treaty are missing, namely, Kuibyshev and Yaroslavsky.[246] It is true that Kuibyshev, former head of the Gosplan [State Planning Commission], is now declared to have been poisoned by the Kremlin doctors. But this does not change the matter. In 1918 this very Kuibyshev evidently intended as Bukharin's friend to poison Lenin, Stalin, and Sverdlov. As for Yaroslavsky, he is not only alive and healthy but is actively participating in all the purges against the Opposition. Evidently it is exactly because of this that Yaroslavsky, this Bukharinist of 1918, has received amnesty. Will this continue for long? If Yagoda himself, yesterday's chief of the GPU, sits on the bench of the defendants then no one can vouch for the fate of Yaroslavsky.

How much low buffoonery in this terrible tragedy!

# ANACHRONISMS[247]

## March 8, 1938

The Moscow judicial frame-ups are full of anachronisms. In the Zinoviev-Kamenev trial (August 1936) the Trotskyists were alleged to have entered into an alliance with the Gestapo during 1932, when the Gestapo had not yet been formed. Leon Sedov in 1932 met the defendant Goltsman in the Hotel Bristol, which had been demolished during 1917.[248] There are many such examples. But even more striking anachronisms constitute the distinguishing feature of the present trial.

The witness Mantsev, dragged from prison, alleged that in 1920 at the Kharkov station within several days after I had been there an attempt was made on the coach of the train in which Stalin was traveling; and that I later urged Mantsev not to busy himself about this inasmuch as "our comrades" could suffer because of this. In order to disentangle at least a part of the absurdities included in this testimony it is necessary to enumerate them:

1. "Our comrades" evidently is supposed to signify the Trotskyists. But in 1920 there were no Trotskyists. The Left Opposition arose only in 1923. The word "Trotskyists" did not appear until a year later.

2. Mantsev, a close collaborator of Dzerzhinsky, the former head of the Cheka, never in general belonged to the Trotskyists, and least of all during a period when Trotskyism didn't exist.

3. The military policy which I carried out met with full support from Lenin and the majority of the Political Bureau. Behind the scenes Stalin led a campaign of intrigue against this policy, supporting Voroshilov,[249] the present people's commissar of defense; Chadenko, the deputy people's commissar of defense; and others who opposed the creation of a centralized army, advocating purely guerrilla detachments. On the Volga, Voroshilov commanded one of the twenty-four armies. Stalin was a member of the military soviet of this army. I dismissed

Voroshilov and recalled Stalin. Later Stalin was stationed on the southern front and again replaced. There was not the least reason for my resorting to terror. A simple order was sufficient to resolve every question.

4. Anyone with the least imagination can readily understand that if in 1920, with actually limitless power concentrated in my hands, I had wished to get rid of Stalin at the front, the matter would scarcely have limited itself to futile attempts about which the world learns now for the first time, eighteen years later.

5. More than once during the years of the civil war I had to resort to severe measures. I did this openly and under my own signature. Stalin intrigued behind the scenes. In July 1919 Lenin upon his own initiative gave me a sheet at the bottom of which appeared the following lines: "Knowing the harsh character of Comrade Trotsky's orders, I am so convinced, so absolutely convinced, of the correctness, expedience, and necessity for the good of our cause, of orders issued by Comrade Trotsky that I give them my full support. V. Ulyanov (Lenin)." Lenin in advance signed his name to each of my orders or actions at the front. I never made use of this carte blanche but it remains in my archives as evidence of the firm moral confidence of Lenin, who, generally speaking, could not be counted among gullible people.

In face of such mutual relations among the individuals concerned, it might be possible to imagine Stalin in 1920 making an attempt upon my life but in no case my making one upon Stalin's. However, we must not forget that one of the tasks of the present trial is to revise the history of the last twenty years and to assign Stalin a position in the past which he never occupied.

# MOSCOW'S DIPLOMATIC PLANS AND THE TRIALS[250]

## March 8, 1938

If human memory were more tenacious, the Moscow trials would be absolutely impossible. The GPU breaks the spine of the defendants, and one has become accustomed to this. But in the same breath the GPU also attempts to break the spine of historical processes; that is more difficult.

In the Zinoviev-Kamenev trial (August 1936), the defendants faced the accusation of having formed a liaison of a purely police character with the German Gestapo. The principal defendants denied this accusation. Public opinion refused to swallow it. In January 1937, Karl Radek and G.L. Pyatakov faced trial in order to revitalize Attorney General Andrei Vyshinsky's all-too-primitive schemata. By their testimony it became no longer a question of sordid espionage, but of an international bloc of Trotskyists with German and Japanese fascism for the purpose of overthrowing the USSR and the Western democracies.

This manner of presentation coincided in time, not accidentally, with the flowering of the policy of the People's Front. Upon the banner of Soviet diplomacy, and consequently of the Communist International, was emblazoned the slogan of a military bloc of the democracies against the fascist countries. At this juncture, the Trotskyists inevitably had to be ticketed as agents of the fascist bloc. The picture was clear and simple.

But surprisingly, the Trotskyists were not accused of having entered into an alliance with fascist Italy. The reason was that Soviet diplomats did not wish to hinder the attempts of England and France to wean Italy from Germany, and allowed for the eventuality that tomorrow Moscow herself might have to present a smiling face to Rome.

In great measure the same considerations applied with respect to Poland; it was hoped that France would maintain Poland in its sphere of influence. In "baring" their international intrigues, the defendants scrupulously conformed to the calculations of Soviet diplomacy. They might try to kill Stalin, but not to maim the politics of Commissar of Foreign Affairs Maxim Litvinov.

The preparations for the present trial coincided with a period of the withering of hopes and illusions in the People's Front and the bloc of democratic powers. England's policy on Spain, the visit of Lord Halifax to Berlin, the about-face of London in the direction of Rome, and finally the substitution of Lord Halifax for Anthony Eden[251]—all these were the diplomatic signposts which determined the new contents of the "voluntary" confessions of the defendants. The design of the Radek-Pyatakov trial, according to which the Trotskyists were agents of the fascist bloc (except Italy), was rejected as inopportune.

The defendants appear now as agents of Germany, Japan, Poland, and England. The liaison with Germany sheds its fascist hue because it is now said to have begun in 1921, when Germany was under the banner of Weimar democracy. The collaboration with England is said to have begun in 1926, eleven years before the Radek-Pyatakov trial. But Karl Radek, who according to Vyshinsky's interpretation is candidate for the post of foreign minister for the Trotskyists, knew nothing of Trotsky's alliance with Great Britain.

At the beginning of 1937, England was a "democracy." With the departure of Eden, it is once again the hub of imperialism. Litvinov has made up his mind to show London his bared teeth. And promptly the defendants echo this in their testimony.

Until very recently, the war in the Far East signified the march of Japanese fascism against the Anglo-Saxon democracies. Now Moscow lets it be known that it is ready to efface the distinction between Japan and Great Britain: both of them are plotting with the Trotskyists against the Soviet regime! The testimony of C.G. Rakovsky, according to which he and I are made out to be agents of the British Intelligence Service, is in reality a diplomatic warning to Prime Minister Neville Chamberlain.[252]

The tardiness in including Poland among the countries compromised by an alliance with the Trotskyists has a twofold cause: a greater and a lesser one. The Polish orientation toward Germany became more definite with the recent about-face of British politics. Forgotten are the times (1933) when Stalin invited Marshal Pilsudski to the celebration of the October Revolution. Moscow gives Warsaw to understand that it entertains no illusions concerning Poland's neutrality, and that, in the event of war, Poland will have to stand prepared to become the arena for clashes between the USSR and Germany. By means of the wagging tongues of the defendants, Litvinov threatens Colonel Jozef Beck.[253]

The second reason why Poland could have been mentioned only in the present trial is that the chief "diplomat" of the second trial in January 1937, Radek, could not have included Poland, which was almost his homeland, in the list of "Trotskyist" countries. It was Radek himself who in 1933 made a triumphal journey to Warsaw, was feted by Pilsudski, and spoke glowingly of the future happy relations between the two countries, both products of revolution.

The world press featured the forthcoming military alliance between the USSR and Poland. Inasmuch as Radek made his theatrical visit not as an agent of Trotsky, but as Stalin's envoy, it was especially difficult for Radek to tie Poland in with Trotskyism in his confession. This task was laid upon the head of the present defendant, V.F. Sharangovich.

The names of France and of the United States have not yet been dragged in. These two countries are being retained as remnants of the "bloc of democracies" against the fascist bloc.

It is true that Rakovsky has confessed to criminal alliances with French industrialists and journalists; but these alliances are with opponents of the People's Front. If through the testimony of Rakovsky concerning the intelligence service, Litvinov is trying to compromise Chamberlain's government, then through the testimony of the same Rakovsky concerning the French industrialist Nicole, and the journalist Bure, Litvinov wishes to perform a friendly service for the government of the People's Front.

In any case, the defendants remained true to themselves; even in their most "perfidious" deals with foreign states they carefully safeguarded the diplomatic plans of the Kremlin.

The silence about France is especially eloquent in its absurdity. France almost until the end of 1933 was considered in Moscow to be the chief enemy of the USSR. Second place was occupied by Great Britain. Germany was counted as a friend. In the trials of the "Industrial Party" (1930) and "Menshevik Union Bureau" (1931)[254] France was invariably found to be a hotbed of hostile intrigue. Meanwhile, the Trotskyists, who had begun to make connections with the enemies of the USSR in 1921 (when they, with Lenin, were in power) completely avoided France, as if they had forgotten its existence. No, they had forgotten nothing;

they simply foresaw the future of the Franco-Soviet pact and were wary about creating any difficulties for Litvinov in 1938.

How fortunate for Vyshinsky that people have such short memories! After my exile to Turkey the Soviet press called me nothing less than "Mister Trotsky." *Pravda* on March 8, 1929, devoted almost a full page to proving "Mister Trotsky" (not Herr Trotsky!) was actually in alliance with Winston Churchill and Wall Street.[255] The article ended with the following words: "It is now clear why the bourgeoisie pays him tens of thousands of dollars!" Payment was then made in dollars, not marks!

On July 2, 1931, *Pravda* printed a forged facsimile, which was to have proved that I was an ally of Pilsudski and the defender of the Versailles treaty against the USSR and Germany. This was at a moment of increasing friction with Warsaw, two years before the plans for the Soviet-Polish alliance had arisen!

On March 4, 1933, when Hitler already sat firmly in the saddle, *Izvestia*, the official organ of the government, announced the USSR to be the only country in the world which does not bear any hostility toward Germany "and this regardless of the form and composition of the government of the Reich." The French semiofficial newspaper *Le Temps* wrote on April 8: "At the time of Hitler's coming to power, European public opinion concerned itself avidly with this event and there were lively commentaries on it; the Moscow papers kept silent."

Stalin was still hoping for friendship with fascist Germany! This is hardly remarkable, since at that time I was still a supposed agent of the Entente.

On July 24, 1933, with the permission of Daladier's government, I came to France. Immediately the Communist newspaper *l'Humanite,* the Paris organ of Soviet diplomacy, proclaimed: "From France, this anti-Soviet hotbed, Trotsky will attack the USSR. France is the strategic point and that is why Mister Trotsky has come here." But at that time I could already have celebrated the twelfth year of my service for Germany!

Such are some of the political landmarks on the road to the present trial. The amount of data and quotations could be increased without end. But even from those cited here the conclusion is clear. The "perfidious" actions of the defendants represent only the negative complement to the diplomatic combinations of the government.

The situation changed; the diplomatic calculations of the Kremlin also changed. Likewise the "betrayals" of the Trotsky-ists changed, or more accurately, the content of their testimony about their alleged betrayals. In addition, and this is most significant, today's events in Moscow make it possible to completely reconstruct the events of the past twenty years.

In 1937, my old friendship with Winston Churchill, Pilsudski, and Daladier was forgotten. I became an ally of Rudolf Hess and a cousin of the Mikado. In the indictment of 1938, my old calling as an agent of France and the United States was found to be completely irrelevant; on the other hand, my forgotten friendship with British imperialism received exceptional prominence.

It can be predicted that if in the last days of the present trial I am yet to be brought into connection with the United States, then surely it will be not as an agent of President Roosevelt, but as the ally of his enemies, the "economic royalists." Thus, even in my "betrayals," I continue to perform a patriotic function.

# STALIN'S ARTICLE
# ON WORLD REVOLUTION[256]

## March 9, 1938

In February, the world press paid no little attention to an article of Stalin's dealing with the question of the dependence of the Soviet Union on the support of the international proletariat. The article was interpreted as a refusal by Stalin of peaceful cooperation with the Western democracies in the name of international revolution. Goebbels's press proclaimed, "Stalin has thrown off his mask. Stalin has shown that his aims do not differ from Trotsky's," etc. The same thought was developed even in the more critical publications of the democratic countries.

Is it necessary today to refute this interpretation? Facts speak louder than words. If Stalin was intending to return to the path of revolution, he would not have exterminated and demoralized revolutionaries. In the last analysis, Mussolini is right when he says in the *Giornale d'Italia* that nobody has hitherto struck such a blow at the idea of communism (proletarian revolution) and has exterminated communists with such bitterness as Stalin.

Viewed on a purely theoretical plane, as is not difficult, the article of February 12 is a simple repetition of the formulas Stalin introduced for the first time into usage in autumn 1924, when he broke with the tradition of Bolshevism: inside the USSR "we" have introduced socialism, inasmuch as we have liquidated the national bourgeoisie and organized the cooperation of proletariat and peasantry; but the USSR is surrounded by bourgeois states which threaten intervention and the restoration of capitalism; it is therefore necessary to strengthen the defense and secure the support of the world proletariat. Stalin has never abandoned these abstract formulas. He has only given them gradually a new interpretation. In 1924, the "help" of the Western proletariat was still occasionally understood as international revolution. In 1938, it began to mean the political and economic cooperation of the Comintern with those bourgeois governments who might show direct or indirect help to the USSR in the event of war. True, this formula presupposes, on the other hand, a revolutionary policy of the so-called "Communist" parties of Germany and Japan. But precisely in these countries the importance of the Comintern is nearly zero.

Nevertheless, it was not by chance that Stalin published his "manifesto" of February 12. The article itself, and the echoes it evoked, were a very essential element in the preparations for the present trial. Renewing the campaign in the courts against the remnants of the old generation of Bolsheviks after a break of a year, Stalin naturally strove to produce the impression in the workers of the USSR and the whole world that he was acting not in the interests of his own clique but in the interests of international revolution. Hence the deliberate ambiguity of certain expressions in the article: without frightening the conservative bourgeoisie, they must put the revolutionary workers at ease.

Thus the assertion that Stalin threw off his peaceful mask in this article is completely false. In fact, he temporarily put on a semirevolutionary mask. For Stalin, international policy is completely subservient to internal. Internal policy means for him, above all, the struggle for self-preservation. Political problems thus take second place to police ones. Only in this field does Stalin's thought work uninterruptedly and untiringly.

In 1936, while secretly preparing the mass purge, Stalin launched the idea of the new constitution, "the most democratic in the world." There really was no lack of eulogies on such a fortunate turn in the policy of the Kremlin! If a collection were published now of articles written by the patented friends of Moscow about the "most democratic constitution," many of the authors could do nothing but burn with shame. The ballyhoo about the constitution served several aims at once; but the chief one, completely prevailing over the others, was the manipulation of public opinion before the trial of Zinoviev and Kamenev.

On March 1, 1936, Stalin gave a notorious interview to Roy Howard. One little point of this conversation completely escaped notice at the time: the future democratic freedoms, said Stalin, were intended for all, but terrorists would not be spared. The same ominous reservation was made by Molotov in an interview given to the director of *Le Temps,* Chastenet. "The present generation," said the head of the government, "is making more and more unnecessary certain strict administrative measures taken in the past. However," added Molotov, following Stalin, "the government must remain strong against terrorists . . ." (*Le Temps,* March 24, 1936). "Terrorists"? But after the episodic murder of Kirov, with the connivance of the GPU, on December 1, 1934, there had been no terrorist acts. "Terrorist" plans? But nobody yet suspected anything about the Trotskyist "centers." The GPU found out about these "plans" and "centers" only from the testimony. Meanwhile, Zinoviev, Kamenev, and the others started to confess their fictitious crimes only in July 1936; Leon Sedov proved this at the time, on the basis of official material, in his *Red Book* (Paris, 1936).

Thus, in the interviews mentioned above, Stalin and Molotov mentioned terrorists by way of "foresight," i.e., inquisitional preparation of the coming confessions. The effusions about democratic freedoms were only an empty shell. The kernel was a barely noticeable reference to anonymous "terrorists." This reference was soon clarified by the shooting of several thousand people.

Parallel with the much-vaunted preparation of the Stalin "constitution" went a series of banquets in the Kremlin, in which members of the government embraced representatives of the workers' and collective farmers' aristocracy ("Stakhanovites"). It was proclaimed at the banquets that for the USSR there had begun at last the epoch of "happy life." Stalin was finally confirmed in the name of "father of the peoples" who loves man and tenderly cares for him. Every day the Soviet press published photographs showing Stalin in a circle of happy people, often with a laughing babe in his arms or on his knees. And I think I can be forgiven for mentioning that on seeing these idyllic photographs I said more than once to my friends, "Evidently something terrible is brewing."

The idea of the stage manager was to give the world a picture of a country which, after bitter years of struggle and deprivation, was finally entering the path of "the most democratic" constitution, created by "the father of the peoples," who loved people, especially children . . . and on this attractive backdrop suddenly present the diabolical figures of the Trotskyists, who are sabotaging the economy, organizing famine, poisoning workers, making an attempt soon on the life of "the father of the peoples," and handing over the happy country to the fascist tyrants to tear to pieces.

Supported by the totalitarian apparatus and unlimited material resources, Stalin thought up a unique plan: to ravish the conscience of the world, and with the approval of the whole of humanity to rid himself forever of all opposition to the Kremlin clique. When this thought was expressed in 1935-36 by way of warning, too many people explained it as "the hatred of Trotsky for Stalin." Personal hatred in questions of historical scale is an utterly paltry and despicable feeling. Furthermore, hatred is blind. But in politics, as in personal life, there is nothing more terrible than blindness. The more difficult the situation, the more necessary is it to follow the advice of old Spinoza, "Not to weep, not to laugh, but to understand."

In the course of the preparation for the present trial, "the most democratic constitution" managed to reveal itself as a bureaucratic farce, as a provincial steal from Goebbels. The liberal and democratic circles in the West began to stop being deceived. Distrust of the Soviet bureaucracy which had unfortunately often coincided with coldness toward the USSR began to seize wider and wider layers. On the other hand, sharp disappointment began to penetrate the workers' organizations. In practical politics the Comintern stands to the right of the Second International. In Spain, the Communist Party stifles the left wing of the working class by GPU methods. In France, the Communists became, in an expression of *Le Temps,* the representatives of "holiday-time chauvinists." This is also seen more or less in the United States and in a series of other countries. The traditional policy of class collaboration, in the struggle with which the Third International arose, now has become, in an exaggerated form, the official policy of Stalinism, with bloody GPU repression used in defense of this policy. Articles and speeches were used solely to mask this fact. That is why in the mouths of the accused are placed theatrical monologues about how they, the Trotskyists, were reactionaries, counterrevolutionaries, fascists, enemies of the working class, over a period of twenty years, and how finally in a GPU prison they had understood the saving character of Stalin's policy. On the other hand, Stalin himself, on the eve of a new bloody hecatomb, found it necessary to say to the working class, "If I am compelled to destroy the old generation of Bolsheviks, that is only in the interests of socialism. I have exterminated the Leninists on the basis of Lenin's doctrine."

This is the real point of the article of February 12. It has no other point. We are faced with an abbreviated repetition of the maneuver with the "democratic constitution." The first blackmail (let's call things by their names) was mainly aimed at the bourgeois democratic circles of the West. The newest blackmail had in view mainly the workers. The conservative authorities of Europe and America have in any case no need to worry. For a revolutionary policy a revolutionary party is necessary. Stalin does not have one. The Bolshevik Party has been killed. The Comintern is entirely demoralized. Mussolini is right in his own way: no one has yet struck the idea of proletarian revolution such blows as the author of the article of February 12.

# MESSAGE TO NEW YORK
# PROTEST MEETING[257]

## March 9, 1938

From inside the fortress won by the proletariat Stalin deals socialism such blows as no one has yet dealt. If anyone sabotages the economic and cultural development of the USSR it is Stalin. If anyone undermines the military power of the USSR it is Stalin. If anyone poisons the ranks of the revolutionary vanguard by treachery and betrayal it is Stalin. Were united world reaction to seek an agent of its own choice, it could find no one more suited than Stalin. The Moscow trials represent the lone attempt in history to deceive all mankind. However, if there is no limit to baseness, there is a limit to gullibility. Strangled thought and horrified conscience are awakening. Progressive mankind is preparing to disgorge the venom of Stalinism. In our thoughts Natalia and I are present at your meeting of protest and challenge. We see in your ranks the spirit of Leon Sedov, fallen at his battle post. With us or without us you will lead our great liberating struggle to victory.

# A KEY TO THE RUSSIAN TRIALS[258]

## March 10, 1938

The Moscow trial had wearied public opinion with its sensational incongruities even before it drew to a close. Even a mediocre journalist could have drafted State Prosecutor Vyshinsky's final plea in advance—except, perhaps, for the profusion of vile slanders.

Vyshinsky has blended a significant element of personal vindictiveness into the political trial. During the years of the revolution he belonged to the White Guard party. When he switched his colors after the final victory of the Bolsheviks, he felt suspect and humiliated. Now he is taking his revenge. He is free to scorn Nikolai Bukharin, Alexei Rykov, C.G. Rakovsky—names he pronounced for years with the most obsequious reverence. And, at the same time, Ambassadors Alexander Troyanovsky, Ivan Maisky, and Jakob Surits,[259] whose pasts resemble Vyshinsky's, proclaim to the civilized world that it is they who have inherited the ideals of the October Revolution while Bukharin, Rykov, Rakovsky, Trotsky, and others betrayed them. Everything is turned on its head.

The only conclusion Vyshinsky must draw from the latest series of Moscow trials is that the Soviet government is nothing but a centralized apparatus for high treason.

The heads of the government and the majority of the people's commissars (Rykov, Kamenev, Rudzutak, Smirnov, Yakovlev,[260] Rosengolts, Chernov, Grinko, Ivanov, Osinsky, and others); the most important Soviet diplomats (Rakovsky, Sokolnikov, Krestinsky, Karakhan, Bogomolov,[261] Yurenev, and others); all the leaders of the Communist International (Zinoviev, Bukharin, Radek); the chief leaders of the economy (Pyatakov, Smirnov, Serebriakov, Lifshits,[262] and others); the best captains and leaders of the army (Tukhachevsky, Gamarnik, Yakir, Uborevich, Kork, Muralov, Mrachkovsky, Alksnis, Admiral Orlov,[263] and others); the most outstanding worker-revolutionists produced by

Bolshevism in thirty-five years (Tomsky, Yevdokimov, Smirnov, Bakaev, Serebriakov, Boguslavsky,[264] Mrachkovsky); the heads and members of the governments of the Russian Soviet Republics (Sulimov,[265] Varvara Yakovleva); the heads of all the thirty Soviet Republics without exception, i.e, the leaders developed by the movement of the liberated nationalities (Budu Mdivani, Okudzhava, Kavtaradze, Chervyakov, Goloded, Skrypnik, Lyubchenko,[266] Nestor Lakoba, Faizul Khodzhaev, Ikramov, and dozens of others); the leaders of the GPU for the past ten years, Yagoda and his collaborators; finally, and this is most important, the members of the all-powerful Political Bureau, actually the supreme power of the country, Trotsky, Zinoviev, Kamenev, Tomsky, Rykov, Bukharin, Rudzutak—all of them were plotting against the Soviet power in the years when they held it in their hands!

All of them, as agents of foreign powers, aimed at ripping to shreds the Soviet federation built by them, and enslaving to fascism the peoples for whom they had fought for dozens of years!

In this criminal activity, ministers, marshals, and ambassadors invariably submitted to one individual; not the official leader, no—an exile! It was sufficient for him but to crook a finger and the veterans of the revolution became agents of Hitler and the Mikado.

Upon the "instructions" of Trotsky through an incidental go-between in the Tass agency, the leaders of industry, transportation, and agriculture destroyed the productive forces of the country and its culture.

Upon an order from the "enemy of the people," sent from Norway or Mexico, the railway workers of the Far East wrecked military trains, and venerable Kremlin physicians poisoned their patients. This is the astonishing picture of the Soviet state that Vyshinsky is obliged to countenance on the basis of the revelations of the latest trials.

But here a difficulty arises. A totalitarian regime is a dictatorship of the bureaucracy. If all the key positions were occupied by Trotskyists who submitted to me, why, in that case, is Stalin in the Kremlin and am I in exile?

In these trials everything is turned on its head. The enemies of the October Revolution array themselves as its executors; careerists beat their chests like champions of ideals; specialists in frame-up stalk in the guise of examining magistrates, prosecutors, and judges.

But nevertheless, says the man of "common sense," it is hard to believe that hundreds of defendants, adults and normal individuals, and endowed, moreover, to a considerable extent with strong characters and exceptional intellects, have senselessly accused themselves before all mankind of terrible and abhorrent crimes.

As often happens in life, "common sense" strains at gnats and swallows camels. Of course it is not easy to comprehend why hundreds of people debased themselves. But is it easier to believe that these same hundreds committed terrible crimes which contradicted their interests, their psychology, the whole cause to which they had devoted their lives? To judge and evaluate, concrete conditions should be taken into mind. These people gave their testimony only after being arrested, with the sword of Damocles poised above them; when they, their wives, mothers, fathers, children, and friends had fallen completely into the power of the GPU; when they had no defense and no glimmer of hope; when they themselves were under a mental strain no human nerves could be capable of withstanding.

On the other hand, these improbable crimes for which they admit guilt were committed—if we are to believe them—at a time when they were completely free, occupied high positions, and had full opportunity calmly to reflect, to ponder, and to choose.

Is it not then self-evident that the most absurd lie uttered under the muzzle of a revolver is immeasurably more natural than the chain of senseless crimes deliberately committed?

Which is the more probable: that a political exile, deprived of power and means, separated from Russia by a veil of slanders, with one movement of his little finger impels ministers, generals, and diplomats over a series of years to betray their country and themselves in the name of hopeless and absurd aims; or that Stalin, having at his disposal unlimited power and an inexhaustible treasury, that is, all means of intimidation and corruption, forced the defendants to bear testimony which carries out Stalin's aims?

In order to overcome definitely the myopic doubts of "common sense" we can put yet one last question. Which is the more probable: that in medieval times, witches actually had traffic with hellish powers and inflicted cholera, the black death, and cattle plague on their villages after nightly consultation with the devil ("the enemy of the people") . . . or that these unfortunate women simply debased themselves under the red-hot iron of the Inquisition? It is sufficient to pose the question clearly for the whole superstructure of Stalin-Vyshinsky to crumble into dust.

In the midst of the unnatural confessions of the defendants there is one which, so far as can be judged from a distance, has passed by with little notice; but which, even when isolated, provides the key not only to the enigmas of the Moscow trial but also to the Stalin regime in its entirety. I have in mind the testimony of Dr. Levin, former head of the Kremlin hospital. This sixty-eight-year-old man declared in court that he willfully abetted in hastening the death of Menzhinsky, Peshkov (son of Gorky), Kuibyshev, and Maxim Gorky himself.

Professor Levin does not speak of himself as a secret "Trotskyist" and no one accuses him of this; not even Prosecutor Vyshinsky attributes to him aspirations to seize power in the interests of Hitler. No, Levin murdered his patients upon the orders of Yagoda, then head of the GPU, who threatened him in case of refusal with severe retaliations.

*Levin feared the "destruction" of his family.* That is literally the testimony that lies at the basis of the indictment.

The assassination of Kirov, committed in turn by all "centers"; the plans to dismember the USSR; malicious wrecking of trains; mass poisoning of workers—all this is nothing in comparison with the testimony of old Levin.

The perpetrators of the crimes specified are supposedly actuated by a thirst for power, hatred, or avarice; in a word, by some similitude to personal ends. Levin, committing the most heinous of all crimes, the perfidious murder of trusting patients, had no personal motives at all! On the contrary, he "loved Gorky and his family." He murdered the son and the father out of fear for his own family. He found no means of saving his own son or daughter other than by consenting to poison an infirm author, the pride of the country.

What is left for us to say then? In a "socialist" state, under the "most democratic" of all constitutions, an old physician, a stranger to political ambition and intrigues, poisons his patients out of fear of the chief of the secret police. The instigator of the crimes is the one in whom is invested the highest power for the struggle against crime. He whose profession is that of safeguarding life is the one who murders. He murders out of fear.

Let us admit for the moment that all this is true. In that case, what is one to say about the whole regime? Levin is not a chance individual. He was physician to Lenin, Stalin, all members of the government. I knew this tranquil and conscientious man well. As with many celebrated physicians, he had intimate, almost sheltering relations with his high-ranking patients. He knew very well how the spines of Messrs. "Leaders" looked, and how their authoritarian kidneys functioned. Levin had free access to every high official. Couldn't he have denounced Yagoda's bloody blackmail to Stalin, Molotov, or any other member of the Political Bureau of the government? It seems that he could not. Instead of exposing the GPU blackguard, the doctor found himself constrained to poison his patients in order to save his own family. Thus, in the Moscow judicial panorama, is revealed the Stalinist regime, at its very summit, in the Kremlin, in the most intimate part of the Kremlin, in the hospital for the members of the government! What is then going on in the rest of the country?

"But all this is a lie," exclaims the reader. "Doctor Levin did not poison anyone! He simply testified falsely under threat of the GPU Mauser." That is completely correct. But because of this the outlook becomes the more sinister.

If a physician threatened by the chief of police actually committed a crime, it would still be possible, forgetting all the rest, to say: a pathological case, a persecution complex, senile dotage—whatever you please. But no, the testimony of Levin constitutes an integral part of the judicial plan inspired by Stalin, and jointly elaborated by Prosecutor Vyshinsky with the new head of the GPU, Yezhov. These people did not fear resorting to so nightmarish a concoction. They did not consider it an impossibility. On the contrary, of all possible variants they chose the most probable, that is, the one most corresponding to the existing conditions and customs. The president of the court would scarcely ask the former head of the Kremlin hospital why he submitted to the criminal instead of exposing him. Even less capable of putting such a question is Vyshinsky.

Each participant in the trial, the whole Soviet press, all wielders of power tacitly confess the full plausibility of the fact that the GPU can force any person to commit any crime, even when that person is free, occupies a high position, and utilizes the protection of the ruling summits. But once the situation is thus clarified, is it then possible to doubt even for a moment that the omnipotent and all-penetrating GPU can force any prisoner in the inner cells of the Lubyanka to confess "voluntarily" guilt for crimes never committed? The testimony of Dr. Levin provides the key to the whole trial. The key opens all Kremlin secrets and at the same time definitely seals the mouths of the advocates of Stalinist justice throughout the world.

Let no one tell us: here is the end to which the October Revolution has brought us! This would be about the same as saying, on seeing the Niagara bridge that recently collapsed: this is the result of our struggle against the waterfall. The October Revolution has not brought us merely judicial frame-ups. It was a powerful impulse to the economic forces and to the culture of a great family of peoples. But it likewise engendered new social antagonisms upon a higher historical level. The backwardness and barbarism, the inheritance of the past, found their most concentrated expression in the new bureaucratic dictatorship. In the struggle with the living and developing society, this dictatorship, without ideas, without honor, and without conscience, has been brought to unprecedented crimes and with that to a fatal crisis.

The accusation of sadism against Doctor Pletnev as an episode in the preparation of the present trial; Yagoda's romantic affairs as the cause for the death of Gorky's son; the religious talisman of the wife of Rosengolts and especially the "confessions" of Doctor Levin—from all these episodes reeks the same odor of decay which arose from the Rasputin affair in the last period of the monarchy.[267]

The ruling layer capable of disgorging such gases is doomed. The present trial is the tragic death struggle of the Stalinist dictatorship.

It is dependent upon the will of the people of the USSR, as upon world public opinion, that in its inevitable downfall this regime shall not drag to the bottom of the historical abyss all the social conquests which a series of generations of the Russian people paid for with innumerable sacrifices.

# THE CASE
# OF PROFESSOR PLETNEV[268]

## March 10, 1938

In this statement we are utilizing exclusively official data taken from the Moscow *Pravda*.

The defendant Pletnev, professor of medicine, is now sixty-six years old. He was the Kremlin physician almost from the days of the October insurrection. He never concerned himself with politics. Lenin, Krupskaya[269] and all the officials of the Kremlin used his services. Pletnev enjoyed not a few distinctions. The Soviet press more than once lavished high praise upon him. But the situation suddenly changed in the middle of 1937: Pletnev was publicly accused of rape and sadism.

In *Pravda* of June 8, 1937, a long article appeared, describing in unusual detail the atrocious violation he allegedly committed upon a woman, "patient B." The article quoted a letter from Mrs. B. to Pletnev which included the following lines: "Be accursed, base criminal, for implanting in me an incurable disease and mutilating my body, . . ." and so on. *Pravda* related that Pletnev, in view of Mrs. B.'s complaints, allegedly attempted to commit her to an insane asylum, and to her reproaches responded: "Get some poison and kill yourself."

The article produced all the more shocking an impression since it was printed prior to any kind of trial of Pletnev. For one who knows the morals of the present Soviet bureaucracy, it is completely clear that such an article against a doctor of high standing could be printed in *Pravda* only with the consent of Stalin or upon his direct command. The suspicion naturally arose even then that the affair was connected with a deep intrigue against Pletnev and that the mysterious "patient B." was in all probability a GPU agent.

Immediately, that is, before any kind of trial, so-called "public opinion" was mobilized from an unseen center; to put it more precisely, the doctors at Moscow, Kiev, Tula, Sverdlovsk, and so on were ordered to pass resolutions demanding the "most severe sentence upon this monster." The resolutions were, of course, published in *Pravda*. We have these numbers of *Pravda* at hand.

On July 17 and 18, 1937, Pletnev's case was considered in closed session by a Moscow court. In the USSR one is often given the death penalty for stealing a bag of flour. All the more reasonable was it to expect a merciless sentence upon a physician-sadist who had implanted an "incurable disease" in and "mutilated" the body of a patient. Meanwhile, in the same *Pravda* of July 19, the readers learned that Pletnev had been "*conditionally* sentenced to two years' deprivation of freedom," that is to say, actually freed from any punishment. The sentence seemed as unexpected as earlier the accusation had seemed.

Within seven months we meet Pletnev as a defendant in the deliberate hastening of the deaths of Menzhinsky, Kuibyshev, and Maxim Gorky. Pletnev of course confesses his guilt. It seems that he committed these monstrous crimes "upon the order" of Yagoda, former head of the GPU. Why did he submit to Yagoda? Out of fear. The Kremlin doctor, knowing all members of the government, did not dare to report the criminal but became his submissive tool. Is this improbable? Such is the testimony. We hear nothing more about the sadist Pletnev. "Patient B." was not called to testify. She had completed her task prior to the trial. Sadism does not interest anyone any more. Now Pletnev, the physician since czarist times, is found to be a terrorist agent of the "Trotskyist-Bukharinist bloc" under the direct leadership of Yagoda, former head of the GPU.

Is it possible to doubt that between the two trials of Pletnev there exists a compact internal relationship? In order to attribute terrorist acts to the Trotskyists, it was necessary to invent them. With this objective, Yagoda, the executioner of the Trotskyists, was metamorphosed into an agent of the Trotskyists, and a doctor was metamorphosed into a poisoner. The accusation of sadism was proclaimed with such deafening ballyhoo seven months ago in order to break the will of the old doctor, father of a family, and to make an obedient tool of him in the hands of the GPU for the forthcoming political trial. Death threatened Pletnev when he was accused of ravishing "patient B." However, behind the scenes an agreement was reached as a result of which only a conditional sentence was meted out to Pletnev. *Such was the price of his fantastic confessions at the trial of the twenty-one.*

Pletnev's case is especially instructive because here all the springs are bared to view.

P.S.—The news has been widely spread through the press to the effect that Stalin supposedly was an agent provocateur during czarist days, and that he is now avenging himself upon his old enemies. I place no trust whatsoever in this gossip. From his youth Stalin was a revolutionist. All the facts about his life bear witness to this. To reconstruct his biography ex post facto means to ape the present Stalin, who from a revolutionist became a leader of the reactionary bureaucracy.

Trotsky during vacation trip in Mexico.

# LETTER TO JEANNE MARTIN[270]

## March 10, 1938

Dearest Jeanne, our little Jeanne:

Natalia just received two letters from you. I have received one letter from you, not counting the report on the progress of Lyova's [Sedov's] illness. Natalia has sent you a telegram. She is still unable to write. She reads and rereads your letters. She weeps, she weeps a great deal. When I can succeed in freeing myself from my work (answering new accusations against Leon and myself) I will join her in weeping. She loves you very much. She has always loved you very much, Jeanne. She thinks and speaks of you with the greatest affection. She imagines you in the small apartment that you shared with Leon until a short time ago. She thinks about these little things, and about you, Jeanne, first of all. For Natalia you are now not just Jeanne, the daughter she loves with such tenderness and with such reserve—as Natalia alone knows how to love—you are now a part of Leon, that which remains of the most intimate side of his personal life in the last few years. My dear little one. . . .

Leon meant a great deal to me. Far more than anyone imagines. He was dearer to me than anyone in the world except Natalia. With Natalia's help I tried to set down on paper the magnitude of the loss we have just suffered. We too cannot accept the idea that he is gone. Ten times a day I catch myself thinking: I have to write to Lyova. . . . I have to ask Lyova. . . . And Natalia? She grieves for herself, she grieves for me, and she grieves for you. Jeanne, we are ready to accept any proposal you have to make concerning your future. If you wish to come here to embrace Natalia, to be embraced by the two of us, we will immediately do everything to make your trip possible. If you decide to stay with us, you will be our beloved daughter. If, after two or three months, you find that it would be better to return to

Paris, we will accept that as only natural. Finally, if you feel that it would be too difficult to be separated from Sieva and the others right now, we will understand how you feel. Sieva's coming here would present certain difficulties—school, language—but we are ready to take that possibility into account as well.

Despite her tears and her grief, Natalia helps in my work. We are fighting for the memory of Leon, for our movement. Leon has already taken his place there, in the history of our movement, forever. From all over the world we receive letters concerning him. The young people are learning to know him and love him. He will become a symbolic figure, our little Lyova, like Karl Liebknecht and others. Yes, dearest Jeanne, our little Jeanne, he is no longer at your side nor will he ever be again. But he has entered into a new life, one that has merged with the liberation movement. We must go on. We must go on with courage. In Paris, or here with us, my dear little child, life will be hard for you. The only way to rise above its blows is through struggle. . . . Natalia will write to you as soon as she is strong enough to hold a pen. But in spirit she has written to you continuously since the terrible news of February 16. Natalia embraces you with all her torn, bleeding heart. I embrace you too, Jeanne. We will send you another telegram tonight. We are thinking of you. We grieve with you.

Yours,
L.T.

[P.S.]—We read your statement to the *Journal* in the Mexican press concerning the "American dollars." It is very good that you have entered the fight. You must continue. It is necessary to write about Lyova . . . about his life in Berlin and in Paris. The three of us together will write his biography. We will gather all the documentation on his life. Lyova had a heroic nature—in the truest sense of the word. He must remain—he will remain—in the memory of humanity. . . . Courage, my little Jeanne.

# THE DEFENDANTS
# ZELENSKY AND IVANOV[271]

## March 11, 1938

The figure of Zelensky has flitted through the trial like a pale shadow. But he is not an unimportant figure. For several years Zelensky was the secretary of the Moscow Committee, the chief section of the party, and a member of the Central Committee. Later on he became head of the cooperative organization of the USSR, the powerful distributing apparatus which deals in billions. Fifteen years ago he was friendly with the now dead Kamenev, a member of the Political Bureau and president of the Council of Labor and Defense; but from the moment of open rupture between Kamenev and Stalin (1926), Zelensky went over to Stalin. In all probability he could not quietly accept the execution of the Old Bolsheviks to whom he himself belonged. This sealed his fate. Within these limits the fate of Zelensky does not differ from the fate of many other defendants. What appears astounding is the character of the accusation presented against him. If we are to believe the indictment, and Zelensky himself, he was an agent of the czarist police in Samara in 1911. A similar accusation is made against Ivanov. Concerning a former member of the Central Committee of the party and people's commissar of the lumber industry, this accusation is truly stunning!

Is it true? We will not concern ourselves over psychological speculation, which in such cases always has an uncertain nature, but will use only unassailable facts. Immediately after the conquest of power by the Bolsheviks (November 1917), the party Central Committee and afterwards the Cheka began the study of the archives of the czarist police department and the local organs of the Okhrana. Numerous provocateurs were discovered, tried by the people's courts, and the most vicious of them shot. The study of the archives, the classification of the material, and the detailed

259

checking were fully completed by 1923. How then could Zelensky's and Ivanov's "provocateur" past have remained in the dark? How could they have occupied such responsible posts and why was the secret suddenly discovered only now, in connection with the present trial, that is, after a delay of twenty years? We consider it necessary here to reveal what the prosecutor of course keeps secret.

Among the revolutionists of the czarist epoch there were not a few who upon police questioning behaved with insufficient courage or lack of caution. Some repudiated their views. Others named their comrades. These people were not agents of the police and still less—provocateurs. They simply displayed cowardice at certain moments. Many of them, upon leaving prison, frankly revealed their mistakes to the leaders of the party organization. Depending upon their further conduct, the party either drove them out forever or accepted them once more into the ranks.

From 1923, Stalin, as the general secretary of the party, concentrated all such material in his archives, and they became in his hands a powerful weapon against hundreds of old revolutionists. Threatening exposure, compromise, or expulsion from the party, Stalin wrung from these people slavish submission and led them step by step toward complete demoralization.

One can fully allow for the possibility that in their political pasts Zelensky, a member of the Central Committee, and Ivanov, a people's commissar, committed errors as characterized above. Stalin could not have failed to know these facts fifteen years ago, since for all responsible appointments the most meticulous inquiries about the candidates were made into the archives. One can say, consequently, with absolute assurance that neither Zelensky nor Ivanov ever were agents of the czarist police. But Stalin nevertheless possessed such documents as gave him the opportunity to break the will of these victims and to force them into the utmost degree of moral degeneration. That is how Stalin's system operates!

# AGAIN ON THE REISS CASE[272]

## March 12, 1938

Dear Comrades:

I am informed that Comrade Vereecken has attempted to embellish Sneevliet's role in the Reiss case by shifting the responsibility to Leon Sedov. I refrain here from characterizing this attempt as it deserves. I simply announce that I have at hand all the correspondence, including Sneevliet's letter, and that this latter document by itself is completely sufficient to judge the matter. I will transmit all this documentation to the International Conference and I will ask for a special commission to establish the responsibility of all the parties to this important and tragic affair.

I wish only to say in advance that Leon Sedov was the embodiment of duty itself. There is not the least stain on his memory. He could indeed serve as an example to all those who are blaming him for mistakes and crimes committed by others. Our International will judge.

# HITLER'S AUSTRIA COUP
# AIDED BY MOSCOW TRIAL[273]

## March 12, 1938

There is tragic symbolism in the fact that the Moscow trial is ending under the fanfare announcing the entry of Hitler into Austria. The coincidence is not accidental. Berlin is of course perfectly informed about the demoralization which the Kremlin clique in its struggle for self-preservation carried into the army and the population of the country. Stalin did not move a finger last year when Japan seized two Russian islands on the Amur river: he was then busy executing the best Red Army generals. With all the more assurance during the new trial could Hitler send his troops into Austria.

No matter what one's attitude toward the defendants at the Moscow trials, no matter how one judges their conduct in the clutches of the GPU, all of them—Zinoviev, Kamenev, Smirnov, Pyatakov, Radek, Rykov, Bukharin, and many others—have by the whole course of their lives proved their disinterested devotion to the Russian people and their struggle for liberation. In executing them and thousands less known, but no less devoted to the cause of the toilers, Stalin continues to weaken the moral strength of the resistance of the country as a whole. Careerists without honor or conscience, on whom he is more and more forced to base himself, will betray the country in a difficult hour. On the contrary the so-called "Trotskyists," who serve the people, but not the bureaucracy, will occupy battle posts in the event of attack upon the USSR as they have occupied them in the past.

But what is all this to Vyshinsky, who, during the years of the revolution, hid himself in the camp of the Whites and joined the Bolsheviks only after their definitive victory, when the possibilities for careers were open? Vyshinsky demands nineteen heads and first of all the head of Bukharin, whom Lenin more than once called "the favorite of the party" and whom in his testament he named "the best theoretician of the party." How stormily the agents of the Communist International applauded Bukharin's speeches when he was still at his zenith! But no sooner had the Kremlin clique overthrown him than yesterday's "Bukharinists" deferentially bowed before the monstrous falsifications of Vyshinsky.

The accuser demands the head of Yagoda. Of all the defendants Yagoda alone undoubtedly deserves severe punishment—although not at all for those crimes of which he has been accused. Vyshinsky compares Yagoda to the American gangster, Al Capone, and adds: "But Russia, thank God, is not America." No traitors could have made a more dangerous comparison! Al Capone was not the head of the federal agents in the United States. But Yagoda for more than ten years stood at the head of the GPU and was Stalin's closest collaborator. According to Vyshinsky, Yagoda was the "organizer and inspirer of monstrous crimes." But all the arrests, exiles, and executions of the Oppositionists, including the trial of Zinoviev-Kamenev, were accomplished under the leadership of this Moscow Al Capone. Is it not then obligatory to review tens of thousands of repressions? Or did the actions of the secret "Trotskyist" Yagoda cease to be "monstrous crimes" when they were directed against Trotskyists? There is no possibility of disentangling from this skein the contradictions and lies.

Vyshinsky demands the head of Levin and the other doctors of the Kremlin, who in place of prolonging life occupied themselves with hastening death. But if we are to believe the judicial investigation, they committed these crimes not for political or personal aims but from fear of this same Yagoda. The head of the GPU, Stalin's majordomo, threatened the doctors with execution of their families if they did not poison the indicated patients, and so great was Yagoda's power that even the Kremlin's high-standing doctors did not dare to expose Capone but instead quietly executed his orders. Vyshinsky builds his accusations on these "confessions." It appears that Capone's power was unlimited in the Soviet Union. It is true that Yezhov has now taken his place. But where are the guarantees that he is any better? In the milieu of a totalitarian despotism, with public opinion strangled, with control completely absent, only the names of the gangsters change, but the system remains the same.

Vyshinsky spoke for five and a half hours, demanding nineteen executions—seventeen minutes for each head. For Rakovsky and

Bessonov the magnanimous prosecutor demanded "only" twenty-five years in prison. Thus Rakovsky, having devoted his energy for fifty years and his considerable personal fortune in the cause of the toilers, can hope to atone for his alleged crimes by his ninetieth birthday!

The only consolation in the face of this terrible and at the same time buffoonish trial is the radical change in public opinion. The voice of the world press is completely unanimous. *No one anywhere anymore believes the accusers.* All understand the real sense of the trial. There can be no doubt that the population of the USSR also does not consist of the blind and the deaf. The organizers of the frame-up isolated themselves from all mankind. The present trial is one of the last convulsions in the political crisis in the USSR. The sooner the dictatorship of Al Capone is converted into the self-government of the workers and peasants, the more strongly will the USSR stand before the threats of fascism from the outside as well as from the inside. The hour of the regeneration of Soviet democracy will give a tremendous impetus to the progress of mankind and will thus sound the death knell for Hitler, Mussolini, and Franco.

# ON HEARST[274]

## March 13, 1938

During the Moscow trial the London *Daily Express* asked me to give them an exclusive article upon the trial. Cabling the article, I did not have the faintest idea that it would return from London and appear in the Hearst papers.

Let the various bigots who support Stalin-Vyshinsky make what they can of this occurrence. I am not greatly moved. It is by no means a question of literary "collaboration" with Hearst. My task and that of my collaborators during these days was to launch into world circulation the greatest possible number of facts and arguments against the executioners and thus attempt to stay their hand. If I should have to post placards, warning the people of a cholera epidemic, I should equally utilize the walls of schools, churches, saloons, gambling houses, and even worse establishments.

# AN EXPLANATION
# FOR FREDA KIRCHWEY[275]

## March 13, 1938

Madam:

In your letter of December 20, 1937, you propose that I give an article to the *Nation* expounding my "philosophy." My answer has been delayed through a series of circumstances which it is unnecessary to specify here.

During the Moscow trials, my name, the name of Leon Sedov, my deceased son, and the names of my friends were, with the help of the "confessions" of the unfortunate victims of the GPU, branded and besmirched and the victims then shot. You occupied a position which in the best case could be classified as benevolent neutrality toward the slanderers, falsifiers, and hangmen. Some of your close collaborators, like the not unknown Louis Fischer, came out as direct literary agents of Stalin, Vyshinsky, Yezhov. You, yourself, madam, left the Trotsky Defense Committee noisily when it appeared to you that the commission, headed by Dr. John Dewey, was capable of casting a shadow upon the chastity of the Soviet Themis.

Since you have now asked me to expound my "philosophy" in the *Nation* you have obviously come to the conclusion that the accusations directed against me are false. Did you declare this openly? The Moscow frame-ups, however, did not fall from the heavens. Have you explained to your readers that you did not have a timely understanding of the meaning of the Moscow proceedings because you falsely assessed the evolution of the Soviet bureaucracy during the whole last period? Have you demarcated yourself from merchants of lies such as Walter Duranty and Louis Fischer, who during a series of years systematically deceived American public opinion and thus facilitated the work of Moscow's falsifiers and hangmen?

You will, I hope, publish in the pages of the *Nation* this letter, which comprises an essential element of my "philosophy."

Leon Trotsky

# NOTES IN THE MARGIN
# OF PRAVDA'S ACCOUNTS[276]

## [March 1938]

1. The accused Bessonov asserts that at the end of December 1936 he sent a letter to L.D. Trotsky, by means of Johanssen. A few days later he received a reply from him.

On December 18, 1936, L.D. Trotsky was secretly brought on board the tanker *Ruth* by the Norwegian police. On December 19 this vessel left Oslo, and reached Tampico (Mexico) only on January 9, 1937. At the end of December 1936, L.D. Trotsky had no possibility of corresponding with anybody. He was also forbidden to use the telegraph.

*Dagbladet,* Oslo, of March 7, 1938, gives incontrovertible proof that Bessonov's testimony about the letter to Trotsky is just as much a figment as the flight of Pyatakov to Oslo. From the beginning of September 1936, all of Trotsky's mail was checked by the head of the central passport bureau, and a copy of every incoming and outgoing letter was taken (testimony of Konstad, head of the central passport bureau). On December 19, L.D. Trotsky left Norway and had no further possibility of communicating with the outside world (testimony of police officer Jonas Lie, who accompanied him on the tanker).

It is true that to avoid this blunder it would have been sufficient to read *Les Crimes de Staline* (pp. 80-81 and 128).

2. *Krestinsky confirms Trotsky's refutation.* Bessonov asserted that Trotsky met Krestinsky in Merano in October 1933. Trotsky immediately refuted this: in October 1933, he was in France at Bagneres (Pyrenees) along with his wife and a friend. His stay at this resort was known to the French police.

During Bessonov's examination, Vyshinsky asked Krestinsky whether he confirmed Bessonov's testimony. Krestinsky confirmed that he was at that time in Merano. "I was there for treatment and *never saw any of the Trotskyists"* (March 2 session—our emphasis). But at the March 4 session (*Pravda*, March 6) during his second examination Krestinsky not only "confesses" that he had met Trotsky in Merano, but even supplies details: "Trotsky arrived in Merano about October 10 along with Sedov." And to avoid all possible refutations by L.D. Trotsky, he states precisely: "Trotsky, as he told me, arrived *on a false French passport . . ."* (our emphasis).

3. *On Sedov's "meetings" with the accused.* (a) *In 1929.* According to Krestinsky's and Rosengolts's testimony (*Pravda*, March 6) Sedov met Krestinsky in Kissingen (Germany) in September 1929. From the time of his exile from the Soviet Union—in February 1929—till February 1931, Sedov, as is clear from his passport and from numerous eyewitness accounts, lived in Turkey and never left it. (b) The same applies to the testimony of Krestinsky, who is supposed, before he left Berlin, to have met Sedov so as to put him in touch with General Seeckt. (c) *In 1933.* The meeting in Velden (Austria) with Rosengolts. In this case Rosengolts is fairly careful and gives no further details. But Sedov was not in Austria in 1933. Till March 1933, he lived in Germany, from which he went straight to France. (d) *In 1934.* The meeting with Rosengolts in Carlsbad (Czechoslovakia). From the time of his arrival in France (1933) Sedov never left that country once. The falsity of this declaration can be proved from documents.

4. Bessonov asserts he met Sedov in Berlin in 1931, after an incident involving Sedov's sister. All newspapers are supposed to have written about L.D. Trotsky and his children at that time in connection with this incident. Sedov's sister, Zinaida, came to Berlin at the very end of 1931; nothing happened to her and not a single newspaper wrote about her then. Only in 1933, when she committed suicide, did all the newspapers write about L.D. Trotsky and his children.

5. As a curiosity we give the total amount of money which, according to the testimony of the accused, was handed to Trotsky and his friends: 2,020,000 gold marks, 930,000 dollars, and 27,000 pounds sterling. This money, according to Krestinsky, went for propaganda abroad, publishing, etc. Comrade Trotsky's interview, which has appeared in the world press, is a sufficient answer to this ridiculous lie.

6. There is no doubt that the accusations of the murder of Gorky, Menzhinsky, and Kuibyshev were invented only two or three weeks before the trial, and the accusation of preparing the

assassination of Lenin, Stalin, and Sverdlov in 1918 only on February 19-20, i.e., three days before the completion of the indictment. (a) Rykov "confessed" the murder of Gorky only on January 10, 1938. (b) The Kremlin doctor Kazakov "confessed" the murder of Menzhinsky only on February 4. (c) The Left SRs Kamkov and Karelin[277] and the former Left Communists Yakovleva, Osinsky, and Mantsev "confessed" only on February 19 and 20 that in 1918 Bukharin intended to kill Lenin, Sverdlov, and Stalin.

7. In the indictment we are informed that Rakovsky became a Japanese spy in 1934, at the time of his journey to Japan. Let us remember that in his testimony to the Commission of Inquiry in April 1937, L.D. Trotsky predicted the possibility of such an accusation. He clearly speaks of this on pages 338-39 of the stenographic record of his examination [*The Case of Leon Trotsky*]; this quotation was included in the last number of the *Biulleten Oppozitsii*—no. 62-63, p. 14.

8. It is curious to note that reports of the course of the trial appear in different lights in the Soviet and foreign press, especially in those papers represented by their own correspondents. Thus, for example, it is interesting to compare Bukharin's examination according to the *Pravda* accounts with the description of a hardly objective correspondent such as M. Berlan of *Le Temps*. On the accusation of spying, Bukharin declared: "I am hearing this for the first time here. Not a word of this was said during the investigation although the prosecutor interrogated me for three months" (*Le Temps*, March 9, 1938). There is not a word of this in *Pravda*.

The following words of Yagoda, not given in the *Pravda* account, should also be noticed: "If I had been a spy, dozens of countries could have let loose their secret agents in the USSR" (*Le Temps*, March 10, 1938). Space forbids us to give more than these two examples.

# CAIN—DZHUGASHVILI
# GOES THE WHOLE WAY[278]

## March 17, 1938

The baseness of the latest show trial at times pales before its stupidity. Stalin still thinks that with the help of a trick invented by him and Yagoda he can deceive all of humanity. The whole idea of the show, the fictitious political plans of the "conspirators," the distribution of roles between them—how crude and vile it all is, even from the angle of legal forgery!

From behind the back of the "great" Stalin there looks at humanity the Tiflis petty-bourgeois Dzhugashvili, a limited and wily boor. The mechanics of worldwide reaction has armed him with unlimited power. No one dares to criticize him or even give him advice. His assistants, the Vyshinskys and Yezhovs, nonentities rotten to the marrow, have not taken up their high posts in the system of totalitarian tyranny and depravity by chance. The accused, the majority of whom are several heads higher than the accusers, ascribe to themselves plans and ideas sprung from the genius of a contemporary Krechinsky and worked out by a clique of gangsters. Driven by the logic of capitulation and degradation, physically and morally crushed, terrorized by fear for dear ones, hypnotized by the political impasse into which the reaction has driven them, Bukharin, Rykov, Rakovsky, Krestinsky, and the others are playing terrible and wretched roles according to the illiterate scripts of Yezhov. And behind the scenes Cain-Dzhugashvili rubs his hands and cackles evilly: what a trick he has thought up to deceive the whole solar system!

But will Stalin be able to go on sniggering behind the wings? Won't an unforeseen turn of events take the wind out of his sails? True, he is fenced off from the world by a wall of ignorance and fawning. True, he is accustomed to think that world public opinion is nothing, the GPU everything. But threatening symptoms are multiplying, visible even to him. Less and less can the Troyanovskys, Maiskys, Suritses—and the Yezhov agents assigned to watch them—report to the Kremlin comforting news from abroad. Ever sharper uneasiness is seizing the working masses of the whole world. Ever more frequently and in increasing numbers the rats called "friends" are hurrying to leave the sinking ship. The international clouds are thickening. Fascism wins victory after victory, and its chief ally on all the world's roads is Stalinism. Terrible military dangers knock at all the gates of the Soviet Union. But Stalin is destroying the army and trampling on the country. Cain is forced to go the whole way. He hastens to besprinkle his hands with the blood of Bukharin and Rykov. Today he can still permit himself that luxury. But he is increasingly less able to taste the "sweetness" of revenge. It is becoming ever more difficult for the old fox of Tiflis, thrown by a turgid wave of history onto the throne of Thermidor, to laugh. Hatred is accumulating around him limitlessly, and terrible revenge hangs over his head.

A terrorist act? It is quite possible that the regime, which has exterminated all the best heads of the country under the pretext of a struggle against terrorism, will indeed encourage terrorism against itself. Yet more can be said: it would be against the laws of history if the ruling gangsters did not bring up against themselves terrorists of despair and revenge. But the Fourth International, the party of world revolution, has nothing in common with despair, and individual revenge is too little for us. What political or moral satisfaction for the proletariat can be given by the murder of Cain-Dzhugashvili, who can be replaced with ease by the next bureaucratic "genius" in turn? To the extent that the personal fate of Stalin interests us at all, we can only wish that he will live to see the destruction of his system. He doesn't have too long to wait. The victorious workers will remove him and his gangster collaborators from under the debris of the totalitarian abomination and make them account for the crimes committed by them at a real court. The human tongue will not find words at the hour of the last judgment which could do service to the most sinister of Cain's stories. The monuments he built to himself will be destroyed or put in museums of totalitarian gangsterism. But the victorious working class will look through all the trials, public and secret, and erect on the squares of the liberated Soviet Union monuments to the unfortunate victims of the Stalin system of baseness and dishonor.

# A REPLY
# TO AMBASSADOR BILMANIS[279]

## March 17, 1938

To the Editor of the *New York Times:*

In a letter to the *New York Times* of March 12, 1938, the Latvian minister in Washington, Alfred Bilmanis, denied "categorically" my statement that according to official Soviet sources the Latvian consul, Bissenieks, gave Nikolaev, the real assassin of Kirov, 5,000 rubles for his terrorist act and asked from him "some letter for Trotsky." (In the *New York Times* of March 8 it was written "from Trotsky," but that is evidently an error in the dispatch, which, moreover, has no importance from the point of view which interests us now.)

The Latvian minister declares that: (1) during Nikolaev's trial he himself was Latvian minister at Moscow and consequently should have possessed first-hand information; (2) "nothing of this nature regarding Mr. Bissenieks ever appeared in the Soviet press"; (3) this fact (the nonpublication in the press) was also confirmed to me "yesterday" (i.e., March 9) by the Soviet Embassy in Washington; finally (4) "Mr. Bissenieks, formerly Latvian consul at Leningrad, is a most honorable person, who never had anything to do with the Nikolaev case."

The "categorical" character of this denial can permit one to imagine that I had invented this entire episode. However, I have invented nothing. The Latvian minister in his denial displayed regrettable imprudence concerning the facts.

The indictment in the Nikolaev affair was published in *Pravda* of December 27, 1934. In this official document it is reported that Nikolaev "visited many times the * * * consul in Leningrad * * * with whom he conferred on the possible forms of help for this (terrorist) group." In the official text the *nationality* and the name of the consul were replaced by asterisks. Later Nikolaev declared that "In the third or fourth visit to the consulate" the above-mentioned consul "gave me 5,000 rubles. Moreover, he said that he could establish a liaison with Trotsky, if I could give him some (!) letter from the group for Trotsky."

The main article of the same issue of *Pravda* (December 27, 1934) explains the political role of the consul: he was the connection between the terrorists and the "international bourgeoisie." The indictment did not say a word about whether or not the unknown-to-me Nikolaev gave to the unknown-to-me consul "some letter for Trotsky."

At the moment of the publication of the indictment the nationality and the name of the consul, for diplomatic considerations, had been, as mentioned, replaced by asterisks. But the matter did not stop here. The Moscow government was obliged within a few days to make public the name of the mysterious consul. In order to save space I am quoting from Leon Sedov's *Red Book* (Paris, 1936) precise data which can easily be verified in any editorial office. Here is what is given on pages 35-36 of Sedov's book: "On December 29, 1934, *Le Temps* reported that 'the foreign circles of Moscow . . . are lost in conjectures on the nationality of this diplomat.' On December 30 a telegraphic agency reported that a 'conference of the consuls was held, at which it was decided . . . to demand that the Soviet authorities give publicly the name of the suspected consul.'

"Stalin was thus constrained, January 2, 1935, to give the name of the consul. 'The foreign consul mentioned in the indictment in the Kirov assassination is the Latvian consul, M. Bissenieks.' And the next day, January 3, Tass agency reported that the Latvian consul, Bissenieks, had been recalled by his government."

The whole world press published the official announcement that the consul who gave 5,000 rubles for the accomplishment of the terrorist act and demanded some kind of "letter for Trotsky" was the Latvian consul in Leningrad, Bissenieks. Having in mind the usual completeness and preciseness of information in the *New York Times,* I do not doubt that the whole episode as well as the name of the consul found a place in the columns of this paper at that time. It is easier, however, to check this in New York than in Coyoacan. Foreign journalists in Moscow then made an attempt to enter into connection with Mr. Bissenieks in order to determine his real role. But Mr. Bissenieks could not be reached. Mr. Bissenieks himself, as far as I know, has nowhere at any time refuted the official Soviet announcement about his role as described in the indictment.

It is impossible not to observe that in all the subsequent trials the consul was not named or mentioned once. Kirov was assassinated in turn by different "centers," but Mr. Bissenieks disappeared without a trace from all the following versions. If Mr. Alfred Bilmanis was at that time a member of the diplomatic corps in Moscow he could not have helped participating in the attempt of the diplomats to determine the identity of the consul accused of a grave crime. He could not but know the announcement of the Commissariat of Foreign Affairs about the identity of the consul as well as the Tass dispatches. I can only regret that his memory has now betrayed him.

The present announcement of Mr. Bilmanis that Consul Bissenieks is a "most honorable person" and did not have any relation to the Nikolaev affair is, to say the least, belated and does not change anything in essence concerning all the facts mentioned above.

Was the name of Mr. Bissenieks mentioned in the Soviet press? Evidently not. But this "omission" is explained by the fact that publication of the name of the *Latvian* consul would have compromised the version about the connection of the terrorists with a foreign *imperialism*. The readers of the Soviet press presumed that the matter concerned a German or Japanese consul, and the head of the Soviet press evidently saw no reason for destroying this impression. But this circumstance changes nothing. The People's Commissariat for Foreign Affairs and Tass are no less official organs than *Izvestia*.

During the time of the two last big trials in Moscow I gave to the press dozens of factual statements and refutations. I gave hundreds of these to the International Commission headed by Dr. John Dewey (see *The Case of Leon Trotsky,* a verbatim report of the hearings held at Coyoacan). Not one of my statements was refuted even partially. The first attempt at factual refutation is the letter of the Latvian minister in Washington. Let public opinion judge to what degree this attempt is convincing.

                                                              Leon Trotsky

# NEW DEFECTORS[280]

## March 17, 1938

After a series of furious purges of foreign Soviet personnel, four big Kremlin agents have become defectors in the last few months: Ignace Reiss, Alexander Barmin, Walter Krivitsky, and finally Fyodor Butenko. If you consider the training, selection, checking, and especially the system of hostages, you have to agree that this percentage is extraordinarily high. It bears witness to the strength of the centrifugal forces which are tearing apart the bureaucracy itself. This fact is highlighted even more sharply if you take a look at the political orientation of the new defectors.

Ignace Reiss immediately took up his stand under the banner of the Bolshevik-Leninists. This clearly indicated his political and moral weight. Only a real revolutionary could have decided on such a step under the present conditions. But at the first steps on his new path Reiss fell, one of the heroes of the Fourth International. He left a wife and child who were indissolubly connected with him in life and remain faithful to his memory after his death. When his son is old enough to pick up the banner fallen from his father's hands, the Fourth International will already be a great historical force.

Alexander Barmin went to the left of the bureaucracy, but has evidently still not finally chosen his path. We have no grounds or right to hasten him. We understand too well the difficulty and responsibility of choice after years spent in the barracks of the Stalin bureaucracy. Let us hope he chooses right!

Walter Krivitsky, if the signs do not deceive us, is drawn to the camp of bourgeois democracy. We do not mean by this that he is going to the *right* of the Stalin bureaucracy. The ranks of the Soviet apparatus are filled with officials with a bourgeois habit of thought. When they throw off the overcoat of Stalinism, they simply disclose their real political nature. If our supposition about Krivitsky proves false, we shall be the first to be delighted thereby.

Fyodor Butenko has made the jump to fascism. Did he have to deny himself much? Wrestle with himself much? We do not think so. A very considerable and growing part of the Soviet apparatus consists of fascists who have not yet recognized themselves. To identify the Soviet regime as a whole with fascism is a crude historical error into which ultraleft dilettantes are inclined to fall, ignoring the difference in social bases. But the symmetry of the political superstructures and the similarity of totalitarian methods and psychological types is striking. Butenko is a symptom of tremendous importance: he shows us the careerists of the Stalin school in their natural form.

If it were possible to X-ray politically the whole Soviet apparatus, we would find in it: concealed Bolsheviks, confused but honest revolutionaries, bourgeois democrats, and finally, candidates for fascism. It can be said with conviction that the more reactionary the nature of the grouping, the faster it is growing within the bureaucracy.

The political riddle of the Moscow trials is whether the apparatus which raised Stalin to power wants to go on carrying him on its back. The centrifugal forces within the bureaucracy only reflect in their turn the deep social antagonisms in the "classless" society and the general hatred of the masses for the bureaucracy. Stalin's own faction is numerically small and consists of the most utter scoundrels, such as Vyshinsky and Yezhov. Bolshevism strove toward a state without bureaucracy, "of the Commune type." Stalin has created a state of a bureaucracy devouring itself, "of the GPU type." That is why the agony of Stalinism is the most frightful and repellent spectacle in human history!

# THE PRIESTS OF HALF-TRUTH[281]

## March 19, 1938

The *Nation* and the *New Republic* are now playing the sorriest and most ignoble role in the American press. These journals lay claim to the role of oracles of "liberal" public opinion. They have no ideas of their own. The social crisis that began in 1929 and caught the "liberals" unaware compelled them to cling to the USSR like a saving anchor. In popularizing the successes of the planning principle and in the cautious counterposing of this principle to capitalist anarchy, these gentlemen temporarily found a mission. They had absolutely no independent program of action for the United States; but for that, they were able to cover up their own muddleheadedness with an idealized image of the USSR.

In fact, the "friendship" with Moscow signified the reconciliation of bourgeois liberalism with the bureaucracy, which had strangled the October Revolution. The more extensive the privileges of the new leading stratum became, and the more conservative it grew in the defense of its privileges—the greater became the number of its friends among the bourgeois intellectuals and the liberals, snobs who keep up with the vogue of the day. The inspirers of this state of mind became Walter Duranty and Louis Fischer, downright sycophants of the Soviet oligarchy. Under their guidance, small-minded professors, mediocre poets, lawyers who had not succeeded in attaining prominence, bored widows, and ordinary lonesome ladies seriously began to take their friendship with the Soviet Embassy in Washington for service in the interests of the October Revolution. Many of them displayed a readiness to defend the Soviet Union to the last drop of blood . . . not theirs, to be sure, but that of the "Trotskyists."

In the heroic epoch of the revolution, the representative of American public opinion in Moscow was John Reed.[282] At that

time, Walter Duranty was located in Riga, working as professional slanderer of the revolution and of its leaders. In later years,
Duranty became the principal link between the Soviet bureaucracy and "liberal" public opinion in the United States. The moral
contrast between John Reed and Walter Duranty well reflects the
political antagonism between Bolshevism and Stalinism. If the
editors of the *Nation* and the *New Republic* tax their ingenuity to
avoid an understanding of this antagonism, it is because such
petty tradesmen in lies as Duranty and Louis Fischer are
incomparably closer to them in spirit than the heroic John Reed.*

Is it surprising that the present bureaucracy of the Kremlin is
incomparably more suitable to the democratic oracles than was
the revolutionary party of Lenin? Just as in the past they did not
understand the laws of revolution, so today they do not
understand the laws of reaction. They hoped that the bureaucracy, not without their benevolent cooperation, would become
increasingly respectable and "human." Faith in uninterrupted
and automatic progress has not been extirpated, to the present
day, from the heads of these people. They have been unable to
draw any conclusions at all even from the fact that the
democratic petty bourgeoisie, whose flesh of the flesh they are,
transformed itself in a few years in Germany into an army of
fascism. They were even less capable of understanding the
malignant evolution of the Stalinist bureaucracy.

Lamentable indeed is the person who, in the great turns of
history, confines himself to empirical conjecture instead of
penetrating into the imminent logic of the class struggle. In the
psychological sense, the defendants were merely instruments in
the hands of the GPU Inquisition. In the historical sense, the
Inquisitor, Stalin, is merely an instrument in the hands of the

---

*W. Duranty, in spite of his genuine Anglo-Saxon "soul," participates
in the Moscow frame-ups in a strictly planned manner, side by side with
the judges, the prosecutor, the defendants, and in general with people who
have a "Russian soul." However, Duranty was not even confronted with
the necessity to choose every day between life and death. His colleague,
Mr. Harold Denny, a man who obviously has an American soul, even if
not of very large dimensions, has speedily adapted himself to the
totalitarian regime. Faced with the need of choosing between the lean-
stomached truth and fat sandwiches, he unhesitatingly took his stand
with the sandwiches and Vyshinsky. It is creatures of his stripe who are
the source of inspiration for "liberal" public opinion.

bureaucracy, which has landed in a blind alley. The bureaucracy itself is merely an instrument of the pressure of world imperialism. The Soviet masses hate the bureaucracy. World imperialism regards it as a tool that has outlived its usefulness and makes preparations to overturn it. The bureaucracy seeks to dupe the masses. It seeks to dupe world imperialism. It lies on both fronts. So that the truth shall not filter out past the frontier nor filter into the country from abroad, the bureaucracy allows only "reliable" people to enter or leave the country.

It surrounds the Soviet Union with a border patrol palisade such as the world has never seen and with countless packs of police dogs.

The period when world imperialism subjected the Soviet land to a blockade is now lost in the past. The blockade of the USSR today is organized by the Soviet bureaucracy itself. Of the revolution as it understands it, the bureaucracy has preserved only the cult of police violence. It thinks that with the aid of police dogs the course of history can be altered. It fights for its existence with a conservative fury such as has not been displayed by any ruling class in history. Along this road, it has arrived in a short time at the commission of crimes such as not even fascism has yet perpetrated. Of this dialectic of the Thermidor, the democratic oracles have understood nothing, understand nothing now, and—let there be no illusions—will not understand anything. Otherwise they would be obliged to shut down the *Nation* and the *New Republic* immediately and thus upset the equilibrium of the solar system!

Since the Thermidorean reaction came out of the revolution, the *Nation* and the *New Republic* have sought tirelessly to prove that revolution and reaction are one and the same thing. They have systematically approved or at least kept silent about the work of falsification, lies, and corruption which the Stalinist bureaucracy has accomplished throughout the world. They have covered up the repression against the Oppositionists, which has been going on now for fifteen years. Yet there has been no lack of warnings. The literature of the Left Opposition is fairly rich, in all languages.

For fifteen years it has shown, step by step, how the methods of the bureaucracy came into increasingly sharp conflict with the requirements of a new society; how the bureaucracy was obliged to screen its own greedy interests, not only by appropriating the mechanics of lying from all the ruling classes, but also by investing these mechanics—in view of the acuteness of the situation in a country scarcely emerged from a revolution—with an unprecedentedly poisonous character. With irrefutable facts and documents we showed how a whole school of falsification came out of the Thermidorean reaction—the school of Stalin—which envenomed every domain of social ideology; we explained how and why it was precisely Stalin ("the cook of peppery dishes," according to Lenin's definition as far back as March 1921) who became head of the avid and conservative caste of usurpers of the revolution; we predicted the Moscow trials ten years before they took place and we explained to the most backward that the judicial frame-ups are only convulsions of the Thermidorean agony.

Finally, in 1937, the International Commission in New York, composed of persons of high moral authority and accustomed to critical judgment, subjected the accusations of Stalin and Vyshinsky to a patient and meticulous analysis. In all the accusations, they found nothing but lies, falsifications, and frame-ups. They stated this openly to the entire world. The verdict of the commission was intended essentially for the "man in the street," the farmer, the small tradesman, the backward worker; in a word, the majority of those whose conditions of existence deprive them of the necessary training and broad horizons.

From the editors of the *Nation* and the *New Republic,* these self-appointed teachers of the people, one might, it would seem, have demanded a critical sense of their own. They might, for example, have recalled from what they learned under their old schoolteachers, that the Thermidorean reaction in France proclaimed the Jacobins to be "Royalists" and "agents of Pitt,"[283] in order to justify in the eyes of the masses the sanguinary repression against them. From these professional moralists, one might, it would seem, have expected some sense of morality. Does not the moral degeneration of the Soviet bureaucracy stink to high heaven? Alas, the moralists have been found to be devoid even of a simple sense of smell.

The Moscow trials not only took this circle of people unawares but have destroyed the tranquility of their souls for a long time to come. A collection of all the articles of the *Nation* and the *New Republic* dealing with the three big trials—what a panorama of narrowness, vanity, hypocrisy, and above all confusion. No, they did not expect them! How could this have happened? Yet, while they lack perspicacity and a sense of smell, they possess to the highest degree the priestly caste's feeling for self-preservation. Thenceforth, their whole behavior was determined by concern with the obliteration of their traces, that is, with seeing to it that the faithful remain unaware of the fact that inside the oracle, all this time, were concealed not very farsighted priests. Theoretically, these pharisees indignantly reject the principle "The end justifies the means," failing to understand that a great historical goal automatically discards those means that are unworthy of it. But in order to bolster up traditional petty prejudices and especially their own authority in the eyes of simpletons, they are always ready to resort to artful dodges and frame-ups of picayune scope.

At first, they tried openly to fulfill their duty as "friends," that is, attorneys for the GPU. But this proved to be too risky. They speedily shifted to the position of philosophical agnosticism and diplomatic nonintervention. They declared the trials to be "puzzling." They refrained from judgment. They warned against premature conclusions. "We cannot decide anything from the outside." "We must not interfere in the affairs of Soviet justice." In a word, they sought evasively to reconcile world public opinion to the abominations that were being concocted in Moscow. These people wanted at all costs to remain on friendly terms with the executioners of the revolution but not to assume direct responsibility for the frame-ups of the GPU.

However, they were unsuccessful in keeping to this second line for any length of time. Under the blows of the disclosures they sang at a continually lower pitch: "Of course, the charges are obviously improbable but . . . but there is 'something' behind them." "We are not with the Stalinists, but we also do not believe the Trotskyists." Only the soothsayers of the *Nation* and the *New Republic* represent the truth. If yesterday and the day before they were blind, that is all the greater guarantee that today their sight is flawless. "There is something behind these charges." Indeed! If the ruling clique is executing all who are left of the Bolshevik Party, it has imperious reasons for doing so. However, we must look for these reasons in the objective interests of the bureaucracy and not in the speeches of Vyshinsky, or in the frame-ups of Yezhov. But we already know that the dialectics of the class struggle remain for these empiricists a book sealed with seven seals. What can you ask or expect from philosophers and publicists who foresaw nothing and see nothing, and were caught completely unawares by the trials? There is nothing left for the bankrupt oracles but to divide the guilt in two: fifty percent is allowed to the executioner, fifty percent to his victim.

The petty bourgeois always stands in the middle and judges a question by the formula: "on the one hand" and "on the other hand." If the capitalists are unbending, still, the workers are too exigent. This line of the golden mean, the *Nation* and the *New Republic* merely draw to its logical conclusion when they wear out half of their moral lymph on the GPU and the other half on the real or fancied "Trotskyists." And in the end, the liberal American finds out from his teachers that Zinoviev and Kamenev were only half-terrorists; that Pyatakov sabotaged industry only six months out of twelve; that Bukharin and Rykov are spies for only two and not four countries; and that Stalin is merely a half-falsifier and a half-scoundrel. Cain? Perhaps he is Cain, but not more than fifty percent.

Their philosophy reflects their own world. By their social nature they are intellectual semibourgeois. They feed upon half-thoughts and half-feelings. They wish to cure society by half-measures. Regarding the historical process as too unstable a phenomenon, they refuse to engage themselves more than fifty percent. Thus, these people, living by half-truths—that is to say, the worst form of falsehood—have become a genuine brake upon truly progressive, i.e., revolutionary thought.

A *New Masses* is simply a garbage can which puts people on their guard by its own odor.[284] The *Nation* and *New Republic* are considerably more "decent" and "nice" and less . . . odorous. But they are all the more dangerous. The best part of the new generation of American intellectuals can proceed on the broad historical highway only if it completely breaks with the oracles of "democratic" half-truth.

# DISCUSSIONS WITH TROTSKY:

## I—International Conference[285]

### March 20, 1938

*Trotsky:* All the sections have had discussions about the events in Spain, the Sino-Japanese war, the class character of the USSR—and some sections have even had their splits, like the German section. Your theses are known by all the sections and the same holds true of the French theses.[286] The question now is only a matter of putting the text in order.

*Cannon:* There remains the question of preparing the text for the conference.

*Trotsky:* We have here prepared the draft of the program—it's possible to get it ready within two or three weeks, then to translate it into English and French. Can your declaration of principles be used for the International Conference?

*Shachtman:* No, it's more the declaration of a national section.

*Trotsky:* Adolphe has sent out his draft of the statutes.[287] The German section has prepared the thesis on the character of the Fourth International. It was sent to every section three months ago and it is now published in *Unser Wort.*[288]

*Shachtman:* We haven't received *Unser Wort* for some months.

*Trotsky:* Perhaps because in your sojourn in the Socialist Party you lost your international connections, and you haven't yet been able fully to reestablish them.
You've also had the thesis of Diego Rivera.[289] The only

objection to be made against it is that it is too long for the conference. I read your suggestion that I write on the war question in the light of the latest events. I accept this suggestion with readiness—to supplement and concretize our thesis in the light of recent events. We have something of importance to do. It can be done in the next few days. We have here a draft but not enough persons who can translate from the Russian.

But what is missing is a program of transitional demands and slogans.[290] It is necessary to make a summary of concrete, precise demands, such as workers' control of industry as opposed to technocracy. From time to time it is mentioned in the paper but only in passing. But I believe it is one of the slogans that is very important for the U.S.

Lundberg writes a book about the sixty families. The *Annalist* says that his statistics are exaggerated. We must ask for the abolition of commercial secrets—that the workers have the right to look into the bookkeeping—as a premise for workers' control of industry. A series of transitional measures which correspond to the stage of monopolistic capitalism and the dictatorship of the proletariat with a section corresponding to colonial and semi-colonial countries. We have prepared such a document. It corresponds to that part of the *Communist Manifesto* of Marx and Engels which they themselves declared outdated. It's only partially outdated, partially it is very good, and is to be replaced by our conference.

Then I also have a draft of a thesis concerning democracy. The gist of it is that democracy is the most aristocratic form of rule— only those countries are able to conserve democracy that have slaves in the world, like Great Britain, whose every citizen has nine slaves; France whose every citizen has one and a half slaves; and the U.S.—I can't reckon the slaves, but it's almost the whole world, beginning with Latin America. The poorer countries, like Italy, gave up their democracy.

It's an analysis of democracy in the light of new events. What is a fascization of democracy? The petty-bourgeois democrats become bankrupt. Only the big ones, the greatest robbers, the richest slaveholders, etc., remain democrats. Such a posing of the question is especially useful for the U.S. Naturally it is not to be written in favor of fascism but in favor of proletarian democracy. Even for the richest country, like the U.S., democracy is becoming less and less workable.

I believe these are almost all we have as propositions for the International Conference. The other important questions, the burning questions of the class character of the Soviet Union, the Sino-Japanese war, the question of Spain, have already been discussed by all the sections. We are well prepared for the conference.

I will prepare, then: (1) transitional demands; (2) the question of democracy; (3) war; (4) manifesto on the world situation; either separately or in the form of one basic pamphlet.

*Cannon:* What about a programmatic manifesto? I wonder whether we should not have such a document?

*Trotsky:* Yes, it would be very good to have one. It can be done from Europe or it can be done from here. It could be adopted by the International Conference itself, or it could be issued by the International Secretariat in the name of the conference.

*Cannon:* On the organizational side of the question—shall we consider this conference as a provisional gathering or as the actual founding of the Fourth International? The prevailing opinion among us is that we would actually form the Fourth International at this conference. We think that the main elements of the Fourth International are by now crystallized. We should put an end to our negotiations and maneuvers with the centrists and henceforth deal with them as separate and alien groupings.

*Trotsky:* I agree absolutely with what Comrade Cannon said. I believe you will meet some opposition from Belgium, particularly from Vereecken. For him life consists of discussions; as soon as a decision is arrived at, it is a catastrophe for him. You will also find some element of opposition from the French comrades at the conference. I don't know about the opinion held by the various British comrades, but I agree entirely that it is absolutely naive to postpone. Naturally we are a weak International but we are an International. This International will become strong by our own action, not by maneuvers with other groups. Naturally, we can attract other intermediary groups, but that would be incidental. The general line is our own development. We had a test in Spain for all these intermediary organizations—the POUM was the most important part of the London Bureau and the same POUM proved to be the most disastrous for the Spanish revolution. I believe that our American section should proclaim its position with energy—we have no reason to boast that we are strong, but we are what we are.

*Cannon:* I think on this point we have to have some explanation for some of the comrades—perhaps in the form of articles or discussions. Some comrades have taken the tactic of maneuvering and making concessions to centrists as a permanent policy, whereas we think that all our maneuvers with the centrists have been exhausted by now. We were justified two, three, or four years ago in delaying organizational actions, in order to complete the maneuvers and experiments with those people, but not now. We noticed in our discussions that there are some comrades who want to carry over the tactic indefinitely—some kinds of maneuvers which are doomed in advance to defeat. And for this reason I believe we have to explain this matter to the comrades.

*Trotsky:* The London Bureau is for us not an arena of action or maneuvers—it's only an obstacle—a petrified centrism without masses. What is of interest to us in the political field is the CP, but there it is not a question of maneuvers but of a resolute struggle.

*Shachtman:* Have you heard any further news about any developments in the POUM in regard to the emergence of a left wing?

*Trotsky:* The leaders are now the Rights—the worst elements of the Maurin group[291]—and have accused those of the Nin wing of being responsible for the catastrophe in Spain by its too revolutionary policy.

*Shachtman:* And in Holland?

*Trotsky:* That is the black spot on our political map. It is a classic example of transformation of a sectarian policy into an opportunistic policy, accompanied by a series of defeats. You know that these left trade unions have existed for the past thirty or forty years. They are not an improvisation of third period Stalinism; they are the result of syndicalist prejudices. Sneevliet became secretary of this organization. It had 25,000 workers and state functionaries—half and half—at its height. But the functions of the state are realized through the trade unions. They are subsidized by the state. In this way the bureaucracy of the trade unions became dependent upon the state. Sneevliet and his friends had an apparatus which didn't and doesn't respond to the

strength of the trade unions and the party but which has as its
base the financial support of the state.

*Cannon:* A direct subsidy?

*Trotsky:* Yes. It gives the trade unions the opportunity to
sustain their apparatus. If the state minister withdraws this
financial support from these trade unions (and he threatened it)
then it's immediately a complete catastrophe. Colijn merely
showed a threatening finger to the left-wing trade unions.[292]
Immediately all the functionaries left it for other trade unions,
and now Sneevliet no longer has 25,000 but a maximum of eleven
to twelve thousand. It is his former radical position, especially on
the colonial question, that gave him authority among the
workers; he was arrested, and when he came out of prison he
became a parliamentary deputy. At that time, in France, we
talked with him and argued that it was impossible for him to
remain a secretary of a trade union, a semifunctionary of the
state, and a member of a revolutionary party. He told me that he
agreed, but he wished to remain as secretary only in order to gain
some 2,000 members from the trade unions to the revolutionary
party. I said: fine, we shall see. But the evolution was a contrary
one. When he entered the parliament we waited for a genuine
revolutionary speech—it was the first time the Fourth International had acquired a parliamentary deputy. But every speech
was equivocal. With his prime minister, Colijn, he was very
gentlemanly—absolutely nonrevolutionary. He will tell you a
thousand reasons for his attitude but he will hide the one real
reason—his obsequiousness to the government in order to retain
financial support for his trade union. Very humiliating, but true.
In this situation he cannot tolerate any criticism. When a
member asks him: Why, in your parliamentary speech, didn't you
say this and that?—he can't answer. He expels every critic. In
order to fight against us—the Fourth International—he turns for
revolutionary camouflage to Spain, and he declares of the POUM,
"That's my party." He went to Spain with 500 gulden to give to
the POUM—everything was photographed in the paper—he went
there and supported the POUM against us.

The POUM had 40,000 members. That's nothing. If you have
only 10,000 members—but members who are connected with the
masses in rebellion—then you can win a revolution. But 40,000
members separated from the masses—that's nothing. But
Sneevliet, Vereecken, Serge turned out to be strikebreakers, in the

true sense of the word "strikebreakers." They were in full
solidarity with the POUM against us in this situation and the
POUM declared: If such important figures are against the official
position of the Fourth International, then it is possible that we
are right. That strengthened the opportunistic tendencies of the
POUM in the most critical situation. Our American friends have
a duty to accuse them energetically, because Spain was a great
historic lesson. The result of the policy of Sneevliet is that from
25,000 members in the trade unions he has now 11,000 and in the
new election he lost his mandate—he no longer had 50,000 votes
but less than 30,000; his diplomatic speeches had no interest for
the workers.

Now he runs to the London Bureau. We can make no
concessions to Sneevliet. We have been patient—it has not been a
question of two or three weeks; it's a question of at least six
years—and we were all very patient, too patient. Now we must
draw a balance sheet, because in the most critical period of the
Spanish revolution he proved to be a strikebreaker—we cannot
pardon him. Remember how he acted during the last international conference. He came, but as a tourist. He participated in one
session; then he telegraphed to Schmidt who approved and later
left the workers' movement completely and within a few months
went over to the bourgeoisie.

*Cannon:* Do we have a group in Holland?

*Trotsky:* Yes, we have a group expelled by Sneevliet and we
have sympathizers in Sneevliet's party. We believe that the
attitude of the conference will be decisive for the Dutch party.
They must be made to understand that it is not a detail.

As for Vereecken, at the time Sneevliet expelled our comrades,
Vereecken approved because, he said, they had developed a
factional attitude inside the Sneevliet party. The Belgian section
also has a Dutch-speaking section, and the comrades there
endorsed our policy, whereupon Vereecken threatened them with
expulsion. They are an international clique; they constantly fight
against the line of the IS. In a certain sense, Vereecken is a
valuable worker, very devoted to the movement and very
energetic, but this worker has all the bad qualities of an
intellectual.

*Cannon:* The thing that does not satisfy us about the European
groups is that they never seem to finish a question—they never

bring their struggle to a conclusion. Half of the success we have had in the U.S. is due to the fact that we come to a point with people who cannot be assimilated. We discuss with them so far only; when they break from the organization, all relations end.

The European comrades don't bring their discussions to a conclusion. It appears to us that they split too lightly and are too quick to unite again. With such people as Vereecken we have followed the policy of coming to a definitive conclusion after thorough discussion. We cannot build the Fourth International with permanent discussion mongers.

I think the conference has to lay down its political line and say to all: Here is our program and platform. Let those who are with us come along on this basis. Let others go their own way.

I believe we must ask the young comrades in the Belgian and French sections to insist on such a position, and terminate all relations with those who reject the conference decisions, no matter who they may be. In the conference itself there should be a discussion on the question of "discussion." We must make it clear that we discuss, not for the sake of discussion but in order to come to a conclusion and to act. It was never clear to us, for example, how Vereecken, after breaking so lightmindedly with the Belgian section and so lightly reuniting, could immediately become political secretary—the highest post in the party. It creates the impression that one can tear the organization to pieces with impunity, then unite and start over again as though nothing had happened. That is a hopeless policy in our opinion. The comrades of the Fourth International must have courage, if a break is made, to make the break definitive.

In the U.S. we consider a break with the organization a capital crime. We do not start all over again with such people the next day. We try to inculcate this spirit in the young comrades so that they will understand that loyalty to the organization is something sacred. They value the unity of the organization in the highest degree. That is why our last discussion was so successful—nobody threatened to split. Consequently the party could allow the greatest amount of freedom in the discussion without fear of split or of dragging the discussion out forever. I think that is one thing the European comrades must develop—the conception that the Fourth International is formed as a definite organization to which every member must be loyal. Those who lightly make splits must be chopped off and cast aside.

*Trotsky:* I subscribe to every word said by Comrade Cannon. I will only add that the situation in the Belgian party was complicated from this point of view, that it contained members from the Socialist Party without revolutionary education. We have Dauge, a young comrade, very active, but educated in the spirit of the Vereecken party, without any spirit of revolutionary discipline.[293] Then there is Lesoil—an excellent comrade who is completely absorbed by his local sphere of action.[294] It was a difficult situation.

That was also the reason why, in this situation, Vereecken could become again the national secretary. The misfortune was that the comrades from the SP, as soon as they split from it, immediately became partisans of independent trade unions. It was the greatest blow for the new party. I exchanged correspondence with Dauge on this question—it was during our stay in Norway and the police got hold of this correspondence, published it, and accused us of Machiavellian schemes; it made the situation more difficult. Vereecken is not interested in the trade union question—only in discussing it. Dauge was in favor of independent unions. Now he has learned a bit, but meanwhile it was a catastrophe for the party. Lesoil was in principle against this attitude but in practice supported Dauge.

I believe that the separation from Sneevliet is complete and that he will not appear at the conference. He didn't answer my last letter in which I stated that, in spite of everything, if he wishes to be with the Fourth International, etc., he should answer and we will do what we can, etc.

As far as Vereecken is concerned he should be given a serious warning by a most responsible party. He will appear at the conference and criticize, but I believe it necessary to issue a sharp, personal warning, enumerating all his errors. He should be warned that our patience is at an end. He is not a young boy; he is forty. He is a chauffeur, works eight hours, then he is very active, writes articles, delivers speeches, etc.; but he is very dangerous for the party.

*Cannon:* What progress has the French section made this year?

*Trotsky:* They haven't recorded great progress during this year—it was a year of People's Front illusions and only the most courageous elements could approach our party. On the other hand, this situation engendered some sectarian tendencies. Some elements look for an explanation for the stagnation and the too slow development not in the objective situation—the great wave of People's Frontism—but in the insufficiency of our slogan, namely, that we consider it our aim to defend the Soviet Union in case of war. This is the tendency of Craipeau, a very good and honest element but dogmatic and with a scholastic kind of mind. In many questions his views coincide with Vereecken's but he is more disciplined in his attitude, more accessible to influence, etc.

The situation in our International is not bad in spite of the sharp discussion on the Russian question. I believe the problem is to check, control, verify their attitude on the trade unions. The trade unions in France, during the last years, became powerful organizations. They had one million in two organizations. Then they merged. Now they have five million in the unified organization; the leadership is more or less in the hands of the Stalinists, and they cover themselves by support of the People's Front. But now the task is to prepare for the approaching crisis in the People's Front. A break between the SP and the CP has already started. This should give a forward impulsion to our French section. They have the correct principles, but the American comrades can help with their practical work.

They had two other incidents which hurt the organization—one member of the National Committee was counterfeiting money—I don't know whether it was to make the party prosperous or for personal reasons. Naturally he was expelled and the party showed it was not done under its direction. But it was a great blow. The second incident was that of two young comrades, Fred Zeller and Corvin.[295] Zeller came to us in Norway with a mandate from the young socialists. I told him, "Now you are the center of attack by the Stalinists, you must be cautious." Immediately he wrote a postcard to a Stalinist and said, "Down with Stalin!" It was reproduced in the Stalinist press. Then he wrote me that he had learned a lesson and would be more cautious with the Stalinists. But he got into the clutches of the Stalinists in some shady intrigue, and so did the other young comrade, and they were both expelled. They were leaders of the youth movement and it was a blow to the movement.

I believe that we should warn our youth in the U.S. We have new elements—devoted but not experienced. They don't know what the Stalinists can do to provoke them. Queer propositions will come from different sides. It is possible that you can find a young revolutionary worker or student involved with genuine fascists (they may be from the Gestapo and the GPU at the same time), and these intrigues can be absolutely fatal for our organization, for revolutionary internationalism.

*R.:*[296] What about Indochina? Don't we have a strong section there?

*Trotsky:* Yes, it's a very good section. The leader is in prison. They had a big weekly and I believe the organization has been declared illegal by our French socialist minister of colonies[297]—I believe that the paper was also—I do not know if it comes out regularly now—I haven't seen it for two months.

*Shachtman:* Yes, it comes out—I've seen copies.

*Cannon:* And Molinier?

*Trotsky:* Molinier publishes a theoretical organ. He declares that he is in principle with us but that our organizational policy is bad and he has a better one. His organization is permeated by hatred of our organization. It is very possible that you will be obliged, objectively, to devote attention to this question, and that at the conference Vereecken will defend him. Molinier should remain outside but the others, his members, can be admitted if they apply individually and if he remains outside. He is an element that can be very useful but only when we have a big organization. In an organization such as ours his people are only disrupters. You can propose to him to come to the U.S. and promise him friendly personal relations and after a year we will see.

As for the German section—it is more a question of organizing their paper. Naturally, as an emigre movement it has no mass basis. It has *Unser Wort,* which appears regularly. The German sections of Switzerland, Austria, and Czechoslovakia have established a theoretical monthly, *Der Einzige Weg* [The Only Road]. The German section proper is not represented but Walter Held participates in it.[298] I have written to him, asking him why the section does not participate, and I await an answer. The best thing would be to transform the organ into one for all German-speaking comrades, and I believe that is feasible. We have very good comrades, Johre and Fischer.[299] Johre is a very good Marxist. In emigration things are very bad. He is embittered—that's why he refused to issue a theoretical monthly for the whole section—but it's necessary. The comrades are very well educated theoretically. Adolphe, for example, was quite green a few years ago, but now he is an educated Marxist. He writes very well in three languages and knows six other languages. But the misfortune is that Sneevliet, Vereecken, and now Serge refuse to recognize the authority of the IS—because it is composed of young boys and their policy is a thousand times better.

*Cannon:* And Maslow-Fischer?[300]

*Trotsky:* They are Maslow-Fischer. On all questions that provoke a discussion—Russia, Spain, China—they are against our line. They have a paper and they sign their articles "Buntari"—insurgents. They're always insurgents; it's a different mentality they have.

Serge is an excellent poet, a literary man. He writes very well and has a long anarchist past. He remained in Russia for years in Stalinist prisons. He was courageous and honest and did not capitulate, which is a very good characteristic. But he didn't follow the development of the Fourth International. He came with some very vague ideas—with the imagination of a poet—to embrace the whole world: the POUM, the anarchists, us. I received a personal letter from him, referring to Sedov, and in it he mentioned that in spite of differences of a secondary nature, etc., etc., he is with us. Only they are not of a secondary nature. It would be very good if our American friends took the initiative in advising him not to enter into politics. I too will try to write to him—it's a very delicate matter—that I consider him one of the best revolutionists and one of the best writers, but not a politician.

Rosmer is very friendly to us. He was connected with Sneevliet but he is now dissatisfied with him. I don't believe that he will take an active part in the movement but his moral authority can be very useful to us.

It is very hard for our French comrades, they live amidst financial misery—there is absolutely no comparison with our rich Yankees. A one-dollar bill—thirty francs—in the IS, is a fortune.

*Cannon:* We have sent fifty dollars; we have a regular monthly pledge for the IS.

*Trotsky:* Oh, that's very, very good. And they are very economical.

It is necessary to have a subsecretariat in New York, with the perspective that the subsecretariat may become the real secretariat. We do not know the fate of Europe if fascism continues to advance. If it does, then America will be the only place and a subsecretariat is necessary.

# DISCUSSIONS WITH TROTSKY:

## II—Defense Organization and Attitude Toward Intellectuals[301]

### March 24, 1938

*Trotsky:* I agree with Comrade Cannon that we must begin immediately with the forces which are at our disposal and with forces we are sure of and not rely on the unreliable elements; thus a choice will be inevitable by the peripheral groups and the liberals, and even our excellent friend Solow will see that he remains a political celibate.[302] If we are successful—and we will have some success—we will win the vacillating elements by and by. It is absolutely certain now that if we make an amalgam with such elements as Freda Kirchwey—the Stalinists will exert more pressure than even during the Defense Committee—these elements will betray us at the most critical moment, just at the moment when our comrades will need defense, in wartime, say. That is why the committee must be a body that educates and selects its elements and puts them to the test. It cannot resemble those liberals who are pacifists during peacetime and when war comes they are all militarists.

When we discussed the question here during the hearings—we must, of course, recognize that the Defense Committee accomplished its task with success in spite of elements who in the critical moment deserted it—I insisted that it was absolutely necessary to surround the committee with workers' groups. Even if we have only 200 such workers, it's better than 1,000 intellectuals, and if these workers are in contact through their delegates with a [Suzanne] La Follette or a Solow, these latter can't act so capricious; the workers discipline them. Our own comrades should join the organization and sympathizers from trade unions. Every liberal is a bit timid when he meets a worker. As to maneuvers with the Lovestoneites, we can abandon them to their own fate. And we can say to Solow: "You are not satisfied with us, create your own committee and we will enter into a united front with you—if you are capable of creating a committee without us."

*Shachtman:* The fact of the matter is that the letter they sent to us is very interesting—it was signed by about twelve—and had something very significant. They referred to the NPLD, which became one with Socialist labor defense when we joined the SP, and stated: you withdrew from the NPLD and as a result the organization collapsed.[303]

*Cannon:* Oh, yes, Solow threatened to write and expose us in the *Modern Monthly*.

*Trotsky:* The *Modern Monthly?* But I believe that you can win even Solow by pursuing a firm policy.

*Shachtman:* As for the attitude toward the intellectuals as a whole, we saw your reply to Rahv.[304] We are discussing the attitude and the relationship of the party towards the radical intellectuals. The great difficulty rests in the fact that they are not homogeneous. They are not a party: you have a type like Sidney Hook,[305] who nine times out of ten agrees with the party. His differences are on the philosophic field; in the committee Hook defended us. It is interesting that even in some details where he did not agree with us he defended us. Then there are the intellectuals who broke with the CP, and they burned their fingers a bit in that experience. There are isolated intellectuals who joined the party and became party people, like Novack[306] and Morrow, but they are very rare. The other intellectuals are represented by Solow. Then there are intellectuals like [James T.] Farrell, who are with us sometimes and not with us at others, but who signed the call for the defense organization.

To what extent should we make efforts to have them speak on our platform, to what extent should we have them collaborate with us on the magazine, and if they collaborate what are the limits of the differences that may be represented, and to what extent should we collaborate on their reviews, like the *Partisan Review?*

It is almost certain that in the inevitable disintegration in the

Stalinist movement the better elements from the CP will tend to come toward us. What attitude should we have in order to bring them close to us? There is another question which Cannon mentioned the other day, and with which I agree, about the *New International:* Is it feasible, correct, preferable to enlarge the magazine from thirty-two to forty-eight pages and use the additional pages for a literary section—not poetry but a section of literary criticism, book reviews, criticisms of other magazines— and to have such a section edited by such elements as Farrell, Rahv, [James] Rorty? Types like those are thus brought closer to the party, and it gives them more elbow room to express different ideas than in the more political section of the periodical. Would this have a tendency to replace such magazines as *Partisan Review* or to function alongside of *Partisan Review,* which is moving toward us? They don't represent the same elements as Solow, who is moving away from us; they represent the elements who have been with the CP and who are coming close to us.

*Trotsky:* I believe the best situation would be a division of labor between the *New International* and *Partisan Review.* To permit the *New International* to be invaded by Marxist dilettantes, even if only on the question of literature, is not free from a certain danger, for the party will carry the responsibility for their cliques, little squabbles, frictions, etc. It would be a bit dangerous and compromising to introduce this into the *New International.* On the other hand, it would be very good to enlarge the *New International,* if not by eight to twelve pages, at least somewhat, not for literary purposes but to follow the ideological events in the workers' movement. There are many magazines, German magazines, Marxist and semi-Marxist; it would be good to mention them and criticize them. It is more important for us than literary criticism.

The *New International* must embrace everything that can interest the workers' movement. But to give a section of some twelve pages to literature would be too dangerous, especially since we devote too few pages to the natural sciences, to the trade union movement, to Marxist theory. It would be better also to establish collaboration with *Partisan Review,* criticize them in a friendly manner, and not take any responsibility for them. Many of the intellectuals will rather adhere to *Partisan Review* than to the *New International,* and we will consider it as a reserve from which we can attract some from time to time to the party.

If the movement toward us is rapid, especially from the

Stalinists, we must have a period of probation of six to twelve months; for the workers no probation, but for the intellectuals, at least six to twelve months. Then give them specific tasks. For example, we won a group of fifteen trade unionists, put some intellectuals to work with them, to find for them materials, statistics, etc. But the intellectuals have only a consultative voice at meetings. They are the ones to be educated by our worker members. If the trade union workers say that the intellectual is useful, has no pretensions, then we can accept him into the party. If we are to have a workers' party we are to make the intellectuals feel that it is a great honor to be accepted by our party and that they will be accepted only if they are approved by the workers. Then they will understand that it is not an intellectual petty-bourgeois party but a workers' movement, which from time to time can use them for its purpose. Otherwise we can be invaded by intellectuals, and if discussions begin with intellectuals coming from the Stalinists, then the workers will avoid our party. We must establish strict rules about intellectuals coming from other parties. We can have a very elastic and liberal policy toward sympathizers; we can have our representative on their editorial board; we can accept the best of them to work on our papers, for the *Appeal,* if it should appear two or three times a week. But let them remain independent; have a very severe attitude toward the intellectuals who enter our party. If it is a matter of a young intellectual who has been in our movement, that's another thing; a worker is also another thing; but an intellectual with an education gained in the Stalinist party, that's a dangerous element for us.

At the same time we must mercilessly attack types like Max Eastman, Eugene Lyons.[307] We must show them that we take things like Marxist theory very seriously, and we must not permit the impression that Max Eastman can be our friend and at the same time, incidentally, an enemy of socialism.

Then it's important that our youth organization have nuclei in colleges for the young intellectuals. We can hope now that America will produce the best Marxists. The crisis will make the American youth think and the American youth will produce the best elements. Such nuclei are not party members but we can survey them, select them, and win the new generation of Marxists for our movement. Most of the old generation is corrupted by the Stalinists, and people who tolerated Stalinism till today are not very critical. The old generation is demoralized and we must begin with the young.

*Dunne:* What about such a man as Liston Oak?[308]

*Trotsky:* Where is he now?

*Cannon:* He tries to be an independent radical; he speaks everywhere, writes everywhere.

*Trotsky:* Possibly it is best to close our papers to him.

*Shachtman:* The trouble is that he comes, gives me an article, asks that it should be printed in *Socialist Appeal;* then I pick up the *Vanguard* and see an article for them.[309]

*Trotsky:* Yes, we should cut off with him. We did that with Ciliga.[310] You know he collaborated in our Russian *Biulleten.* Then he went to the Mensheviks, and we immediately cut him off.

*Karsner:* It seems to me that we need something for these types, a peripheral organization.

*Trotsky:* Yes, they can work in an organization like the NPLD. We can explain, even when we reject their articles, that the journalist for a workers' paper must be a teacher. How can he, if he himself does not have a program? If he wishes to help in movements like the NPLD, all right, but he cannot work on the paper, cannot pretend to be a teacher before he knows his own way. Even if we lose one or two of them by such a measure we will teach many others, and they will become more serious.

*Cannon:* Organizationally we are in a much better position to follow a firmer policy right now. When we were such a small group and the CP had not yet disintegrated and the SP seemed to move to the left, we did not have such an advantageous position. Now the SP is killed, the Lovestoneites can't expand; all the sectarian groups who tried to fight us are wiped out. In the whole anti-Stalinite field we are now the clearly established leaders. People who used to wonder whether the WP or the SP would prevail,[311] whether the Fieldites, Oehlerites, or we would prevail, know that that has all been settled. Then we have a youth movement, a most significant and promising movement. The Lovestoneites and the SP have no youth movements.

*Trotsky:* From the Communist youth we have new adherents—

that's of the greatest historical importance.

*Cannon:* There is great self-confidence in our youth—the Stalinists are much more on the defensive than ever before.

*Trotsky:* I don't know the structure of our youth organization; it's necessary to have a section for the intellectuals and students and an organization for workers.

*Shachtman:* Our youth is predominantly student; there is now going on an intense discussion on the ways and means of reaching the working youth. There is only one point on which I do not agree with Jim. It is true the Lovestoneites are essentially a New York movement. Nevertheless, there is an unmistakable, though not big, increase in their movement: in Philadelphia they had fifteen members of the Young Communist League. As a result of their collaboration with Homer Martin they have a small organization in Detroit.[312] They are going through an interesting turn in policy. They speak now of the dead Third International. They are orienting along with the whole Brandler movement to the London Bureau.

There is no doubt in my mind that in New York the Lovestoneites have some very serious trade union posts—unfortunately, more serious than ours. It is confined, it is true, to the needle trades, but they have fairly substantial influence there; we have virtually none. If the Lovestoneites announce a meeting, his people boost it in the needle trades section and he gets a few hundred.

Our comrades report a friendlier attitude on the part of the Lovestoneite rank-and-file comrades toward us. One of them said: "We don't support the Comintern now. We are against the Moscow trials; why don't we have a united organization?" You understand of course that I'm not proposing a united organization; the remark is just symptomatic of the feeling in their ranks. We are still stronger, far stronger, than they in our youth movement, in our membership, in our meetings. The question is one of trying to get some of their rank-and-file elements into our organization. The fact that Wolfe came to our meeting is very signficant.

[Here there was some more discussion on work in the Stalinist ranks but the question was left over in connection with the Russian question, which was to be discussed the next day.]

James P. Cannon, Martin Abern, and Max Shachtman in
New York, 1938.

# DISCUSSIONS WITH TROTSKY:

## III—The Russian Question[313]

### March 25, 1938

*Trotsky:* It is very difficult to say something in concrete form about the evolution of social relations in the Soviet Union, something new, because in the past years the data and statistics become more and more false, more fictitious, than ever before. We have absolutely the same frame-ups in the press as in the court. The press is absolutely false concerning the social line-up in the Soviet Union. The last census was ordered burned; I don't know if the news penetrated into the American press; it is of the greatest importance.

In *Revolution Betrayed* I criticized the statistics, the data which had the purpose of hiding the social stratification, the salary of a bureaucrat and of a worker, the salary of an agricultural worker and the manager of the kolkhoz [collective farm], or the number of house servants. I suppose there are no fewer than five million bureaucratic families and aristocrats in the kolkhozes who have domestic servants, and in the towns they have two or three more, including a chauffeur and a nurse for the children; it is a social class of servants in the service of the higher strata and all this is not included in the census report.

A census took place in January, and then the world learned of a special decree to burn it because it was gathered by "Trotskyites, falsifiers, enemies of the people," etc. And the most elementary thing, the most important measure of conditions in the USSR—the size of the population—was not published. Walter Krivitsky gave a full explanation of this in the French press and Miliukov's paper published it too. There was a decrease in the population [growth] to a very high degree. The population grows yearly by three million.

*Shachtman*: When was the last census?

*Trotsky*: In the 1920s, and then too it showed the same increase, and the population was then estimated at 117-18 million. But Krivitsky claims that last year's census showed that there were only 130 million. The result of this is a total catastrophe, because it is the best test of the living conditions of the people. This number indicates that the collectivization, deportation, assassination of tens of thousands of peasants, and then the famine and epidemics in 1931-32, ran into the millions. I believe that this is only part of the truth. This indicates that the normal conditions are very bad, that mortality is very high, that the population grows not by three million yearly but by one million, and this is the balance of the whole period of the "great happiness and prosperity" proclaimed by the five year plan.

In *Revolution Betrayed* I used the data in local papers that Sedov had secured for me—and that made it possible to partially establish the truth. Since that time you cannot find any concrete approximation to reality in the press. In Miliukov's paper in Paris I found a very interesting article, an interview with a semi-Trotskyite—he is not named, but I believe it is Walter Krivitsky, who inclines toward bourgeois democracy—which states that the situation of the peasant is becoming better but the situation of the worker is very bad; that the division of the national income, which is systematically in favor of the peasants, is against the workers. That is true if we mean by peasants the aristocracy in the collective farm—the situation of the administrator is close to the situation of a boss; he is a merchant because the collective farmer has the right to buy and sell at least a part of the material on the market. The administrator is a semifunctionary and a semiboss. His income is very important; and at the same time he is a representative of the GPU. You can imagine what power is concentrated by such an administrator. The situation of the worker on the farm, as in the factories, is totally different, and the relationship of economic forces is changing in favor of the higher stratum, the collective farmer. This signifies an aggravation of the social stratification of society. At the same time the bureaucracy concentrates economic power in its hands.

The Moscow trials are one of the expressions of this process and the political contradictions naturally reflect the social conditions. The bureaucracy has a tremendous fear of the population—a hatred, more than the czar had—because the population has the tradition of two revolutions and is not so illiterate. In the population too there are social antagonisms and political frictions. Very important are the internal antagonisms in the bureaucracy; the trials are a direct expression of that; part of the bureaucracy exterminated another part.

*Shachtman*: Why?

*Trotsky*: Because the discontent of the masses produces different currents even in the bureaucracy. One section says, "Let's make some concessions," and the other says, "No." As everywhere, the pressure of the masses produces disintegration in the ruling caste.

It is hard to give an account of the political differences in the bureaucracy, but there is a good hint of this in the Moscow trials. Some wish to restore capitalism; others are against it. The accusations have a symbolic significance.

Another incident, small in size but extremely instructive, gives us a hint of the differences: the people who broke with Moscow. We had Reiss, Barmin, a representative in Greece, Krivitsky, who was the chief of all military espionage in Germany—there were only four or five of such importance as Krivitsky—and then Butenko, who fled from Rumania to Italy. We know that the diplomatic staff was selected and purged at least ten times during the past few years, and you know how many they recalled and assassinated, and yet after the great purge we have four who have escaped. This percentage is very high; it shows that the centrifugal forces in the bureaucracy are tremendous. These aren't the first four people we met on the street: one was a minister in Greece, another chief of the secret service in Germany, Reiss was of the same level as Krivitsky, almost of the same importance. Now, the direction of these people: Reiss immediately declared for the Fourth International; Barmin remains friendly; Krivitsky is oriented toward bourgeois democracy (he is connected with the Mensheviks, liberals—he broke all connections with us, especially after our son's death—it was for him a pretext); Butenko became a fascist. Only four people, but extremely symptomatic—it is a rainbow of all political colors inside the bureaucracy itself. It explains why Stalin by and by passed from the party machine to the GPU. Now it is not the Political Bureau but Stalin-Yezhov. A member of the Politburo can be named by a defendant in the trial and brought to trial—we have had an example of that in Rudzutak: he was a candidate for the Political Bureau, which I am sure did not name him; he was named by Yezhov.

Then there is an important question for us, which was very widely discussed by the Russian White Guards: whether there are Trotskyists in Russia or not. Even Victor Serge affirmed that Stalin, with reason, terribly exaggerates the number of Trotskyites. The people coming from Russia affirm there are only right tendencies in the Soviet Union—no left tendencies—and Trotskyism is only a phantom. It is both true and not true: it is true that inside the bureaucracy the right tendencies are growing and even becoming fascist. The social basis is different in the masses. But if we take an isolated young bureaucrat—there is a totally fascist type: he has no tradition of the October Revolution. He is only disciplined, disciplined to shoot, disciplined to purge, and disciplined to proceed by trials—all for the glory of the fatherland. The personage of Butenko is very important in the ranks of the bureaucrats. The percentage of such comrades as Reiss is very small. In the masses the tendencies are more elementary but they are directed against the bureaucracy, against the new aristocracy; in this sense they are Trotskyist. They are not real Trotskyists but their attitude coincides in the essential general criticism. It is simply a matter of not being able to establish connections because of the totalitarian regime.

We can see the same thing in Spain very clearly. The working masses in July 1936 developed activity absolutely in our direction but our comrades were very few, and to the degree that the POUM reflected a little the movement in the masses, it was called Trotskyist. That is the reason for the terrible hatred against us.

I believe that individual terrorism is inevitable in Russia. By their trials they provoke terrorism even as the czar did. It is impossible to imagine that of all the thousands shot there will not be some brother or sister who will shoot a bureaucrat. The bureaucrats do everything to abolish the Marxist tradition against terrorism; the tendency of the individual toward terrorism is propagated by the trials. They will reap the harvest they have sown in the form of individual terrorism. That's absolutely possible because there is no party for the mass movement. Terrorist acts are numerous in the provinces. The personage of Nikolaev, who killed Kirov, is unknown—perhaps it was a general reason, a woman. Slutsky, who was chief of the GPU service abroad, told Krivitsky, who asked him for the reason Nikolaev did it, "Don't ask, it is so enigmatic; it's better not to ask." Then he told him that Stalin left for Leningrad and led the first investigation of the assassins in order to give the necessary direction to the investigation.

*Shachtman:* We have discussed it many times among ourselves: how is it that Stalin has not been assassinated in the past period?

*Trotsky:* Two reasons: (1) The honest and serious elements, who don't believe anything can be accomplished by that and say, "Who will replace him? Molotov? Is he any better?" (2) He is personally well guarded. Not one of the czars was so well guarded. But in spite of everything, the pressure from below and from above is so terrible that terrorist explosions must arise in the next period. It is very doubtful that they can change anything fundamentally; they can accelerate the overthrow of the Stalin clique, but in favor of more consciously bourgeois elements who are also not prepared. We can't expect that the revolutionary elements could utilize such an act as we did in the fight against the czar. We rejected the method of the SRs; but every time a terrorist act was committed we declared that we sympathized with the SRs, we explained the reasons, and mobilized the feeling against the czar. Now we have no organization which could do that propaganda.

A war would at first inevitably strengthen the position of Stalin in that the spirit of self-preservation by the bureaucracy and by the people will give new spirit to the Kremlin gang. But during the war it will be the same as in other countries. The disintegration of the regime, and the war, will signify the inevitable death of this regime. What regime will replace it is part of the general question. If the war produces a revolution in the capitalist countries, then the fall of the Stalinist clique will be only a secondary episode in the war—if it should not be immediately replaced by workers' organizations (soviets). If we admit for a moment this hypothesis, that the war should signify the end of our civilization, then naturally Russia will fall. But that's not very probable. The death agony of Stalinism, we wrote—and it is not an exaggeration—also signifies the death of the Comintern. It is not only possible but probable, almost sure, that the Comintern will end its career as a vigorous movement before the definite fall of the Kremlin clique in the Soviet Union. But it depends also to a certain extent on our own policy.

What is the Comintern? It is three streams: (1) the apparatus, which consists of rascals and limited fanatics; (2) then the petty-bourgeois intellectuals attracted during this period; (3) the workers, the most important part of whom were attracted to the party before. Now it is possible that from the first two streams— from the apparatus and the intellectuals—part will go to the

Lovestoneites (it's too difficult for them to approach us, and we hope we will not be too hospitable to the functionaries and intellectuals—I can only repeat that we should establish very strict rules in relation to them, at least a year's probationary period).

As for the third stream, the worker in the Stalinist party, the worker who is not a functionary but a rank-and-file member. If such a worker has remained till today, it is not because he supported the Moscow trials but because a worker has a very profound feeling of devotion, gratitude, psychologically more stable. He remains in the party in spite of everything. In his modesty he says he did not understand. It is possible that the intellectual will separate from the party before the workers. But when the workers will break they will rush to us and not the Lovestoneites.

That's why it is important to have a nucleus in the Stalinist party, to explain and to prepare some elements, and to have information. I believe we don't have such information now, and it is absolutely necessary to establish a general staff to fight the Stalinists in the party, naturally under the direction of our party. To have some young comrades first get information, study the whole Stalinist press from this point of view: what's happening in the party, the conflicts, expulsions, etc. Then to have direct agents in the party, and agents in the good sense. I believe that in their staffs, in the offices, the differentiation between the technical personnel and the big leaders must be very sharp. Browder is a caricature of Stalin—the technical service consists of absolutely insignificant personalities. We can find elements beginning with the janitor. Possibly the janitor is an agent of the GPU; very well, then another of a less responsible post. Then the typists. There are very privileged typists who belong to the service of Browder and the GPU but there are others in completely technical jobs who are totally neglected; we must find our agents there, systematically look for these people, penetrate, find out, enter into friendly contact with the Communist worker, and then by and by create a service of information.

*Cannon:* What kind of comrade would you put as chief of such work? What characteristics should he possess?

*Trotsky:* A comrade like Abern would be good.[314] I never met him, I don't know him, but that's my impression. A comrade who can do systematic work; he must have young collaborators. You can use devoted women with success, but women who are intelligent. They have other methods of entering into connection with Communist worker elements.

*Shachtman:* Do you mean to send people into the CP?

*Trotsky:* Yes, if possible. You know the example in France. The Russian youth came with the purpose of winning over the Socialist youth. They had a secret meeting, but the secretary of Fred Zeller was our comrade. We had discussion with this comrade and asked her to publish the stenogram immediately. She had some second thoughts, but then consented to publish. After we published that, we won all the youth. Zeller hesitated but the rank and file immediately had the warmest sympathy for us, and then Zeller came with them.

*Cannon:* The stenogram was published without authorization?

*Trotsky:* Of course. Then Fred Zeller said, "My secretary was more intelligent than I." A very important question in the fight against the Stalinists is the war question. Here I believe that the Ludlow amendment is very important; it is a touchstone, naturally, not sufficient. And the Ludlow amendment receives ten times greater importance than if the Stalinists favored it. Our first approach was a bit doctrinaire and sectarian, but the best way is to announce openly that we changed our line. The best is to say what is. You can say we changed our program and you can give the example of Lenin on the agrarian question. We play no tricks with the workers. We proposed a more revolutionary fight but we are a small minority. You believe in the Ludlow amendment as a check to big business and the administration; we will go along with you. But the last resolution of the National Committee is equivocal and McKinney's statement that we haven't changed anything is untrue, not frank.[315] You can't make a turn and not tell the masses—then it is no turn. We have to say: "Yes, we made this turn because we wish to be with you." You underline this in such a manner that the Lovestoneites lose the courage to reproach you. And the Lovestoneites are of no importance. It concerns our relationship to the working class—that is of importance.

[Here there was a discussion of what our position should be if the Ludlow amendment is brought back (to Congress) in a revised and watered-down form. Trotsky stated that he would have to see the new one but that in any case we should *now* agitate for the bill as is and point out that already the initiators are incapable of fighting for it.]

*Shachtman:* And you distinguish between our support of the Ludlow amendment and disarmament?

*Trotsky:* Disarmament is absolutely different. That is absolutely false; the proposal for disarmament is fictitious. But with the Ludlow amendment it is different; the workers wish to check the administration. That has nothing to do with the League of Nations, arbitration courts, the talk about disarmament. I propose that we connect the amendment with the demand that the youth have right to vote at the age of eighteen.

*Dunne:* The boys of eighteen will be twenty-one tomorrow when war comes.

*Trotsky:* Yes, yes, that's another argument.

*Cannon:* Do you think that the Stalinist movement has any prospects for further growth in the U.S.—for further expansion? During the past few years they have grown tremendously not only in membership but in ramifications. I'm inclined to think that they have reached their apex in the U.S. unless, in connection with a war, they receive government blessings, as professional patriots and influential police agents against us. But in general the terrible reception the Moscow trials have received and the collapse of the People's Front policy and their foreign policy in general have dealt serious blows to the Stalinist movement in the U.S. There is a much broader attack against Stalinism now. Then also in many trade unions where they have had control a powerful opposition has developed. Now our comrades tell us that the hatred against the Stalinists, in the painters' union for example, where they combine with the worst gangster elements, is growing.

*Shachtman:* There are a few other important symptoms. Two liberal papers in New York, the *World Telegram* and the *Evening Post,* edited by Stern, who is a strong Roosevelt man.[316] But up to yesterday the *Post* especially was very tolerant of the Stalinists, very friendly.

*Trotsky:* I read the dispute between Mayer and the editor on the question of Russia; it was very interesting.

*Shachtman:* Yes, and now the *Post* opened a campaign against the Moscow trials. And the *World Telegram* published the articles of Stolberg and it hurt the Stalinists in the trade unions.

*Trotsky:* I believe the defeat in Spain which is approaching now—the desertion of the government will occur in the coming weeks—will produce the greatest impression and will be directed against the Stalinists. After the defeat the component parts will accuse one another. The hatred in Spain from the Socialists is terrible. Then the volunteers will come back and we will have hundreds of Beattys because the civil war is a great school. Then the People's Front in France, it's a total collapse. Today the cables show that the American stock exchange is again nervous, that it dropped. That signifies the last convulsions of the New Deal policy with all illusions. These three factors—the defeat in Spain, the defeat of the People's Front in France, and, with your permission, the bankruptcy of the New Deal—signify the mortal blow for the democrats. Naturally it depends also on our activity. After the World War the Second International seemed to be totally dead and during the first years the Third International grew and grew. And I hope now . . .

*Karsner:* The Third International grew when there was victory. But wherever the workers look now there are defeats. The workers are disillusioned not only with Stalinism but with Communism. I wonder whether these hundreds of people from Spain will come to us or leave the movement.

*Trotsky:* That's absolutely correct. It gives us great difficulties. The selection of our cadres is different, occurs in a different period. Then the cadres adhered to a victorious state, now they adhere only to a revolutionary program; our development is much slower than the Comintern. On the other hand, we will have a new generation. We must not forget the new generation, which didn't pass through the Stalinists. The whole question for us is to find the connection between our cadres and the workers. The young generation is not exhausted, not tired, that's why it's symptomatic that we won the young from the CP and the Communist youth is beginning to turn to us. That is the first important move toward us and we will grow.

# ROOSEVELT'S STATEMENT ON TROTSKYISTS IN RUSSIA[317]

## March 29, 1938

On March 25, President Roosevelt announced to press representatives that the United States remains, as formerly, a land of refuge for all those subjected to political or religious persecution: for instance, "Catholics in Barcelona; anti-fascists in Italy; Trotskyists in Russia; Jews, Protestants and Catholics in Germany and Austria. . . ."

Every thinking person will understand the significance of the reference in this connection to the "Trotskyists in Russia." No one will suspect the president of the United States of sympathy for so-called "Trotskyism." But it is not a question of this. Neither is it a question merely of the simple right of asylum. For if the Trotskyists were but one percent of what Moscow justice pictures them to be they could not lay claim to the right of asylum. No country would open the gates to people who under cover of false political slogans occupy themselves with espionage, sabotage, poisoning, and crimes of a like nature. In addition, during the last two trials, the Moscow accusers tried especially to prove that "Trotskyists" are in alliance with Japan against the United States. If in spite of all this the president of the U.S. has mentioned "Trotskyists" among those persecuted political currents which can count upon the right of asylum in the U.S., that merely means that Mr. Roosevelt does not believe the Moscow accusations. The political and moral weight of this fact is the more significant in that Mr. Roosevelt expresses in the present instance the firmly crystallized conviction of the overwhelming majority of civilized humanity.

# LETTER TO
# THE LEAGUE OF NATIONS[318]

## March 31, 1938

On October 22, 1936, through my Norwegian attorney, the late Michael Puntervold, I had the honor of appealing to you in a letter, receipt of which you were kind enough to acknowledge in your reply No. 3A-15105-15085. I am not informed as to the present status of the question of creating a tribunal against terrorists under the League of Nations. I do not know whether it already exists, or whether it is expected to start working in the near future. In any case, I consider it my duty not only to repeat the considerations which I had the honor of bringing to your attention nearly a year and a half ago, but also to supplement them with a new, fully concrete proposal.

It was the Soviet government which initiated the creation of a tribunal against terrorists under the League of Nations. The people's commissar of foreign affairs for the USSR, Mr. M. Litvinov, displayed at the League of Nations sessions an especially keen and, as it might then have appeared, an inexplicable interest in this question. However, to informed people the matter was clear even then. Preparing the trial against "Trotskyist terrorists" over a number of years, the GPU was fully convinced that the monotonous "confessions" of the accused would persuade the whole world, including the future tribunal of the League of Nations, as to the correctness of the accusations and offer the opportunity of obtaining the legal deliverance of myself and my son Leon Sedov into the hands of the GPU. This was the immediate and direct aim of Moscow's initiative on the question of an international tribunal.

In my letter of October 22, 1936, I expressed the thought that a tribunal dedicated to the defense of governments in various countries from terrorists cannot, on the other hand, refuse defense to private individuals if they, because of purely political

311

motives, are falsely accused of terrorism by an ill-intentioned government. I therefore considered then, and still consider, that I have the right to plead for an examination of my case by the future tribunal under the League of Nations, in spite of the fact that the Soviet government has apparently definitely renounced the thought of seeking help in Geneva against my alleged "conspiracies."

The impartial International Commission headed by the well-known American philosopher and educator, John Dewey, after almost nine months of work, came to a final conclusion in regard to the Moscow trials, declaring them deliberate frame-ups. Armed with numerous and irrefutable proofs which are at the disposal of the above-mentioned commission, I am ready at any time to appear before the tribunal of the League of Nations in order once more and definitively to convert my accusers into accused.

But I make bold to think that by this time it is already impossible to stop merely at the first step. During the last half year, the world has been witness to a series of *actual* terrorist acts committed in various countries according to a general plan and with undoubted singleness of purpose. I have in mind not the legal and extralegal murders in the USSR, where the question, thus or otherwise, concerns the legalized actions of the state apparatus, but acts of downright banditry on the international arena.

The murder of Ignace Reiss, former agent of the GPU, on September 4, 1937, near Lausanne, Switzerland, can in no sense be viewed as a legal act. The Swiss and French authorities have complete, exhaustive data unmasking the real organizer of this murder: the GPU, the secret police in the USSR.

During the judicial investigation of the murder of Ignace Reiss it was disclosed in passing that this same gang, in conducting systematic espionage upon my son, Leon Sedov, attempted to kill him at Mulhouse in January 1937. What relationship the GPU had to the sudden death of my son on February 16 of this year is still subject to general investigation.

Among the documents of the chief murderer of Ignace Reiss, a so-called Rossi, who succeeded in fleeing in time, proofs were found of his attempts to enter Mexico for purposes not difficult to determine on the basis of the aforementioned circumstances. The actual name of this professional murderer in the service of the GPU is Roland Abbiatte.

Witnesses of unimpeachable authority can relate before the tribunal the preparation by GPU agents of terroristic acts against me during my sojourn in Europe and Mexico. I can further cite the kidnaping in Spain of my former collaborator, Erwin Wolf, a Czechoslovakian citizen who has disappeared without a trace; the terrorist acts in Spain against the Catalonian revolutionist, Andres Nin; the Austrian emigre, Kurt Landau;[319] the son of a Russian emigre, Mark Rein; and a number of other individuals have received worldwide publicity. Even that part of the legal and extralegal investigation which has been accessible to public opinion to date is completely sufficient to warrant the intervention of an international tribunal against a centralized Mafia of terrorists working on the territory of several states other than their own.

With the help of documents, testimony of witnesses, and irrefutable political considerations I take it upon myself to prove what public opinion has been in no doubt of for some time: that is, that the head of this criminal band is Joseph Stalin, general secretary of the Communist Party of the USSR.

Inasmuch as the people's commissar of foreign affairs of the USSR, Mr. Litvinov, has very eloquently insisted upon the necessity for governments to mutually obligate themselves to extradite terrorists, he, we can hope, will not refuse to employ his influence to place the above-mentioned Joseph Stalin, as head of the international terrorist band, at the disposal of the tribunal under the League of Nations.

For my part, I am ready to place all my energy, information, documents, and personal connections at the disposal of the tribunal in order that the truth may be fully disclosed.

# FOR THE REORGANIZATION
# OF THE MEXICAN SECTION[320]

## April 15, 1938

Dear Comrade Cannon:

May I make some proposals concerning the Mexican "situation"?

1. It would be good if our party addressed the British Labour Party, the trade unions, the Independent Labour Party, and so on, with the proposition to oppose vigorously Chamberlain's policy in the oil matter.[321] Our party could take the leading role in this affair.

2. Your participation in the meeting here had one "unexpected" result. Galicia, in the name of the revived League, published a manifesto in which he attacked Cardenas for his policy of compensating the expropriated capitalists, and posted this manifesto principally on the walls of the Casa del Pueblo.[322] This is the "policy" of these people.

I don't know whether they have answered your last letter about the expulsion of the Fernandez group. In any case, they continue to call themselves a section of the Fourth International. In my opinion the Pan-American Conference should not recognize them but appoint a commission for the reorganization of the Mexican section. But it is necessary to send at least one responsible comrade who could remain here at least two or three months. The sooner you send him the better.[323] You know that the project of a Spanish theoretical magazine should not, at least in the beginning, be an official organ of the Fourth International, but an organ of a bloc of the Fourth International people with some sympathizers such as the Zamora brothers and others, in order to safeguard the magazine from the attempts of the local groups and cliques. It should be organized not as a Mexican but as a Latin American magazine under the official control of the Pan-American Committee, which can appoint Diego [Rivera] and its representative (Curtiss) as editors of the magazine. Such a decision is very urgent.[324]

My best greetings,
Hansen [Trotsky]

# TOWARD A GENUINE BRITISH SECTION[325]

## April 15, 1938

Dear Comrade Sumner:

I haven't written you for a long time but you understand the reasons. We received your cable and your letter and both Natalia and I warmly appreciate your friendly feelings. . . .

I don't know whether you have been informed about the trip of Comrade Cannon to Europe and in the first place to London. It is possible that Comrade Shachtman will also go with Cannon. I ascribe great importance to this trip especially for things in England. Cannon and Shachtman are our best comrades in the States, with a broad outlook and with serious organizational experience. One of their tasks is to meet all the English groups who belong or wish to belong to the Fourth International and to try to normalize the situation among these groups in order to help the crystallization of a genuine British section of the Fourth International. I hope that you and your group will give Cannon and Shachtman your full cooperation in their task.

I doubt that they can remain in London for more than a week, possibly less. It is absolutely necessary to use this time as well as possible. The best procedure it seems to me would be to enter now into connection with the other groups and even to establish a technical committee with the purpose of arranging the meeting of the American friends with each of the British groups separately, and then with all of them together. You will surely receive in time a communication specifying the precise day of arrival of the American friends in London. I should be very glad to have a note from you about the preparation for the discussions with "C" and "S" and also later about the results of these discussions.

I receive your publications. Thanks. But I write today only on the "C-S" trip.

Best greetings from Natalia and me to you and all friends.

Yours fraternally,

Leon Trotsky

P.S.—I have received a letter from Frank Maitland in the name of the "Revolutionary Socialist Party." He wishes to publish my article on Spain as a pamphlet and is ready to do it in cooperation with one of our British groups.[326] The evolution of his party, he writes me, is totally in the direction of the Fourth International. Are you in contact with them? I am writing to Maitland today.

# LETTER TO JAMES P. CANNON[327]

## April 15, 1938

Dear Comrade Cannon:

1. We are sending you copies of letters concerning your trip to London. I hope that you will inform them in time so that they can prepare the meetings and so that you can use your time in London with full efficiency.

2. Please arrange to send Maitland a copy of my article on Spain, but not the printed copy in the *Socialist Appeal* (there are some errors), rather a corrected typewritten copy.

3. We have sent you the transitional program draft and a short statement about the labor party. Without your visit to Mexico, I could never have written the program draft because I learned during the discussions many important things which permitted me to be more explicit and concrete. I should be very glad to have the opinion of the friends upon the document.

4. I am enclosing some small corrections to the text of the program draft.

5. I am now finishing the article "Their Morals and Ours." In two days we will begin the translation. This article will be my swan song for at least half a year. I am going to work on my books and will reduce my collaboration on the press and even my correspondence to the strictest minimum.

6. I must mention that Comrade Pincus was and remains very helpful to us in our work here especially in the editing of translations and I am sure he will be very useful to our movement in the States.

7. We heard vaguely about your automobile accident and were very sorry about this disagreeable complication to your trip. The friends assured me in any case that none of you were hurt personally. All of us hope that this disagreeable accident will not darken the remembrance of your sojourn in Mexico. We remember your visit with the warmest feelings.

8. I am a bit astonished about the kind of publicity given to Eastman's letter in the *New International.* The publication of the letter is all right, but the prominence given it on the cover, combined with the silence about Eastman's article in *Harpers,* seems to me a bit compromising for the *New International.* Many people will interpret this fact as our willingness to close our eyes on principles when friendship is concerned.[328]

9. In my Kronstadt article there is a very disagreeable error on page 106, the last paragraph. It is printed: "conscious of their importance on the arena . . ." and so on. It should read: "conscious of their impotence on the arena." It would be well to annotate this sense-distorting error in the next issue.

                              Best regards to all friends,
                              Yours,
                              L.D. [Trotsky]

# THOUGHTS ON
# THE FRENCH SECTION[329]

## April 19, 1938

Dear Friends:

Personally we had not sufficiently discussed here the French question. This is now the most important of all. The development of our French section is not satisfactory. They do not communicate any statistics to us, which is a bad sign in itself. The newspaper does not appear regularly. The same is true of the so-called monthly. They have not a single man with organizational capacities. At the same time they have suffered severe blows through Stalinist or fascist or Stalinist-fascist conspiracy against them.

I know practically nothing about the real state of the *Commune* organization, but their paper is incomparably richer. Until last month it appeared weekly; now it appears in small format *three times a week*. They published a thick "theoretical" symposium and numerous leaflets and pamphlets. This competition is causing general confusion and is extremely prejudicial to our section. We can't simply ignore the *Commune* organization. We must help our section vanquish the *Commune* organization. It can be done only by a very thorough combination of positive and negative measures.

*Concerning our section*

1. A special commission with your participation should verify their organization, the administration and bookkeeping, especially that of both publications.

2. Very concrete organizational measures should be demanded as a condition for international help to them.

3. The French section should be put in the center of attention of the whole International. (It is my opinion that it is more important now to send money to France than to China.)

4. If Sh. [Shachtman] remains in Europe he should devote the greater part of his time to the French question, especially to the theoretical monthly.

*Concerning the* Commune *group*

1. They will surely appeal in one form or another to the conference. It would be good to provoke such an appeal some weeks prior to the conference. We should not repulse them in advance. On the contrary, we should show them that we are ready to reconsider relations—of course, on the basis of certain principles and conditions.

2. Here also we must begin with the verification of their bookkeeping, but naturally from another point of view. We must explain to them that the elimination of every suspicion in this respect is for us as an international organization an imperative condition for any further discussions. If they oppose this verification in spite of our insistence, they doom themselves: we will then publish the news that the discussions were interrupted because they could not tolerate international control of their financial sources. This would be for them a mortal blow. That is why they would not reject intervention of a control commission if it is at all possible for them to bare their own "commercial secrets." This point seems to me to be of the greatest importance and has great advantage for us in either case: whether they accept or reject our control.

3. If the control commission establishes that *La Commune* exists only thanks to the commercial affairs of M. [Raymond Molinier], as I suppose, the commission should declare, on the basis of all previous decisions, that we cannot tolerate a situation where a leading comrade makes money through dubious affairs and then determines policy by means of this money. In my opinion the decision should be that M. must abandon work in France for at least two years. If he or they reject this proposition we should make public the fact that the discussions were interrupted as a result of their refusal to separate revolutionary politics from the commercial affairs of M. Such a declaration in the name of the international organization would deal a mortal blow to them.

4. If they accept both above-mentioned conditions, the situation would be very favorable. We then enter into political and organizational discussions. We condemn their organizational methods. We condemn their political errors, intrigues, etc. We create, under the IS, a commission with the purpose of promoting

unification. If Sh. remains in Europe, he should be chairman of this commission.

I believe it would be the best way of helping the French section. For the transitional period, after the acceptance of all above-mentioned conditions, we could, until the merger, accept the *Commune* organization as a sympathizing group. It would give the IS more right and possibilities to intervene in the internal life of this organization.

The whole procedure is very delicate. That is why absolute secrecy of the whole plan is necessary. At the same time we should be very firm toward our leading French comrades who will surely reject in advance every maneuver on a large scale as a "capitulation," etc. We must make them understand that we are not ready any longer to tolerate the miserable state of the French section in such a decisive political situation.

Please let me know if you agree with the general line of this plan.

Comradely yours,
Hansen [Trotsky]

# MORE ON EUROPEAN PROBLEMS[330]

## April 20, 1938

Dear Friends:

In my last letter about the French question I forgot to mention what to do personally with M. in case they accept our propositions. You could propose to him that he go to the States for two years with the perspective of being readmitted to the Fourth International after a certain test period.

It could be possible to send him with the same purpose to Belgium, especially in view of the fact that Vereecken seems to be in an unofficial alliance with him. But Brussels is too near Paris and from there M. would surely intervene in the inner life of the French section. I believe that it is necessary to act in this respect openly and firmly without important concessions.

We have received a letter from Held. His legal position in Norway is not very stable, especially with the approach of the "national" government. His plan is to go for some months to France to arrange there the regular appearance of *Unser Wort* and then try to go to the States directly or via Mexico. Held is a very valuable comrade. His presence in Paris would be very useful to C. [Cannon] in view of his knowledge of different languages, of the European situation, and of his reasonable approach to every question. It seems to me that C. should write to Held and fix a rendezvous with him.

Held belongs to the Johre-Fischer group but at the same time he is collaborating on *Der Einzige Weg*. He could be very helpful to you in settling the German question.

An international youth conference in connection with the general conference could be organized very well with the participation of Held. For the new IS he is one of the best candidates.

I believe therefore that he should remain in France as long as possible (if he can now enter France). To have him in the States is a luxury, in Europe a necessity. Of course when the soil becomes too hot under his feet he should go to the new world.

Yours,

Hansen [Trotsky]

# THE MEXICAN
# OIL EXPROPRIATIONS[331]

## A Challenge to the British Labour Party

### April 23, 1938

The Editor
*Daily Herald*
London

Dear Sir:

In the vocabulary of all civilized nations there exists the word "cynicism." As a classic example of brazen cynicism, the British government's defense of the interests of a clique of capitalist exploiters should be introduced into all encyclopedias. I am therefore not mistaken if I say that world public opinion awaits the voice of the British Labour Party regarding the scandalous role of British diplomacy in the question of the expropriation of the Eagle joint-stock oil company by the Mexican government.

The juridical side of the question is clear to a child. With the aim of exploiting the natural wealth of Mexico, the British capitalists placed themselves under the protection and at the same time under the control of Mexican laws and the Mexican authorities. No one compelled Messrs. Capitalists to do this, either by military force or through diplomatic notes. They acted entirely voluntarily and consciously. Now Mr. Chamberlain and Lord Halifax wish to force mankind into believing that the British capitalists have pledged themselves to recognize Mexican laws only within those limits where they find it necessary. Moreover, it accidentally occurs that the completely "impartial" interpretation of the Mexican laws by Chamberlain-Halifax coincides exactly with the interpretation of the interested capitalists.

The British government cannot, however, deny that only the *Mexican* government and the Supreme Court of the country are competent to interpret the laws of Mexico. To Lord Halifax, who nourishes warm sympathies for the laws and courts of Hitler, the Mexican laws and courts may seem unjust. But who gave the British government the right to control the inner politics and legal procedure of an independent state? This question already contains part of the answer: the British government, accustomed to command hundreds of millions of colonial slaves and semislaves, is trying to fit those same methods also to Mexico. Having encountered courageous resistance, it instructs its lawyers hurriedly to invent arguments in which juridical logic is replaced by imperialist cynicism.

The economic and social side of the problem is as clear as its juridical side. The executive committee of your party would, in my opinion, act correctly if it created a special commission for studying what British, and in general foreign, capital has contributed to Mexico and what it has extracted. Such a commission could within a short period present to the British public the stunning balance sheet of imperialist exploitation!

A small clique of foreign magnates, in the full sense of the word, pumps out the living sap of Mexico as well as of a series of other backward or weak countries. The solemn speeches about foreign capital contributing "civilization," about its assisting in the development of national economy, and so forth, are the sheerest pharisaism. The question, in actuality, concerns plundering the natural wealth of the country. Nature required many millions of years in order to deposit gold, silver, and oil in the subsoil of Mexico. The foreign imperialists wish to plunder these riches in the shortest possible time, making use of cheap labor power and the protection of their diplomacy and their fleet.

Visit any center of the mining industry: hundreds of millions of dollars, extracted by foreign capital from the earth, have given nothing, nothing whatever, to the culture of the country; neither highways nor buildings nor good development of the cities. Even the premises of the companies themselves often resemble barracks. Why, indeed, should one spend Mexican oil, Mexican gold, Mexican silver on the needs of faraway and alien Mexico, when with the profits obtained it is possible to build palaces, museums, theaters in London or in Monaco? Such are the civilizers! In the place of historical riches they leave shafts in the Mexican soil and ill health among the Mexican workers.

The notes of the British government refer to "international

law." Even irony powerlessly drops its hands in the face of this argument. About what kind of international law are we talking? Evidently about the law which triumphed in Ethiopia and to which the British government is now preparing to give its sanction. Evidently about that same law which the airplanes and tanks of Mussolini and Hitler are already announcing in Spain for the second year with the British government's invariable support.

The latter held endless conversations about the evacuation of foreign "volunteers" from Spain. Naive public opinion long thought this meant the halting of intervention by the foreign fascist bandits. Actually the British government demanded of Mussolini only one thing: that he remove his armies from Spain only *after* he guaranteed the victory of Franco. In this case, as in all others, the problem consisted not in defending "international law" or "democracy" but in safeguarding the interests of British capitalists in the Spanish mining industry from possible attempts on the part of Italy.

In Mexico, the British government carries on basically the same politics as in Spain—passively in relation to Spain, actively in Mexico. We are now witnessing the first steps of this activity. What will be its further development? No one can yet foretell. Chamberlain himself does not yet know. One thing we can affirm with assurance: the *further development* of the attempts of British imperialism against the independence of Mexico will to a great degree depend upon the conduct of the British working class. Here it is impossible to evade the issue by resort to indefinite formulas. Firm resoluteness is necessary to paralyze the criminal hand of imperialist violence. I therefore finish as I began: world public opinion awaits the firm voice of the British Labour Party!

L. Trotsky

P.S.—Several imperialist newspapers have attempted to represent me . . . as the initiator of the expropriation. Such nonsense does not even deserve refutation. I, a private person, enjoying the hospitality of this country, have learned only from the papers all the stages of the struggle of the foreign capitalists against the Mexican laws. But this was completely sufficient to form an opinion. To state this opinion aloud is the elementary duty of every participant in the liberating struggle of the proletariat.

L.T.

# EUROPE OR SAN FRANCISCO?[332]

## May 12, 1938

Dear Jim:

1. It is not easy for me to give advice on the alternative, Europe or San Francisco. But I believe that in spite of everything, you could be replaced by other comrades with more success in California than in Europe. I do not doubt that the situation on the Coast is critical and important; but it is, nevertheless, only a local situation, which tomorrow will be repeated in other parts of the States. The question in Europe has a universal character: it is possibly the last meeting before the war; the conference will also give the American section reinforced authority for its action in California as elsewhere. That is why it is my hypothetical opinion that you could send to Frisco such people as Widick or Dobbs or both[333] and that you go to Europe as quickly as possible. You see that I conclude more categorically than I began but it seems to me that it is the only one correct conclusion.

2. We haven't as yet heard a single word concerning the Pan-American Conference and especially its decision on the Mexican question. What is the score? We are all very disquieted about your silence on this matter. Did you forget your obligations? The Galicia clique began a systematic campaign and published a bulletin directed against Diego Rivera and all of us. The lack of a formal decision and of a representative of the Pan-American Secretariat paralyzes our friends here in every respect and can produce the worst results. Please answer *immediately* on this question.

3. We haven't as yet received the resolutions of the last plenum. But as we understand, it accepted the turn on the labor party question.[334] If so, it is necessary in my opinion immediately to utilize this turn in respect to the Lovestoneites. Some of our comrades seem to be especially embarrassed by the fact that we may have the appearance of capitulating before the Lovestone-

ites. This appearance can be used with the purpose of sapping the last fundamental base on this matter. We don't deny it. It is purely a tactical question. The situation changed and our attitude also. "But what is now the reason for *your* opposition to the Fourth International?" and so on. Such an attitude could in one way or another eliminate this obstacle on our path.

4. Suzanne La Follette writes me in a personal way that she is looking for money in order to create a weekly for combatting the *Nation* and the *New Republic*. She adds also that she reads with great interest and "profit" the publications of our party. It is an interesting symptom.

Fraternally,
Hansen [Trotsky]

# FOR AN IMMEDIATE
# TRIP TO EUROPE[335]

## May 16, 1938

Dear Jim:

The latest news from Europe shows that your immediate trip to Europe is absolutely necessary. Vereecken seems to be very active in his factional work on the international arena. After his attempt to take the side of Eiffel against the Mexicans, he is now trying to take the side of the Mexicans against Diego.[336] The announcement of the conference put all the differences on the agenda and inevitably gave them an acute character. Your absence now from Europe will facilitate the work of the disrupters and in the last analysis create a difficult situation for the American party. The more I think about the question the more it becomes clear to me that in the next two months the fate of the American party will be decided not on the Pacific Coast but in Europe. You should go there at any price.

The lack of decisions of the Pan-American Conference is a terrible handicap here and in certain respects a rehearsal of what can happen in Europe if the matter is not carried to a conclusion.

After your intervention here all the questions developed an acute character. Now Diego has an expectant attitude and Galicia is working nationally as well as internationally. This situation is absolutely intolerable. Your immediate answer by airmail on this whole question is absolutely necessary.

Fraternally,

Hansen [Trotsky]

# ON C.L.R. JAMES[337]

## May 17, 1938

Dear Jim:

I enclose an excerpt of a letter from Alexander, who is now in France, not in England, but connected with the English organization. This letter gives a picture of the state of the English groups. The very important point concerns James. In his book, which I unfortunately never read, he criticizes Comrade T[rotsky] very sharply from an organizational point of view, as I have been told by a friend. I suppose that this criticism at that time was a theoretical justification of his own policy toward the Independent Labour Party, but that is not of importance. I suppose that he now considers his own criticism as a hindrance to friendly collaboration with us. That was one of the reasons why I insisted that you invite him to the Pan-American Conference (a proposition you accepted), but it seems that this decision like some others was forgotten during the trip from Mexico to New York. In any case it is very important to convince James that his criticisms are not considered by any one of us as an item of hostility or an obstacle to friendly collaboration in the future. It would be very bad if under the influence of this fact and some others he finished with a rupture from us and an alliance with Field, with whom he is, as Alexander affirms, already in contact.

I should also add that some British comrades at one time had the impression of having been treated a bit without respect by Comrade Shachtman during his visit to London. They haven't forgotten it even to this day. We can regret such a mood but it is necessary to reckon with it in the future.

We wait with the greatest impatience a letter from you concerning your trip to Europe.

Comradely,
Hansen [Trotsky]

# LEARN TO THINK[338]

## A Friendly Suggestion
## to Certain Ultraleftists

### May 22, 1938

Certain professional ultraleft phrasemongers are attempting at all cost to "correct" the theses of the secretariat of the Fourth International on war in accordance with their own ossified prejudices. They especially attack that part of the theses which states that in all imperialist countries the revolutionary party, while remaining in irreconcilable opposition to its own government in time of war, should nevertheless mold its practical politics in each country to the internal situation and to the international groupings, sharply differentiating a workers' state from a bourgeois state, a colonial country from an imperialist country.

"The proletariat of a capitalist country that finds itself in an alliance with the USSR* [state the theses] must retain fully and completely its irreconcilable *hostility to the imperialist government of its own country.* In this sense its policy will not differ from that of the proletariat in a country fighting against the USSR. But in the nature of practical actions considerable differences may arise depending on the concrete war situation"

---

*We can leave aside here the question of the class character of the USSR. We are interested in the question of policy in relation to a workers' state *in general* or to a colonial country fighting for its independence. So far as the class nature of the USSR is concerned we can incidentally recommend to the ultraleftists that they gaze upon themselves in the mirror of A. Ciliga's book, *In the Country of the Big Lie.* The ultraleft author, completely lacking any Marxist schooling, pursues his idea to the very end, that is, to liberal-anarchic abstraction.

["War and the Fourth International," in *Writings 33-34*].

The ultraleftists consider this postulate, the correctness of which has been confirmed by the entire course of development, as the starting point of . . . social patriotism.* Since the attitude toward imperialist governments should be "the same" in all countries, these strategists ban any distinctions beyond the boundaries of their own imperialist country. Theoretically, their mistake arises from an attempt to construct fundamentally different bases for wartime and peacetime policies.

Let us assume that rebellion breaks out tomorrow in the French colony of Algeria under the banner of national independence and that the Italian government, motivated by its own imperialist interests, prepares to send weapons to the rebels. What should the attitude of the Italian workers be in this case? I have purposely taken an example of rebellion against a *democratic* imperialism with intervention on the side of the rebels from a *fascist* imperialism. Should the Italian workers prevent the shipping of arms to the Algerians? Let any ultraleftists dare answer this question in the affirmative. Every revolutionist, together with the Italian workers and the rebellious Algerians, would spurn such an answer with indignation. Even if a general maritime strike broke out in fascist Italy at the same time, even in this event the strikers should make an exception in favor of those ships carrying aid to the colonial slaves in revolt; otherwise they would be no more than wretched trade unionists—not proletarian revolutionists.

At the same time, the French maritime workers, even though not faced with any strike whatsoever, would be compelled to exert every effort to block the shipment of ammunition intended for use against the rebels. Only such a policy on the part of the Italian and French workers constitutes the policy of revolutionary internationalism.

Does this not signify, however, that the Italian workers moderate their struggle in this event against the fascist regime? Not in the slightest. Fascism renders "aid" to the Algerians only in order to weaken its enemy, France, and to lay its rapacious hand on her colonies. The revolutionary Italian workers do not forget this for a single moment. They call upon the Algerians not to trust their treacherous "ally" and at the same time continue

---

*Mrs. Simone Weil even writes that our position is the same as Plekhanov's in 1914-18.[339] Simone Weil, of course, has a right to understand nothing. Yet it is not necessary to abuse this right.

their own irreconcilable struggle against fascism, "the main enemy in their own country." Only in this way can they gain the confidence of the rebels, help the rebellion, and strengthen their own revolutionary position.

If the above is correct in peacetime, why does it become false in wartime? Everyone knows the postulate of the famous German military theoretician, Clausewitz, that war is the continuation of politics by other means. This profound thought leads naturally to the conclusion that the struggle against war is but the continuation of the general proletarian struggle during peacetime. Does the proletariat in peacetime reject and sabotage *all* the acts and measures of the bourgeois government? Even during a strike which embraces an entire city, the workers take measures to insure the delivery of food to their own districts, make sure that they have water, that the hospitals do not suffer, etc. Such measures are dictated not by opportunism in relation to the bourgeoisie but by concern for the interests of the strike itself, by concern for the sympathy of the submerged city masses, etc. These elementary rules of proletarian strategy in peacetime retain full force in time of war as well.

An irreconcilable attitude against bourgeois militarism does not signify at all that the proletariat *in all cases* enters into a struggle against its own "national" army. At least the workers would not interfere with soldiers who are extinguishing a fire or rescuing drowning people during a flood; on the contrary, they would help side by side with the soldiers and fraternize with them. And the question is not exhausted merely by cases of natural calamities. If the French fascists should make an attempt today at a coup d'etat and the Daladier government found itself forced to move troops against the fascists, the revolutionary workers, while maintaining their complete political independence, would fight against the fascists alongside of these troops. Thus in a number of cases the workers are forced not only to permit and tolerate, but actively to support the practical measures of the bourgeois government.

In ninety cases out of a hundred the workers actually place a minus sign where the bourgeoisie places a plus sign. In ten cases however they are forced to fix the same sign as the bourgeoisie but with their own seal, in which is expressed their mistrust of the bourgeoisie. The policy of the proletariat is not at all automatically derived from the policy of the bourgeoisie, bearing only the opposite sign (this would make every sectarian a master strategist). No, the revolutionary party must each time orient itself *independently* in the internal as well as in the external situation, arriving at those decisions which correspond best to the interests of the proletariat. This rule applies just as much to the war period as to the period of peace.

Let us imagine that in the next European war the Belgian proletariat conquers power sooner than the proletariat of France. Undoubtedly Hitler will try to crush proletarian Belgium. In order to cover up its own flank, the French bourgeois government might find itself compelled to help the Belgian workers' government with arms. The Belgian soviets of course reach for these weapons with both hands. But, actuated by the principle of defeatism, perhaps the French workers ought to block their bourgeoisie from shipping arms to proletarian Belgium? Only direct traitors or out-and-out idiots can reason thus.

The French bourgeoisie could send arms to proletarian Belgium only out of fear of the greatest military danger and only in expectation of later crushing the proletarian revolution with their own weapons. To the French workers, on the contrary, proletarian Belgium is the greatest support in the struggle against their own bourgeoisie. The outcome of the struggle would be decided, in the final analysis, by the relationship of forces, into which correct policies enter as a very important factor. The revolutionary party's first task is to utilize the contradiction between two imperialist countries, France and Germany, in order to save proletarian Belgium.

Ultraleft scholastics think not in concrete terms but in empty abstractions. They have transformed the idea of defeatism into such a vacuum. They can see vividly neither the process of war nor the process of revolution. They seek a hermetically sealed formula which excludes fresh air. But a formula of this kind can offer no orientation for the proletarian vanguard.

To carry the class struggle to its highest form—civil war—this is the task of defeatism. But this task can be solved only through the revolutionary mobilization of the masses, that is, by widening, deepening, and sharpening those revolutionary methods which constitute the content of class struggle in "peacetime." The proletarian party does not resort to artificial methods, such as burning warehouses, setting off bombs, wrecking trains, etc., in order to bring about the defeat of its own government. Even if it were successful on this road, the military defeat would not at all lead to revolutionary success, a success which can be assured only by the independent movement of the proletariat. Revolutionary defeatism signifies only that in its class struggle the proletarian party does not stop at any "patriotic" considerations, since defeat of its own imperialist government, brought about or hastened by the revolutionary movement of the masses, is an incomparably *lesser evil* than victory gained at the price of national unity, that is, the political prostration of the proletariat. Therein lies the complete meaning of defeatism and this meaning is entirely sufficient.

The methods of struggle change, of course, when the struggle enters the openly revolutionary phase. Civil war is a war, and in this aspect has its particular laws. In civil war, bombing warehouses, wrecking trains, and all other forms of military "sabotage" are inevitable. Their appropriateness is decided by purely military considerations—civil war continues revolutionary politics but by other—precisely military—means.

However, during an imperialist war there may be cases where a revolutionary party will be forced to resort to military-technical means, though they do not as yet follow directly from the revolutionary movement in their *own* country. Thus, if it is a question of sending arms or troops against a workers' government or a rebellious colony, not only such methods as boycott and strike, but direct military sabotage may become entirely practical and obligatory. Resorting or not resorting to such measures will be a matter of practical possibilities. If the Belgian workers, conquering power in wartime, have their own military agents on German soil, it would be the duty of these agents not to hesitate at any technical means in order to stop Hitler's troops. It is absolutely clear that the revolutionary German workers also are duty-bound (if they are able) to perform this task in the interests of the Belgian revolution, irrespective of the general course of the revolutionary movement in Germany itself.

Defeatist policy, that is, the policy of irreconcilable class struggle in wartime, cannot consequently be "the same" in all countries, just as the policy of the proletariat cannot be the same in peacetime. Only the Comintern of the epigones has established a regime in which the parties of all countries break into march simultaneously with the left foot. In struggle against this bureaucratic cretinism we have attempted more than once to prove that the general principles and tasks must be realized in each country in accordance with its internal and external conditions. This principle retains its complete force for wartime as well.

Those ultraleftists who do not want to think as Marxists—that is, concretely—will be caught unawares by war. Their policy in time of war will be a fatal consummation of their policy in peacetime. The first artillery shots will either blow the ultraleftists into political nonexistence, or else drive them into the camp of social patriotism, exactly like the Spanish anarchists, those absolute "deniers" of the state, who found themselves for the same reasons bourgeois ministers when war came. In order to carry on a correct policy in wartime one must learn to think correctly in time of peace.

# ONCE MORE ON COMRADES SNEEVLIET AND VEREECKEN[340]

## May 24, 1938

### I

I raised the question of the erroneous conduct of Comrade Sneevliet in the Reiss case privately in a strictly confidential letter to Sneevliet. My purpose was to give Sneevliet himself the chance to understand the error he had made.

Comrade Vereecken deemed it necessary to inject this confidential letter into the discussion with the Brussels organization on the policy of the Dutch RSAP. In other words, Comrade Vereecken, for factional purposes, *manifestly abused* my letter—after which he complains about the contamination of a principled struggle by false "methods." But now that this question has been raised in the open I must give an explanation.

Sneevliet's first error was to evaluate in a completely false manner the political and practical situation surrounding the Reiss case, and he was unable to give Comrade Reiss the necessary advice. I spoke of that, without naming Sneevliet, in the article "A Tragic Lesson," which was printed in different languages, including in the press of the Belgian section. I will not repeat my arguments here. Walter Krivitsky and A. Barmin used precisely the mode of operation I suggested in the article "A Tragic Lesson." Up to now the results have been infinitely more favorable, as much in the area of politics as in the area of personal security.

Sneevliet's second error was to subordinate a political fact of enormous importance (Reiss's break with Moscow) to secondary considerations with respect to the priority of his organization, his newspaper, his "enterprise." Not only did he not consult with the representatives of the Russian section, in particular with me, on what path to choose, but on the contrary he put off the meeting between Reiss and Sedov by all possible means and under different pretexts.

Anyone who knows Sneevliet's politics and his modes of action will also understand with no trouble that Sneevliet was motivated by hostility toward our international organization.

Reiss addressed himself to Sneevliet not as an individual but as a representative of the Fourth International. He saw in Sneevliet a *liaison* with our international organization, in particular with me. Sneevliet could not or would not tell him that in reality he had already broken with our organization and was leading a struggle against it on an international scale. Without explaining to Reiss the situation that had come about, Sneevliet maneuvered, stalled, and blocked with all the forces at his command a meeting and an agreement between Reiss and ourselves. *Sneevliet's ambiguous relationship to the Fourth International created a doubly ambiguous relationship between Sneevliet and Reiss.*

If Reiss had known that Sneevliet was locked in combat with the Fourth International, he would undoubtedly have found other channels and we might perhaps have succeeded in giving him good political advice in time.

This leads us to our own collective mistake: we have tolerated Sneevliet's ambiguous attitude for too long; that is, we allowed him to appear in the spotlight as one of the leaders of the Fourth International and at the same time to ignore our international organization and to undermine it with all the means at his disposal. A revolutionary organization does not have the right to allow such ambiguities, for they can always result in serious and even tragic consequences.

We must get to the bottom of this lesson in a serious way. We can provide evidence of the greatest good will and patience toward parties which are outside our international organization but are moving in our direction. We can and must prove ourselves capable of the greatest patience when it comes to resolving internal questions in our organization. *But we cannot allow dual accountability*, that is, give our ideological opponents the right to hide behind the banner of the Fourth International, and at the same time at each step violate its internal discipline and trample underfoot the elementary duty of loyalty.

This lesson shows in particular that we must reject once and for all the ridiculous and obsolete expression *"for* the Fourth International." *Our organization is the organization of the*

*Fourth International.* Let those who do not wish to understand this retain their independence for a while. But we cannot permit anyone to have one foot in our organization and the other outside, all the more freely to strike blows at us.

## II

Vereecken's attempt, for purely factional reasons, to whitewash Sneevliet at the expense of Sedov is disgraceful in the fullest sense of the word. The factual history of the affair has been very well brought to light by Comrades Etienne and Paulsen in their letter printed in Bulletin No. 14 of the PSR.[341] Only a blind person or one with no conscience whatever could propose—after this letter, which contains numerous facts and quotations—a resolution in the style of Vereecken.

After innumerable delays on Sneevliet's part, Sedov, who was quite ill, did not have the strength to go to Rheims to meet with Reiss on September 6, as he informed Sneevliet. But Sneevliet, in his usual manner, stormed "Now or never." In a letter to me Sneevliet speaks with irony of the fondness people in Paris have for vacations. Vereecken expounds the same theme. In fact, Sedov was never acquainted with vacations, for he worked for the movement not less, but more than many others. If he found it necessary to leave Paris for two weeks, it was only because his physical condition had become intolerable, as the physicians revealed while Sedov struggled against death. To speak of Sedov's "vacations" is not only disgraceful but absurd as well, for by September 6, the date fixed for the meeting in Rheims, Reiss had already been killed. Consequently, Sedov's physical inability to be at the meeting had not the slightest effect on the fate of Reiss.

The first meeting of Reiss and Sneevliet took place July 10. Between this meeting and the meeting set for Rheims, Reiss spent a large portion of his time in Paris, that is, right where Sedov was. The fact that they did not meet during that time is entirely Sneevliet's fault. All of Sedov's letters which are relevant to this affair are in my hands. If necessary, I will publish them.

Sneevliet's errors in the Reiss case are not accidental. Sneevliet has broken completely with the revolutionary perspective. He approaches all questions from the point of view of his little bureaucratic apparatus. Sneevliet is not a Marxist but a pure-and-simple trade unionist. He is concerned only with the interests of his little enterprise: the NAS. To him, the party is no more than an appendage of the NAS, and the name of the Fourth International is no more than a cover for public view. During the last International Conference, in 1936, Sneevliet, who was there as a delegate from the city of P., boycotted the sessions under the pretext that I had been allowed to criticize his policies in a letter to the conference. Such a lack of respect for fraternal delegations is sufficient evidence that Sneevliet is an outsider within our movement. It is in this same way that Sneevliet approached the Reiss case, not from the point of view of the general tasks of the revolutionary struggle, but from the point of view of the secondary interests of his little enterprise. Only factional attorneys can defend Sneevliet's conduct in this affair.

### III

Comrade Vereecken is waging a struggle against "a factional spirit." This has almost become his specialty. He wants to forbid the Bolsheviks from doing "factional" work in the centrist POUM. He wants to prevent members of the Fourth International from doing factional work in Sneevliet's centrist party. He is concerned, "aside from factions," with the reputation of the dirty schemer Eiffel, with whom even the Oehler sect publicly broke. Finally, Vereecken states that all criticism of his own politics is something "factional." Isn't all that appalling? For the revolutionary a Marxist faction in an opportunist party is a *positive* thing; a centrist faction in a revolutionary party is a *negative* thing. The Dutch Bolshevik who refuses to carry out "factional" (how horrible!) work against Sneevliet, who has disloyally broken with our organization, is a traitor and not a revolutionary. Is that not clear?

However, the most remarkable thing is that the most indefatigable factional work against the Fourth International is carried out precisely by Vereecken. With his little faction he split from our Belgian and international organization when the Belgian section temporarily entered the Socialist Party [POB—Belgian Labor Party]. Vereecken's factional and completely disloyal criticism hindered our Belgian section from doing more fruitful work within the Socialist Party. Having finally returned to the organization, Vereecken joined forces with all the ultraleft and centrist opponents of Bolshevism in various countries. Together with Sneevliet he supported Oehler and Muste against our

American section.[342] Where is Oehler now? Where is Muste? All the while our American section has reported important success—against Vereecken and his international faction.

All the attempts to lead Sneevliet to an honest discussion were shattered against the obstinate resistance of this trade union bureaucrat. And each time, Vereecken found some argument to take up the defense of Sneevliet against Marxism. Oh, of course, Vereecken is "not in complete agreement" with Sneevliet. But that doesn't hinder him from always supporting Sneevliet, as in general all those who are preparing to abandon the Fourth International or are abandoning it already. Vereecken goes with them amicably right to the door; sometimes he himself stays outside, to return later and accuse the Fourth International of bad methods.

IV

We must make a list of the names of all the deserters and turncoats to whom, in their turn, Vereecken has extended his sympathy. We must, on the other hand, make a list of all the faithful and intransigent revolutionaries in struggle against whom Vereecken has never restrained himself in the choice of means. Defending the POUM, he portrayed our devoted Spanish comrades as adventurers. Defending Sneevliet, he attempted to cast a shadow on Sedov. In France he tried to put our section into the same bag with the Molinier group. He is already anxious to know if Diego Rivera did not offend the innocent Eiffel. Toward the International Secretariat Vereecken permits himself an absolutely inadmissible tone. What does all that mean?

Most recently, our "impartial" and "anti-factional" Vereecken accused me in public of "not understanding the Belgian organization." What is the basis of this accusation? A letter from Diego Rivera was sent to Lesoil's address and not to Vereecken's. Now, I never had anything to do with the sending of this letter and in general I do not occupy myself with addresses. Comrade Van explained all that in detail in his recent statement. This little episode indicates how loyal Vereecken is and how well founded are the accusations he levels. It is noteworthy also that the accusations are invariably directed not against the ultralefts or centrists but against those who defend the Marxist line of the Fourth International.

No, the problem is not any supposed bad methods of the IS, but the *very foundation of Vereecken's ideas.* In his factional struggle he has removed himself far from the principles of Marxism. The Bolshevik position makes him feel ashamed and embarrassed at every step. Vereecken does not feel at ease. This is why he complains of our "methods," attacking the revolutionaries and defending the opportunists.

In my opinion, the International Conference will render a very great service to our Belgian section if it gives a proper assessment of Vereecken's factional work on the national and international levels. We accuse Vereecken not of having a factional attitude—a factional attitude against opportunism and sectarianism is honorable!—but of losing his footing on the ground of principle; of heading an *anti-Marxist* faction, which played and still plays the role of a brake on the development of the Fourth International. Let us hope that if the International Conference says that loud and clear, its warning will encourage Comrade Vereecken to radically revise his position, and especially his intolerable methods.

V

At the same time, as important as the personal question of Comrade Vereecken is, the question of the fate of our Belgian section as a whole is incomparably more important. Its development seems to be stagnating temporarily. As much as can be judged from afar, the cause of this stagnation is to a considerable degree the erroneous policies of Comrade Vereecken, which focused the attention of the party in a completely false direction. To assure the Belgian section's entry into the mainstream, the following measures in my opinion are necessary:

1. It is necessary to explain to all the members of the section the dead-end character of Sneevliet's trade union policy and its absolute incompatibility with the tasks of a revolutionary party. Those who want to build or maintain their own caricature of a trade union have no place in the Fourth International.

2. The principal and fundamental task of the Belgian section must be serious, systematic, and tenacious work inside the reformist trade unions. Any abandonment of this work, whatever the arguments or pretexts, must be considered desertion from the battlefield.

3. Through the intermediary of the trade unions we must penetrate into the internal life of the Socialist Party, form a close

alliance with the socialist workers and make our agitation correspond to the internal life of the mass workers' organizations.

4. In the same manner we must penetrate the labor youth organizations.

5. The newspaper must reflect, to a much greater degree than at present, the internal life of the mass organizations, and must be concerned with their internal problems.

6. Raising the level of theoretical understanding within the section is the indispensable condition for saving it from the sectarian and centrist tendencies of various leaders. Toward this end it is necessary to set up a serious theoretical monthly in French. If such an enterprise is not within the means of the Belgian section alone it may be necessary to have a single theoretical magazine for all the French-speaking countries.

The objective conditions for the development of the Belgian section are extremely favorable. It is only necessary to put aside the subjective obstacles in time.

# NO OBSTACLE TO COMMON VOTE[343]

## May 25, 1938

Dear Comrade Cannon:

I am very glad to learn that you are going to Europe. You didn't name the other delegate or delegates. I hope that Shachtman will go also because his work not only during but after the conference will be of the greatest value. Permit me again to call your attention to the French section. The new split in the Socialist Party shows the tremendous pressure from the workers. But our section happens to be incapable of attracting new fresh elements. Some leading comrades seem to be tired: no systematic work, no organization, not even the capacity to collect money where it is possible. The management of *Quatrieme Internationale* is miserable, the management of *Lutte ouvriere* not much better. The situation in Britain, in Holland, is nothing in comparison with the situation in France.

I don't see as yet the weight and importance of the differences in your National Committee concerning the draft program and the labor party issue. Both matters necessarily contain at present some *hypothetical* elements. We enter into a new stage with a new plan which has in the first place the value of a *working hypothesis*. The general line of this hypothesis is common to all of us but different parts can be and surely will be modified in the fire of experience. That is why I cannot well understand what can be the obstacle or hindrance for a common vote with the purpose of imposing the general line of the draft program against the centrists on one side and the ultralefts on the other. That is the primordial task from the point of view of the international conference.

The labor party question is now a specific American issue. Vereecken and his consorts will try to interpret the "turn" as a premeditated plan to dissolve the Socialist Workers Party into the coming labor party, to abdicate the independence of the party, and so on. But nobody in our American section, I hope, has such an idea. That is why in spite of some nuances—which have more a preliminary or preventive character, no more—the American delegation can be absolutely solid before the international conference, even on this specific American issue.

Concerning the draft program itself the most disputable chapter will thus be on the trade unions, on the war, on sectarianism, and on the defense of the USSR. On all these questions the American section is as good as unanimous. In this case what can prevent you from giving a unanimous statement, which—without entering into the specific or secondary matters—confirms the general line as directed against the centrists and ultraleftists?

It is very good that three young comrades go to Europe. They will be very useful during the preparation of both conferences. It is only necessary to immediately elaborate a plan for their itinerary, in order that every one of them can be utilized to the fullest extent.

My best greetings and wishes,
Hansen [Trotsky]

# 'FOR' THE FOURTH INTERNATIONAL? NO! THE FOURTH INTERNATIONAL![344]

## May 31, 1938

Dear Comrade:

The proclaiming of the Fourth International seems "premature" to you. You consider that it is more "modest" and more accurate to retain the name "Movement *for* the Fourth International." I cannot agree with this at all. This name seemed pedantic, unfitting, and slightly ridiculous to me even two years ago, when it was first adopted. The experience of the last two years has fully proved it a mistake. The best proof lies in the fact that *it has not been accepted at all.* No one calls us by this name. The bourgeois press, the Comintern, Social Democrats, all speak in one voice simply of the Fourth International. No one sees the little word "for." Our own organizations with minor exceptions act likewise, calling themselves sections of the Fourth International. This is so, in any case, with the French, the Germans, the Russians, the Americans, the Mexicans, the Cubans, and others. Only Sneevliet and Vereecken have fashioned their banner out of the little word "for." But this very fact best emphasizes the mistake in the old name, a name which to the overwhelming majority proved absolutely impracticable.

You are completely in accord with me that the Fourth International is being built only by us, that no other grouping is capable of fulfilling or will undertake to fulfill this task. On the other hand, I least of all am inclined to close my eyes to the fact that our International is still young and weak. But this is no reason for renouncing our name. In civilized societies a person carries one and the same name in childhood, in adulthood, and in old age, and this name merges with his individuality.

To you the little word "for" seems an expression of political "modesty." To me it seems an expression of indecision and lack of self-confidence. A revolutionary party that is not sure of its own significance cannot gain the confidence of the masses. The circumstance that class enemies as well as wide circles of workers already refer to us as the Fourth International shows that they have more confidence in this "firm" than some of the skeptics or semiskeptics in our own ranks.

It seems to you that the name Fourth International will prevent sympathetic or semisympathetic organizations from approaching us. This is radically wrong. We can attract others to us only by a correct and clear policy. And for this we must have an organization and not a nebulous blot. Our national organizations call themselves *parties* or leagues. Here, too, it could be said that the "proclaiming" of a Revolutionary Socialist Party in Belgium makes it more difficult for sympathetic or semisympathetic groupings to approach us. If the principle of "modesty" is to be observed, our Belgian party, for instance, should have been called "the movement for a Revolutionary Socialist Party." But I think that even Comrade Vereecken would not agree to such a ridiculous name! Why then in our international organization should we apply principles different from those in our national organizations? It is unworthy of a Marxist to have two standards: one for national politics and the other—for international.

No doubt in Belgium, as in any other country, groups could arise that are sympathetic to us but are not yet ready today to enter formally into our ranks. We must be ready to establish friendly relations with them and, if they wish, to include them within the framework of the Fourth International on the basis of *sympathizing* organizations, that is, with a consultative vote.

You point to the fact that we have not as yet made a theoretical analysis of the latest stage of imperialism, etc. But if this is an argument against "proclaiming" the Fourth International, it is no less an argument against the existence of national parties. Again two standards! But the Fourth International as a whole is undoubtedly much better equipped theoretically and to a much greater degree assured against vacillations than any of the national sections separately.

The relation between theory and practice bears not a one-sided but a two-sided—that is, dialectical—character. We are sufficiently equipped theoretically for action; at any rate much better than any other organization. Our action will push our theoretical work forward, will arouse and attract new theoreticians, etc. The Fourth International will never spring from our hands ready made like Minerva from the head of Jupiter. It will grow and develop in theory as well as in action.

Let me remind you that the Communist League was created by Marx and Engels before they wrote the *Communist Manifesto.* That the First International was created before the appearance of the first volume of *Capital.* The Second International—before the publication of all the volumes of *Capital.* The Third International existed during its best period without a finished program, etc.

The historic process does not wait for "final," "finished," "exhaustive" Marxian research. We had to take a position on the Spanish revolution without awaiting Marxist studies on Spain. The war will demand an answer from us irrespective of whether or not our theoreticians have issued one, two, or three volumes of research work. Just as war cannot be postponed until the discovery of the most perfect weapon, so the revolution and the Fourth International cannot be postponed until the appearance of the most perfect theoretical work. Theory is very important. But pedantic fetishism of theory is good for nothing.

The paradox lies in the fact that those who call themselves "for the Fourth International" in reality carry on an ever-sharpening struggle *against* the Fourth International. In the example of Sneevliet this is most clear. He is "for" the POUM and "for" the London Bureau and in order to retain his equilibrium he is, in addition, "for" the Fourth International. We have no need for such confusion. The policy of Sneevliet only compromises the Fourth International in Holland as well as internationally. In Spain Sneevliet's policy took the form of direct strikebreaking at the most critical moment. And all this is covered up by the little word "for"! Vereecken's policy is only 51 percent of Sneevliet's policy. The question stands not very much different with Maslow. All of them are "for." In reality they all carry on a struggle against the basic principles of the Fourth International, furtively looking to the right and to the left in search of such allies as can help them overthrow these principles. We cannot permit this at all. We must devote the greatest attention to all the vacillating and immature working class groupings that are developing in our direction. But we cannot make principled concessions to sectarian-centrist leaders who want to recognize neither our international organization nor our discipline.

"That means you want a monolithic International?" someone will say in holy fear. No, least of all that, I will reply calmly to this suspicion. The entire history of the Fourth International and of each of its sections shows a constant, uninterrupted, and free struggle of points of view and tendencies. But as our experience testifies, this struggle retains a sane character only when its participants consider themselves members of one and the same national and international organization which has its program and its constitution. We can, on the other hand, carry on a comradely discussion with groups who stand outside of our organization. But as the experience with Sneevliet and Vereecken indicates, the discussion inevitably assumes a poisoned character when some leaders stand with one foot in our organization, the other—outside of it. To allow the development of such a regime would be suicidal.

Because of all these considerations I stand completely for calling ourselves as we are called by the workers and by class enemies, that is, the *Fourth International!*

L. Trotsky

# REVOLUTIONARY ART AND
# THE FOURTH INTERNATIONAL[345]

## June 1, 1938

Dear Comrades:

I deeply regret that unfavorable circumstances do not allow me to participate in your conference. The vanguard of the workers of the whole world awaits its answers to the most burning problems of their struggle for freedom.

I am, however, sufficiently acquainted with the discussion that is going on in different countries on the fundamental problems of the workers' movement, and with the documents which have been submitted for your appraisal, to have the right to assure you of my complete solidarity with the work which you are called to do.

In the whole course of its history, the proletariat has never yet been as completely deceived and betrayed by its organizations as it is today, twenty-five years after the start of the First World War and a few years, perhaps only a few months, before the start of the Second World War.

The Social Democratic International, as illustrated by the last and most recent governmental experience of Leon Blum in France, is an adjunct of the bourgeois state apparatus, which summons it to its aid in the most difficult periods for the most shameful work: in particular, to prepare a new imperialist war.

The role of the Third International is—if such a thing is possible—even more criminal and injurious, because it covers the services it renders to imperialism with the authority stolen from the October Revolution and Bolshevism.

On the soil of Spain, Stalinism has shown with particular clarity that it has assumed the role of international policeman against the proletarian revolution, the same role that czarism played against the bourgeois revolution.

Official anarchism, by its shameful policy in Spain, has

With Andre Breton on an outing in Mexico, 1938; in background, Jean van Heijenoort and Frida Kahlo Rivera.

convinced the masses of workers of the entire world that they can no longer count on it. Like the bureaucracy of the two pseudo-Marxist Internationals, the anarchist bureaucracy has succeeded in making itself one with bourgeois society.

To prevent the shipwreck and rotting away of humanity, the proletariat needs a perspicacious, honest, and fearless revolutionary leadership. No one can provide this leadership except the Fourth International, basing itself on the entire experience of past defeats and victories.

Permit me, nevertheless, to cast a glance at the historic mission of the Fourth International, not only with the eyes of a proletarian revolutionist but with the eyes of the artist which I am by profession. I have never separated these two spheres of my activity. My pen has never served me as a toy for my personal diversion or that of the ruling classes. I have always forced myself to depict the sufferings, hopes, and struggles of the working classes because that is how I approach life, and therefore art, which is an inseparable part of it. The present unresolved crisis of capitalism carries with it a crisis of all human culture, including that of art.

In a certain way the whole world situation impels talented and sensitive artists onto the road of revolutionary creativeness. But this road, alas, is obstructed with the rotting corpses of reformism and Stalinism.

If the vanguard of the world proletariat finds its leadership, avant-garde art will find new perspectives and new hope. Meanwhile, the so-called Communist International, which brings nothing to the proletariat but defeats and humiliations, continues directing the intellectual life and the artistic activity of the left wing of the international intelligentsia.

The results of this hegemony are particularly striking in the USSR, that is to say, in the country where creative revolutionary activity should have attained its highest development. The dictatorship of the reactionary bureaucracy has stifled or prostituted the intellectual activity of a whole generation. It is impossible to look without physical repugnance at the reproductions of Soviet paintings and sculpture, in which functionaries armed with brushes, under the surveillance of functionaries armed with guns, glorify as "great" men and "geniuses" their chiefs, who in reality are without the slightest spark of genius or greatness. The art of the Stalinist epoch will go down in history as the most spectacular expression of the most abysmal decline that the proletarian revolution has ever undergone.

Only a new upsurge of the revolutionary movement can enrich art with new perspectives and possibilities. The Fourth International obviously cannot take on the task of directing art, that is to say, give orders or prescribe methods. Such an attitude toward art could only enter the skulls of Moscow bureaucrats drunk with omnipotence. Art and science do not find their fundamental nature through patrons; art, by its very existence, rejects them. Creative revolutionary activity has its own internal laws even when it consciously serves social development. Revolutionary art is incompatible with falsehood, hypocrisy, and the spirit of accommodation. Poets, artists, sculptors, musicians will themselves find their paths and methods, if the revolutionary movement of the masses dissipates the clouds of skepticism and pessimism which darken humanity's horizon today. The new generation of creators must be convinced that the face of the old Internationals represents the past of humanity and not its future.

# REMARKS ON CZECHOSLOVAKIA[346]

## June 2, 1938

*Question:* What would be the tactics of the Bolshevik-Leninists in Czechoslovakia in face of the aggression from fascist Germany? Where do these tactics differ from those pursued, for example, in Spain and China?

*Trotsky:* Why is the question especially put for Czechoslovakia? We can ask the same about France or any other country. I believe that Czechoslovakia is a small country and in the event of war her existence would be directly threatened. But the difference between Czechoslovakia and France lies in the fact that France has colonies. It is an imperialist country. Czechoslovakia has no colonies. But this difference is only apparent. Czechoslovakia is an imperialist country in every respect. It is a highly developed country with finance capital in a leading position in a very concentrated industry, the very important war industry. This is why Czechoslovakia is a developed capitalist country, but not only that.

In Czechoslovakia we now have a population of about 15 million. It is not a big country. Under European conditions it is a medium-sized country. Of this 15 million population there are only 6 million Czechs. The official state statistics record the Czechs and Slovaks together (they are different nations). This reckoning them together is done only to give a false impression. The Slovaks, numbering about 3.5 million, feel like oppressed people and fight for autonomy. Then the Germans, the Sudeten Germans, number 3.5 million, and the Hungarians almost a million. Seven or eight hundred thousand are Ruthenians (really part of Russia). Then there are Poles and Jews, but in small numbers. You see that they have 6 million Czechs and 9 million of different minorities who are oppressed by the Czechs—severely oppressed. In a national and economic sense the Czechs have different privileges and during the last crisis the pressure on the minorities became terrible.

You see that if they don't have foreign colonies they have internal colonies, and the relation arithmetically between the Czechs and the internal colonies is approximately the same as with France and her colonies, the same six to nine. Now the Stalinists wish to force these 15 million people to defend democracy, but they do not speak of the fact that the Czech democracy is one of the shabbiest in this epoch, when all democracies have doubtful status. These national minorities under the national oppression of Czech democracy should no more defend democracy than the Algerians or Moroccans or the Indians in their relation to England. Now if we question Czechoslovakia as a "democracy" for 6 million—then for the 9 million it is a machine of oppression.

These general statistics are necessary as an introduction to the political questions. In the first period, with the creation of Czechoslovakia after the war, the bourgeois classes of the minority nations looked with hope toward the new Czechoslovakian state. They became patriotic. Hungarians, Germans, Ruthenians, Slovakians all became patriotic for the following reasons: First, it was more profitable to be in the camp of the victors (and furthermore the situation in Germany was very bad from the point of view of the bourgeoisie). From this point we have the paradox that the German minority looked for aid not to Germany but to Prague. Second, the situation in Germany was very disquieting. In Hungary we even had a soviet republic in 1919 and it was not clear whether the counterrevolution was stable.

That was the reason why the German bourgeoisie became Czech patriots. The bourgeois class in this respect is more flexible in that it subordinates its national sympathies and antipathies to its economic interests. It was not so with the workers. It was possible to unite the workers of different nations in Czechoslovakia only by separating the workers as a class on the basis of their class interests, that is, on the basis of revolutionary policy, which meant irreconcilable opposition to the state. This was the only way of having a united proletariat in Czechoslovakia. But thanks to the national petty-bourgeois prejudices and the false policies determined by these prejudices and the interests of the higher strata of the workers, the proletarian party was divided into national camps. We have had a Czech Social Democracy, a German Social Democracy, German trade unions and Czech trade unions. Then these trade unions were divided by the Czechs to correspond to different political parties, but that is a second element of the whole picture.

Now the situation has changed since the conquest of power by Hitler. Germany became a solid, strong state with a population of 68 million or so and the German bourgeoisie of Czechoslovakia, oppressed to a certain degree, began to put its hopes and its patriotism not in Prague but in Berlin. The reasons for this are entirely clear. It is a large arena for capitalist development, it is German—the same language, no national oppression, a surer existence. It is a stronger state. But what is very important is that this turn of German capital to Germany attracted the German petty bourgeoisie and not only the petty bourgeoisie but also the German workers and German Social Democrats. Why? Because the German workers can hope for nothing in Czechoslovakia. They see that the dominant bourgeoisie is supported by the Czech trade unions. They are democratic (patriotic) and the German workers, who are oppressed doubly as a class and as a nationality, cannot become Czech patriots.

Moreover, in Czechoslovakia there is no longer a revolutionary party because the Stalinists also are patriots. They say to the 9 million: "You must support the Czech government." They can deceive the Czech workers but it is not so easy with the German workers. By this democratic-patriotic policy, they, like the Social Democrats of the Second International, transformed the German population into cannon fodder for fascism, and we see in the latest cables that Henlein has had the greatest success in the elections.[347] He fully dominates the Germans. It is a classical example of the fact that the People's Front policy brings about fascism. Not only the Sudeten workers but the lower classes of the cities could be won against the state, but People's Front democracy-patriotism divides the workers according to national lines and transforms them into cannon fodder. That is the situation in Czechoslovakia.

Now, in time of peace as in time of war, what must be the policy of the proletarian party? Naturally, irreconcilable opposition to the state, the bourgeoisie, and to advance the slogan that the main enemy is in our own country—the ruling class. One can say that this policy would help Hitler. The same could be said of France or any other country. But Czechoslovakia is even now a prisoner of Hitler. On the map, since the Anschluss, Germany forms a pincers upon Czechoslovakia. She has no access to her allies to the west, and is a country which must import food, wheat, etc. It is a country which, from the military point of view, is doomed to catastrophe. Czechoslovakia can be saved only through a revolution in Europe, including Czechoslovakia and Germany. If we can theoretically accept the defeatist position of the working class, the working class can serve the military purposes of Hitler. It can add to his advantage at first. But this is a question only of the military map. It is a question not only of where the military lines will be formed during the war but also of the fate of nations and peoples.

Czechoslovakia can be saved from fascism only by revolution and revolution can be provoked in Germany only by the revolutionary attitude of workers in other countries, because the strength of Hitler consists in that "we were vanquished," "we have no colonies," "we are the oppressed country," "in all other countries the workers support the bourgeoisie." In Czechoslovakia the People's Front policy furnished Henlein with his army. The People's Front policy in France and in Czechoslovakia is the best service that can be rendered Hitler. If we had a revolutionary party, it would sap the ideology of the fascists insofar as it could affect the workers. On the other hand, a revolutionary policy has a contagious nature. Imagine in Czechoslovakia that we have a revolutionary policy and that it leads to the conquest of power. It would be a hundred times more dangerous to Hitler than patriotic support of Czechoslovakia. That is why it is absolutely obligatory that our comrades follow a defeatist policy.

In China we do not have an imperialist country but a backward country which is being changed into a colonial country by Japan. (I forgot to add that Czechoslovakia is a partner of a world corporation of imperialist countries. If it doesn't have colonies, it has loans from Britain. These loans are possible because of Britain's colonies; likewise with military support from France. It is a link in the imperialist chain.) China is an isolated country and with the imperialists it is only a question of China's division.

There is no analogy between China and Spain. In Spain we have a civil war between two groups of the bourgeoisie. Because the workers do not have an independent policy we see the victory of fascism. It is a civil war in one capitalist country. It is a different kind of situation. It is important in this respect that on the internal scale of a state there can be a fight between two parts of the ruling class as to what form of rule is best. But whether in the fascist or democratic form they exploit the people. In this sense it is a fight between fascism and democracy. But when two countries enter a war, with its international complications, it can never be a war between democracy and fascism. The war is always for colonies, etc. That is why it is absolutely stupid to say that Czechoslovakia would enter into war to save democracy. If Czechoslovakia is victorious it is likely that the military clique will dominate the oppressed minorities which would become very rebellious during the war. It can be victorious only as an absolutist military machine.

For Czechoslovakia what is important is not its economic-political-military salvation. What shall be the slogan? The United Socialist States of Europe. For Czechoslovakia this is a burning question. The United Socialist States of Europe can be organized only by an independent working class policy, and that independent working class policy cannot support the bourgeoisie.

*Question:* What should be the policy of the Bolshevik-Leninists when the government sent troops to the German region? Would a revolutionary party fight against it?

*Trotsky:* It is a question of practical possibilities. If we can do it, if we have the strength, of course we fight against sending troops into the German region.

# MEXICO
# AND BRITISH IMPERIALISM[348]

## June 5, 1938

The international campaign which imperialist circles are waging over the expropriation of Mexican oil enterprises by the Mexican government has been distinguished by all the features of imperialism's propagandistic bacchanalias—combining impudence, deceitfulness, speculation in ignorance, with cocksureness in its own impunity.

The signal for this campaign was given by the British government when it declared a boycott of Mexican oil. Boycott, as is known, always involves self-boycott, and is therefore accompanied by great sacrifices on the part of the boycotter. Great Britain was until recently the largest consumer of Mexican oil; naturally not out of sympathy for the Mexican people, but out of consideration for her own advantage.

Heaviest consumer of oil in Great Britain itself is the state, with its gigantic navy and rapidly growing air force. A boycott of Mexican oil by the British government signifies, therefore, a simultaneous boycott not only of British industry but also of national defense. Mr. Chamberlain's government has shown with unusual frankness that the profits of Britain's capitalist robbers loom above state interests themselves. Oppressed classes and oppressed peoples must thoroughly learn this fundamental conclusion.

Both chronologically and logically the uprising of General Cedillo grew out of Chamberlain's policy. The Monroe Doctrine prevents the British admiralty from applying a military-naval blockade of the Mexican coast.[349] They must act through internal agents, who, it is true, do not openly fly the British flag, yet serve the same interests as Chamberlain—the interests of a clique of oil magnates. In the White Book issued by British diplomacy just a few days ago we may be sure that the negotiations of its agents with General Cedillo are not included. Imperialist diplomacy carries on its major business under cover of secrecy.

In order to compromise the expropriation in the eyes of bourgeois public opinion, they represent it as a "Communist" measure. Historical ignorance combines here with conscious deceit. Semicolonial Mexico is fighting for its national independence, political and economic. This is the basic meaning of the Mexican revolution at *this* stage. The oil magnates are not rank-and-file capitalists, not ordinary bourgeoisie. Having seized the richest natural resources of a foreign country, standing on their billions and supported by the military and diplomatic forces of their metropolis, they strive to establish in the subjugated country a regime of imperialistic feudalism, subordinating to themselves legislation, jurisprudence, and administration. Under these conditions expropriation is the only effective means of safeguarding national independence and the elementary conditions of democracy.

What direction the further economic development of Mexico may take depends decisively upon factors of an international character. But this is a question of the future. The Mexican revolution is now carrying out the same work as, for instance, the United States of America accomplished in three-quarters of a century, beginning with the Revolutionary War for independence and finishing with the Civil War for the abolition of slavery and for national unification. The British government not only did everything at the end of the eighteenth century to retain the United States under the status of a colony, but later, in the years of the Civil War, supported the slaveholders of the South against the abolitionists of the North, striving for the sake of its imperialist interests to thrust the young republic into a state of economic backwardness and national disunity.

To the Chamberlains of that time, too, the expropriation of the slaveholders seemed a diabolical "Bolshevik" measure. In reality the historic task of the Northerners consisted in clearing the arena for the independent democratic development of bourgeois society. Precisely this task is being solved at this stage by the government of Mexico. General Cardenas stands among those statesmen of his country who have been fulfilling work comparable to that of Washington, Jefferson, Abraham Lincoln, and General Grant. And, of course, it is not accidental that the British government, in this case, too, finds itself on the other side of the historic trench.

The world press, in particular the French, preposterous as it may seem, continues to drag my name into the question of the expropriation of the oil industry. If I have already refuted this nonsense once it is not at all because I fear "responsibility," as was insinuated by one talkative agent of the GPU. On the contrary, I would consider it an honor to carry even a part of the responsibility for this courageous and progressive measure of the Mexican government. But I do not have the least basis for it. I first learned of the decree of expropriation from the newspapers. But, naturally, this is not the question.

Two aims are pursued in interjecting my name. First, the organizers of the campaign wish to impart to the expropriation a "Bolshevik" coloration. Second, they are attempting to strike a blow at the national self-respect of Mexico. The imperialists are endeavoring to represent the affair as if Mexico's statesmen were incapable of determining their own road. A wretched and ignoble hereditary slaveholders' psychology! Precisely because Mexico today still belongs to those backward nations which are only now impelled to fight for their independence, greater audacity of thought is engendered among its statesmen than is granted to the conservative dregs of a great past. We have witnessed similar phenomena in history more than once!

The French weekly *Marianne,* a notorious organ of the French People's Front, even asserts that on the oil question the government of General Cardenas acted not only as one with Trotsky but also . . . in the interests of Hitler. It is a question, you see, of depriving the great-hearted "democracies" of oil in case of war and, contrariwise, of supplying Germany and other fascist nations. This is not one whit more clever than the Moscow trials. Humanity learns, not without amazement, that Great Britain is being deprived of Mexican oil because of the ill-will of General Cardenas and not because of Chamberlain's self-boycott. But then the "democracies" possess a simple way of paralyzing this "fascist" plot: let them buy Mexican oil, once more Mexican oil, and again Mexican oil! To every honest and sensible person it is now beyond all doubt that if Mexico should find itself forced to sell liquid gold to fascist countries, the responsibility for this act would fall fully and completely upon the governments of the imperialist "democracies."

Behind the back of *Marianne* and its ilk stand the Moscow prompters. At first glance this seems preposterous, since other prompters of the same school use diametrically opposed librettos. But the whole secret consists in the fact that the friends of the

GPU adapt their views to geographic gradations of latitude and longitude. If some of them promise support to Mexico, others picture General Cardenas as an ally of Hitler. From the latter point of view, Cedillo's oil rebellion should be viewed, it would seem, as a struggle in the interests of world democracy.

Let us, however, leave the clowns and intriguers to their own fate. We do not have them in mind, but the class-conscious workers of the entire world. Without succumbing to illusions and without fear of slander, the advanced workers will completely support the Mexican people in their struggle against the imperialists. The expropriation of oil is neither socialism nor communism. But it is a highly progressive measure of national self-defense. Marx did not, of course, consider Abraham Lincoln a communist; this did not, however, prevent Marx from entertaining the deepest sympathy for the struggle that Lincoln headed. The First International sent the Civil War president a message of greeting, and Lincoln in his answer greatly appreciated this moral support.

The international proletariat has no reason to identify its program with the program of the Mexican government. Revolutionists have no need of changing color, adapting themselves, and rendering flattery in the manner of the GPU school of courtiers, who in a moment of danger will sell out and betray the weaker side. Without giving up its own identity, every honest working class organization of the entire world, and first of all in Great Britain, is duty-bound to take an irreconcilable position against the imperialist robbers, their diplomacy, their press, and their fascist hirelings. The cause of Mexico, like the cause of Spain, like the cause of China, is the cause of the international working class. The struggle over Mexican oil is only one of the advance-line skirmishes of future battles between the oppressors and the oppressed.

# ON THE EDGE
# OF A PRECIPICE[350]

## June 12, 1938

Dear Comrade Lesoil:

I consider the situation in the Belgian section to be quite delicate. I find that Comrade Vereecken's politics are developing in an increasingly anti-Marxist direction. Since 1933 there has not been one important question where we have not seen him take a wrong position—sometimes sectarian, other times opportunist. It seems to me that his own zigzags and flights of fancy have embittered him so much that he tries to pick fights with anyone—except the opponents of the Fourth International. What can possibly come of this attitude? It is absurd to think that the national sections can accept the proposal to turn themselves into a collection of groups and cliques that "proclaim allegiance" to the Fourth International. Such a course would mean simply canceling out the theoretical and political struggle we have conducted for the past ten years, the lines of demarcation, the ruptures and splits that were the product of this struggle, in order to wipe the slate clean and begin the whole business afresh. No, really, such a nihilistic attitude toward one's own political tendency is astounding even in the case of such an individualistic and capricious man as Comrade Vereecken. I repeat: What can come of all this? Moreover, I do not see an adequate reaction from the Belgian section. It is in no way a matter of secondary questions or of "method," as Vereecken insists with rather naive obstinacy. It concerns the very cornerstones of our movement. No one in our ranks, as far as I know, is any longer inclined to allow Vereecken to play games with principles that have been established at such great cost. No indeed!

You ask me whether perhaps I want a split with Vereecken and his faction. I will reply quite frankly—no. I tried to do everything possible to prevent in time the criminal split Vereecken provoked. I have tried to help the Belgian section restore its unity. I have not lost hope of saving Vereecken for our movement, but I must tell you frankly that I regard the next conference as the last opportunity to remedy the situation.

You are well acquainted with the Molinier affair. Those we lost were his closest friends. I had a hundred discussions with them (Henri M., Frank, Meichler, and others),[351] attempting to persuade them that Molinier could only be saved for the movement by subjecting him to the firmest discipline. I did not succeed. I felt duty-bound to give the same advice to Vereecken's friends and associates. He is standing on the edge of a precipice. It is necessary to seize him firmly by the shoulders, shake him in a friendly way, and make him understand that one cannot practice politics with flights of fancy, improvisations, and petty personal combinations. That is my opinion, my dear friend. You can use this letter in any way you see fit. It is inspired solely by concern for the interests of our Belgian organization.

Best greetings,
L. Trotsky

# NO, IT IS NOT THE SAME[352]

## June 18, 1938

The *Workers Age* of June 11 carries an article in defense of Lovestone and Company's long years of subservience to the Thermidorean bureaucracy. This article proves once again that these people are incorrigible.

In my study on morals, I pointed out the criminal attitude of Brandler and Lovestone toward the Moscow trials. Lovestone's answer to this is: "Yes, we erred, but Trotsky, too, erred with regard to the trial of the Mensheviks in 1931. Where is the difference?"

We will explain briefly the difference to these gentlemen. The Mensheviks are a conservative, petty-bourgeois party, tied up with imperialism. In the October Revolution they united with the bourgeoisie against the proletariat. During the civil war, the right wing of the Mensheviks (Maisky, Troyanovsky, and many others) stood on the side of the imperialists—some even with weapons in hand.

The Menshevik emigres in Paris consider Leon Blum, the clerk of the trusts and the executioner of colonial peoples, to be their friend and leader. Under these circumstances, different forms of a bloc of Russian Mensheviks, especially of their individual representatives and groups, with imperialists, are politically entirely possible, both at present and in the future, just as they were possible in the past.

The defendants in the trial of the Mensheviks in 1931 were little-known or completely unknown people, whose political past did not offer any guarantee and whose political views at the time of the trial remained entirely unknown.

If, in view of the stated circumstances, I admitted the possibility that these or other Mensheviks, or former Mensheviks, were really involved in imperialist intrigues and combinations, I did not at all, however, come out as the defender of the Stalinist bureaucracy and of Stalinist justice. On the contrary, I continued in irreconcilable struggle against the Moscow oligarchy.

The case was—with Mr. Lovestone's permission—somewhat different in the trials against the "Trotskyists." By its entire past, this grouping had shown that it was little inclined to friendship with the bourgeoisie and with imperialism. The literature of the "Trotskyists" has been and still is accessible to all. Zinoviev and Kamenev were figures of international magnitude. I believe Lovestone knew them personally sufficiently well. The accusation against them was politically and psychologically preposterous.

The trials against the "Trotskyists" took place five years after the trial of the Mensheviks. During those five years, our literature succeeded in completely unmasking the Thermidorean bureaucracy with its methods of frame-up and amalgam.

Not to know and to see all this was possible only to those who did not want to know and see. Precisely in this category belong Brandler, Lovestone, and their friends. They did not believe for a single moment that Trotsky, Zinoviev, Kamenev, Smirnov, Radek, Pyatakov, and the others were counterrevolutionary terrorists, allies of the fascists, etc.

Lovestone and Company are good for nothing as Marxists, but no one considers them idiots. *They knew very well that we were confronted with a gigantic frame-up.* But since in their petty-bourgeois, cowardly, and conservative policy they had firmly bound their reputation with that of the Thermidorean bureaucracy, they made an attempt to follow it to the very end, in the hope that Stalin would succeed in his violation of public opinion. In their hearts they hoped that for this service the Kremlin would finally "recognize" them and call them to "office." Only when they saw that the Moscow superfalsifier had failed ignominiously did they step aside and recognize in a half-voice their "slight" mistake.

In France, at the end of the last century, a Jewish officer, Dreyfus, was accused of espionage. Dreyfus was a figure unknown to anyone. One could be thoroughly sincere, a democrat, a socialist, an opponent of anti-Semitism, etc., and still admit the possibility that Dreyfus might really be a spy: such cases are not at all infrequent among officers. But it is quite another thing to come out in defense of the French general staff, and of all kinds of reactionary scoundrels, and to take part in the anti-Semitic newspaper campaign.

Between these two "mistakes" there is some difference,

gentlemen of the *Workers Age!* One mistake has an episodic character; the other flows organically from a policy shot through and through with rottenness.

I am not writing this for Lovestone and his clique. These people are hopeless. For fifteen years they were only shadows of different groups in the Soviet bureaucracy. Lovestone was a Zinovievite with Zinoviev, a Bukharinite with Bukharin, a Stalinist with Stalin. For fifteen years he repeated all the slanders and falsifications against the so-called "Trotskyists." His fraternization with Vyshinsky and Yagoda in 1936 was a natural link in this shameful chain. Lovestone cannot be reeducated. But in the ranks of the so-called Lovestoneites there are undoubtedly entirely sincere people who are being systematically misled. For them, I write these lines.

# TO THE CONGRESS OF THE REVOLUTIONARY SOCIALIST PARTY OF BELGIUM[353]

## June 22, 1938

Dear Comrades:

I have just now received the news that Comrade Vereecken has resigned as a member of the party. This is quite a sad thing for our movement, for Vereecken has uncommon qualities of devotion and energy. But it is an especially tragic thing for Vereecken himself; because our movement, which is thoroughly revolutionary and no less thoroughly realistic, is the only one that could save him from his own negative characteristics: his sectarianism, lack of solidarity, and a quite exceptional sensitivity. Vereecken is gravely mistaken if he thinks he can "serve his class" outside our movement. For my part I can only hope that, now or later, he will again find the road of the Fourth International, for that is the one and only way to serve the proletariat in our epoch.

The reasons Vereecken gives for his resignation are far from permissible and only expose the state of permanent frenzy that has become so characteristic of Vereecken. He accuses T., the IS, and "those who support them unconditionally" (?) of wishing to "liquidate" him at all costs. What could be the reasons for such an inexplicable and abominable purpose? We are not wealthy in comrades, especially in experienced comrades who devote themselves completely to our movement. On the contrary, I think that all the leading comrades of our movement have done and are prepared to do everything in their power to keep Vereecken in our ranks. Everything but one thing: to give way to him on the very principles of the Fourth International. It would be easy to show that far from being attacked or persecuted by others, it is Vereecken himself who has attacked the IS and the leaderships of nearly all the sections, except for those who trampled on the principles of Marxism, made a mockery of our international discipline, and fraternized with our worst enemies. The documents that serve as the immediate pretext for Vereecken's resignation were nothing but acts of self-defense against the absolutely unjustified attacks coming from Vereecken. By means of these attacks he sought to cover up his own past mistakes. This state of frenzy is not at all an individual quirk. Rather, it is characteristic of a particular political state of mind. This is what the draft Transitional Program says about it: "Since sectarians, as in general every kind of blunderer and miracle-man, are toppled by reality at each step, they live in a state of perpetual exasperation, complaining about the 'regime' and 'the methods' and ceaselessly wallowing in small intrigues."

Several days ago I received the statement of Comrade V. concerning the municipal elections. V.'s arguments against participation seemed to me false from beginning to end. You know that I considered and still consider our party's support to Van Zeeland to be an extremely serious and dangerous error.[354] When V. reaffirms this he is right. But this mistake is no reason for abstentionism. If the party, because of the sectarian tendencies of its leadership, is so weakened that it cannot participate in the elections, it must say so openly and not cover its weakness with artificial and scholastic arguments.

"The labor notes (for *La Lutte*) grow fewer week by week." I read that in your minutes of June 8, 1938. This simple fact sums up an entire political line, that is, its weaknesses. When the party turns its back on the workers, the workers respond in kind. It is necessary at all costs to sink roots in the unions. You must sink roots in the youth. In my opinion the orientation of your congress should be: enough hollow phrases, enough repetition of abstract formulas for their own sake. To the masses; again to the masses; always to the masses!

We observed in France in 1936 a movement of incomparable power and vigor. We said: this is a prerevolutionary situation in the most concrete and immediate sense of the term. Can one doubt for a minute that if this movement had found a leadership that had expressed its aspirations even the least bit the proletarian revolution in France would today be an accomplished fact? But all the official organizations joined together to trick, break, mislead, sabotage, and paralyze the revolutionary movement. Have they succeeded? Yes, at least to a certain extent; that is, they have lessened the chances of proletarian revolution in favor of fascism. We have had a new demonstration of the power of the apparatuses of three Internationals—the Second, the Third, and the Amsterdam—power which has its most basic source in the bureaucracy in Moscow and the crude and perfidious treachery of the Comintern. Under these conditions to wish to remain outside the working class, waiting for it to turn its eyes definitively toward us, is a program fit for the most sterile sectarians, who are revolutionaries only, as Engels put it, in their own imagination.

I think, dear comrades, that the draft program presented by the IS in its general outline speaks well to the needs of our Belgian party. It is only a question of not being content with an abstract *acceptance* of the program, but of passing over to its immediate *application*. The prerequisite is ruthlessly to have done with all the vestiges of sectarianism. In this situation the resignation of Vereecken can take on a symbolic character.

Comrades, time is more precious than ever. Do not waste it. Carry out a courageous turn. Let the hesitant, the weak, the dilettantes leave! Sink roots in the unions; sink roots in the youth; make your newspaper into the instrument and the expression of your work among the masses. If you succeed in executing this turn, your congress will mark a crucial stage in the development of your party.

My best revolutionary greetings accompany your work.

Fraternally,
Leon Trotsky

# FOR AN OPEN POLEMIC
## WITH THE LIBERALS[355]

## June 29, 1938

Dear Rae:

Joe communicated to me the news from your letter that my article on morals provoked great dissatisfaction in Dr. Dewey, Sidney Hook, and others, and that they intend to smash my bad philosophy. I am very glad to hear this.

With the honest liberals and radicals we have a "united front" with a practical aim: to unmask a frame-up. But in every honest united front neither of the two parties renounces its right to free criticism. Dr. Dewey made great use of this even in his announcement of the verdict over the broadcasting system. In this respect our comrades were more reserved, even too reserved, in my opinion. An open polemic will reestablish things in their natural proportions and relations. I hope that Max Eastman also will answer. The very confused and equivocal character of his friendship to us is extremely prejudicial to our movement. Friends who say about us: "They are very good people, intelligent, honest, admirably courageous, but . . . their theory is bad, their politics are false, they are incapable of creating an organization, etc., etc.," are the worst, most dangerous enemies of the Fourth International. Better to say that they are the more dangerous the more diplomatic and tolerant we are.

An open delimitation from these friends is absolutely necessary. Every young worker or intellectual who is interested in us must know that those friends belong to the camp of the radical bourgeois democracy and not to the revolutionary camp of the proletariat. Only under these conditions can the "friendship" in certain cases be useful for both sides. The same is doubly true in regard to such a miserable philistine as Eugene Lyons, who participates in the banquets of Pioneer Publishers and immedi-

370

ately after this makes a lecture before the White Guard Russians and explains to them that the poor "Trotskyites" are only remnants of a condemned past. No, God save us from such friends.

My warmest greetings to you and Max. Where are you? Have you found a job? We here are working hard with Sara on the Stalin book, which is progressing very rapidly.

Best greetings,
Leon Trotsky

# STALIN AND ACCOMPLICES
# CONDEMNED[356]

## July 5, 1938

You desire a statement from me concerning the interview Lombardo Toledano gave while he was in Oslo and the dispatch which *Aftenposten* published on June 10, dealing with the coming trial of the Soviet diplomats.

Your paper's attitude toward me has always been one of unvarnished hostility, expressed in the nastiest fashion. I regard this hostility as well deserved. Therefore, I can only answer your questions on the condition that my answers will be published without omissions, in toto, including this introduction. As far as your paper's commentary is concerned, it is all the same to me.

I will begin with the trial of the diplomats. I do not know whether this trial, in which your paper seems to think Yakubovich will play the leading role, will actually take place. If it does, Yakubovich's role will not be determined by his third-rate importance (in a political sense) but with reference to political geography. He was ambassador in Norway, where I resided for a year and a half. Of those who apparently will go to trial, I was personally well acquainted with the former ambassador to Berlin and Tokyo, Yurenev, the former ambassador to Warsaw and general consul in Barcelona, Antonov-Ovseenko, and the former chief of the Military Department of the Commissariat of Foreign Affairs, General Gekker. But Yakubovich I didn't know at all. Of course, I may have met him in Moscow at some official conference or other, but I don't recall it. In any case, any possible connection or contact between us while I was in Norway would have been just as impossible for me as it was for him. My attorney, the late Mr. Puntervold, told me while I was interned in Hurum that, according to "reliable sources," Yakubovich took a very aggressive stand in the Norwegian Foreign Ministry, where he slammed his fist on the table and demanded first my

372

internment and then my expulsion from Norway. He won his first demand; the second was denied him. This is all that I know, secondhand, about Yakubovich's activities in Norway.

It is very likely that Yakubovich has been implicated solely in order to correct the blunder with Pyatakov's famous plane trip, where he allegedly landed at the Kjeller airport. Pyatakov's thoroughly fantastic and extremely ill-considered testimony was refuted at the time by the Norwegian press. Soviet justice has not yet recovered from this blow. It is possible that it will be Yakubovich's task to present a new version of this journey to the world. Yakubovich could, for example, say that Pyatakov made a geographical error, or that he intentionally concealed the real facts about the airport in order to protect an accomplice, perhaps the very same Yakubovich. We will be presented with a new set of circumstances which, naturally, will contain new errors. Moscow justice will in time correct these errors too—after Yakubovich's death. These are, of course, all suppositions. But I regard them as quite likely if the diplomat's trial takes place.

As for the interview Lombardo Toledano gave to *Arbeiderbladet* (May 25), it can be said that it compromises the paper as much as the object of the interview. In this conversation, Lombardo does not speak a word of the truth, just like in most of his political speeches. He distorts the truth not just for the purpose of political slander, but apparently totally without purpose—because he is incapable of anything else.

According to Toledano, Diego Rivera "invited" me to Mexico so that—I would create publicity for Rivera. Don't these words characterize Toledano's own ethics and moral stature?

Replying to the question about whether I have friends in Mexico, Toledano says: "When he arrived, he had possibly five friends; now he has only two, Diego Rivera and his wife." This does not prevent the same Toledano from declaring at a public meeting in Mexico that I am preparing *a general strike against General Cardenas's regime*. In which of these two instances is Toledano lying? I am obliged to say—as usual, in both.

Toledano undertakes to ridicule the "trial" which my friends allegedly put on in Coyoacan. He goes into fantastic details about how the lady of the house, Frida Rivera, gave the judges and the witnesses tea (apparently in order to bribe them). There is not a word of truth in this. There was no trial in Coyoacan. A commission of inquiry came there for a week to interrogate me as a witness. The stenographic report of the meetings of the Commission of Inquiry have been published in a 617-page book, *The Case of Leon Trotsky*. Even a superficial acquaintance with this book will serve to unmask Mr. Toledano's lies from beginning to end.

Under the title *Not Guilty* (Harper and Brothers, New York, 1938) there has been published the text of the verdict of the International Commission of Inquiry, nominally into the case of Leon Trotsky and Leon Sedov, but in reality into the case of Stalin and his accomplices. We recall first of all the composition of the judges:

John Dewey, president of the commission, well-known American philosopher, professor emeritus of Columbia University, international authority on pedagogical questions;

John Chamberlain, American writer, long-time literary critic of the *New York Times,* lecturer at Columbia University on journalism;

Edward Ross, dean of American sociologists, professor emeritus of Wisconsin University;

Benjamin Stolberg, well-known American publicist on questions of the workers' movement;

Carlo Tresca, leader of American anarcho-syndicalism, publisher of the magazine *Il Martello,* leader of a number of strikes;

Suzanne La Follette, secretary of the commission, well-known writer, editor of radical journals;

Alfred Rosmer, well-known figure in the French workers' movement, member of the Executive Committee of the Comintern (1920-21), chief editor of *l'Humanite* (1923-24);

Otto Ruehle, old member of the left wing of the German Social Democracy, associate of Karl Liebknecht, author of a biography of Karl Marx;

Wendelin Thomas, leader of the revolt of the German sailors on November 7, 1918, subsequently Communist deputy in the Reichstag (1920-24);

Francisco Zamora, former member of the executive committee of the Mexican Confederation of Workers, professor of political economy, eminent Marxist publicist.

As legal adviser to the commission figured John Finerty, well-known liberal attorney in the United States.

All the participants in the commission have a long and distinguished past in various fields of social life, science, and political activity. They all defended the October Revolution in its time from the sharp tongues of reaction. Many of them took part in campaigns around the sensational trials of Sacco-Vanzetti, Tom Mooney, etc.[357] Apart from A. Rosmer, who at certain times was politically linked with L. Trotsky, all the other participants in the commission, both its liberal majority and its Marxist minority, were and remain opponents of the so-called Trotskyists.

The commission worked under very high pressure for more than eight months, questioned directly and through a special subcommission in Paris numerous witnesses, studied many hundreds of documents, and formulated its final conclusion in the verdict, which takes up 422 pages of closely printed text.

Each point of the accusation against Trotsky and Sedov, each "admission" by the accused, all the testimonies of the witnesses, are arranged in exhaustive fullness in separate paragraphs. The text of the verdict takes up 247 such paragraphs.

There is, of course, no possibility of exhausting in this note the contents of the book, which will always remain a monument of ideal honesty, legal and political acumen, and painstaking thoroughness. All the facts, dates, testimonies, and arguments scattered over the pages of the official account of the Moscow trials, and in critical and polemical productions of the friends of the GPU and its opponents, are here subjected to careful analysis. Everything doubtful is sifted out and only unshakable facts remain, from which unshakable conclusions are drawn. They are already known.

Paragraph 246 says: "On the basis of all the evidence herein examined and all the conclusions stated, we find that the trials of August 1936 and January 1937 were frame-ups."

Paragraph 247, the last one, says: "On the basis of all the evidence herein examined and all the conclusions stated, we find Leon Trotsky and Leon Sedov not guilty."

No force will be able to erase this book from the currents of world public opinion. Friends and apologists of the GPU will break their teeth on its unconquerable arguments. The verdict has been given and there is no appeal from it. A brand has been burned on the forehead of Stalin, organizer of the greatest legal forgery in world history!

L. Sedov, who applied all his strength to the revelation of the truth about the Moscow trials, did not live to see the appearance of this historic book. He had at least the satisfaction of acquainting himself with a short text of the verdict, published on September 20 of last year. Now the truth about the accusers of Sedov is finally revealed. It remains to reveal the truth about his murderers. We will not rest until that work is finished!

Neither Lombardo Toledano nor any other of Stalin's agents will be able to keep world public opinion from being affected by this book.

# MORE ON THE SUPPRESSION
# OF KRONSTADT[358]

## July 6, 1938

In my recent article on Kronstadt I tried to pose the question on a political plane. But many are interested in the problem of personal "responsibility." Souvarine,[359] who from a sluggish Marxist became an exalted sycophant, asserts in his book on Stalin that in my autobiography I consciously kept silent on the Kronstadt rebellion; there are exploits—he says sarcastically—of which one does not boast. Ciliga, in his book *In the Country of the Big Lie,* recounts that in the suppression of Kronstadt "more than ten thousand seamen" were shot by me (I doubt whether the whole Baltic fleet at that time had that many). Other critics express themselves in this manner: yes, objectively the rebellion had a counterrevolutionary character but why did Trotsky use such merciless repressions in the pacification and subsequently?

I have never touched on this question. Not because I had anything to conceal but, on the contrary, precisely because I had nothing to say. The truth of the matter is that *I personally did not participate in the least in the suppression of the Kronstadt rebellion, nor in the repressions following the suppression.* In my eyes this very fact is of no political significance. I was a member of the government, I considered the quelling of the rebellion necessary and therefore bear responsibility for the suppression. Only within these limits have I replied to criticism up to now. But when moralists begin to annoy me personally, accusing me of exceeding cruelty, not called forth by circumstance, I consider that I have a right to say: "Messrs. moralists, you are lying a bit."

The rebellion broke out during my stay in the Urals. From the Urals I came directly to Moscow for the Tenth Congress of the party. The decision to suppress the rebellion by military force, *if the fortress could not be induced to surrender, first by peace negotiations, then through an ultimatum*—this general decision was adopted with my direct participation. But after the decision was taken, I continued to remain in Moscow and took no part, direct or indirect, in the military operations. Concerning the subsequent repressions, they were completely the affair of the Cheka.

How did it happen that I did not go personally to Kronstadt? The reason was of a political nature. The rebellion broke out during the discussion on the so-called "trade union" question. The political work in Kronstadt was wholly in the hands of the Petrograd committee, at the head of which stood Zinoviev. The same Zinoviev was the chief, most untiring, and most passionate leader in the struggle against me in the discussion. Before my departure for the Urals I was in Petrograd and spoke at a meeting of Communist seamen. The general spirit of the meeting made an extremely unfavorable impression upon me. Dandified and well-fed sailors, Communists in name only, produced the impression of parasites in comparison with the workers and Red Army men of that time. On the part of the Petrograd committee the campaign was carried on in an extremely demagogic manner. The commanding personnel of the fleet was isolated and terrified. Zinoviev's resolution received, probably, 90 percent of the votes. I recall having said to Zinoviev on this occasion: "Everything is very good here, until it becomes very bad." Subsequent to this Zinoviev was with me in the Urals where he received an urgent message that in Kronstadt things were getting "very bad." The overwhelming majority of the sailor "Communists" who supported Zinoviev's resolution took part in the rebellion. I considered, and the Political Bureau made no objections, that negotiations with the sailors and, in case of necessity, their pacification, should be placed with those leaders who only yesterday enjoyed the political confidence of these sailors. Otherwise, the Kronstadters would consider the matter as though I had come to take "revenge" upon them for their voting against me during the party discussion.

Whether correct or not, in any case it was precisely these considerations which determined my attitude. *I stepped aside completely and demonstratively from this affair.* Concerning the repressions, as far as I remember, Dzerzhinsky had personal charge of them and Dzerzhinsky could not tolerate anyone's interference with his functions (and properly so).

Whether there were any needless victims I do not know. On this score I trust Dzerzhinsky more than his belated critics. For lack of data I cannot undertake to decide now, a posteriori, who should have been punished and how. Victor Serge's conclusions on this score—from third hand—have no value in my eyes. But I am ready to recognize that civil war is no school of humanism. Idealists and pacifists always accused the revolution of "excesses." But the main point is that "excesses" flow from the very nature of revolution, which in itself is but an "excess" of history. Whoever so desires may on this basis reject (in little articles) revolution in general. I do not reject it. In this sense I carry full and complete responsibility for the suppression of the Kronstadt rebellion.

# FOR FREEDOM IN EDUCATION[360]

## July 10, 1938

I sincerely thank the editors of *Vida* for having asked me to express my opinion on the tasks of Mexican educators. My knowledge of the life of this country is still insufficient for me to formulate concrete judgments. But there is a general consideration which I can state here:

In backward countries, which include not only Mexico but to a certain extent the USSR as well, the activity of schoolteachers is not simply a profession but an exalted mission. The task of cultural education consists in awakening and developing the critical personality among the oppressed and downtrodden masses. The indispensable condition for this is that the educator himself must possess a personality developed in the critical sense. A person who does not have seriously worked-out convictions cannot be a leader of the people. That is why a regime that is totalitarian in all its forms—in the state, in the trade union, in the party—strikes irreparable blows at culture and education. Where convictions are imposed from above like a military command, the educator loses his mental individuality and cannot inspire either children or adults with respect or trust in the profession he exercises.

This is at present happening not only in the fascist countries, but also in the USSR. The bases created by the October Revolution are still—fortunately—not completely destroyed. But the political system has already definitively assumed a totalitarian character. The Soviet bureaucracy which has done violence to the revolution wants the people to consider it infallible. It is to the schoolteacher that it has entrusted this task of deceiving the people as priests do. To stifle the voice of criticism, it has introduced the totalitarian system into the education workers' trade unions. The police functionaries put at the head of the unions wage a furious campaign of slanders and repression against educators with a critical mind, accusing them of being counterrevolutionaries, "Trotskyists," and "fascists." Those who do not yield, the GPU suppresses. What is more, the Soviet bureaucracy is striving to extend the same system to the whole world. In every nation it has its agents who are seeking to establish the totalitarian system inside the trade unions of those countries. This is the terrible danger which is threatening the cause of revolution and threatening culture, particularly in the young, backward countries, where the population is all too ready, even as it is, to bend the knee to feudalism, clericalism, and imperialism.

The most fervent wish I can express is for Mexican education not to be subjected to a totalitarian system in its trade unions, with the lies, slanders, repressions, and strangling of critical thought this brings in its train. Only an honorable and tenacious ideological struggle can secure the elaboration of firmly rooted, serious convictions. Only education armed with these convictions is capable of winning unshakable authority and completing its great historical mission.

# ON THE ANNIVERSARY
# OF REISS'S DEATH[361]

## July 17, 1938

The more time passes the clearer emerges the figure of Reiss, who fell so tragically on the threshold of the Fourth International. The break with the Bonapartist clique did not mean for him desertion into private life, as for certain other scared and demoralized bureaucrats. Reiss did not for a minute intend to turn aside with a mien of feigned superiority for those who continued the struggle. Before taking measures to ensure his personal safety, he wrote a principled declaration of the reasons for his shift to the banner of the Fourth International. In the very days when he was just preparing the open break with the Kremlin, he was already busy with propaganda and recruiting among his former collaborators and colleagues. One must clearly imagine the grave internal convulsions he had to go through, to understand what strength of spirit was hidden in this revolutionary fighter!

The figure of Ludwig [Reiss] becomes nearer and dearer to us the more we see of "disillusioned" and "tired" bureaucrats who, you see, are so tormented by Stalin and their own pasts that, without changing their spirit, they go straight over to the camp of bourgeois democracy or liberal semianarchism. Under the stresses of life these gentlemen come to the conclusion that the October Revolution was just a "mistake" and that you must therefore think up something new, unseen and unheard of, completely, hermetically protected from all weaknesses and failures. And in expectation of this doctrine of salvation, the ultraleft dilettantes, allied with more open fascists, busy themselves with gossip and intrigue against revolutionaries. Are examples necessary?

Ludwig died at the very beginning of a new chapter of his life.

We all feel his death as one of the heaviest blows—and there have been many of them. It would, however, be an inadmissible error to think that his sacrifice was fruitless. By the heroic character of his conversion—from Thermidor to the revolution—Reiss brought to the treasure-house of proletarian struggle a much greater contribution than all the "disillusioned" exposers of Stalin put together. The figure of Reiss will stay alive in the memory of the young generations as a lesson and example, and inspire them all and lead them on.

# TO THE CONFERENCE
# OF THE YOUNG PEOPLE'S
# SOCIALIST LEAGUE[362]

## July 18, 1938

A revolutionary party must of necessity base itself on the youth. It can even be said that the revolutionary character of a party can be judged in the first instance by its capacity to attract to its banner the working class youth. The basic attribute of socialist youth—and I have in mind the *genuine* youth and not old men of twenty—lies in its readiness to give itself fully and completely to the cause of socialism. Without heroic self-sacrifice, courage, resoluteness, history in general does not move forward.

But self-sacrifice alone is not enough. What is necessary is to have a clear understanding of the unfolding course of development and the appropriate methods of action. This can be gained only through theory and through living experience. The most flaming enthusiasm soon cools off and evaporates if it does not find timely support in a clear understanding of the laws of historic development. How often have we not observed how young enthusiasts, having bumped their heads, become wise opportunists, how disappointed ultraleftists turn in very short time into conservative bureaucrats, just as an outlaw settles down and becomes transformed into an excellent gendarme. To acquire knowledge and experience and at the same time not to dissipate the fighting spirit, revolutionary self-sacrifice, and readiness to go to the very end—that is the task of education and self-education of revolutionary youth.

Revolutionary irreconcilability is a precious quality once it is directed against opportunist adaptation to the bourgeoisie and against the theoretical flabbiness and fainthearted hesitation of all sorts of office and parlor Communists and Socialists of the type of Browder, Norman Thomas, Lovestone, and the like. But

Writings of Leon Trotsky (1937-38)

"irreconcilability" turns into its opposite when it merely serves the sectarians and confusionists as a platonic consolation for their inability to link themselves up with the masses.

Fealty to the ideological banner is the indispensable and fundamental quality of the genuine revolutionist. But woe to him who turns this "fealty" into doctrinaire stubbornness, into repetition of ready-made, once-and-for-all learned formulas, without the capacity to give heed to life and respond to its needs. Genuine Marxist policy means carrying the ideas of the proletarian revolution to ever wider masses, through ever changing and ever new and frequently unexpected combinations of historic conditions.

The main enemy within the ranks of the proletariat remains, of course, opportunism, especially its most vicious and malignant form—Stalinism, that syphilis of the working class movement. But for a successful struggle against opportunism it is essential that we do away with the vices of sectarianism and pedantic phrase-mongering in our own ranks. The history of the Fourth International, including the section in the United States, has afforded us not a few lessons on this score; we must understand and apply them. The ancient Greeks used to parade drunken helots in order to turn their youth away from alcoholism. All the Oehlers, Fields, Vereeckens, and Company are the helots of sectarianism who fashion their grimaces and leaps as if with the special aim of repelling our youth from sterile and annoying sectarianism.

It remains to be hoped that the next conference of the League will become an important stage on the road of acquiring political experience on the granite basis of Marxist program. Only with this condition will the fate of the great historic movement of which the youth League is one of the advance sections be assured.

Leon Trotsky

# THE DISAPPEARANCE
# OF RUDOLF KLEMENT[363]

## July 18, 1938

My friends in Paris informed New York yesterday by telephone about the disappearance of Rudolf Klement, a German exile living in Paris. Klement, a former Hamburg student, was for two years my secretary at Prinkipo and in France. He was a well-educated young man, twenty-eight years old, possessing a fluent knowledge of several languages. From Paris he had continued to give me a great deal of assistance in my literary work. Like Erwin Wolf, my Czechoslovakian secretary, Klement took an active part in the unmasking of the Moscow frame-ups and through this provoked the violent hatred of the GPU.

My Parisian friends say that they received a copy of a letter from Perpignan addressed to me by Klement. I have not received this letter yet. But from Klement's previous letters it is clear that he had no intention of going anywhere. My Parisian friends think that Klement was kidnaped by the GPU, just as Erwin Wolf was some time ago. If this is so, it is entirely possible that the GPU forcibly carried him to Spain for bloody revenge. I hesitated whether or not to give this information to the press before final verification. But since every hour lost may spell doom to my young friend, I consider it my duty to make public right now the information received by me.

# WAS LEON SEDOV MURDERED?[364]

## July 19, 1938

To M. Pagenel
Examining Magistrate of the Lower Court
Department of the Seine

Dear Sir:

This morning I received from my attorneys, Messrs. Rosenthal and Rous,[365] materials relating to the preliminary investigation and the medical findings on the death of my son Leon Sedov. In so important and tragic a case I deem it my right to speak with complete frankness, without any diplomatic subterfuges. The transmitted documents have astonished me by their reticences. The police investigation, as well as the medical experts' report, is obviously pursuing the line of least resistance. In this way the truth cannot be revealed.

The medical experts arrive at the conclusion that Sedov's death may be explained by natural causes. This conclusion, in the present circumstances, is almost void of meaning. Any sickness may *under certain conditions* lead to death. On the other hand, there is no sickness or almost none that must necessarily result in death exactly at a given moment. The judicial investigation is not faced with a theoretical question of whether a given sickness could of itself have resulted in death but rather with a practical question of whether somebody had deliberately aggravated the sickness in order to do away with Sedov as quickly as possible.

During the Bukharin-Rykov trial this year in Moscow, it was revealed with cynical frankness that one of the methods of the GPU is to assist a disease in expediting death. The former head of the GPU, Menzhinsky, and the writer Gorky were not young and were ill; their death, consequently, might have been readily explained by "natural causes." That is what the official findings of the physicians originally declared. However, from the Moscow judicial trials mankind learned that the shining lights of the Moscow medical world, under the guidance of the former head of the secret police, Yagoda, had hastened the death of sick people by methods that either are not subject to or are very difficult of detection. From the standpoint of the question that concerns us it is almost a matter of indifference whether the testimony of the accused was truthful or false in the particular concrete instances. It suffices that secret methods of poisoning, spreading infection, causing chills, and generally expediting death are included in the arsenal of the GPU. Without going into further details, I take the liberty of calling your attention to the verbatim report of the Bukharin-Rykov trial published by the Soviet Commissariat of Justice.

The experts declare that death "might have" also resulted from natural causes. Of course, it might have. However, as is evident from all the circumstances of the case, none of the physicians expected Sedov's death. It is clear that the GPU itself, trailing every step of Sedov's, could not have pinned its hopes on the possibility that "natural causes" would accomplish their work of destruction without extraneous assistance. Meanwhile, Sedov's illness and his surgical operation offered exceptionally favorable conditions for an intervention of the GPU.

My attorneys have placed at your disposal, Your Honor, all the necessary data proving that the GPU considered the extermination of Sedov as one of its most important tasks. Generally speaking, French judicial authorities can hardly entertain any doubt on this score, following the three Moscow trials and especially after the revelations made by the Swiss and French police in connection with the murder of Ignace Reiss. For a long period of time, and especially for the last two years, Sedov lived in a constant state of siege by a GPU gang which operates on Parisian territory almost as freely as in Moscow. Hired assassins had prepared a trap for Sedov at Mulhouse similar in all respects to the trap in which Reiss fell victim. Only chance saved Sedov on that occasion. The names of the criminals and their roles are known to you, Your Honor, and I do not need to dwell on this point.

On February 4, 1937, Sedov published an article in the French periodical *Confessions* in which he warned that he was in excellent health; that his spirit had not been broken by the persecutions; that he inclined neither to despair nor suicide; and that should death suddenly strike him, those responsible for it must be sought in Stalin's camp. I forwarded the issue of *Confessions* to Paris to be placed in your hands, Your Honor, and that is why I am quoting from memory. Sedov's prophetic warning, flowing from unimpeachable and universally known facts of a historic magnitude, should, in my opinion, have determined the course and character of the judicial investigation. The conspiracy of the GPU to shoot, strangle, drown, poison, or infect Sedov was a constant and basic fact in the last two years of his life. His sickness was only an episode. Even in the hospital Sedov was compelled to register under a fictitious name of Martin, in order thus to render more difficult, if only partially, the work of the bandits who were dogging his steps. In these conditions justice has no right to mollify itself with an abstract formula: "Sedov *might have* died from natural causes," so long as the contrary has not been established, namely, that the powerful GPU had let slip a favorable opportunity to aid the "natural causes."

It may be argued that the above-developed considerations, however weighty in themselves, cannot alter the negative results of expert medical examination. I reserve the right to return to this question in a special document, after a consultation with competent physicians. That no traces of poison were found does not imply that no poisoning took place, and in any case it does not imply that the GPU did not resort to some other measures to prevent the organism, after an operation, from overcoming the illness. If in question here were an ordinary case, under normal living conditions, then the findings of medical experts, while not exhausting the question, would have preserved their full force of conviction. But we have before us a case quite out of the ordinary, namely, a death, unexpected by the physicians themselves, of an isolated exile, following a prolonged duel between him and a mighty state machine armed with inexhaustible material, technical, and scientific resources.

The formal medical examination is all the more inadequate because it stubbornly overlooks the central moment in the history of the illness. The first four days after the operation were days of obvious improvement in the health of the patient, whose condition was considered so favorable that the hospital administration discharged the special nurse. Yet on the night of February 14 the patient, left to himself, was found wandering nude and in a state of wild delirium through the corridors and premises of the hospital. Doesn't this monstrous fact merit the attention of experts?

If natural causes must have (*must have,* not *might have*) led to the tragic denouement, then by what and how can the optimism of the physicians, owing to which the patient was left completely unattended at the most critical moment, be explained? It is of course possible to try to reduce the whole case to an error of prognosis and poor medical care. However, in the materials of the investigation there is not even a mention of it. It is not difficult to understand why: if there was inadequate supervision, then does not the conclusion force itself automatically that his enemies, who never lost sight of Sedov, could have utilized this favorable situation for their criminal ends?

The staff of the clinic made an attempt, it is true, to list those who had come in contact with the sick man. But what value have these testimonies, if the patient had the opportunity, unknown to the staff, of leaving his bed and room, and wandering without hindrance on anybody's part through the hospital building in a condition of delirious excitement?

At all events, M. Thalheimer, the surgeon who operated on Sedov, was taken unawares by the events of the fatal night. He asked Sedov's wife, Jeanne Martin des Pallieres: "Hasn't the patient tried to commit suicide?" To this question, which cannot be deleted from the general history of the sickness, Sedov himself had supplied an answer in advance in the above-cited article, a year prior to his death. The turn for the worse in the patient's condition was so sudden and unexpected that the surgeon, who was acquainted neither with the identity of the sick man nor with the conditions of his life, found himself compelled to resort to the hypothesis of suicide. This fact, I repeat, cannot be deleted from the general picture of the illness and death of my son! One might, if one were inclined, say that the suspicions of Sedov's relatives and intimates arise from their apprehensiveness. But we have before us a physician for whom Sedov was an ordinary patient, an unknown engineer by the name of Martin. Consequently the surgeon could not have been infected with either apprehensiveness or political bias. He guided himself solely by those symptoms which came from the organism of the sick man. And the first reaction of this eminent and experienced physician to the unexpected, i.e., unaccounted for by any *"natural* causes," turn in the case was to suspect an attempt at suicide on the part of the patient. Isn't it clear, isn't it most palpably evident that had the surgeon known at that moment the identity of his patient and the conditions of his life he would instantly have asked: "Couldn't this be the work of assassins?"

This is precisely the question that is posed in all its force before the judicial investigation. The question is formulated, Your Honor, not by myself but by the surgeon Thalheimer, even if involuntarily. And to this question I find no answer at all in the materials of the preliminary investigation forwarded to me. I do not find even an attempt to seek an answer. I find no interest even in the question itself.

Truly astonishing is the fact that the enigma of the crucial night has remained thus far not only unexplained but even unprobed. That time is allowed to lapse, rendering extremely difficult the work of any subsequent investigation, cannot be explained away as an accident. The administration of the clinic has naturally tried to avoid any investigation of this point, for it could not fail to bring to light gross negligence owing to which a gravely sick man was left without any attendance and could have committed acts fatal to himself or *could have been subjected* to such acts. The expert doctors, for their part, did not at all insist upon clarifying the events of the tragic night. The police investigation was confined to superficial depositions of individuals who were guilty at least of negligence and therefore interested in covering it up. Yet behind the negligence of some might easily have lurked the criminal will of others.

French jurisprudence follows the formula for investigation "against X." Under this very formula the investigation is now being conducted into the death of Sedov. But X in this case does not at all remain an "unknown," in the literal sense of the term. It is not a question of a chance cutthroat who murders a wayfarer on a highway, and vanishes after the murder. It is a question of a very definite international gang which has already committed more than one crime on the territory of France, and which makes use of and cloaks itself with friendly diplomatic relations. That is the real reason why the investigations of the theft of my archives, the persecution of Sedov, and the attempt to kill him at Mulhouse, and, finally, that is the reason why the present investigation of Sedov's death, which has already lasted five months, have brought and are bringing no results. Seeking to avoid being involved in the completely real and powerful political factors and forces behind the crime, the investigation proceeds from a fiction that in question here is a simple episode of a private life; it labels the criminal "X" and—fails to find him.

The criminals will be exposed, Your Honor; the radius of the crime is far too great, far too great a number of people and interests often contradictory to each other have been drawn into it; the revelations have already begun, and they will disclose that the threads of a series of crimes lead to the GPU and, through the GPU, directly to Stalin. I cannot tell whether French justice will take an active part in these disclosures. I would heartily welcome it, and am prepared for my part to do everything in my power to assist. But, in one way or another, the truth will be discovered!

From the above it follows quite obviously that the investigation into the death of Sedov has hardly begun as yet. In consideration of all the circumstances in the case and the prophetic words written by Sedov himself on February 4, 1937, the investigation cannot but proceed from the assumption that the death was of a violent character. The organizers of the crime were GPU agents, the fake functionaries of Soviet institutions in Paris. The perpetrators were the agents of these agents recruited from among the White emigres, French or foreign Stalinists, and so on. The GPU could not fail to have its agents in a Russian clinic in Paris or among circles closest to it. Such are the paths along which the investigation must proceed, if it, as I should like to hope, seeks to uncover the crime and not pursue the line of least resistance.

> I remain, Your Honor,
> Most sincerely yours,
> Leon Trotsky

# MY CONSPIRACY[366]

## July 19, 1938

During the eighteen months of my stay in this hospitable country I have been accused of a number of dreadful conspiracies.

A few months back Mr. Toledano declared at various meetings that I was preparing a general strike against the government of General Cardenas. No more and no less! The leader of the Communist Party (his name, I think, is Laborde) declared at a public mass meeting in the presence of the president of the republic that I was in a fascist conspiracy with Generals Cedillo and . . . Villareal. On the morrow each of the accusers cast aside his own accusation like a cigarette butt, forgot about it, and passed on to new inventions.

At present my vacation trip to Patzcuaro, Jiquilpan, Guadalajara, and Morelia is placed on the agenda. Now I am no longer accused of preparing a general strike and a fascist uprising but of . . . a trip through Mexico, stopping at hotels, and meeting and conversing with Mexican citizens. Yes, I have actually committed all these crimes. And, I must add, I committed them with great pleasure.

On the part of the various layers of the population—workers, teachers, army men, artists, government and municipal authorities—I met nothing but consideration and hospitality, which in general so brilliantly distinguish the Mexicans. In Patzcuaro, a few teachers, who visited Diego Rivera and myself on their own initiative, conversed with me concerning the situation in the USSR and in particular about public education. I expressed to them the same views which I have expressed many times in my books and articles. In order to assure complete clarity of exposition, I gave them a written statement. None of these teachers, so far as I know, considered or called himself a "Trotskyite."

In Jiquilpan, Guadalajara, and Morelia, I am sorry to say, I had no such meetings, since at each of these places I stopped for only a few hours.

In Guadalajara, the field of operation for my "conspiracy" was the government palace, the university, and the orphan asylum, where I examined the frescoes of Orozco. Various people approached me asking for autographs or simply to press my hand. Some of them I asked jestingly, just as I asked the teachers in Patzcuaro: "Aren't you afraid to approach a counterrevolutionist and fascist?" Almost invariably I received the answer, "Not a single sensible person believes this." Needless to say, this answer gave me great moral satisfaction.

So far as the conspiracy with Dr. Atl is concerned,[367] I can only say that I heard his name for the first time from the "unmaskers." I never met Dr. Atl and do not have the honor of knowing him.

I do not doubt that this statement, containing in itself the refutation of a false denunciation, will also be interpreted by my detractors as "interference in the internal life of Mexico." But this trick will fool no one. I gave a definite obligation to the government of this country, that is, to the government of General Cardenas and not to the government of Lombardo Toledano. No one has informed me that the task of keeping my behavior under observation has been conferred upon Mr. Toledano. I never obligated myself to keep silent on slanders and slanderers. I retain the right in my house as well as during trips to breathe the Mexican air, to meet citizens of this country, to enter into conversations with them, to visit monuments of art—and in such cases as I find it necessary, to brand openly and by name those "democrats," "socialists," and "revolutionists," who have shamefully taken upon themselves the assignment to obtain, by lies and slander, my deliverance into the hands of the GPU.

# FINANCING THE
# REVOLUTIONARY MOVEMENT[368]

## July 23, 1938

. . . I have the impression that our practical methods of action are not in accordance with our revolutionary program, that we are too passive in our practical activity. It is not only a question concerning the fascist danger or the question of activity in the trade unions, but also in such matters as the publishing of our paper and our whole activity. I cannot understand how this very revolutionary YPSL organization is not capable of publishing the *Challenge* once a month. It is due to financial difficulties. I absolutely cannot understand why.

In Paris during the war we published a daily paper beginning with a capital of thirty francs ($8.00) and we published it for almost three years. How? We had three devoted comrades in a printing shop, and they worked it. When we had money, we paid them. When we had no money, they waited for better times. I believe that at least our young comrades should make the same effort, not only to have a central printing shop in New York, but one in every important region, such as we had in czarist Russia in every important town. We must have such printing shops if we have nothing else. For example, our English comrades now have their own printing shop, but to have such a printing shop with two or three devoted comrades, we can put out not only the *Socialist Appeal* at least twice a week, but also pamphlets, leaflets, etc. The trouble is that the party work is too much based on petty-bourgeois conceptions.

We must educate our youth for more of a spirit of sacrifice. We already have so many young bureaucrats in our movement. For example, the *Challenge* needs $300. If they lack it, good, they wait. That is not the revolutionary way. It is a very opportunistic policy, far more opportunistic than advocating a labor party. You know that the reason we don't have the revolution is because the workers are held back by bourgeois prejudices—democratic prejudices. We don't have these prejudices, but in the matter of approaching practical things we have the bourgeois manner. It is very useful for the bourgeois class.

The American workers consider it a degradation not to have a Ford, fine clothes, for they think they must do the same as the bourgeois. It is disgraceful to imitate the upper class. We Marxists understand this very well. Absolutely bad, in a revolutionary situation particularly. But in practical methods we act the same way. We don't have the revolutionary courage to break this tradition, to break the bourgeois norms of conduct and set up our own rules of moral duty, etc. This is especially true for youth, and it is extremely important, not only to educate themselves theoretically, but to educate themselves as militants, as men and women.

# THE FORTHCOMING TRIAL
# OF THE DIPLOMATS[369]

## July 25, 1938

At one time it might have seemed that Moscow had given up further political trials with their monotonous confessions. During the last period, however, rumors persistently speak of continued preparation for a show trial of diplomats.

The political situation on the international arena as well as inside the USSR is such that these rumors must be considered as entirely probable.

It was the aim of the preceding trials to clear Stalin of responsibility for the mistakes and breakdowns in industry, agriculture, the government apparatus, and the Red Army.

The new trial apparently will have as its task the shifting of responsibility from Stalin to his subordinates for the severe failures which Soviet diplomacy and the Comintern have suffered on the international arena.

The "People's Front" policy in Spain ended in catastrophe. In the Far East Moscow has revealed only too clearly her impotence. She has been almost entirely pushed out of European politics. Nothing remains but to blame the decline in prestige of the Soviets upon new scapegoats in the form of docile diplomats. Doubtless this is the basic idea of the forthcoming trial.

Defendants named are the former Soviet representatives in the Far East (Yurenev, Bogomolov), in Berlin (the same Yurenev), in Spain (Antonov-Ovseenko and Rosenberg).[370] Rakovsky is expected to appear in court as witness and possibly as accused. The roles marked out for these accused are evident in advance in their main outline: the diplomats disclosed state secrets, entered into alliance with enemies, betrayed their fatherland, etc.

However, in this trial the role of Yakubovich, the former ambassador in Norway, remains enigmatic. In distinction to Antonov-Ovseenko, to Rakovsky, and to a certain extent to

Yurenev, Yakubovich never belonged to any opposition. In essence he was a political officeholder of the diplomatic corps. Even as an officeholder he remained always in the background. For a number of years he served as secretary to the Soviet Embassy in Berlin, before obtaining an independent assignment in Oslo.

This third-rate diplomatic post suddenly assumed political significance in 1936 in connection with the attempts of the Moscow government to oust me from Norway. Through the deceased Norwegian lawyer Puntervold, who was close to government circles, I was quite well informed at the time about what was going on behind the scenes.

Yakubovich threatened boycott of the merchant marine and of the fishing trade and, according to Puntervold's account, violently banged the table in the Ministry of Foreign Affairs. The frightened Norwegian government consented to intern me, but did not dare go so far as to deliver me up. This failure, no doubt, was chalked up against Yakubovich, since the Zinoviev-Kamenev trial was so timed as to obtain my immediate deliverance into the hands of the GPU.

Another lapse was ascribed to Yakubovich in connection with the second trial (February 1937), the pivotal point of which was Pyatakov's flight to Oslo in a German airplane for criminal conference with me. As is well known, facts established with absolute exactitude by the Norwegian authorities as well as others entirely refute Pyatakov's testimony: not a single foreign plane landed at the Oslo airport during the entire month of December 1935.

The International Commission in New York established all facts referring to this incident with exhaustive fullness and irreproachable accuracy (see *Not Guilty*, pp. 173-91). The breakdown of Soviet justice in this central point could not but be imputed as a lapse of Yakubovich's, since no doubt precisely through him the GPU was gathering information about my life in Norway, conditions of that country, the airport in Oslo in particular. Yakubovich for his part did what he could. But the blunders disclosed at the trial were more than enough for the shooting of an unfortunate diplomat.

Of course, in court Yakubovich will not repent the fact that he supplied the GPU with careless or slipshod information. In all probability another task will be imposed upon him, namely, that of giving *new* information which should even partially smooth out the deadly impression produced by the breakdown in Pyatakov's testimony. What will be the nature of Yakubovich's "confession" now being prepared? It is not difficult to suppose several variants here. We will take one of them hypothetically in order to show by a concrete example the methods of Stalinist justice.

Yakubovich might admit that he actually belonged to a Trotskyist conspiracy, and was the closest friend and ally of Pyatakov. Precisely he, Yakubovich, organized Pyatakov's flight from Berlin to Oslo. The landing did not at all take place at the airport but on one of the fjords and moreover he, Yakubovich, brought Pyatakov in his own car to his apartment and then took him to meet Trotsky. Pyatakov testified falsely in court regarding the time and place of the landing in order to shield his friend Yakubovich. The new data on the imaginary flight which Yakubovich will be assigned will most likely be built on more careful research and combinations. Possibly even with some "chance" witnesses arranged in advance.

Of course, for our part we deal with only a hypothesis. The future trial if held will bring verification. It is quite likely that this article will force Vyshinsky to choose some other variant and introduce corresponding changes in his accusation and in Yakubovich's testimony. We shall try to discover the traces of these alternatives in time.

The work of the GPU is sufficiently crude and invariably leaves dirty marks. At any rate only the hypothesis advanced above permits us to understand how a third-rate diplomatic job-holder, devoid of any political interest, occupying a peaceful post in superpeaceful Norway, could—according to information from various sources—be placed almost at the head of a diplomatic conspiracy.

In any case, I should add that I have never met Yakubovich, that I have had no political relations with him either directly or indirectly, and during my stay in Norway considered him my worst enemy, who led a campaign of slander against me without sparing any expense.

Apparently Yakubovich's successors on the bench of the accused will have to answer for his inevitable fresh blunders should Stalin manage for any length of time to keep in motion his conveyor belt of falsifications.

# A 'LETTER'
# FROM RUDOLF KLEMENT[371]

## August 1, 1938

This morning, August 1, I received a letter apparently in the handwriting of Rudolf Klement, in German. The letter is dated July 14 and presumably went via Paris and New York. The handwriting is undoubtedly similar to the handwriting of Klement but bears an extremely uneven, sickly and feverish character. The letter peculiarly is signed, "Frederic." As to its contents it is one of the most fantastic documents that I have ever held in my hands. To start with, the salutation. All the preceding letters of Klement, including those written just a few days before, begin with the words, "Dear Comrade" or "Dear L.D." (my initials). This last letter begins with the words, "Mr. Trotsky." From beginning to end the letter presents an incoherent piling up of accusations against the Fourth International, against me personally, and against my deceased son.

The accusations are of two kinds: the first—clearly dictated by the GPU—the inevitable "bloc" with fascism and connection with the Gestapo; the second—a series of accusations concerning single episodes from the internal life of the Fourth International which seem to make an attempt at explaining the sudden change in Klement's position.

What is most striking is that the content of the letter in all its details stands in direct and clear contradiction to hundreds of letters written by the same Klement up until a very short time ago to me personally and to mutual friends. The letter is written as if the past had not existed at all. Only a person tied hand and foot, physically and morally, could write like this, and then only under the dictation of other people absolutely unfamiliar with Klement's past who wanted to make use of him for their purposes.

Theoretically it could still be assumed that Klement has lost his mind. But in this case the puzzle remains as to why his delirium should contain the elements of the well-known "accusations" of the GPU. We must not forget for one moment that Klement was closely familiar with the life and work of the Fourth International, that he was especially indignant at these "accusations," and that his indignation found inimitable expression in dozens of letters. Klement took an active part in the unmasking of the Moscow trials, and this work, again, is imprinted in numerous letters and documents.

It is most probable, however, that the letter is written in the grip of the GPU and that Klement, in fear for his life or for the lives of people dear to him, or finally, under the influence of some drugs, submissively wrote down what he was ordered, not bothering to correct obvious absurdities. It is even possible that Klement included these absurdities with complete readiness in order, in this fashion, to compromise the GPU's plot beforehand. In any case this letter, written and transmitted to me, testifies that this affair will have its aftermath. The very fact of Klement's disappearance remains of course the chief mystery. Where is he? What has happened to him? The letter bears no indication of the place of mailing. Apparently the letter passed from city to city; the inner envelope bears only my initials. I will endeavor of course to obtain the necessary information about the postal route of this letter.

The letter ends with the words: "I have no intention to come out openly against you." Needless to say, I wish more than anything else that the unfortunate Klement could speak and come out "openly" if . . . he is still alive. I am immediately sending a photostatic copy of the letter for the disposal of the French authorities and the New York commission of Dr. John Dewey. Let us trust that the solution of this mysterious case will be found and that complete light will be shed upon it.

# ON THE FATE OF RUDOLF KLEMENT

## August 3, 1938

1. I received by mail via New York City on August 1 the letter in German signed "Frederic." The letter is dated July 14, without indicating the mailing place. The inner envelope bears in German the words, "for L.D." It is necessary to establish from where and by what route the letter reached New York. Let me add that the marks and lines on the margin which appear on the photostatic copy were made by me in red pencil upon first reading the letter.

2. Klement began his letters to me with the words, "Dear Comrade L.D." The present letter begins with the salutation, "Mr. Trotsky." This salutation, apparently, should correspond to the hostile tone of the letter which announces the "break in relations."

3. The handwriting of the letter is very similar to the handwriting of Klement. But after more careful comparison with old letters the difference becomes very striking. The handwriting of the last letter is not free, but studied, uneven; individual characters are drawn too carefully, others, on the contrary, are hesitating. Absence of erasures and careful spacing of words, especially at the end of lines, show beyond any doubt that the letter has been copied from a draft.

Was the letter really written by Klement? I shall not presume to deny it categorically. The handwriting is similar if each character is taken by itself; but the manuscript as a whole lacks naturalness and ease. If this is Klement's handwriting, then it can be so only under very exceptional circumstances; more likely, however, it is *skillful forgery.*

4. From the point of view of the handwriting, the *salutation* and the *signature* draw attention. Clearly they have been written at different times (different shade of ink) and in a somewhat different hand. There is only one alternative: either the author of the letter hesitated a long time as to what salutation and what

Rudolf Klement.

signature to use, and resolved the question only after the letter had been finished; or the forger already had samples of the words "Trotsky" and "Frederic" before him from old correspondence while the rest of the letter had to be composed from individual characters. Therefore the greater naturalness and ease in the outline of the salutation and signature.

5. The name "Frederic" as a signature is difficult to explain. It is true that Klement once really used this pseudonym, but he abandoned it more than two years ago when he grew suspicious that the name had become known to the GPU or the Gestapo. The letters which I have received from Klement in Mexico for the last year and a half have been signed either "Adolphe" or "Camille," but never "Frederic." What made Klement return to a long abandoned pseudonym, especially in a letter to me? Here the hypothesis naturally arises that the forgers of the letter had in their possession *old* letters of Klement signed "Frederic," and that they were not aware of the change in pseudonym. For the investigation this circumstance is of very great importance.

6. In the content of the letter there are something like two levels which are mechanically connected with one another. On the one hand, the letter repeats the vile falsifications of the GPU in reference to my connections with fascism, relations with the Gestapo, etc.; on the other hand, it criticizes my policy seemingly from the point of view of the interests of the Fourth International, and tries in this manner to give an explanation for Klement's "turn." This ambiguity threads the entire letter.

7. On the fabricated conversations between Klement and me concerning the admissibility of "temporary concessions to fascist heads for the sake of the proletarian revolution," the letter represents only a belated repetition of corresponding "confessions" at the Moscow trials. "Frederic" does not even attempt to introduce any vital, concrete feature into the Moscow frame-up. More than that, he declares simply that the "bloc" with fascism was concluded on "a basis not altogether clear to me" (Frederic), as if thus renouncing in advance any attempt to understand or explain the methods, tasks, and purposes of this fantastic bloc. Thus it seems that somehow I found it necessary in the past to initiate "Frederic" into my alliance with Berlin, but did not initiate him into the meaning of this alliance. In other words, my "frankness" had the single purpose of helping out the GPU.

"Frederic" writes further on the same score that "what was called using fascism was direct collaboration with the Gestapo." Not a word on what this collaboration consisted of and precisely how "Frederic" learned about it. In this part "Frederic" follows strictly the shameless methods of Vyshinsky-Yezhov.

8. Then follow accusations of an "internal" character intended to serve as motivation for Klement's break with the Fourth International and with me personally. It is curious that this part of the letter should begin with a reference to my "Bonapartistic manners," that is, it seems to return the epithet applied by me to the Stalinist regime. In passing, all the accusations in the trials against the Trotskyites are built on this pattern: Stalin plasters his political opponents with crimes of which he himself is guilty or with accusations which are advanced against him. Vyshinsky, the GPU and its agents carry out this operation almost automatically. "Frederic" submissively follows the strictly set pattern.

9. The letter further lists all the negative consequences of my "Bonapartist" methods. "In the past," he states, "we were abandoned by such people as Nin, Roman Well, Jacob Frank."[373] The combination of these three names is strange. Roman Well and Jacob Frank openly returned in their time to the Comintern after having attempted for a while to act in our ranks as secret agents of the Comintern. On the contrary, Andres Nin, after his break with us, maintained an independent position, remained hostile to the Comintern, and fell victim to the GPU. Klement knows this distinction very well. But "Frederic" ignores it or does not know it.

10. "You have delivered the POUM," continues "Frederic," "to the mangling of the Stalinists." This phrase is absolutely enigmatic, not to say senseless. Despite the POUM's open break with the Fourth International, the GPU persecuted the members of the POUM precisely as if they were Trotskyites; in other words, the POUM is subjected to "mangling" on the same basis as the adherents of the Fourth International. "Frederic's" enigmatic phrase is apparently dictated by the desire to set against Trotskyism those members of the POUM who have not yet been murdered by the GPU.

11. The accusations which refer to a later period are of no less false a character. "Recently our organization was abandoned by such people as Sneevliet and Vereecken, who showed such great political sense and wisdom in the Spanish question." Sneevliet and Vereecken in reality showed their sympathy for the POUM, which was accused by the Stalinists of being connected with fascism. Thus it seems that "Frederic" on the one hand solidarizes himself with the POUM, Sneevliet, and Vereecken; and on the other, repeats the accusations against the opponents

of the GPU (among them, consequently, also against the POUM) of connections with fascism. It must be added that during the last several years Klement often reproached me in friendly fashion with being too tolerant and patient in regard to Sneevliet and Vereecken. But apparently "Frederic" knows nothing about this.

12. "We were abandoned," he continues, "by Molinier, Jan Bur with his group,[374] Ruth Fischer, Maslow, Brandler, and others." In this list the name of Brandler, who never belonged to the Trotskyist camp but on the contrary was always its irreconcilable and open enemy, strikes the eye immediately. Years of open struggle in which he invariably defended Stalinism against us testify to his animosity. Klement well knew the political figure of Brandler and our attitude toward him. He knew only too well, at the same time, the inner life of the Fourth International. Why did "Frederic" introduce Brandler's name among the people who belonged to our movement and then broke with it? Two explanations are possible. If we grant that the letter was written by Klement, we must assume that he wrote it under the muzzle of a revolver and included Brandler's name in order to show the forced character of his letter. If we proceed from the fact that the letter was forged, the explanation is indicated by the entire technique of the GPU, where ignorance is combined with brazenness. In the Moscow trials all opponents of Stalin were thrown into one heap. Among the members of the nonexistent "Right-Trotskyite" bloc were included not only Bukharin but also Brandler and even Souvarine. In accordance with the same logic Brandler finds himself among people who broke with the Fourth International, to which he never belonged.

13. "It is puerile to think," continues "Frederic," "that public opinion will allow itself to be pacified by the simple declaration that they are all agents of the GPU." This phrase is even less understandable. None of us have said that Nin and other leaders of the POUM, being annihilated by the GPU, were agents of the GPU. This applies as well to the other people mentioned in the letter, except Roman Well, who through his activity openly distinguished himself in the service of the GPU. Klement knew very well that none of us advanced such preposterous accusations against the people listed in the letter. But the whole thing is that by attempting, in passing, to defend the American, Carleton Beals, and other friends and agents of the GPU, "Frederic" must consequently compromise the very accusation of connection with the GPU. Hence, this clumsy trick, by means of which the suspicion is extended—in my name—to people to whom it

obviously cannot be applied at all. This again is the style of Stalin-Vyshinsky-Yagoda-Yezhov.

14. The name "Beals" is spelled incorrectly in the letter: "Bills." Only a person not familiar with the English spelling could write in such a manner. But Klement knew the English language well, knew the name Beals, and was very pedantic in spelling out names.

15. The German of the letter is correct; but it seems to me much more primitive and unwieldy than the language of Klement, who possessed stylistic abilities.

16. Worthy of attention, too, is the reference to the forthcoming International Conference, by means of which I hope, in the words of the letter, "to save the situation" for the Fourth International. In reality, as can be seen from ample correspondence, Klement was the initiator of the conference and took the most active part in its organization. The GPU, insofar as it was aware of the internal affairs of the Fourth International (through the press, internal bulletins, and possibly through secret agents), might have hoped by kidnaping Klement prior to the conference to stop the organizational work and prevent the conference itself.

17. This same part of the letter contains a reference to the proposal of including Walter Held in the International Secretariat "apparently by orders from over there." In other words the author of the letter wishes to impute that Walter Held is an agent of the Gestapo. The absurdity of this information is apparent to all who know Held. But naturally, casting a shadow upon one of the prominent adherents of the Fourth International is one of the designs of the GPU.

18. The letter ends with these words: "I have no wish whatever to come out openly against you: I have had enough of it all, I am tired. I go and leave my place for Walter Held." The falsity of these phrases is absolutely evident. "Frederic" would not have written this letter if he or his masters did not intend in some way or another to utilize it subsequently. In what way? This is not yet apparent. Possibly it may be used in particular in the Barcelona trial held behind closed doors against the "Trotskyites."[375] But possibly too it is for a larger purpose.

What conclusions follow from the foregoing analysis? At first, upon receipt of the letter, I had almost no doubt that it was written by Klement's own hand, but in a very nervous condition. My impression is explainable from the fact that I was accustomed to receiving letters from Klement and had never had any reason to question their authenticity. The more I scrutinized the text, however, and the more I compared it with his preceding letters, the more I became convinced of the fact that the letter is only a very skillful forgery. The GPU has no lack of specialists of all kinds. My friend Diego Rivera, who has the refined eye of a painter, does not at all doubt that the handwriting is forged. To solve this question we can and must utilize the services of a handwriting expert.

If it should be established, as I believe, that the letter is a forgery, all the rest will become clear of itself.

Klement was kidnaped, spirited away, and probably killed. The GPU fabricated the letter, representing Klement as a traitor to the Fourth International, possibly with the aim of shifting responsibility for his murder upon the "Trotskyites." All this is entirely within the practices of this international gang. I consider this variant the most likely.

At first, as I have already stated, I assumed that the letter was written by Klement—at the point of a revolver or out of fear for the fate of people dear to him; or more correctly, not written but copied from an original placed before him by GPU agents. In case this hypothesis is confirmed, the possibility is not excluded that Klement is still alive and that the GPU in the near future will attempt to extract further "voluntary" confessions from him. "Confessions" of this kind dictate their own reply from public opinion: let Klement, if he is alive, come out openly before the police, the judicial authorities, or an impartial commission and tell them all he knows. We can predict in advance that the GPU will in no case let Klement out of their hands.

Theoretically a third supposition is possible: namely, that Klement had suddenly radically altered his views and gone over voluntarily to the side of the GPU, drawing from this all the practical conclusions, that is, consenting to support all the frame-ups of this institution. One can go even further and assume that Klement has always been a GPU agent. But all the facts, including the letter of July 14, make this hypothesis absolutely inconceivable. Not a few times Klement could have granted the GPU the greatest services, so far as it was a question of taking my life, the life of Leon Sedov, or determining the fate of my collaborators and my documents. He had the opportunity to come out openly during the Moscow trials with his "revelations," which in those days at least would have made a much greater impression than now. But during the Moscow trials Klement did what he could to unmask the frame-ups, actively helping Sedov in gathering data. Klement showed great devotion for the movement and a serious theoretical interest in the discussion of debatable questions. To his pen belong a series of articles and letters showing that he had a very earnest, even ardent attitude toward the program of the Fourth International. To feign devotion and theoretical interest for a movement for a number of years—that task is more than difficult.

It is just as difficult to accept the hypothesis of a "sudden" turn within the last period. If Klement had voluntarily gone over to the Comintern and the GPU—no matter for what reason—he would have had no basis whatsoever for hiding. The above-mentioned Roman Well and Jacob Frank, as well as Senin, the brother of Well,[376] did not at all hide after their "turn"; on the contrary, they came out openly in the press, and Well and Senin (the brothers Sobolevicius) have even made a career. Finally, in the case of his voluntarily going over to the side of the Comintern, Klement as a capable and informed person should have written a much more coherent letter without self-evident incongruities and absurdities which any investigating magistrate, any impartial commission, armed with the necessary documents can easily refute.

These are the considerations which led to the conclusion that Klement was kidnaped by the GPU and that his letter to me is a forgery, fabricated by the specialists of the GPU. It is very easy to refute this hypothesis: *"Frederic" must emerge from his hiding place and come out with open accusations.* If he will not do this, it means that Klement is in the clutches of the GPU, and probably already "liquidated," as have been so many others.

The chief responsibility in solving the mystery of Rudolf Klement's disappearance lies with the French police. Let up hope, no matter how difficult this may be, that they will this time prove themselves more persistent and more successful than they have been in solving all the preceding crimes of the GPU on French soil.

August 4, 1938

P.S.—All the above had already been written when I received from Paris a letter by Comrade Rous, dated July 21, each line of which confirms the above conclusions.

1. Rous received a copy of the letter addressed to me, but signed "Rudolf Klement" and "Adolphe." Assuming the same signature to be on the original addressed to me, Rous expressed legitimate astonishment over the letter being signed with the name "Adolphe" and not "Camille," the signature Klement used during

the entire last period. In fighting against the espionage of the GPU and the Gestapo, Klement changed his pseudonyms three times during the last few years in the following order: Frederic, "Adolphe," Camille. Obviously, the GPU fell into a trap. Possessing the names Klement, Frederic, and "Adolphe," to lend more plausibility they placed on different copies all three of the names (which is absurd in itself), but did not use the only name which Klement actually utilized as his signature during the last period.

2. On July 8, that is five days prior to Klement's disappearance, his portfolio of papers vanished in the subway. It is understood, of course, that the portfolio could not be found. Klement, who well knew that the GPU in Paris acts as if it were in its own home, immediately informed every section of the Fourth International of the theft of the portfolio, suggesting that they cease sending letters to the old addresses.

3. On July 15, after receiving "Adolphe's" letter postmarked Perpignan, the French comrades visited Klement's room. His table was set, everything was in order, not the least sign of preparation for departure! The importance of this circumstance does not need any elucidation.

4. Comrade Rous points out that the address on the letter from Perpignan was written as the Russians write it, first the name of the city, then at the bottom of the envelope the name of the street. It can be considered beyond all doubt that Klement, as a German and a European, never wrote addresses in this manner.

5. Why, asks Rous, is the name "Beals" written as in Russian, "Bills" (in other words, the Russian transliteration of the name is simply written in Latin characters)?

Omitting other remarks from Rous's letter (Rous and other French comrades will themselves bring these considerations to the attention of the public and of the French authorities), I shall limit myself now to stating that the first factual information received directly from France fully confirms the conclusions at which I arrived on the basis of the analysis of the letter signed "Frederic"; that is, *Rudolf Klement has been kidnaped by the GPU.*

# THE SINO-JAPANESE STRUGGLE[377]

## August 11, 1938

On August 6, Mr. S. Nanjo, representing the two largest newspapers of Japan, the *Tokyo-Nichinichi* and the *Osaka-Mainichi,* made a written request of me for an interview. His questions concerned the relations between the USSR, Japan, and China; how the recent purges affected the Red Army; and what internal changes could be expected in the USSR in the future. My answer to Mr. Nanjo was as follows:

August 7, 1938
Mr. S. Nanjo
Representative of *Tokyo-Nichinichi* and *Osaka-Mainichi*
Hotel Montejo
Paseo de la Reforma 240
Mexico, D.F.

Sir:
It would give me great pleasure to express my views on the situation in the Far East as well as on the relations between the USSR and Japan before the wide reading public of the newspapers represented by you. I am afraid, however, that the obstacles which stand in the road are virtually insurmountable. As I see from your list of questions, your newspapers assume that my answers could be utilized in the interests of the foreign policy of Japan and of her internal regime. The directors of your newspapers could have arrived at this conclusion only on the basis of the false information in the Soviet press. My real views have nothing in common with what the Moscow press says about them.

In the struggle between Japan and China I stand fully and completely on the side of China. With all my irreconcilability toward the Stalinist regime, I consider that in the clash between the USSR and Japan, the USSR represents progress; Japan—the worst reaction. I do not doubt that in the next armed clash of great magnitude, Japan will suffer a social and political catastrophe, similar to the one suffered by the czarist empire during the World War.

These are my real views, which I would be willing to develop and elaborate for the information of the Japanese people, who are forcibly held in a state of complete ignorance. But I doubt very much that your newspapers would agree to print a truthful elucidation of the situation in the Far East.

If I am mistaken on this score, I should, naturally, be completely ready to admit my mistake. But in this case I would request you to furnish me with full and specific guarantees that my answers to your questions would be printed in full and without the least alteration.

Sincerely yours,
Leon Trotsky

Upon receiving this letter, Mr. Nanjo found himself incapable of publishing my answer to his questions and declined the interview.

# THE USSR AND JAPAN[378]

## August 11, 1938

The feeling of satisfaction over the truce between the USSR and Japan should not inspire optimism about the near future. Japan cannot move deeper into China and at the same time tolerate the USSR in Vladivostok. No diplomatic art can remove this antagonism. Tokyo would prefer to postpone settling its accounts with the USSR until its position in China is secure. But on the other hand, internal events in the USSR tempt Japan to strike while the iron is hot, that is, to test its strength immediately. Hence the ambiguous policy of Japan: provocations, border violations, bandit raids, and simultaneously—diplomatic negotiations so as to retain the possibility for temporary semiretreats in case the USSR proves stronger than Japan would like.

In Moscow the inevitability of a Far Eastern war has long been understood. Generally speaking, Moscow has always been interested in delaying the war, as much because rapid industrialization strengthened the military power of the Soviets as because the inner contradictions of Japan, where a semifeudal regime still exists, are preparing the greatest social and political catastrophe.

Military difficulties which Japan encountered in China and which the Japanese militarists in their extreme shortsightedness did not foresee, gave rise, however, to a new situation. The vital interests of the USSR require that it help China with all its might, consciously facing the risk flowing from this. This is understood in the Kremlin, since a definite opinion upon the Far Eastern problem has been shaping itself during the entire twenty years of the Soviet regime. But the Kremlin oligarchy fears war. This does not mean that it fears Japan. No one in Moscow doubts that the Mikado could not withstand a big war. But in Moscow they give themselves no less clear an accounting of the fact that a

412

war will inevitably lead to the collapse of the Stalinist dictatorship.

Stalin is willing to grant any concessions in foreign policy in order the more ruthlessly to maintain his power within the country. But these concessions and the failures of Soviet diplomacy in the last two years kindle discontent within the country and force Stalin to demonstrative gestures of force intended to hide his readiness to make new concessions. This is the explanation for the latest bloody conflicts on the Manchurian and Korean border, as well as for the fact that so far these conflicts have ended in truce and not in a new war.

The key to the situation is now in the hands of Tokyo. The Japanese government is ruled by generals. The Japanese generals are commanded by lieutenants. This constitutes the immediate danger in the situation. The lieutenants grasp neither the position of Japan, nor the position of the USSR. Despite the Chinese lesson—and partly because of the Chinese lesson—they are seeking easy victories at the expense of the USSR. They are generally mistaken. If they provoke a war, it will not produce the immediate collapse of Stalin; on the contrary, it will strengthen his position for a year or two, and this period is more than sufficient to reveal in reality the full internal bankruptcy of Japan's social and political regime. A big war will bring to Japan a revolutionary catastrophe similar to the one which befell czarist Russia in the last great war. The collapse of the Stalinist dictatorship will come only in a second turn. That is why for the rulers of Japan it would not be wise to force Stalin into doing what he does not want, that is, defending the USSR with arms in hand.

# ANSWERS TO THE QUESTIONS
# OF LLOYD TUPLING[379]

## August 12, 1938

*Question:* Since your retirement do you spend your days writing? Or more precisely, what activities do you undertake in an average day?

*Answer:* My time is devoted almost exclusively to writing. I am working now simultaneously on two books: one on Stalin, the other on Lenin. The first will be published by Harper and Brothers at the beginning of next year, the second a year later.

*Q.* Do you believe that the cessation of firing between USSR and Japanese troops along the Manchurian border will mean a lasting and definite end to hostilities? What do you believe were the motives of the USSR in opening the battles?

*A.* I feel no optimism about the truce between the USSR and Japan. It is impossible for Japan to move deeper into China without coming into greater conflict with the USSR in Vladivostok. While Japan would prefer postponing the eventual settlement of accounts with the USSR until her position is more secure in China, the internal events in the USSR tempt Japan to strike now. It is for this reason that Japan has been following a double policy: provocations, violations of the border, raids, and at the same time—negotiations through diplomatic channels in order to keep the road clear for temporary semiretreats in case the USSR should prove too strong for Japan's liking.

*Q.* In the last decade we have seen a most rapid change in the political systems governing various peoples. How long do you believe it will be, if ever, until the United States evolves into a society governed by Marxist principles?

*A.* If the general line of development is clear, the attempts to fix in advance the terms of historic change is futile. One thing, nevertheless, can be affirmed with assurance: the rhythm of development in our time is incomparably more rapid, convulsive, catastrophic than in any previous epoch.

*Q.* Would you care to give me a definition of a "Trotskyite"?

*A.* A "Trotskyite" is one who, staying theoretically on Marx's point of view, connects his activity with the fight of the workers for their emancipation; who bases his hopes for a better future exclusively on the consciousness of the toiling masses; who is free from any considerations of careerism or personal interest; who is strong enough to support slanders, persecutions, and frame-ups; who finds his highest satisfaction not in personal advantages but in the general progress of mankind.

*Q.* In the United States it has long been believed by many that the 1935 change in the Communist Party line which allowed cooperation with bourgeois governments has set back the development of all leftist movements to the position they held a decade ago. Do you believe that the reversal of tactics was a discredit to Marxian aims?

*A.* The Communist International follows the degeneration of the ruling caste in the USSR. Fifteen years ago it was a revolutionary vanguard of the working class. Now it is a bureaucratic appendage to the Moscow oligarchy. Mr. Browder and his followers have nothing in common with the teachings of Marx and Lenin. They represent now a conservative petty-bourgeois party which misleads a part of the workers.

*Q.* After the next great war, which seems to be growing closer day by day, under what political principles will people organize? What do you believe the general effects of that war will be?

*A.* The new world war will inevitably lead to a social revolution. Japan, Germany, and Italy, in view of the terrible internal tensions in these countries, will be the first on the road to catastrophe. But the others will follow them. The ruling classes cannot help but see this perspective and their fear of it is the only "pacifist" factor of our time.

*Q.* During the Moscow trials of late 1937 and early 1938, why did the GPU connect the political activities of their prisoners with "Trotskyism"?

*A.* The GPU tries to discredit "Trotskyism" at any price because so-called "Trotskyism" is the tradition of the October Revolution and the hope of the toiling masses for final liberation. The new aristocratic caste fears the masses and hates "Trotskyism."

*Q.* Concerning this question, I have read many answers, many of which conflict. I am seeking your views because you are the one person in the world who can answer authoritatively. What prevented you from returning to Moscow for the funeral of Lenin? How was your exile plotted?

*A.* I received the announcement of Lenin's death in a code telegram from Stalin when I was very sick in the Caucasus. I asked by code immediately if I would have time to return to the funeral. Stalin answered me that the funeral would take place Saturday, and that in view of my sickness the Political Bureau considered it not advisable for me to return to Moscow. In reality the funeral took place Sunday. Stalin's communication was consciously false and prevented me from participating in the funeral services. It would be, nevertheless, very naive to overestimate the political importance of this episode. The "plot" against me had a profound social basis. The new aristocracy issued from the revolution and sought to smash every old revolutionary who remained true to the toiling masses.

# FREEDOM OF THE PRESS AND THE WORKING CLASS[380]

## August 21, 1938

A campaign against the reactionary press is underway in Mexico. The attack is being directed by the CTM leaders, or, more precisely, by Mr. Lombardo Toledano personally. The objective is to "curb" the reactionary press, either by placing it under a democratic censorship or by banning it altogether. The trade unions have been mobilized for war. The incurable democrats, corrupted by their experience with a Stalinized Moscow and headed by "friends" of the GPU, have hailed this campaign, which cannot be regarded as anything but suicidal. In fact, it is not difficult to foresee that even if this campaign triumphs and leads to practical results that suit the taste of Lombardo Toledano, the ultimate consequences will be borne primarily by the working class.

Both theory and historical experience testify that any restriction of democracy in bourgeois society is, in the final analysis, invariably directed against the proletariat, just as any taxes that are imposed also fall on the shoulders of the working class. Bourgeois democracy is of use to the proletariat only insofar as it opens up the way for the development of the class struggle. Consequently, any working class "leader" who arms the bourgeois state with special means for controlling public opinion in general and the press in particular is, precisely, a traitor. In the last analysis, the sharpening of the class struggle will impel the bourgeoisie of every stripe to reach an agreement among themselves; they will then pass special laws, all sorts of restrictive measures, and all kinds of "democratic" censorship against the working class. Anyone who has not yet understood this should get out of the ranks of the working class.

"But at times," some "friends" of the USSR will object, "the dictatorship of the proletariat is forced to resort to special measures, particularly against the reactionary press."

"This objection," we reply, "comes down primarily to trying to identify a workers' state with a bourgeois state. Even though Mexico is a semicolonial country, it is also a bourgeois state, and in no way a workers' state. However, even from the standpoint of the interests of the dictatorship of the proletariat, banning bourgeois newspapers or censoring them does not in the least constitute a 'program,' or a 'principle,' or an ideal setup. Measures of this kind can only be a temporary, unavoidable evil."

Once at the helm, the proletariat may find itself forced, for a certain time, to take special measures against the bourgeoisie, if the bourgeoisie assumes an attitude of open rebellion against the workers' state. In that case, restricting freedom of the press goes hand in hand with all the other measures employed in waging a civil war. Naturally, if you are forced to use artillery and planes against the enemy, you cannot permit this same enemy to maintain his own centers of news and propaganda within the armed camp of the proletariat. Nonetheless, in this instance, too, if the special measures are extended until they become an enduring pattern, they in themselves carry the danger of getting out of hand and of the workers' bureaucracy gaining a political monopoly that would be one of the sources of its degeneration.

We have a living example of such a dynamic before us in the detestable suppression of freedom of speech and of the press that is now the rule in the Soviet Union. This has nothing to do with the interests of the dictatorship of the proletariat. On the contrary, it is designed to protect the interests of the new governing caste from the worker and peasant opposition. That very Bonapartist bureaucracy in Moscow is now being aped by Mr. Lombardo Toledano and Company, who equate their personal careers with the interests of socialism.

The real tasks of the workers' state lie not in clamping a police gag on public opinion but rather in freeing it from the yoke of capital. This can be done only by placing the means of production, including the production of public information, in the hands of society as a whole. Once this fundamental socialist step has been taken, all currents of public opinion that have not taken up arms against the dictatorship of the proletariat must be given the opportunity to express themselves freely. It is the duty of the workers' state to make available to them, in proportion to their numbers, all the technical means they may require, such as presses, paper, and transport. One of the main causes of the degeneration of the state apparatus is the Stalinist bureaucracy's monopolization of the press, which threatens to reduce all the gains of the October Revolution to utter ruin.

If we were to go looking for examples of the Comintern's fatal influence on the workers' movements in various countries, the present campaign by Lombardo Toledano would provide one of the oddest. Toledano and his fellow doctrinaires are trying essentially to introduce into a bourgeois democratic system means and methods that might in certain temporary conditions prove unavoidable under a dictatorship of the proletariat. What is more, they are not really borrowing these methods from the dictatorship of the proletariat but rather from its Bonapartist usurpers. In other words, they are infecting an already ailing bourgeois democracy with the virus of decaying Stalinist bureaucracy.

Mexico's anemic democracy faces a constant and deadly threat from two directions—first, from foreign imperialism, and second, from the agents of reaction within the country, who control the publications with the widest circulation. But only the blind or feebleminded could think that as the result of a ban on the reactionary press the workers and peasants can free themselves from the influence of reactionary ideas. In reality, only the greatest freedom of speech, of the press, and of assembly can create favorable conditions for the advance of the revolutionary movement of the working class.

It is essential to wage a relentless struggle against the reactionary press. But workers cannot let the repressive fist of the bourgeois state substitute for the struggle that they must wage through their own organizations and their own press. Today the state may appear to be "kindly" disposed to the workers' organizations; tomorrow the government may fall, will inevitably fall, into the hands of the most reactionary elements of the bourgeoisie. In that case, whatever restrictive legislation that exists will be thrown at the workers. Only adventurers with no thought other than for the needs of the moment would fail to heed such a danger.

The most effective way to combat the bourgeois press is to expand the working class press. Of course, yellow journals of *El Popular*'s ilk are incapable of taking up such a task. Such sheets have no place among the workers' press, the revolutionary press, or even the reputable democratic press. *El Popular* serves the personal ambitions of Mr. Lombardo Toledano, who in turn serves the Stalinist bureaucracy. Its methods—lies, slander, witch-hunting campaigns, and falsification—are also Toledano's methods. His newspaper has neither program nor ideas. Obviously such a sheet can never strike a responsive chord in the working class or win the proletariat away from the bourgeois papers.

So, we come to the unavoidable conclusion that the fight against the bourgeois press starts with throwing out the degenerate "leaders" of the working class organizations, in particular with freeing the workers' press from the tutelage of Lombardo Toledano and other bourgeois place seekers. The Mexican proletariat has to have an honest newspaper to express its needs, defend its interests, broaden its horizon, and prepare the way for the socialist revolution in Mexico. This is what *Clave* proposes to do. So, we are starting out by declaring an unrelenting war against Toledano's wretched Bonapartist pretensions. And in this effort we are looking forward to the support of all the advanced workers, Marxists, and genuine democrats.

# FURTHER EVIDENCE
# OF GPU GUILT IN SEDOV DEATH[381]

## August 24, 1938

Your Honor:

Supplementing my statement of July 19, I have the honor to add the following considerations:

1. I have consulted competent physicians. None of them, naturally, would venture to counterpose their opinion from afar to the opinion of the highly qualified French specialists who performed the autopsy. But the physicians whom I have consulted agree unanimously that the course of the illness and the causes of death were not established by the investigation with the necessary fullness demanded by the extraordinary circumstances of this case.

2. The incompleteness of the investigation is most clearly confirmed by the attitude of the surgeon, Mr. Thalheimer, himself. He refused to give explanations, appealing to "professional secrecy." The law grants a physician this right. But the law does not obligate a physician to make use of this right. In the present case the physician must have had some special reason for hiding behind professional secrecy. What is Mr. Thalheimer's reason? There cannot be any question at all in the present case of safeguarding the secrets of the patient or of his relatives. It is therefore a question of safeguarding the secret of the physician himself. What does this secret consist of? I have no reasons whatever to suspect Mr. Thalheimer of criminal actions. But it is quite evident that *had the death of Sedov followed naturally and inevitably from the nature of his illness, the surgeon would not have the least interest or psychological inclination for refusing to give the necessary explanations.* In hiding behind professional secrecy Mr. Thalheimer says that there are particular circumstances in the course of the illness and the causes of death, the clarification of which he does not wish to assist. It is impossible

to give any other interpretation to Mr. Thalheimer's attitude. Reasoning in a purely logical manner, we can only come to the conclusion in the present circumstances that the physician could invoke professional secrecy in one of the three cases:

a. if he was interested in hiding his own crime;

b. if he was interested in hiding his own negligence;

c. if he was interested in hiding the crime or negligence of his colleagues, collaborators, etc.

Mr. Thalheimer's demonstrative silence should in itself have indicated the course of the investigation. It is necessary by all means to uncover the circumstances which motivated the surgeon to hide behind "professional secrecy."

3. The testimony of the owner of the clinic, Mr. Simkov, is unclear, scanty, and partly contradictory. *Did he or did he not know who his patient was?* This question is not clarified at all. Sedov was admitted to the clinic under the name "Martin, French engineer." But in the clinic Dr. Simkov conversed with Sedov in Russian. It is precisely thanks to this that the nurse Eismont, according to her own words, learned that "Martin" was a Russian or knew Russian. As the investigating documents themselves point out, Sedov was registered under a different name for purposes of security. Was Dr. Simkov aware of these purposes? And if he was, why did he address the patient in Russian in the presence of the nurse Eismont? If it was through carelessness, did not he reveal the same carelessness in other aspects as well?

4. According to police information Dr. Zhirmunsky, the director of the clinic, was considered a "Bolshevik sympathizer." Nowadays this is a very definite characterization. It signifies a friend of the Kremlin bureaucracy and of its agencies. Zhirmunsky declared that he learned the real identity of the patient only on the eve of his death from Mrs. Molinier. If these words are to be taken on faith, we should have to conclude that Mr. Simkov, who informed Zhirmunsky in advance over the telephone of the arrival of the patient, concealed from his closest collaborator the real identity of the "French engineer, Martin." Is this likely? In the presence of the nurse Eismont, Simkov, as has already been pointed out, spoke with the patient in Russian. Zhirmunsky knows the Russian language. Or did Simkov have special reasons to beware of Zhirmunsky? What reasons precisely?

5. A "Bolshevik sympathizer"—this is a definite characterization. Here the investigation clearly stops midway. Under the conditions of Russian emigration this "sympathy" does not remain nowadays a platonic one. Generally the "sympathizer"

assumes a hostile atttitude with regard to White emigration. From what circles does Mr. Zhirmunsky draw his clients? Does he mix with the circles of the Soviet Embassy, of the trade representation, etc.? If so, then without any doubt the most important agents of the GPU enter among his clients.

6. Somehow nothing is said in the documents about the political sympathies of the owner of the clinic, Mr. Simkov. This is a grave omission. The close collaboration between Mr. Simkov and Zhirmunsky impels us to suppose that Mr. Simkov too was not hostile to Soviet circles and possibly had connections in these spheres.

7. Dr. Simkov is a contributor to the medical periodical *Oeuvre Chirurgicale Franco-Russe*. What character does this publication bear—is it a product of a bloc of French physicians with the Soviet government or, on the contrary, do White emigres appear in the name of Russian medicine? This question remains entirely unclarified. Moreover, not only the police but even infants know that under cover of all kinds of medical, juridical, literary, pacifist, and other organizations and publications, the GPU creates bases of support which serve it, especially in France, for committing crimes with impunity.

8. We cannot proceed without mentioning one exceptionally significant circumstance which I permit myself, Your Honor, to bring to your special attention. As is known, Mr. Simkov had the misfortune this year to lose two sons, victims of a landslide. During the time when the real fate of the boys still remained unknown, Mr. Simkov declared in an interview given by him to the French press, that if his sons were kidnaped this *could only be done by "Trotskyites" in revenge for Sedov's death.* At the time this struck me by its monstrosity. I must say frankly that such a supposition could only enter the mind of a person whose conscience was not altogether clean, or to a person who mixed in political circles deadly hostile to me and Sedov, where agents of the GPU could direct the thought of the unfortunate father to this fantastic and revolting conjecture. But if Mr. Simkov is on friendly terms with circles which preoccupy themselves with systematic physical extermination of "Trotskyites," it is also not difficult to suppose that these friendly relations could, even without the knowledge of Mr. Simkov, have been utilized for a crime against Sedov.

9. With regard to the personnel of the clinic, beginning with Mr. Zhirmunsky, the police investigation invariably repeats the formula of the "nonparticipation" of these people in active political life, apparently considering that this circumstance frees

them from the necessity of further investigation. This view is absolutely false. It is not a question of open political activity but of carrying out the most clandestine and criminal assignments of the GPU. Agents of this kind, like military spies, naturally cannot compromise themselves by participation in agitation, etc. On the contrary, in the interests of conspiracy, they lead an extremely peaceful existence. Monotonous references to "nonparticipation" of all the interrogated persons in active political struggle would testify to the extreme naivete of the police, if the wish to avoid an earnest investigation were not concealed behind it.

10. But, Your Honor, without an earnest, intensive, and courageous investigation, the crimes of the GPU cannot be uncovered. To give an approximate idea of the mores and methods of this institution I am obliged to quote from the official Soviet magazine *Oktyabr* [October] of March 3 of this year. The article is devoted to the show trial which resulted in the shooting of the former head of the GPU, Yagoda. "When he used to remain in his study," the Soviet magazine says of Yagoda, "alone or with his henchman Bulanov, he threw off his mask. He moved to the darkest corner of the room and opened up his treasured closet. Poisons. He contemplated them. This beast in human image admired the flasks in the light, apportioning them among his future victims." Yagoda is the one who organized my own, my wife's, and our son's deportation; the Bulanov mentioned in the quotation accompanied us from Central Asia to Turkey as the representative of the authorities. I do not enter into a discussion of whether Yagoda and Bulanov were guilty of the crimes of which it was deemed necessary to accuse them. I call attention to the quotation simply to characterize in the words of the official publication the environment, atmosphere, and methods of Stalin's secret agency. The present head of the GPU, Yezhov, the attorney Vyshinsky, and their foreign agents of course are not one whit better than Yagoda and Bulanov.

11. Yagoda drove one of my daughters to untimely death, the other—to suicide. He imprisoned my two sons-in-law,[382] who subsequently disappeared without a trace. The GPU arrested my youngest son, Sergei, on a preposterous charge of poisoning workers, after which he disappeared. By its persecutions the GPU drove to suicide two of my secretaries, Glazman and Butov, who preferred death to ignominious testimony under Yagoda's dictation.[383] Two others of my Russian secretaries, Poznansky and Sermuks, disappeared in Siberia without leaving a trace.[384] In Spain the agents of the GPU arrested my former secretary, a

Czechoslovakian citizen, Erwin Wolf, who disappeared without a trace. Just very recently in France the GPU kidnaped another of my former secretaries, Rudolf Klement. Will the French police find him? Will they care to make any effort to search for him? I permit myself to doubt this. The above-mentioned list of victims embraces only the people closest to me. I do not speak of the thousands and tens of thousands of those who perished in the USSR at the hands of the GPU as "Trotskyites."

12. Among the enemies of the GPU and its marked victims, Leon Sedov ranked first with me. The GPU did not take its eyes off him. During at least two years the gangsters of the GPU tracked Sedov like game. These facts are irrefutably established in connection with the murder case of I. Reiss. Can we suppose even for a moment that the GPU lost sight of Sedov during his stay at the clinic and passed up such an exceptionally favorable moment? The investigating authorities have no right to such suppositions.

13. Your Honor, one cannot read the report of the police signed by Hauret and Boilet without indignation. Regarding the preparation of a series of attempts on Sedov's life the report states: "Apparently, his political activity really was the subject of sufficiently close observation on the part of his adversaries." This phrase alone gives the police away completely! Where it is a question of preparing the murder of Sedov in France the French police speak of "sufficiently close observation" on the part of anonymous "adversaries," and add the word "apparently." Your Honor! The police do not want to uncover the truth as they did not uncover it in the theft of my archives, as they uncovered nothing in the case of the murder of I. Reiss, as they do not intend to uncover anything in the matter of the kidnaping of Rudolf Klement. In the French police and in their higher-ups the GPU has powerful accomplices. Millions of rubles are expended only to safeguard the impunity of the Stalinist Mafia in France. To this must be added considerations of a "patriotic" and "diplomatic" nature which are conveniently utilized by the murderers in Stalin's service who operate in Paris as if in their own home. That is why the investigation in the case of Sedov's death bears a fictitious character.

L. Trotsky

# TRADE UNION CONGRESS
# STAGED BY CP[385]

## August 27, 1938

*Question:* What is your opinion of the coming Pan-American workers' congress, which will be celebrated in this capital?

*Answer:* The closest unification of the workers of the American continent is a vital necessity. Only such unity can assure the influence of the workers of each of the American countries on internal as well as on foreign policy. In particular, only a firm and decisive policy of the united proletariat can prevent America's being involved in a war. Will the forthcoming congress accomplish this aim? I doubt it.

*Q:* What in your opinion is the real aim of this congress?

*A:* In the convocation of the Pan-American workers' congress different elements pursue different aims. The working class masses semi-instinctively strive for unification and independent policy. Some of the leaders pursue entirely different aims. In the name of the Mexican proletariat appears, as stage manager, Mr. Lombardo Toledano. He is a "pure" politician, foreign to the working class and pursuing his own personal aims. Toledano's ambition is to climb to the Mexican presidency on the backs of the workers. In pursuit of this aim, Toledano has closely intertwined his fate with the fate of the Kremlin oligarchy. From there he receives instructions and all kinds of aid. Moscow subjected the Mexican Communists to Mr. Toledano, that is, to his struggle for power. Toledano's recent trip to the United States and to Europe as well as the forthcoming congresses in September have as one of their aims to provide a springboard for Toledano. In this field Toledano works completely hand in hand with Moscow. One need not doubt that at the forthcoming congresses in Mexico all international agents of Moscow, open and secret ones, will participate.

*Q:* What do you believe will be its practical result?

*A:* The results of the Pan-American Trade Union Congress will depend to a great extent on whether or not Lombardo Toledano will succeed in subordinating the working class movement of this continent to the orders of his Moscow chiefs. I am convinced that he will not succeed. In tying his fate to the GPU, Lombardo Toledano is preparing a catastrophe for his policy and for his career.

*Q:* How does the opposition look upon the congress?

*A:* It is very doubtful whether the opposition will be able to enter the congress. The congress does not consist of delegates elected by the masses. The tasks of the congress were not discussed by the masses. The organizational work is carried on behind the stage with the GPU agency performing the greater part of the work. Consequently there is every reason to believe that the congress will be a congress of a carefully selected workers' bureaucracy. I shall be glad to be mistaken.

*Q:* In recent declarations William Green declared that it would be a congress of Communists and extreme leftists, and said that the AFL would not accept the invitation to attend.

*A:* William Green falsely represents the congress as a "revolutionary" one in order to justify his own reactionary policy. Green does not want the unification of the workers of all the Americas because he himself represents the workers' aristocracy of the United States and views with contempt the Indo-American workers.

*Q:* What significance does the presence of John L. Lewis of the CIO have at the congress?[386]

*A:* What aims Lewis pursues in his participation at the congress I cannot say as yet. This will become clear from his attitude at the congress itself. It is absolutely clear, however, that Lombardo Toledano and other agents of Moscow—North American and Mexican—have as their aim the submission of the CIO

to the dictates of Moscow. For Moscow diplomacy this question is
now of decisive importance. *It is a question of transforming the
workers' organizations of all America into obedient instruments
of Stalin and his GPU.* With this aim the Comintern, as is known,
sharply changed its policy. Browder became a Rooseveltian,
Toledano—a Cardenist. But this is only to lull the adversary.
Their real aim is to penetrate the state apparatus at any price.
Precisely because of this Moscow supports the ambitions of
Toledano. If these aims should be achieved, this would mean, in
the full sense of the word, *a catastrophe for the American
working class and for American culture.* We do not want the
transformation of Mexico into Catalonia, where the hirelings of
the GPU, no better than any fascist, now strangle all that is
honest and independent in the proletariat and in the intelligentsia. As I have already said, I firmly trust that these designs will
suffer a fiasco. The GPU and its methods are far too compromised, in particular, due to the investigation of the New York
commission headed by Dr. Dewey. The American working class
will find its own road and methods of unification for the defense
of its historic interests.

# THE CONGRESS AGAINST WAR AND FASCISM[387]

## August 1938

In order to clearly realize the significance of the Congress Against War and Fascism, it is necessary to proceed from the following circumstances:

1. The congress was organized by the GPU, on Stalin's orders, for his diplomatic purposes. Those participating in the congress can be divided into six groups: (1) the Kremlin's secret agents, including the most responsible GPU agents; (2) members of various Comintern subsidiary organizations (of youth, etc.); (3) liberal and radical intellectuals, trade union officials, etc., who receive direct or indirect doles from Moscow; (4) agents of the "democratic" governments; (5) secret agents of the fascist governments; and (6) all kinds of dilettantes, pacifist ladies, publicity seekers, etc.

The first group, of course, plays the decisive role. The second group is subordinated to the first along lines of military discipline. The third group consciously closes its eyes to all problematic circumstances. The fourth and fifth groups are pursuing the objectives of espionage. The sixth group understands nothing and is enlisted to serve as a cover for all the others.

2. The majority of these "pacifists" are patriotic political figures from the imperialist countries. When these gentlemen talk about "democracy" or "culture," they have in mind exclusively their imperialist democracy and their imperialist culture. Thus, for example, Mr. Jouhaux (whom Lenin in the press called nothing but a traitor) believes it self-evident that France's sixty million colonial slaves ought to die for the "democracy" of their slaveholders in the next war. The British "pacifists," like the North American, defend peace only to the extent that and as long

as their imperialist fatherlands are interested in it. Moreover, in their heart of hearts they all regard the colonial and semicolonial peoples as historical manure, destined to be the fertilizer of *their* democracy and *their* culture.

3. Of course, the workers and peasants of all countries honestly and sincerely want peace. It is possible to attain it, however, only by a revolutionary struggle against the imperialist governments. It is precisely in order to paralyze this revolutionary anti-imperialist struggle that Jouhaux and those like him organize "People's Fronts," i.e., subordinate the proletariat to the "left" wing of the *imperialist* bourgeoisie. This gives the imperialists an opportunity to use pacifist congresses as a cover and prepare a new war in which all the backward and weak peoples and states will be the first to be crushed.

4. The privileged imperialist countries (the U.S., Great Britain, and France) believe they have a monopoly on democracy and are not at all inclined to bolster democracy and progress in the weaker and more backward countries. In Spain, England prefers to have General Franco, who will inevitably become financially dependent upon the London bankers and grant them more advantageous and stable conditions for exploitation than a Spanish democracy could. The Washington government gets along exceptionally well with certain Latin American dictatorships, turning each of them into its own obedient agent. It is improper, therefore, to speak of democracy "in general." *Imperialist* "democracy" is fully directed against democracy for backward and weak colonial and semicolonial peoples.

5. In peacetime, the imperialist "pacifists" are not sparing of magnanimous phrases; but in the event of a conflict, they will take their stand on the side of their government and tell the broad masses: "We did all we could to preserve peace but the intransigence of Mexico (or some other opponent) doomed our efforts to failure." With the emergence of conflict or the outbreak of war they all become open advocates of their own national imperialism.

6. Stalin's international policy, based on the oppression of the peoples of the USSR, by and large coincides with or seeks to coincide with the policies of the democratic imperialists. Stalin is looking for rapprochement with the present-day governments of France, Great Britain, and the United States. Toward this end, he has transformed the corresponding sections of the Comintern into social-imperialist parties. Stalin seeks to prove to the ruling classes of the most powerful countries that he is not a threat to

their imperialist interests. Stalin can carry out such a policy only by sacrificing the interests of the world working class and of all colonial and semicolonial peoples. It is impermissible to be deceived by conventional phrases and relics of the old revolutionary slogans. Stalin is supporting a "revolutionary" and "national" policy in colonial and semicolonial countries precisely within the limits that will frighten the imperialist country concerned and show it the high value of his friendship. The most striking example is in the New World: the *United States* and *Mexico*. Stalin's real aim is to win the confidence and friendship of the White House. In this game Mexico is only one of his pawns. Stalin seeks to show that he can, if he wants, be very dangerous for the United States in Mexico and in Latin America in general. But all this is to make it possible for him to later sell out the interests of Mexico and Latin America to North American imperialism on suitable terms.

7. Nor are things going better in the struggle against *fascism*. At the present time there is no need to discuss this question on a theoretical level. It is enough to point to the living example of Spain. Nothing helped Franco so much as Stalin's bloc with the imperialist "democracies." In order to demonstrate to the French and British bourgeoisie his reliability as a conservative, Stalin— with the assistance of the Spanish Toledanos, Labordes, and the others, and with the aid of the GPU apparatus—strangled the Spanish agrarian revolution and the socialist movement of the workers. By this and this only was Franco's victory made possible.

8. The Spanish experience is only a rehearsal. The very same danger threatens other countries. On the question of oil and land the antagonism between the interests of Mexico and the interests of the two most powerful imperialist "democracies" is vividly revealed. In the present case, Mexico serves as the representative of all oppressed, backward, and exploited peoples. The imperialist democrats will, when the opportunity offers, especially at staged congresses, talk profusely about the "Good Neighbor" policy, peace, friendship of peoples, etc. This does not prevent them, in the event of a sharp conflict of interests, from ending up on the side of their imperialist governments. As regards Stalin, in the interest of friendship with the imperialist "democracies," he does not hesitate for an instant to betray any colonial or semicolonial country.

9. The congress in Mexico was conceived, ordered, and organized by Moscow. In view of the extremely strained relations

with Japan, Stalin wants at precisely this time to show his potential strength on the United States border. It is as if he were playing with a revolver, letting it be understood that the muzzle could be aimed at Washington, but that he is ready at any moment to flip on the safety catch or to open fire in the opposite direction, in perfect accord with the North American or British military headquarters. This is the essence of the matter. All else is simply words, rhetorical phrases, or empty gestures.

# FASCISM AND
# THE COLONIAL WORLD[388]

## August 1938

1. Fascism is the most savage and abominable form of imperialism. But this does not at all mean that the working classes and oppressed peoples must put up with imperialism when it puts on its democratic mask. The Latin American peoples do not want to fall under the domination of Japanese, Italian, or German imperialism. But this does not at all mean that Mexico can tolerate British or North American imperialism controlling its natural resources or its national policies. The working classes and peoples of the backward countries do not want to be garrotted by either a fascist or a "democratic" executioner.

2. Japan is attempting to make China a colony. Italy and Germany are reaching out toward the French and British colonies. In this sense they are "the aggressors." But this does not at all mean that the working classes and oppressed peoples have a duty to defend the colonial rights of France, Great Britain, Holland, Belgium, and the others. The task of genuine revolutionaries is to get rid of the oppressive colonial regimes. Our slogan: *the right of all nations to self-determination, not in word, but in deed; the full and genuine liberation of all colonies!*

3. The future of humanity is inseparably linked with the destiny of India, China, Indochina, Latin America, and Africa. The active sympathy, friendship, and support of genuine revolutionists, socialists, and honest democrats is completely on the side of these peoples—who constitute the majority of humanity—and not on the side of their oppressors, no matter what kind of political masks they appear in. Those who actively or even passively support a colonial regime under the pretext of defending their own "democracy" are the worst enemies of the working classes and oppressed peoples. We and they are traveling very different roads.

4. We are wholeheartedly with the Spanish people in their struggle against fascism. But the elementary condition for the victory of the Spanish revolution is the expulsion of the GPU from Republican Spain and the unhindered development of the revolutionary initiative of the Spanish workers and peasants. Only in this way can the masses of Spanish people again be mobilized against the domestic and foreign fascists; only in this way will the social and military ground be torn out from under Franco's feet.

6. For the backward countries, the road for opposing fascism is above all the road of revolutionary struggle for national independence and for the radical transformation of agrarian relations. Without agrarian revolution there is neither national independence nor salvation from fascism. Anyone who stands in the way of the expropriation of landed property and national resources for the benefit of the peasants and the people as a whole is abetting fascism. Vague generalities about friendship and democracy are not enough. One must have a clear position: either with the magnates of capital and their "democracy" for show; or with the genuine democracy of the workers, peasants, and oppressed peoples.

The Mexican socialist or democrat who finds it possible to believe in the "pacifism" of the bloc between the Stalinist bureaucracy and the imperialist democracy is at best distinguished by political blindness. Gentlemen of the Lombardo Toledano variety who seek to subordinate the working class of Mexico to the bloc between the GPU and the imperialist pacifists are outright traitors not only to the interests of the Mexican proletariat but to the national interests of the Mexican people.

If Mexico lets itself be lured onto the political course of Lombardo Toledano, i.e., voluntarily lets itself be used as small change in the dealings between the Kremlin and the White House, it would mean the destruction not only of Mexican democracy but of the country's national independence.

The Mexican people do not want and cannot allow the methods used in Spain to be transferred to their soil—neither the methods of Franco nor those of Stalin.

Hand in hand with hundreds of millions of oppressed, nonwhite races, hand in hand with hundreds of millions of workers in the imperialist countries, the workers and peasants of Mexico will fight for the peace, freedom, independence, and well-being of their country as well as for the happiness of all humanity.

# A GREAT ACHIEVEMENT[389]

## August 30, 1938

When these lines appear in the press, the conference of the Fourth International will probably have concluded its labors. The calling of this conference is a major achievement. The irreconcilable revolutionary tendency, subjected to persecutions no other political tendency in world history has in all likelihood suffered, has again given proof of its power. Surmounting all obstacles, it has under the blows of its mighty enemies convened its International Conference. This fact constitutes unimpeachable evidence of the profound viability and unwavering perseverance of the international Bolshevik-Leninists. The very possibility of a successful conference was first of all assured by the spirit of revolutionary internationalism which imbues all our sections. As a matter of fact, it is necessary to place extremely great value upon the international ties of the proletarian vanguard in order to gather together the international revolutionary staff at the present time, when Europe and the entire world live in the expectation of the approaching war. The fumes of national hatreds and racial persecutions today compose the political atmosphere of our planet. Fascism and racism are merely the most extreme expressions of the bacchanalia of chauvinism which seeks to overcome or stifle the intolerable class contradictions. The resurgence of social patriotism in France and other countries, or, rather, its new open and shameless manifestation, pertains to the same category as fascism, but with an adaptation to democratic ideology or its vestiges.

Also pertaining to the same circle of events is the open fostering of nationalism in the USSR at meetings, in the press, and in the schools. It is not at all a question of the so-called "socialist patriotism," i.e., defense of the conquests of the October Revolution against imperialism. No, it is a question of restoring preeminence to the patriotic traditions of old Russia. And here the task is likewise one of creating suprasocial, supraclass values, so as thereby more successfully to discipline the toilers and subject them to the greedy bureaucratic vermin. The official ideology of the present Kremlin appeals to the exploits of Prince Alexander Nevski, to the heroism of the army of Suvorov-Rymniksky or Kutuzov-Smolensky,[390] while it shuts its eyes to the fact that this "heroism" was based on the enslavement and benightedness of the popular masses, and that for this very reason the old Russian army was victorious only in struggles against the still more backward Asiatic peoples, or the weak and disintegrating states on the Western border. On the other hand, in conflicts with advanced countries of Europe the valiant czarist soldiery always proved bankrupt. Obviously, the experience of the last imperialist war has already been buried in the Kremlin, just as it has forgotten the not unimportant fact that the October Revolution grew directly from defeatism. What do Thermidoreans and Bonapartists care about all this? They require nationalistic fetishes. Alexander Nevski must come to the aid of Nikolai Yezhov.

The theory of socialism in one country, which liquidated the program of the international revolutionary struggle of the proletariat, could not fail to terminate in a wave of nationalism in the USSR and could not but engender a responsive wave of the same nature in the "Communist" parties of other countries. Only two or three years ago it was maintained that the sections of the Comintern were obliged to support their governments only in the so-called "democratic" states that were prepared to support the USSR in the struggle against fascism. The task of defending the workers' state was intended to serve as a justification for social patriotism. Today, Browder, who has been no more and no less prostituted than other "leaders" of the Stalintern, declares before a Congressional investigating committee that in the event of a war between the U.S. and the USSR, he, Browder, and his party will be on the side of their own democratic fatherland. In all probability this answer was prompted by Stalin. But the case is not altered thereby. Betrayal has a logic of its own. Entering the path of social patriotism, the Third International is now being clearly torn from the hands of the Kremlin clique. "Communists" have become social imperialists, and they differ from their "Social Democratic" allies and competitors only in that their cynicism is greater.

Betrayal has a logic of its own. The Third International following the Second has completely perished as an International. It is no longer capable of displaying any kind of initiative in the sphere of world proletarian politics. It is, of course, no accident that after fifteen years of progressive demoralization, the Comintern revealed its complete internal rottenness at the moment of the approaching world war, i.e., precisely at a time when the proletariat is most urgently in need of its international revolutionary unification.

History has piled up monstrous obstacles before the Fourth International. Moribund tradition is being aimed against the living revolution. For a century and a half, the radiations of the Great French Revolution have served the bourgeoisie and its petty-bourgeois agency—the Second International—as a means of shattering and paralyzing the revolutionary will of the proletariat. The Third International is now exploiting the incomparably more fresh and more powerful traditions of the October Revolution to the same end. The memory of the first victorious uprising of the proletariat against bourgeois democracy serves the usurpers to save bourgeois democracy from the proletarian uprising. Confronted with the approach of the new imperialist war, the social patriotic organizations have joined forces with the left wing of the bourgeoisie under the label of the People's Front, which represents nothing else but an attempt on the part of the bourgeoisie, in its death agony, once again to subject the proletariat to its rule just as the revolutionary bourgeoisie had subjected it at the dawn of capitalism. What was once a progressive historical manifestation now appears before us as a revolting reactionary farce. But while the "People's Fronts" are impotent to cure a capitalism that is rotten to the core, while they are incapable of even checking the military aggression of fascism—the example of Spain is full of symbolic meaning!—they nevertheless still prove sufficiently powerful to sow illusions among the ranks of the toilers, to paralyze and shatter their will to fight, and thereby create the greatest difficulties in the path of the Fourth International.

The working class, especially in Europe, is still in retreat, or at best, in a state of hesitation. Defeats are still too fresh, and their number far from exhausted. They have assumed their sharpest form in Spain. Such are the conditions in which the Fourth International is developing. Is it any wonder that its growth proceeds more slowly than we should like? Dilettantes, charlatans, or blockheads, incapable of probing into the dialectic of historic ebbs and flows, have more than once brought in their verdict: "The ideas of the Bolshevik-Leninists may perhaps be correct but they are incapable of building a mass organization." As if a mass organization can be built under any and all

conditions! As if a revolutionary program does not render it
obligatory for us to remain in the minority and swim against the
stream in an epoch of reaction! The revolutionist who uses his
own impatience as a measuring stick for the tempo of an epoch is
worthless. Never before has the path of the world revolutionary
movement been blocked with such monstrous obstacles as today,
on the eve of a new epoch of the greatest revolutionary
convulsions. A correct Marxist appraisal of the situation prompts
the conclusion that we have achieved inestimable successes in
recent years, despite everything.

The Russian "Left Opposition" originated fifteen years ago.
Correct work on the international arena does not add up as yet
even to a complete decade. The prehistory of the Fourth
International properly falls into three stages. In the course of the
first period, the "Left Opposition" still placed hopes in the
possibility of regenerating the Comintern, and viewed itself as its
Marxist faction. The revolting capitulation of the Comintern in
Germany, tacitly accepted by all its sections, posed openly the
question of the necessity of building the Fourth International.
However, our small organizations, which grew through individual selection in the process of theoretical criticism practically
outside of the labor movement itself, proved as yet unprepared for
independent activity. The second period is characterized by the
efforts to find a real political milieu for these isolated propagandist groups, even if at the price of a temporary renunciation of
formal independence. Entry into the Socialist parties immediately increased our ranks, although in respect to quantity the gains
were not as great as they could have been. But this entry
signified an extremely important stage in the political education
of our sections, which tested themselves and their ideas for the
first time face to face with the realities of the political struggle
and its living requirements. As a result of the experience acquired
our cadres grew a head taller. A not unimportant conquest was
also the fact that we parted company with incorrigible sectarians,
muddlers, and tricksters who are wont to join every new
movement in the beginning only to do everything in their power
to compromise and paralyze it.

The stages of development of our sections in various countries
cannot of course coincide chronologically. Nevertheless, the
creation of the American Socialist Workers Party can be
recognized as the termination of the second period. Henceforth
the Fourth International stands face to face with the tasks of the
mass movement. The transitional program is a reflection of this
important turn. Its significance lies in this, that instead of

providing an a priori theoretical plan, it draws the balance of the already accumulated experience of our national sections and on the basis of this experience opens up broader international perspectives.

The acceptance of this program, prepared and assured by a lengthy previous discussion—or rather, a whole series of discussions—represents our most important conquest. The Fourth International is now the only international organization which not only takes clearly into account the driving forces of the imperialist epoch, but is armed with a system of transitional demands capable of uniting the masses for a revolutionary struggle for power. We do not need any self-deceptions. The discrepancy between our forces today and the tasks on the morrow is much more clearly perceived by us than by our critics. But the harsh and tragic dialectic of our epoch is working in our favor. Brought to the extreme pitch of exasperation and indignation, the masses will find no other leadership than that offered them by the Fourth International.

# ANOTHER STALINIST PLOY[391]

## September 4, 1938

Dear Friends:

This very moment we received from the United States from an absolutely reliable source the following information which we request that you give the widest possible publicity. Our informant for considerations of security did not venture to approach you directly and preferred to address us. But you could safely declare that you received this information on the spot, in New York.

A few months ago Hernan Laborde, leader of the Mexican Stalinist party, "left for Moscow." At least that is what the entire Mexican press carried. In reality, Laborde remained all the time illegally in the United States. His task, as will be seen from what follows, was to utilize the preparation for the September congresses in Mexico for a decisive blow against Trotsky, Diego Rivera, and their friends. In connection with the work of the Congressional committee, the police apparently stumbled on Laborde's tracks. At any rate, that was the impression of the leaders of the Communist Party, who became terrified of an international scandal and of compromising the New York agency of the GPU. Laborde received an order to leave the United States immediately. There is no reason to believe that he went to the USSR. On the contrary, there are data that he returned clandestinely to Mexico where he kept his incognito in order to support the version of his stay in the USSR.

The Mexican Communist Party is now fully subordinated to the leaders of the Communist Party of the United States and through these latter receives all orders from Moscow. This strange order of things is very easily explainable. Mexico has no Soviet institutions and the agents of the GPU in Mexico, having no diplomatic coverage, are obliged to the strictest secrecy. They therefore avoid any direct contact with the local Communist Party, fearing that it might harbor police agents. In the United States the most important agents of the GPU enjoy diplomatic immunity and can therefore transmit the most secret instructions to those leaders of the Communist Party who enjoy the unquestioned confidence of the GPU. These trusted persons, in turn, transmit the instructions to Mexico.

The latest instructions received by Laborde in the middle of August were to strengthen the campaign of persecutions against Trotsky and his friends, not confining it to political and bureaucratic measures, but passing over to "direct action" (literal expression). In connection with the murders of Trotskyites in France, Switzerland, and especially in Spain, it is not hard to guess what "direct action" means.

The Central Committee of the Mexican Communist Party has already informed New York that they have started to carry out the received instructions. A strictly conspiratorial meeting was convoked with the participation of only certain members of the Central Committee and organizers of "fighting actions," among them two or three foreigners who arrived in Mexico in connection with the preparation of the congress "against war and fascism." At this meeting the reporter (apparently Laborde himself) demanded not only that the political campaign against the Trotskyites be strengthened tenfold but that the necessary atmosphere be created "for the physical liquidation of Trotsky and some of his friends" (literal expression). In regard to the "political" campaign the reporter promised full material assistance on the part of the Minister of Education, Mr. Vazquez Vela, and his nearest assistants. A parallel campaign, in the words of the reporter, is being carried on by the trade union secretary, Lombardo Toledano, who during his recent trip to Europe received all the necessary instructions from the GPU and also the necessary material means (in particular a slanderous film against Trotsky). Among the deputies in the congress there are a great number of foreign agents of the GPU whose main task consists in creating in Mexico a "favorable atmosphere" for carrying out the latest Moscow instructions.

We repeat once more—we absolutely guarantee the trustworthiness of our source. You can safely begin a campaign, with all necessary energy, drawing all our friends into it. It is very important not to lose a moment's time. It is necessary, in particular, to invite the representatives of the Mexican press in New York and transmit to them the facts given above.

Hansen [Trotsky]

# THE TOTALITARIAN DEFEATIST
# IN THE KREMLIN[392]

## September 12, 1938

Beginning with the year 1933 the international importance of the USSR began to rise rapidly. Often one could hear then from European journalists the opinion: "The Kremlin holds the fate of Europe in its hands," "Stalin has become a world arbiter," and so on. No matter how exaggerated these estimates may have been even at that time, they arose from two undeniable factors—the sharpening of world antagonisms and the growing strength of the Red Army. The relative success of the first five year plan, the tangible program of industrialization which created a material base for the army and navy, the halting of the progressive paralysis of the railways, the first favorable crops on the basis of the kolkhoz, the increase in the amount of livestock, the decrease in want and starvation—these were the internal prerequisites for the successes of Soviet diplomacy. Stalin's words—"life has become easier, life has become happier"—refer to this period. For the toiling masses life indeed became somewhat easier. For the bureaucracy life became a great deal happier.

Meanwhile a great part of the national income was being consumed for defense. The peacetime army of 800,000 men was raised to a million and a half. The navy began to revive. During the years of the Soviet regime a new commanding staff, from lieutenants to marshals, had time to form itself. To this must be added a political factor—the opposition, from the left as well as from the right, was routed. Victory over the opposition seemed to find its objective justification in economic achievements. Stalin's power appeared unshakable. All this taken together transformed the Soviet government if not into the arbiter of Europe, then at any rate into a significant international factor.

The last two years have left not a trace of this situation. The specific weight of Soviet diplomacy is lower at present than in the most critical months of the first five year plan. London has not only turned its face toward Rome and Berlin but even demands that Paris turn her back on Moscow. Thus Hitler, through Chamberlain, now has the opportunity to carry out his policy of isolating the USSR. Although France has not abrogated her agreement with the USSR, she has reduced it to a second-rate reserve. Having lost faith in assistance from Moscow, the Third Republic unfailingly trails on the heels of England. Conservative French patriots complain not without bitterness that France has become Great Britain's "last dominion." Italy and Germany, with the consent of the very same Chamberlain, intend to root themselves firmly in Spain, where only recently Stalin had seemed—and not only to himself—to be the master of fate. In the Far East, where Japan met unexpected difficulties of gigantic magnitude, Moscow proved incapable of anything more than frontier skirmishes, and these always on the initiative of Japan.

The cause for the decline in the international role of the Soviets within the last two years surely cannot be sought in the reconciliation or softening of international contradictions. No matter what the episodic oscillations may be, the imperialist countries are fatally approaching a world war. The conclusion is obvious: Stalin's weakness on the world arena is above all the result of the internal development of the USSR. What then has occurred in the Soviet Union during the last two years to turn strength into impotence? The economy seems to be growing; industry, despite so-called "sabotage," continues to laud its successes; crops improve; military supplies accumulate. Stalin successfully puts down internal enemies. What then is the matter?

Not so long ago the world judged the Soviet Union almost exclusively from the figures of Soviet statistics. These figures, although grossly exaggerated, nevertheless testified to undeniable achievements. It was taken for granted that behind the paper screen of figures existed an ever-growing prosperity of the people and of authority. But it has not turned out this way at all. In the final analysis, the processes of economics, of politics, and of culture are relations among living people, among groups and classes. The Moscow judicial tragedies revealed that these relations were wretched, or more correctly said, intolerable.

The army is the quintessence of a regime, not in the sense that it expresses only its "best" qualities, but in the sense that it imparts a most concentrated expression to its positive as well as negative tendencies. When the contradictions and antagonisms of a regime reach a certain acuteness, they begin to undermine the army from within. The opposite conclusion is that when the army—the most disciplined organ of the ruling class—begins to be torn by internal contradictions, this is an unmistakable sign of the intolerable crisis in society itself.

The economic successes of the Soviet Union, which at a certain time strengthened its army and its diplomacy, have above all raised up and strengthened the ruling bureaucratic layer. Historically, no class in society has ever concentrated in its hands in such a short period such wealth and power as the bureaucracy has concentrated during the two five year plans. But precisely through this it has placed itself in ever-growing contradiction to the people, who have passed through three revolutions and overthrown the czarist monarchy, the nobility, and the bourgeoisie. The Soviet bureaucracy now combines in itself, in a certain sense, the features of all the overthrown classes without either their social roots or their traditions. It can defend its monstrous privileges only by organized terror, and it can justify its terror only by judicial frame-ups. Having grown out of economic successes, the autocratic rule of the bureaucracy has become the chief obstacle on the future road of these achievements. Further growth of the country is impossible without the general growth of culture, that is, without the independence of each and all, without free criticism and free research. These elementary conditions of progress are necessary for the army, even to a greater degree than for the economy, because in the army the reality or sham of statistical data are tested in blood. But the political regime in the USSR has definitely approached that of a punitive battalion. All progressive and creative elements, genuinely devoted to the interests of the economy, public education, and national defense, invariably come into conflict with the ruling oligarchy. Thus it was in its time under czarism, thus it occurs at an incomparably higher tempo now under the regime of Stalin. Economy, culture, the army, need people with initiative, builders, creators. The Kremlin needs faithful executors, reliable and merciless agents. These human types—agent and creator—are irreconcilably hostile to one another.

During the last fifteen months the Red Army has lost almost its entire commanding staff, originally recruited in the years of civil war (1918-20), then educated, trained, and replenished in the following fifteen years. The thoroughly renewed and constantly changed officers' corps Stalin subjected to the open police surveillance of new commissars. Tukhachevsky, and with him the flower of the commanding staff, fell in struggle against the police dictatorship over the Red Army officers' corps. In the navy, where the strong and the weak sides of the armed forces assume an especially concentrated character, the annihilation of the highest officers has had an even more wholesale character than in the land forces. One must repeat again and again: the armed forces of the USSR are beheaded. The arrests and executions continue. A protracted duel is being waged between the Kremlin and the officers' corps, in which the right to shoot belongs to the Kremlin alone. The causes for this tragic duel are not of a temporary or accidental but of an organic nature. The totalitarian bureaucracy concentrates in its hands two functions—*power* and *administration*. These two functions have now come into sharp conflict. In order to assure good administration it is necessary to abolish totalitarian power. To uphold Stalin's power it is necessary to smash independent and capable administrators, military as well as civil.

The system of commissars, first introduced in the period when the Red Army was built out of nothing, signified, of necessity, a regime of dual command. The inconveniences and dangers of such an arrangement were absolutely clear even then, but they were considered a lesser and moreover a temporary evil. The very necessity of dual command in the army grew out of the collapse of the czarist army and out of the conditions of civil war. What does the new dual command signify? The first stage in the collapse of the Red Army and the beginning of a new civil war in the country?

Commissars of the first conscription expressed the control of the working class over alien and mostly hostile military specialists. Commissars of the new formation signify the control of the Bonapartist clique over military and civil administration and through it over the people.

Commissars of the first epoch were enlisted from the most earnest and sincere revolutionists, genuinely devoted to the cause of socialism. The commanders, who came in their majority from the ranks of old officers and sergeants, oriented themselves poorly under the new conditions, and the best of them themselves sought counsel and support from the commissars. Though not without friction and conflicts, dual command at that time led to friendly collaboration.

The matter is altogether different now. The present commanders grew out of the Red Army, are indissolubly connected with it, and enjoy an authority gained through the years. The commissars on the contrary are drafted from sons of bureaucrats, with neither revolutionary experience, military knowledge, nor moral endowment. They are purely a type of careerist of the new school. They are given commands only because they represent "vigilance," that is, Stalin's police supervision over the army. Commanders view them with merited contempt. The regime of dual command turns itself into a struggle between the political police and the army, with the central power on the side of the police.

The historic film unwinds in reverse, and what was a progressive measure of the revolution is revived as a revolting reactionary caricature. The new dual command permeates the government apparatus from top to bottom. At the head of the army nominally stands Voroshilov, the people's commissar, marshal, cavalier of many orders, and so on, and so on. But actual power is concentrated in the hands of a nonentity, Mekhlis,[393] who on direct instructions from Stalin is turning the army topsy-turvy. This occurs in every military district, in every division, in every regiment. The same is true in the navy and air force. Every place has its own Mekhlis, who is instilling "vigilance" instead of knowledge, order, and discipline. All relations in the army assume a fluctuating, unsteady, floating character. Nobody knows where patriotism ends and betrayal begins. Nobody is certain of what one may or may not do. In case of discrepancy in the orders of the commander and the commissar, everybody must guess which of the two roads leads to reward and which to prison. Everybody waits expectantly and anxiously looks about himself. Honest workers lose all ambition. Rogues, thieves, and careerists do their work under cover of patriotic denunciations. The army foundations are loosened. In big things and small devastation reigns. Weapons are not cleaned and not inspected. Barracks take on a filthy uninhabited air. Roofs leak, there is a lack of bathhouses, the Red Army soldiers have no clean linen. Food becomes worse in quality and is not served at the appointed hours. The commander responds to complaints by passing them on to the commissar; real offenders cover themselves up by denouncing "wreckers." Drunkenness is on the increase among the commanders. The commissars vie with them in this respect also. The regime of anarchy cloaked by police despotism now saps all sides of Soviet life. It is particularly disastrous in the army, which can exist only under a sound regime and complete transparency of all relations. This is the reason, among others, why the big army maneuvers were cancelled this year.

The diagnosis is clear. The growth of the country, especially the growth of its new wants, is incompatible with the totalitarian abomination. It therefore shows a tendency to eject, expel, cast out the bureaucracy from all spheres. When Stalin accuses this or that section of the apparatus of lack of "vigilance" he says by this: "You are concerned about the interests of the economy, science, or the army, but you are not concerned about my personal interests!" Stalinists in all parts of the country and in all strata of the bureaucratic pyramid find themselves in the same position. The bureaucracy can no longer uphold its position in any other way than by undermining the foundations of economic and cultural progress. The struggle for totalitarian power resulted in the annihilation of the best men of the country by its most degraded scoundrels.

Fortunately for the USSR, the internal situation of its potential enemies—already tense now—will become ever more critical in the coming period. But this does not change the analysis of the internal situation in the USSR. Stalin's totalitarian system has become a true breeding place for cultural sabotage and military defeatism. To say this bluntly is an elementary duty to the peoples of the USSR and to world public opinion. Politics, military politics in particular, cannot reconcile itself to fictions. The enemies know only too well what goes on in Stalin's realm. There exists a category of "friends" who prefer blindly to believe the Kremlin's agents. We write not for them but for those who choose to face the approaching stormy epoch squarely.

# LETTER TO ROSE KARSNER[394]

## September 13, 1938

Dear Comrade Rose:

It seems that Jim is doing an excellent job in Europe. The news concerning the Greek section is very agreeable.[395] I regret very much that we don't have a couple of Jims more. At least one for Europe.

Joe wrote you about the situation here. We are waiting for Otto [Schuessler] and the Austrian and this waiting makes uncertain all our plans and combinations. Only you in New York with the help of Jim if he is still in Europe could clarify the situation and thus create a base for concrete decisions.

My best greetings.

Yours,
L. Trotsky

# YES OR NO?[396]

## September 14, 1938

On September 8, the well-known Chicago attorney, Albert Goldman, informed the press of a GPU plot in connection with the congresses in Mexico. The heart of the plot, according to Goldman, was New York, where the leader of the Mexican Stalinist party, Hernan Laborde, was summoned under greatest secrecy. In order better to hide his participation in the plot against Trotsky and his friends, Hernan Laborde spread the rumor that he was leaving for several months in the USSR.

In reality, however, he remained during this entire time in New York in close contact with the most important representatives of the GPU in the United States. Under their direction Laborde worked out a campaign of persecution and slander against Trotsky and his friends. The practical aim of this campaign was either to achieve the expulsion of Trotsky from Mexico—that is, his actual deliverance into the hands of the hangmen of the GPU—or the creation of a favorable atmosphere for doing away with him in Mexico itself. This was Moscow's order.

Goldman is a very experienced and responsible attorney and if he gave this information to the press it means that it emanates from an irreproachable source.

At any rate, at the same time Goldman made these revelations, Laborde suddenly appeared in Mexico. I say "suddenly" since *the press did not carry a single word about his return*. Where did Laborde come from? Had he really been in the USSR? This is not difficult to prove by passport visas. Or did Laborde, as Goldman's source states, remain secretly in the United States? What did he do there? No one will suspect Laborde of preparing a coup d'etat against the regime of the U.S. What did he do there? And why did he return with the utmost secrecy at the very moment of the opening of the congress?

Mr. Laborde has full opportunity to refute Albert Goldman's statement. He only needs to answer clearly where he has been in the last months. In Moscow or in New York? No subterfuges will help. Silence will help just as little. Public opinion will force the plotters to give a clear and precise answer to the question: Did Laborde hide in the United States? Yes or no? If yes, then for what purposes?

# 'TOWARD A DECISION'[397]

## September 17, 1938

Under this title there has appeared in Brun, Czechoslovakia, a book of 191 pages in the German language devoted to an analysis of the world situation, the internal condition of Czechoslovakia, and the problems of the world proletariat. The author of this book, Jaroslav Cerny, who published this work on the assignment of the "Vanguard" group, stands fully on the positions of revolutionary Marxism. It is natural therefore that he is also a convinced partisan of the Fourth International. It is just as natural that the bourgeois, Social Democratic, and Stalinist press should completely neglect this outstanding work, deserving of the most careful attention.

This note in no way pretends to assume the role of a critical article on Comrade Cerny's book. To this task I hope to return later. I wish to point out here that I do not agree with the author on everything. Thus his estimate of the last economic rise seems to me greatly exaggerated. But this is just a question of the analysis of the factual material, and now that the United States has again entered into a deep crisis it is much less difficult to judge the preceding rise than in the days when Comrade Cerny was writing his book. There are several other partial questions which in my opinion require additional treatment. But all these, after all, are only details which do not violate our basic solidarity with the author of the study.

However, there is one question of a timely political nature which must be clarified immediately. Cerny writes: "So far as the Trotskyists are concerned, they have shown themselves in the last ten years to be the only Marxist current which correctly assessed fascism and demanded in time a proletarian united front for struggle against it, while Stalin was at that period still calling Social Democracy the twin of fascism. This assessment of

Trotskyism was shared not so long ago by quite a few functionaries of the Second International, among them by Otto Bauer."[398] Here one should add that the left Social Democrats began to view us with "benevolence" beginning with the blissful third period, when our Marxist criticism was directed in the main against the ultraleft goat leaps of the Comintern. But from the moment when the Comintern made what seemed at first glance a sudden—though in reality an absolutely inevitable—turn to the basest opportunism, the left Social Democratic functionaries, not excepting the late Bauer, hastily became semi-Stalinists and thus turned hostilely against the Fourth International. An analogous zigzag was made by Messrs. Walcher,[399] Fenner Brockway, and other "left" imitators of Otto Bauer.

"We do not doubt for a moment," continues Comrade Cerny, "that in the future also the Trotskyists will continue to make a very valuable contribution to the process of revolutionizing the international proletarian movement and in the re-creation of its world organization."

If the programmatic unity of the author and the "Vanguard" group with the Bolshevik-Leninists can therefore be considered as firmly established on all basic questions, the organizational side of the matter appears much less clear. In this connection the author writes: "We do not think, however, that it would be correct to create a new 'Trotskyist' party. . . . The world revolutionary proletariat must create a new and therefore a fourth International. However, it will be created not outside the big proletarian organizations, but through them and on the basis of them. In this view we differ from the official Trotskyists."

The great practical significance of this statement needs no proof. And precisely because of this we would wish a clearer, that is, a more concrete formulation of the question. Cerny and his group, as may be judged from the book, continue to remain in the Czechoslovakian Social Democracy. We have never been principled opponents of the formation of factions of the Fourth International within reformist or centrist parties; on the contrary, for many countries we considered this stage unavoidable. The experiment passed through in several countries brought undoubtedly positive results, which nevertheless did not by far transform our sections into mass parties. How long our cothinkers can or should remain a faction of the Czechoslovakian Social Democracy is a question of concrete conditions and possibilities and not at all of principles. That is why the motives which prompted the author to counterpose his group to the "official Trotskyists" are not clear to us. In our opinion it can be only a question of a division of labor, of a temporary distribution of "spheres of influence" but in no case of counterposing two organizational methods.

From the history of the Third International we know a case where the Communist faction succeeded in gaining the majority of a Socialist party and included it officially in the Comintern; this was the case in France. Of course such a case is theoretically possible in the building of the Fourth International. Does Cerny want to say that his closest cothinkers have a chance of converting the Czechoslovakian Social Democracy? From here, from afar, this perspective seems to be more than doubtful. In any case there cannot be any question of extending this method to all countries in the hope of building the Fourth International directly on the "basis" of present Social Democratic or Stalinist "big proletarian organizations."

However, if Cerny wants to say that revolutionary Marxists, those who make up independent sections of the Fourth International as well as those who temporarily work as factions within two other Internationals, are obliged to concentrate their main effort within the mass organizations, and in the first place in trade unions, we would be in full and unconditional solidarity with him on this. Those "partisans" of the Fourth International who under one excuse or another remain outside of mass organizations can only compromise the banner of the Fourth International. Our roads are not the same.

The purpose of this note, we repeat, is not to retell or give a critical evaluation of the rich and valuable content of this book of Comrade Cerny. We wish only to draw the attention of our sections and of all thinking Marxists in general to this study. The second part of Cerny's book is wholly devoted to the "problems of the working class movement in Czechoslovakia." The theoretical organs of our sections should, in my opinion, bring this second part, even if only in brief, before their readers.

I most warmly recommend Cerny's book to all Marxists, to all class-conscious workers who know the German language.

# NOTES AND ACKNOWLEDGMENTS

1. "Ninety Years of the Communist Manifesto." Introduction to the first Afrikaans translation of the *Communist Manifesto*. The original version, in *New International*, January 1938, contained several errors; a corrected version was printed the following month. **New International** was the magazine of the Socialist Workers Party until April 1940, when it was taken over by Max Shachtman and his followers, who split from the SWP to form their own organization. The SWP then began publishing *Fourth International*, whose name was later changed to *International Socialist Review*.

2. **Karl Marx** (1818-1883) and **Frederick Engels** (1820-1895) were the founders of scientific socialism and leaders of the First International, 1864-76.

3. **The Communist (or Third) International—the Comintern—** was organized under Lenin's leadership in 1919 as the revolutionary successor to the Second International. Stalin dissolved the Comintern in 1943 as a gesture of goodwill to his imperialist allies. The **"People's Front"** or (Popular Front) was a governmental coalition of the Communist and Socialist parties with bourgeois parties around a program of liberal capitalism. The Comintern adopted its People's Front policy at its Seventh Congress in 1935.

4. **Eduard Bernstein** (1850-1932) was the leading theoretician of revisionism in the German Social Democracy. He held that Marxism was no longer valid and had to be "revised": socialism would come about not through class struggle and revolution but through the gradual reform of capitalism achieved by parliamentary means; the workers' movement, therefore, had to abandon the policy of class struggle for one of class collaboration. Bernstein invented the term "theory of impoverishment" in 1890 in a criticism of Marx's assertion, in the *Communist Manifesto*, that the poverty of the proletariat as a whole tends to increase with the development of capitalism. **Karl Kautsky** (1854-1938) was regarded as the outstanding Marxist theoretician until World War I, when he abandoned internationalism and opposed the October Revolution.

5. **Leon Blum** (1872-1950) was the head of the French Socialist Party in the thirties and premier of the first People's Front government in 1936. **Camille Chautemps** (1885-1963), a Radical Socialist, was French premier, 1930 and 1933-34, but retired in disgrace because of his

involvement in financial scandals. He was premier again in 1937-38. **Francisco Largo Caballero** (1869-1946) was a leader of the left wing of the Spanish SP. He was premier from September 1936 until May 1937. He was succeeded by **Juan Negrin Lopez** (1889-1956) who was the final premier of the Spanish Republic, resigning in exile in France after the Spanish Civil War.

6. **Bonapartism** was a central concept in Trotsky's writings during the 1930s. He used the term to describe a dictatorship, or a regime with certain features of a dictatorship, during periods when class rule is not secure; it is based on the military, police, and state bureaucracy, rather than on parliamentary parties or a mass movement. Trotsky saw two types—bourgeois and Soviet. His most extensive writings on bourgeois Bonapartism are in *The Struggle Against Fascism in Germany* (Pathfinder, 1970). His views on Soviet Bonapartism reached their final form in his essay "The Workers' State, Thermidor and Bonapartism," reprinted in *Writings 34-35*. **"Socialism in one country"** was Stalin's theory, introduced into the Communist movement in 1924, that a socialist society could be achieved inside the borders of a single country. Later, when it was incorporated into the program and tactics of the Comintern, it became the ideological cover for the abandonment of revolutionary internationalism and was used to justify the conversion of Communist parties throughout the world into docile pawns of the Kremlin's foreign policy. A comprehensive critique by Trotsky is in his 1928 book *The Third International After Lenin* (Pathfinder, 1970).

7. **The Second International** began in 1889 as a loose association of national Social Democratic and labor parties, uniting both revolutionary and reformist elements; its strongest and most authoritative section was the German Social Democracy. Its progressive role ended in 1914, when its major sections violated the most elementary socialist principles and supported their own imperialist governments in World War I. It fell apart during the war, but was revived as the Labor and Socialist International, a completely reformist organization, in 1923.

8. In **1848** struggles for bourgeois democratic rights, national independence, and constitutional reforms took place throughout Europe. **The Paris Commune** was the first example of a workers' government. It was in power March 18–May 28, 1871, just seventy-two days, before it was overthrown in a bloody series of battles.

9. **Vladimir Ilyich Lenin** (1870-1924) restored Marxism as the theory and practice of revolution in the imperialist epoch after it had been debased by the opportunists, revisionists, and fatalists of the Second International. He initiated the Bolshevik tendency, which was the first to build the kind of party needed to lead a working class revolution. He led the first victorious workers' revolution in 1917, and served as the head of the first Soviet government. He founded the Communist International and helped elaborate its principles, strategy, and tactics. He prepared a fight against the bureaucratization of the Russian CP and the Soviet state, but died before he could carry it out. His book *Imperialism: The Highest Stage of Capitalism* was written in 1916.

10. **The Fourth International** (World Party of Socialist Revolution) was the political movement led by Trotsky during his third exile. It was called the International Left Opposition (ILO—Bolshevik-Leninists) until 1933. After Hitler came to power, it discontinued its original policy of working for the reform of the Comintern, proclaimed the need for a new International, changed its name to the International Communist League (ICL—Bolshevik-Leninists), and set to work gathering forces for revolutionary parties throughout the world. Trotsky proposed that the Fourth International be founded at an ICL conference in July 1936, but the conference instead established the Movement for the Fourth International (MFI). The founding conference of the FI was held in France in September 1938.

11. "It Is High Time to Launch a World Offensive Against Stalinism." *Socialist Appeal,* November 20, 1937. **Socialist Appeal** was the paper of the left wing of the Socialist Party in 1936-37; after the left wing was expelled, it became the paper of the newly formed Socialist Workers Party.

12. **GPU** was one of the abbreviated names for the Soviet political police; other names were Cheka, NKVD, MVD, KGB, etc., but GPU is often used in their place.

13. From 1936 to 1938 Stalin conducted three big **Moscow confession show trials,** in which most of the leaders of the Russian Revolution were accused of plotting to restore capitalism. The main defendants in the proceedings, in absentia, were Trotsky and his son Leon Sedov. Through these trials, Stalin consolidated his personal rule over the Soviet Union.

14. **The POUM** (Workers Party of Marxist Unification) was founded in Spain in 1935, when the Spanish Left Opposition broke with Trotsky and merged with the centrist Workers and Peasants Bloc. Trotsky severed all relations with it when it joined the Spanish People's Front government.

15. **Gregory Zinoviev** (1883-1936) and **Leon Kamenev** (1883-1936) helped Stalin initiate the crusade against Trotskyism in 1923, but they blocked with the Left Opposition from 1926 until they were expelled from the party in 1927. They capitulated, were readmitted, but were expelled again in 1932. They repented again, but became the victims of the first big Moscow show trial and were executed. Zinoviev was the first head of the Comintern (1919-26).

16. **Jacques Duclos** (1896-1975) was a Stalinist deputy and a member of the Political Bureau of the French CP.

17. **Mikhail Koltsov** (1898-1942) was a Stalinist agent in Spain during the Civil War. As a staff writer for *Pravda* after his return to the USSR, he defended the frame-up trials until he was himself arrested in December 1938 on charges of having ties with Spanish Trotskyists. His book *Spanish Diaries* was published posthumously. **Willi Muenzenberg** (1889-1940), an organizer of the Young Communist International, masterminded many propaganda enterprises for the German CP and the Kremlin. He broke with the Stalinists in 1937 and died under mysterious

circumstances during the German invasion of France.

18. **Andres Nin** (1892-1937) was a founder of the Spanish CP and secretary of the Red International of Labor Unions. He supported the Left Opposition and was expelled from the CP in 1927. He participated in the formation of the International Left Opposition and was the leader of its Spanish section until its break with the ILO in 1935, when it merged with the Workers and Peasants Bloc of Joaquin Maurin to form the POUM. For a brief time in 1936 he was minister of justice in the Catalan government, but he was then arrested by the Stalinists and assassinated. **Erwin Wolf,** a Czech, served as Trotsky's secretary in Norway. He was kidnaped and killed by the GPU in Spain in 1937. **Mark Rein** had gone to Spain to cover the Civil War for a socialist newspaper and vanished, evidently a victim of the GPU.

19. **Rudolf Hess** (1894-    ) was head of the political section of the Nazi party from 1932, and a member of Hitler's cabinet council from 1934. In 1941, he flew to Scotland where he was held as a prisoner of war; in 1946 he was sentenced to life imprisonment by the Nuremburg war crimes tribunal.

20. **Anton Grylewicz** was a leading Oppositionist in Germany, listed as the "official editor" of the *Biulleten Oppozitsii* (Bulletin of the Opposition, the Russian-language organ of the ILO) when it was published in Berlin.

21. **Ignace Reiss** was the pseudonym of Ignace Poretsky, a GPU agent who broke with Stalin in the summer of 1937 and joined the Fourth Internationalists. He was murdered by GPU agents near Lausanne, Switzerland, on September 4, 1937 (see *Writings 36-37*). He is the subject of a memoir by his widow, Elizabeth K. Poretsky, entitled *Our Own People* (1970).

22. **White Guards,** or Whites, was the name given the Russian counterrevolutionary forces after the October Revolution.

23. **Andrei Vyshinsky** (1883-1954) was a Menshevik from 1902 until 1920. He received international notoriety as the prosecuting attorney in the Moscow trials and then was Soviet foreign minister, 1949-53. **David Zaslavsky** (1880-1965) was a journalist on the Central Committee of the Bund who came out against the Bolsheviks during the October Revolution. In 1919 he supported the Soviet government. **Alexander Troyanovsky** (1882-1955) and **Ivan Maisky** (1884-1975) were both prominent right-wing Mensheviks, hostile to the October Revolution, who became Soviet diplomats in the late twenties. Troyanovsky was a member of the Menshevik Central Committee who denounced the Bolsheviks in the Constituent Assembly in 1918 as German agents. He later became Soviet ambassador to the U.S. Maisky had been a minister in the White government in Siberia, and later became Soviet ambassador to London.

24. **Joseph Stalin** (1879-1953) became a Social Democrat in 1898, joined the Bolshevik faction in 1904, and was a member of its Central Committee from 1912. After the February revolution and before Lenin returned and reoriented the Bolsheviks toward winning power, he favored

a conciliatory attitude to the Provisional Government. He was commissar of nationalities in the first Soviet government and became general secretary of the CP in 1922. Lenin called in 1923 for his removal from that post because he was using it to bureaucratize the party and state apparatuses. After Lenin's death in 1924, Stalin gradually eliminated his major opponents, starting with Trotsky, until he became virtual dictator of the party and the Soviet Union in the 1930s. The chief concepts associated with his name are "socialism in one country," "social fascism," and "peaceful coexistence."

25. **Chiang Kai-shek** (1887-1975) was the right-wing military leader of the Kuomintang during the Chinese revolution of 1925-27. The Stalinists hailed him as a great revolutionary until April 1927, when he conducted a bloody massacre of the Shanghai Communists and trade unionists. He ruled over China until overthrown by the Chinese CP in 1949.

26. **Walter Duranty** (1884-1957) was a *New York Times* correspondent in Moscow for many years, and supported the Stalinists against the Opposition. **Louis Fischer** (1896-1970) was a European correspondent for the *Nation,* serving chiefly in the Soviet Union, and was the author of several books on European politics. Trotsky viewed him as an apologist for the Stalinists.

27. **Romain Rolland** (1866-1944), a novelist and dramatist, was a leading spirit of the "left" ever since his pacifist denunciation of World War I. In his later years he lent his name to Stalinist literary congresses and manifestoes. **Henri Barbusse** (1873-1935) was a pacifist novelist who joined the French CP in 1923 and wrote biographies of Stalin and Christ. **Andre Malraux** (1901-    ) had expressed sympathy for Trotsky in 1933-34, but became a collaborator of the Stalinists in the People's Front period and refused to speak up for Trotsky against the Moscow trial slanders. After World War II he became a Gaullist government official. **Heinrich Mann** (1871-1950), the brother of Thomas Mann and also a writer, was exiled to France 1933-40 and subsequently lived in the U.S. until his death. **Lion Feuchtwanger** (1884-1958) was another expatriot German writer living in London and France who came to the U.S. in 1940. He attended the 1937 Moscow trial and wrote *Moscow 1937: My Visit Described for My Friends* (London, 1937).

28. **Leon Jouhaux** (1870-1954) was general secretary of the CGT (General Confederation of Labor), the chief union federation in France. He was a reformist, social patriot, and class collaborationist. **Emile Vandervelde** (1866-1938) was a Belgian Labor Party leader and president of the Second International, 1929-36. He was in the cabinet during World War I, and signed the Versailles treaty as Belgium's representative.

29. **Indalecio Prieto y Tuero** (1883-1962) was a leader of the right wing of the Spanish SP. He was the minister of navy and air in Largo Caballero's cabinet and remained in Negrin's cabinet until the Stalinists insisted on his expulsion in 1938.

30. "Once Again: The USSR and Its Defense." *Internal Bulletin,* Organizing Committee for the Socialist Party Convention, no. 2, November 1937. This was the bulletin (hereafter called the OCSPC) of the American SP left wing, which had been expelled and was preparing for the convention that was to form the Socialist Workers Party at the end of the year. While the nature of the Soviet state was being debated in the SP left wing too, Trotsky wrote this article specifically in answer to one by **Yvan Craipeau** (1912-     ), a leader of the French section of the MFI. Craipeau left the FI in 1946, and wrote a history, *Le Mouvement trotskyste en France* (1971).

31. **Thermidor** 1794 was the month in the new French calendar when the revolutionary Jacobins headed by Robespierre were overthrown by a reactionary wing of the revolution that did not go so far, however, as to restore the feudal regime. Trotsky used the term as a historical analogy to designate the seizure of power by the conservative Stalinist bureaucracy within the framework of nationalized property relations.

32. **Adolph Hitler** (1889-1945) was appointed chancellor of Germany in January 1933 and, at the head of the National Socialist (Nazi) Party, led Germany into World War II.

33. The German **Spartacists** mentioned here were a small emigre group in the 1930s and should not be confused with the Spartacus League, which was organized by Rosa Luxemburg and Karl Liebknecht as the antiwar wing of the German Social Democracy and was the predecessor of the German CP. The name derives from Spartacus, the leader of a slave uprising at the end of the Roman Republic. **Hugo Urbahns** (1890-1946), a leader of the German CP, was expelled in 1928 and helped to found the Leninbund, which was associated with the ILO until 1930. In 1933 he moved to Sweden, where he died.

34. In 1923 a revolutionary situation developed in Germany, due to a severe economic crisis and the French invasion of the Ruhr. A majority of the German working class turned toward support of the CP, but the CP leadership vacillated, missed an exceptionally favorable opportunity to conduct a struggle for power, and permitted the German capitalists to recover their balance before the year ended. The Kremlin's responsibility for this wasted opportunity was one of the factors that led to the formation of the Russian Left Opposition at the end of 1923.

35. The first **five year plan** for economic development in the Soviet Union, begun in 1928, projected a modest acceleration of industrial growth and an irresolute policy toward the peasantry. Suddenly the Political Bureau reversed its position and called for fulfilling the five year plan in four years. The resultant speed-up and forced collectivization of the peasantry led to a period of economic chaos and great hardship for the population. **The great rumblings in Germany (1931-33)** refers to the stormy crises that toppled several cabinets before Hitler; the thought seems to be that the Kremlin's sectarian sabotage of revolutionary opportunities in Germany undermined Stalin's authority even among a section of the Soviet bureaucracy.

36. **The Spanish revolution** began in 1931 when the monarchy was overthrown and a republic proclaimed. In 1936 the People's Front government was elected and civil war broke out, ending in 1939 when Franco's fascist forces defeated the Republican troops. All the organizations of the Spanish left participated in the bourgeois People's Front government, leaving the insurgent masses leaderless in their struggle. Trotsky's writings on this are collected in *The Spanish Revolution (1931-39)* (Pathfinder, 1973). During June 1936 a massive strike wave broke out in France, with as many as seven million workers on strike at one time, many on sit-down strikes. Another upsurge of strike activity took place in July 1936.

37. **M. Yvon** was a French worker who spent eleven years in the Soviet Union at the bench and as a manager. In his "What Has Become of the Russian Revolution?" he painted a dismal picture of the Russian workers' poverty and misery.

38. **Revolution proletarienne** was a syndicalist journal published by former members of the French CP who had been expelled in the mid-twenties for sympathizing with the Left Opposition.

39. **Proudhonists** were followers of **Pierre-Joseph Proudhon** (1809-1865), one of the first theoreticians of anarchism. He argued for a society based on fair exchange between independent producers and considered the state less important than the workshops that he believed would replace it. The Russian **Left Opposition** (Bolshevik-Leninists or "Trotskyists") was formed in 1923 to oppose the Stalinization of the Russian CP. It was the first nucleus of the International Left Opposition and Fourth International.

40. **Maxim Litvinov** (1876-1951) was people's commissar of foreign affairs, 1930-39, ambassador to the U.S., 1941-43, and deputy commissar for foreign affairs, 1943-46. Stalin used him to personify "collective security" when he sought alliances with democratic imperialists, and shelved him during the period of the Stalin-Hitler pact and the cold war.

41. "War and the Fourth International," theses adopted by the International Secretariat in 1934, is in *Writings 33-34*.

42. **Italy invaded Ethiopia** in 1935. **The Sino-Japanese war,** which began in 1931 when Japan invaded Manchuria, was expanded and intensified by the Japanese in the summer of 1937 (see *Writings 36-37*). American and British aid and supplies to China did not begin until after the Japanese attack on Pearl Harbor in 1941.

43. "An 'Attempt' on Stalin's Life." By permission of the Harvard College Library. This statement to the press does not appear to have been printed anywhere.

44. **Georgi Pyatakov** (1890-1937) and **Karl Radek** (1885-1939) were expelled from the Russian CP in 1927 for membership in the Left Opposition. They capitulated and were reinstated and given important party and industrial posts, but were victims of the second Moscow trial.

45. **Konon B. Berman-Yurin** (1901-1936) and **Fritz David** (1897-

1936) were sentenced to death in the first Moscow trial. They were accused of meeting Trotsky in 1932 in Copenhagen to get instructions from him for Stalin's assassination. Berman-Yurin was a Russian newspaper correspondent in Germany. David had been a member of the German CP and trade union editor of its newspaper, *Rote Fahne* (Red Flag).

46. **Valentin Olberg** (1907-1936) joined the Left Opposition in 1930, but was expelled as a suspected member of the GPU. He was sentenced to death in the first Moscow trial.

47. "America's Sixty Families." From the archives of James P. Cannon. A letter to **James T. Farrell** (1904-    ), the author of *Studs Lonigan* and other novels, and a sympathizer of the SWP for some years during the thirties and early forties. **America's Sixty Families,** by Ferdinand Lundberg (Vanguard Press, 1937), documented the existence of an economic oligarchy in the U.S. headed by sixty families of immense wealth. The author brought the work up to date in 1968 with *The Rich and the Super-Rich.*

48. **Socialist Call** was the official newspaper of the SP.

49. **Partisan Review** was a left-wing magazine which first leaned toward Stalinism, then shook off Stalinist influence, and finally rejected Marxism altogether. In "Discussions with Trotsky: II—Defense Organization and Attitude Toward Intellectuals" (pages 294-300), *Partisan Review* is discussed in more detail.

50. "Letter on American Problems." From the archives of James P. Cannon, to whom it was addressed. **Cannon** (1890-1974) was an IWW organizer, a leader of the left wing in the SP, and a founder of the American CP. Expelled in 1928 for expressing solidarity with Trotsky, he led in the formation of the Left Opposition and later the SWP and the FI. At the time this letter was written, he was occupied with the preconvention discussion by the SP left wing and preparations for the founding convention of the SWP at the end of 1937.

51. **The National Committee** refers to the leading committee of the SP left wing, soon to become the SWP. Trotsky is concerned here with the choice of an additional comrade to come to Coyoacan as a guard.

52. **Harry Milton** was a Trotskyist active in the New York garment workers' union, who went to Spain as an antifascist volunteer and, at the front, was arrested by the Stalinists and deported.

53. **Joseph Hansen** (1910-    ) joined the Trotskyist movement in 1934, was active in a maritime union, and served as Trotsky's secretary 1937-40. His accounts of Trotsky's stay in Mexico, including his assassination, are in *Leon Trotsky, The Man and His Work* (Merit Publishers, 1969) and the introduction to Pathfinder's 1970 edition of *My Life.* After serving for many years as editor of *The Militant* and *International Socialist Review,* and as international representative of the Socialist Workers Party, he became the editor of *Intercontinental Press.*

54. **The Latin American conference** was planned as a regional agency to help prepare the international conference that was to found the FI. A Latin American conference was held in May 1938, and adopted a number of resolutions which were submitted to the international conference held in September 1938.

55. **Diego Rivera** (1886-1957) was the noted Mexican painter whose murals were removed from Rockefeller Center in New York because of their Communist subject matter. A founder of the Mexican CP and a member of its Central Committee since 1922, he left the CP in 1927 over the expulsion of the Left Opposition. He was Trotsky's host in Mexico when Trotsky first arrived there, but Trotsky was forced to break with him publicly in 1939 over the issues of dual unionism, the class nature of the Soviet state, and the Mexican presidential campaign of 1940, in which Rivera supported the candidacy of a right-wing general. The split is documented in *Writings 38-39.*

56. **Hugo Oehler** led a sectarian faction in the Workers Party of the United States that had opposed on principle the WP's entry into the SP, which was proposed as a way of reaching the growing left wing in that party. He and his group were expelled in 1935 for violating party discipline and formed the Revolutionary Workers League.

57. "Letter to Comrade Wasserman." From the archives of James P. Cannon. **Jac Wasserman** was the manager of Pioneer Publishers until 1940, when he joined the Shachtmanite Workers Party.

58. **Pioneer Publishers** was the American publisher of most of Trotsky's books in English and many other radical books and pamphlets from 1931 to 1965, when it was succeeded by Merit Publishers, which later became Pathfinder Press.

59. The **Kronstadt** naval base was the site of an uprising of sailors against the Bolshevik regime in 1921. The rebels demanded soviets without Communists and opposed many of the stern measures the Bolsheviks had taken during the civil war to safeguard the revolution. The uprising, suppressed by the Bolsheviks, led to the concessions of the New Economic Policy. Two articles on Kronstadt by Trotsky appear later in this volume.

60. "Coming Trials to Reveal Secret Plans of GPU." *Socialist Appeal,* November 27, 1937.

61. **Leon Sedov** (1906-1938), Trotsky's elder son, joined the Left Opposition and accompanied his parents in their last exile. He was Trotsky's closest collaborator and co-editor of the Russian *Biulleten Oppozitsii.* He lived in Germany from 1931 to 1933, and then in Paris until his death at the hands of the GPU. Trotsky's obituary for him begins on p. 166.

62. Trotsky's archives were stolen from the Paris office of the International Institute of Social History (Amsterdam) a day after they were deposited there.

63. **General Eugene Miller** had been named chief of the Union of Czarist Army Veterans—a White Guard organization—in January 1930, when the current chief had disappeared in Paris, presumably abducted by the Soviet secret police. Miller was in turn kidnaped on September 22, 1937. He left a note implicating General Eugene Skoblin, a GPU agent functioning in White Guard emigre circles in France, but Skoblin escaped.

64. Trotsky's cable to Premier Chautemps, published in *Socialist Appeal,* November 27, 1937, ran as follows: "In affairs assassination Ignace Reiss, my stolen archives, and analogous crimes, permit me to insist on the necessity of submitting at least as witness Jacques Duclos, vice-president Chamber of Deputies and an old GPU agent. Trotsky."

65. "How to Struggle Against War." Only part of this letter to the editors of *Challenge of Youth* was published in *Challenge of Youth,* September 20, 1940. The remainder was translated from the Russian for this volume by Marilyn Vogt, by permission of the Harvard College Library. **Challenge of Youth** was the paper of the Young People's Socialist League, retained when a majority of the organization broke with the Social Democracy and adhered to the Fourth International in the summer of 1937, when the SP's left wing was expelled and began the process of organizing the SWP. *Challenge* continued to be published as a Fourth Internationalist paper until the spring of 1940, when a majority of the YPSL split away under the leadership of Max Shachtman and James Burnham.

66. **The International Secretariat** (IS) was the administrative leadership of the international Trotskyist movement.

67. "Bertram Wolfe on the Moscow Trials." *Socialist Appeal,* December 4, 1937. **Bertram Wolfe** (1896-    ) was a leader of the Lovestone faction in the American CP, which expelled the Trotskyists in 1928 and was itself expelled the following year on orders from Stalin. He was an apologist for the Moscow trials until late 1937, when he publicly changed his position in a review of *The Case of Leon Trotsky,* the transcript of the Dewey Commission's hearings in Coyoacan, Mexico. He later moved to the right and eventually supported Nixon in the 1972 elections. He wrote *Three Who Made a Revolution* (1948), about Lenin, Trotsky, and Stalin.

68. **Heinrich Brandler** (1881-1967) was a founder of the German CP and its principal leader when it failed to take advantage of the revolutionary crisis of 1923. He was made a scapegoat by the Kremlin and removed from the party leadership in 1924. He aligned himself with Bukharin's Right Opposition in the USSR, and was expelled from the CP in 1929. He maintained an independent organization until World War II. **Jay Lovestone** (1898-    ), a leader of the American CP in the twenties, was expelled in 1929 shortly after the downfall of his international ally, Bukharin. The Lovestoneites served as a Right Opposition to the CP in the thirties but dissolved their organization at the beginning of World

War II. Lovestone later became cold-war adviser in foreign affairs for AFL-CIO President George Meany.

69. "Not a Workers' and Not a Bourgeois State?" *Internal Bulletin* (OCSPC), no. 3, December 1937. This was a contribution by Trotsky to the internal discussion that preceded the founding convention of the SWP. *Internal Bulletin* (OCSPC), no. 2, November 1937, had published a draft resolution on the Soviet Union by the Convention Arrangements Committee, and a longer amendment by Burnham and Carter, which Trotsky analyzes here. (*Internal Bulletin,* no. 3, December 1937, was to contain Burnham and Carter's answers to Trotsky.)

70. **James Burnham** and **Joseph Carter** were leaders of the Trotskyist faction of the SP left wing and later of the SWP. In the preconvention discussion they represented a tendency in the leadership that sought to change the party's characterization of the Soviet Union as a workers' state, but insisted that they continued to support the defense of the USSR against imperialist attack. In addition, they were beginning to express apprehensions about the centralist aspects of Bolshevik organizational policy. At the SWP convention their resolution on the USSR received the votes of three delegates against sixty-nine for the majority resolution, supported by Cannon, Shachtman, and Abern. The Burnham-Carter resolution on the organization question was withdrawn when the majority agreed to minor amendments in its resolution. In 1940 Burnham and Carter, this time joined by Shachtman and Abern, broke with the SWP over the class nature of the Soviet state. Burnham soon withdrew from the Shachtmanite Workers Party, and later became a propagandist for McCarthyism and other ultraright movements and an editor of the right-wing *National Review.*

71. **The New Leader** was the paper of the British **Independent Labour Party.** The ILP was founded in 1893 and helped to found the Labour Party, left it in 1931, and was now associated with the centrist London Bureau. It returned to the Labour Party in 1939. **Fenner Brockway** (1890-      ) was an opponent of the Fourth International and secretary of the London Bureau. He was also a leader of the ILP.

72. **The American Federation of Labor** (AFL) was a conservative craft union federation whose president was **William Green** (1873-1952) and one of whose vice presidents was **Matthew Woll** (1880-1956).

73. The Congress of Industrial Organizations (**CIO**) was originally set up in 1935 as a committee within the AFL. The AFL leaders refused to respond to the demand for powerful new organizations to represent radicalizing workers on an industry-wide basis, and expelled the CIO unions in 1938, forcing them to establish their own national organization. The AFL and CIO merged in 1955.

74. **Sir Walter Citrine** (1887-      ) was the general secretary of the British Trades Union Congress from 1926 to 1946. He was knighted for his service to British capitalism in 1935, and was made a baronet in 1946.

75. "For a Revolutionary Publishing House." *Socialist Appeal,* January

1, 1938, where it had the title "Trotsky Urges Backing for Pioneer Publishers." The occasion was the sixth anniversary of the founding of Pioneer Publishers.

76. "Moscow-Amsterdam 'Unity.'" *Socialist Appeal,* December 11, 1937. This was part of an interview by *El Universal* (Mexico City), shortly after a report had appeared in the press about the opening of negotiations for the unification of the Stalinist-dominated and Social Democratic-dominated union federations. Such a unification did not actually take place until 1945 and did not last long after the start of the cold war.

77. **Amsterdam International** was the popular name of the Social Democratic-dominated International Federation of Trade Unions, with headquarters in Amsterdam.

78. **Mikhail Tomsky** (1886-1936) was a right-wing Bolshevik who opposed the October 1917 insurrection. He was the head of the Soviet trade unions and a member of the Politburo until he joined the right-wing fight against Stalin led by Bukharin. He committed suicide during the first Moscow trial.

79. **N.M. Shvernik** (1888-    ) was the presiding judge at the trial of Mensheviks in 1931. He became a candidate member of the Politburo in 1939 and remained on it until 1966.

80. **Nicholas Yezhov** became the head of the GPU in 1936 but disappeared after the third Moscow trial.

81. "An FBI Agent's Story." From the archives of James P. Cannon. Unsigned. Accompanied by the following cover letter, signed "Joe Hansen": "Dear Comrades: I am enclosing a copy of the reply of Comrade Trotsky to a letter from Comrade Weber concerning the information obtained from a G-man relative to a campaign to exterminate the Trotskyites. The essential part of the information is as follows: 'In the further course of the conversation he . . . stated that ever since Roosevelt's Chicago war speech, the G-men had been set to gather information on the Marxists and Trotskyists, particularly in the two centers, New York and San Francisco, and that they were going to clamp down on the Trotskyists in three months. In addition, he added that there would also be a move that would bring the expulsion of Trotsky from Mexico in six months.'" **Jack Weber** at this time was a leader of the SP left wing in New Jersey; he left the SWP after World War II. The term "G-men" (for "government men") was widely used for FBI agents in the thirties. Contrary to Trotsky's suggestion, it was decided not to comment on the incident publicly.

82. **Machete** was the newspaper of the Mexican CP, whose name was later changed to *Voz de Mexico.* **General Antonio Villareal** was a former militant labor organizer and initiator of the Mexican Revolution in 1910. Because the Commission of Inquiry had approached him to participate in its hearings, the Stalinists linked his name to Trotsky and to the right wing in order to slander and discredit him. **General Saturnino Cedillo** was a right-wing army officer who led an unsuccess-

ful uprising against the Mexican government in May 1938 and was killed the following January by government troops.

83. **Hernan Laborde** was the chief leader of the Mexican CP until early 1940, when he was purged in a reorganization of the party which was related to preparations for the Trotsky assassination.

84. The Commission of Inquiry into the Charges Made Against Leon Trotsky in the Moscow Trials was called the **Dewey Commission** after its chairman, **John Dewey** (1859-1952), the noted American philosopher and educator. The commission conducted hearings in Mexico, April 10-17, 1937, and issued the verdict that Trotsky and his son Leon Sedov were not guilty of the charges against them. The summary of its findings was published in *Not Guilty* (Monad Press, 1972).

85. **Sara** was Sara Weber, who had been Trotsky's Russian-language secretary in Turkey and France.

86. "A Few Words on *Lutte ouvriere.*" *Bulletin Interieur,* POI (Internationalist Workers Party, the French section of the MFI), no. 3, January 21, 1938. An excerpt. Signed "Crux." Translated for this volume from the French by Naomi Allen. **Lutte ouvriere** (Workers' Struggle) was the POI newspaper.

87. **Quatrieme Internationale** was the POI's occasional theoretical review.

88. "The Future of the Dutch Section." *Internal Bulletin,* Socialist Workers Party, no. 5, August 1938. A letter to **Henricus Sneevliet** (1883-1942), a founder of the Dutch and Indonesian CPs who left the CP in 1927. In 1933 his group allied itself with the ILO. However, he broke with the MFI in 1938 because of differences over trade union policy and the Spanish Civil War. During World War II he was arrested by the Nazis and shot.

89. Beginning in 1933, the threat of fascism spurred the development of significant left wings in the old Social Democratic parties. Trotsky proposed the temporary entry of the Left Oppositionists into certain Socialist parties to link up with the new youthful revolutionaries.

90. The first **International Conference** for the Fourth International was held in Geneva in July 1936. The theses, resolutions, and appeals adopted by the conference are in *Documents of the Fourth International (1933-40),* and Trotsky's letters about the conference are in *Writings 35-36.*

91. **The Dutch NAS** (National Labor Organization) was a small left-wing union movement which Sneevliet led during the 1930s.

92. "A Letter to the *New York Times.*" *New York Times,* December 7, 1937, where it had the title "Mr. Trotsky on the Far East."

93. "Defeatism vs. Defensism." From the archives of James P. Cannon. A letter to Burnham and Carter, who had just sent Trotsky a copy of Burnham's first draft of the Declaration of Principles later adopted by the SWP convention and of their document defending the right of defeatists

to remain members even though the party adopted a "defensist" position on the Soviet state. It is necessary to note the special use of these terms in the discussion then going on: a **defensist** was one (like Trotsky) who defended the Soviet Union against all imperialist or capitalist assaults, despite opposition to the Soviet leadership, while a **defeatist** was one who, denying that the Soviet Union was a workers' state, would not support the Soviet Union any more than any capitalist state in a war. The more prevalent usage of these terms dates from World War I, before the first workers' state existed, when the radical movement was divided between defensists, who supported their capitalist governments, and defeatists (like Lenin and Trotsky) who opposed the capitalist governments in war as in peace. In the present letter Trotsky also uses the terms in that sense, as in the fourth paragraph. There were only two delegates at the SWP convention who favored defeatism toward the USSR.

94. **B.J. Field** was expelled from the Communist League of America after violating party discipline in 1934. He organized the League for a Revolutionary Workers Party, which soon disappeared. **Albert Weisbord** (1900-    ), who was expelled from the American CP in 1929, organized a small group, the Communist League of Struggle, which proclaimed its adherence to the ILO in the early 1930s although its politics vacillated between those of the Right and Left Oppositions. He later broke with Marxism and became an AFL organizer.

95. "A Suggestion on Burnham." A letter to James P. Cannon, from his archives. Marked "confidential." As this and other letters here show, even while he was refuting Burnham's ideas on the USSR and the organization question, Trotsky made special efforts to draw Burnham close, as long as Burnham declared himself a Soviet defensist. Two years later, when the war began and Burnham and Shachtman abandoned their defensism, Trotsky's attitude became completely irreconcilable.

96. **Max** was Max Shachtman (1903-1972), a leader of the American CP and a cofounder of the American Trotskyist movement. In 1940 he split from the SWP because of differences over the defense of the Soviet Union, and formed the Workers Party. In 1958 he joined the Socialist Party.

97. Burnham did not make the trip to Coyoacan and never met Trotsky.

98. "On Democratic Centralism." *Internal Bulletin* (OCSPC), no. 5, December 1937. This was another of Trotsky's contributions to the preconvention discussion.

99. "Two Defections in One Week." By permission of the Harvard College Library. Translated for this volume from the Russian by Pat Galligan.

100. **Walter Krivitsky** (1889-1941) was chief of the Soviet military intelligence in Western Europe before his defection in December 1937. He revealed numerous secrets of Soviet intelligence and was the author of *In Stalin's Secret Service* (1939). His political evolution was to the right and

he later became associated with the Mensheviks. He died in Washington under mysterious circumstances six months after the assassination of Trotsky.

101. "Telegram to the Dewey Commission." *Socialist Appeal,* December 25, 1937. The commission's verdict of "not guilty" was actually reached on September 21, 1937, but was not to be made public until December 13, 1937.

102. "Statement to Journalists on the Dewey Verdict." The text of the statement was published in the Scottish *Forward,* January 15, 1938, and the text of the answers to questions in *Socialist Appeal,* December 25, 1937. Both versions omitted the brief introduction, which was translated for this volume from the Spanish by Russell Block, by permission of the Harvard College Library.

103. **Wilhelm Liebknecht** (1826-1900) was a founder of the German Social Democracy in 1869, and a member of the Reichstag 1867-1870 and from 1874 until his death. He was imprisoned for two years for opposing the Franco-Prussian War.

104. **Alfred Rosmer** (1877-1964) was a friend of Trotsky from before World War I and a member of the Left Opposition until 1930, when he resigned because of political and organizational differences with the majority. He and Trotsky became personally reconciled in 1936.

105. **Denis N. Pritt** (1888-1972) was a British lawyer and a member of Parliament, 1935-50, and an uncritical admirer of Stalin. **Vicente Lombardo Toledano** (1893-1968), a Stalinist, was the head of the Mexican Confederation of Workers, the major trade union federation in Mexico. He was an active participant in the slander campaign carried out by the Mexican Stalinists against Trotsky, which was designed to prepare public opinion for his assassination.

106. **Carleton Beals** (1893-      ) was an American journalist and publicist. An original member of the Commission of Inquiry, Beals resigned after the eleventh session (see *The Case of Leon Trotsky* and *Writings 36-37*).

107. **Emile Zola** (1840-1902), the French novelist, wrote *J'Accuse* (I Accuse) in defense of Alfred Dreyfus, an army officer who was a victim of anti-Semitism.

108. "Permission to Use Articles." From the archives of Joseph Hansen. A letter to **Emrys Hughes** (1894-1969), editor (1936-41) of the Scottish *Forward,* one of the few public journals that would print Trotsky's writings during the Moscow trials. From 1947 until his death he was a member of Parliament.

109. **Charles Sumner** was the head of the Revolutionary Socialist League in England and a secretary at the founding conference of the FI in 1938.

110. "How to Conduct a Political Discussion." From the archives of James P. Cannon. A letter to James Burnham.

111. **Burnham's article in Symposium,** July 1932, a review of Trotsky's *History of the Russian Revolution,* was discussed by Trotsky in "A Proposal to an American Editor," reprinted in *Writings 32.* **Prinkipo** is an island in the Sea of Marmara off Turkey where Trotsky spent the first four and a half years of his final exile. **Max Eastman** (1883-1969) was an early sympathizer of the Left Opposition and a translator of several of Trotsky's books. His rejection of dialectical materialism in the 1920s was followed by his rejection of socialism in the 1930s. He became an anti-Communist and an editor of *Reader's Digest.*

112. "Letter to the *New International.*" From the archives of James P. Cannon. Copies were sent to Shachtman, Cannon, and Abern, along with a list of corrections for the published text of "Ninety Years of the *Communist Manifesto.*" The *New International* published a corrected version of the article in its February 1938 issue.

113. The note read: "Preface to the first edition of the *Manifesto* ever to be published in Afrikaans, the language of the natives of the Union of South Africa." Afrikaans is the language spoken by the people of Dutch or Huguenot ancestry in South Africa.

114. "Greetings to Norway." *Oktober,* no. 1, January 1938. Translated from the Norwegian for this volume by Russell Block.

115. **Trygve Lie** (1896-1968), former legal adviser to the Norwegian Labor Party (which was once affiliated to the Third International), was Norwegian minister of justice, 1935-39, and was responsible for arresting Trotsky while he was in Norway and holding him incommunicado. He was later minister of foreign affairs (1941-46) and became secretary-general of the United Nations after World War II (1946-53). **Jonas Lie** was the Norwegian police officer assigned to guard Trotsky and his wife during the trip across the Atlantic from Norway to Mexico. On January 1, 1937, during the voyage, the police officer received a telegram of greetings from the minister. Under the Nazi occupation government, Jonas Lie became chief of police.

116. **R. Konstad** was the reactionary director of the Norwegian passport bureau who prevented Trotsky from sending or getting mail during his 1936 internment and even tried to deny him the right to listen to the radio.

117. "Answers to the Questions of *Marianne.*" By permission of the Harvard College Library. Translated for this volume from the French by Jeff White. **Marianne** was a French journal which was supporting the People's Front at this time. It is not known whether *Marianne* published Trotsky's answers.

118. **Hendrik De Man** (1885-1953) was a leader of the Belgian Labor

Party's right wing and author of a 1933 "labor plan" to end the depression and promote production. Trotsky's comments on the "De Man plan" are in *Writings 33-34.*

119. The French **Radical Party,** or **Radical Socialists,** neither radical nor socialist, was the principal capitalist party of France between the two world wars, and was comparable to the Democratic Party in the U.S.

120. The **"third period,"** according to the schema proclaimed by the Stalinists in 1928, was the final period of capitalism, the period of its immediately impending demise and replacement by soviets. Flowing from this, the Comintern's tactics during the years 1928-34 were marked by ultraleftism and sectarianism, including refusing to join the mass labor unions in the capitalist countries and building smaller "red" unions instead, as well as refusing to build united fronts with other working class organizations. The Stalinists abandoned this policy in 1934, and the following year adopted the People's Front policy.

121. **Edouard Daladier** (1884-1970), a Radical Socialist, was French premier from 1933 until 1934, when he was ousted during an attempted fascist coup d'etat. He was minister of war under Leon Blum. Later he became premier again and signed the Munich Pact with Hitler in September 1938. **Jean Zyromsky** (1890-    ) was a leader of the French SP with pro-Stalinist leanings. An advocate of "organic unity" with the Stalinsits in the mid-thirties, he joined the CP after World War II.

122. **Les Crimes de Staline** (1937), published in France, has never been printed as a book in English, but its entire contents are in English in *Writings 36-37* (except for Trotsky's speech to the Dewey Commission of April 17, 1937, which is in *The Case of Leon Trotsky*).

123. The **League for the Rights of Man** was a French civil liberties organization which whitewashed the Moscow trials. **Victor Basch** was its head. **R. Rosenmark** was a lawyer used by the Stalinists as an apologist for the trials.

124. "Intellectuals and the Party Milieu." From the archives of James P. Cannon, to whom this letter was addressed. "B" was James Burnham.

125. **Mikhail N. Pokrovsky** (1868-1932) and **Nikolai Rozhkov** (1868-1927) were prominent Soviet historians. Pokrovsky was a member of the Bolshevik Party from 1905. He became a leading Stalinist apologist in the late twenties.

126. **The Robinson case** refers to two Americans who disappeared in Moscow. Their passports, with the name Robinson, were faked. Their disappearance seemed to be linked to the preparations for a new frame-up trial, this time aimed at the American anti-Stalinist movement and antiwar sentiment. Cannon's "memo" on the case was in *New International,* February 1938.

127. "Letter to Australians." *Fourth International,* July 1942.

128. "The Spanish Lesson for the Fourth International." From the archives of James P. Cannon.

129. The article, "The Lessons of Spain—The Last Warning," written December 17, 1937, was printed in *Socialist Appeal* in a translation by John G. Wright, and was reprinted in Trotsky's *The Spanish Revolution (1931-39)*.

130. **Georges Vereecken** was the representative of a sectarian tendency in the Belgian section of the MFI. He broke with Trotsky when the Belgian section entered the Belgian Labor Party, rejoined later, and again split on the eve of the founding congress to form his own group. **Victor Serge** (1890-1947) was an anarchist in his youth. After the Bolshevik revolution he moved to the Soviet Union and worked for the Comintern. Arrrested as an Oppositionist and then freed in 1928, he was rearrested in 1933. Thanks to a campaign by intellectuals in France, he was released and allowed to leave the USSR in 1936. He soon developed differences with the MFI and left it. He wrote several important historical works, including *The Year One of the Russian Revolution* (Holt, Rinehart & Winston, 1972) and *From Lenin to Stalin* (Pathfinder, 1973).

131. **Felix Morrow** was a leader of the SWP. His book **Revolution and Counter-Revolution in Spain** (second edition, Pathfinder, 1974) was published without Trotsky's article. Morrow was one of the defendants in the Minneapolis Smith Act trial in 1941, during which he was also editor of *The Militant,* successor of *Socialist Appeal.* He was expelled from the SWP for violating discipline in 1946.

132. "For a Permanent Defense Committee." From the archives of James P. Cannon. This was addressed to the SWP leadership in New York.

133. **The conference** was the founding convention of the Socialist Workers Party, which ended January 3, 1938.

134. "On *Modern Monthly.*" From the archives of James P. Cannon. A letter to the SWP leadership in New York. **Modern Monthly** (later called *Modern Quarterly*) was an independent radical journal edited by V.F. Calverton from 1923 to 1940. It featured diverse political commentary, as well as literary criticism and fiction. Trotsky wrote for it in the early thirties, but he later dissociated himself from it because he felt that it did not have a sufficiently critical position on the Moscow trials (see "To the Editor of *Modern Monthly,*" in *Writings 36-37*).

135. **Anita Brenner** (1905-1974) was a journalist and author of books on Mexico. She was friendly with Mexican President Cardenas and was the first foreign reporter to get a policy statement from him during the oil expropriations in 1938.

136. "Letter on Defeatism." *Internal Bulletin,* SWP, no. 3, 1938. A letter to **Jean Van Heijenoort,** who had served as one of Trotsky's secretaries

in all four countries of his last exile. He rejected Marxism after World War II and became a professor of philosophy.

137. **Benjamin Stolberg** (1891-1951), a member of the Dewey Commission, was an author and journalist. **John F. Finerty,** the commission's attorney, was the former counsel for Sacco and Vanzetti and for Tom Mooney.

138. **Amadeo Bordiga** (1889-1970), a founder of the Italian CP, was expelled on charges of "Trotskyism" in 1929. The ILO tried to work with the Bordigists but failed because of the latters' inveterate sectarianism: they opposed the tactic of the united front, for example, "on principle."

139. **The London Bureau** (International Bureau of Revolutionary Socialist Parties), established in 1935, was the successor of the International Labor Community (IAG). It was a loose association of centrist parties not affiliated to either the Second or the Third International but opposed to the formation of a Fourth International. Among its members were the SAP (Socialist Workers Party) of Germany, the British ILP, the Spanish POUM; later in 1938 they were joined by the German Brandlerites, the French PSOP (Workers and Peasants Socialist Party), and the American Lovestoneites.

140. "Does the Soviet Government Still Follow the Principles Adopted Twenty Years Ago?" Scottish *Forward,* February 12 and 19, 1938.

141. The **Stakhanovist** movement was a special system of speedup in Soviet production named after a coal miner, Alexei Stakhanov, who reportedly exceeded his quota sixteen-fold by sheer effort. The system was introduced in the Soviet Union in 1935, and led to great wage disparities and widespread discontent among the masses of workers. For his reward Stakhanov was made a full member of the CP and a deputy to the Supreme Soviet of the USSR.

142. **Ivan N. Smirnov** (1881-1936) was expelled from the CP in 1927 as a Left Oppositionist, but capitulated in 1929 and was reinstated in the party. He was rearrested in 1933 and executed after the first Moscow trial. **Leonid Serebriakov** (1890-1937) also capitulated after being expelled in 1927 and was given responsible posts, but was shot after the second trial. **Grigory Sokolnikov** (1888-1939) for a short time supported the Zinovievists on the issue of the party regime. For that he was shot after the second trial. **Mikhail Tukhachevsky** (1893-1937) was among the Red Army generals charged with treason and executed in 1937. **Christian Rakovsky** (1873-1941), an early leader of the Left Opposition, was deported to Siberia in 1928; in 1934 he capitulated. In 1938 he was one of the major defendants in the third Moscow trial, where he was sentenced to twenty years' imprisonment. **Nikolai Krestinsky** (1883-1938) renounced the Left Opposition in 1927 but was killed after the third Moscow trial.

143. **Alexander V. Kolchak** (1874-1920) commanded one of the Eastern counterrevolutionary fronts during the Russian civil war.

144. **Joseph Goebbels** (1897-1945) was the Nazi minister for propa-

ganda and national enlightenment from 1933, and a member of Hitler's cabinet council from 1938. He committed suicide upon Germany's defeat.

145. "Hue and Cry Over Kronstadt." *New International,* April 1938.

146. **Pavel Miliukov** (1859-1943), a leader of the liberal Constitutional Democrats (Cadets), was minister of foreign affairs in the Russian Provisional Government, March-May 1917, and an outstanding enemy of the Bolshevik Revolution. His paper was called *Poslednya Novosti* (Latest News).

147. **Wendelin Thomas** was a former Communist deputy to the German Reichstag (1920-24) and a member of the International Commission investigating the Moscow trials. For Trotsky's answer to him, see "The Questions of Wendelin Thomas," July 6, 1937, in *Writings 36-37.*

148. **The New Economic Policy** (NEP) was adopted as a temporary measure in 1921 to replace the policy of "Military Communism," which had prevailed during the civil war. The NEP allowed a limited growth of free trade inside the Soviet Union and foreign concessions alongside the nationalized and state-controlled sections of the economy. The NEP stimulated the growth of a class of wealthy peasants and of a commercial bourgeoisie (NEPmen), and produced a long series of political and economic concessions to private farming and trade.

149. **The Social Revolutionary Party** (SRs) was founded in Russia in 1900, emerging in 1901-02 as the political expression of all the earlier populist currents; it had the largest share of influence among the peasantry prior to the revolution in 1917.

150. **John G. Wright** (1902-1956) was a leader and educator of the SWP, who translated many of Trotsky's works into English. The title of his article was "The Truth About Kronstadt."

151. **Nikolai Yudenich** (1862-1933) was a czarist general who in 1919 organized an offensive against Petrograd with Allied aid.

152. **Anton Denikin** (1872-1947) was one of the leaders of the counterrevolution in southern Russia during the civil war.

153. **Alexander Berkman** (1870-1936) was a Polish-born Anarchist who lived in the U.S. He spent fourteen years in prison for stabbing Henry Clay Frick during the Homestead Steel strike. Along with **Emma Goldman** (1869-1940) he was imprisoned for antiwar activity during World War I and deported to Russia. Both disliked the Soviet regime and moved elsewhere.

154. **Nestor Makhno** (1884-1934) was the leader of small partisan bands of peasants who fought against Ukrainian reactionaries and German occupation forces during the Russian civil war. He refused to integrate his forces into the Red Army and ultimately came into conflict with it. His forces were finally dispersed by the Soviet government in 1921.

155. **Luis Companys y Jover** (1883-1940) became the head of the local government in Catalonia in 1933. His party was the bourgeois nationalist Catalan Esquerra. **Jose Garcia Oliver** (1901-  ) was a right-wing

Spanish Anarchist leader who collaborated with the Stalinists to crush the revolutionary wing of the loyalists. He was minister of justice in the central government from 1936 until the end of the Civil War.

156. **"Military Communism"** was the policy followed by the Soviet government during the civil war, which subordinated all production to the needs of the front and included the confiscation of grain from the peasants. It led to a drastic decline in production.

157. "Sneevliet's Role." From the personal archives of James P. Cannon.

158. "An Open Letter to *De Nieuwe Fakkel.*" *Internal Bulletin,* SWP, no. 5, August 1938. **De Nieuwe Fakkel** (The New Torch) was the paper of the Dutch section of the MFI and **De Internationale** was its magazine.

159. **The RSAP** (Revolutionary Socialist Workers Party), formed in 1935, was the Dutch section of the MFI. Because of differences over the issues listed in Trotsky's open letter, the RSAP broke with the MFI and did not participate in the FI's founding conference in 1938.

160. "Conclusion of a Long Experience." *Internal Bulletin,* SWP, no. 5, August 1938. A letter to the IS.

161. The resolution, "The International Bureau of Revolutionary Socialist Parties ('London Bureau') and the Fourth International," is in *Writings 35-36* (second edition).

162. "An Excellent Article on Defeatism." *Internal Bulletin,* SWP, no. 3, 1938. A letter to the IS, with copies to all sections.

163. The article by W. St. (Rudolf Klement) appeared, with some revisions, in *New International,* May 1938, under the title "Principles and Tactics in War."

164. W. St. noted: "I discarded the slogan of 'mass desertion' after the remark of Comrade T. Indeed, if we cannot reproach those soldiers who, lacking all enthusiasm for the cause of 'their' imperialism and rather sympathizing with the cause of the nonimperialist 'adversary,' pass over to the other side, it would be false to make a *slogan* out of it for the reasons given by Comrade Trotsky" (*Internal Bulletin,* SWP, no. 3, 1938, p. 9, in comments on his own article and Trotsky's remarks).

165. "Factory Papers and a Theoretical Journal." *Bulletin Interieur,* POI (Internationalist Workers Party, French section of the MFI). Translated for this volume from the French by Richard Lesnik.

166. **Raymond Molinier** (1904-    ) was a cofounder of the French Trotskyist movement with whom Trotsky collaborated until 1935, when his group was expelled for violating discipline by publishing its own newspaper, *La Commune,* the "mass paper." Attempts at reunification were made several times in the following years, but proved unsuccessful until the middle of World War II. The discussion on "a mass paper" is

documented in *Writings 35-36* (second edition). **Nicolle Braun** was Erwin
Wolf. His pamphlet *L'Organe de masse* (A Mass Paper), with an
introduction by Trotsky, was published by the International Secretariat.
Trotsky refers to him as "our poor N. Braun" because he had recently
been kidnaped and killed by the GPU in Spain (see note 18).

167. "The Ludlow Amendment." From the archives of James P.
Cannon, to whom it was addressed. **The Ludlow Amendment** was a
proposed amendment to the U.S. Constitution that would require a direct
referendum by the people before the U.S. government could declare war. It
was introduced by Democratic Representative Louis Ludlow of Indiana,
and was voted down in the House of Representatives by a close vote on
January 10, 1938. Earlier that week, a Gallup public opinion poll had
shown 72 percent of the American people favored the amendment. The
SWP Political Committee was opposed to support of the amendment, with
the exception of Burnham. In these letters Trotsky explained why he
disagreed with the PC majority; thinking that the defeat in the House had
removed the amendment as a practical political issue, he stressed the
methodological importance of a correct approach to it and left it up to
Cannon as to whether to carry the matter further. Cannon not only
showed the letters to Burnham but referred them to the PC, which
considered the issue again in February and changed its position from
opposition toward the amendment to abstention in disputes over it.
Trotsky took the issue up again in March during talks with an SWP
delegation, and at a plenum in April the SWP National Committee voted
in favor of critical support of the amendment.

168. "Letter to an American Youth." *Challenge of Youth,* March 1938.
A reply to a student in New York who could not decide between the
findings of the Moscow trials and the Commission of Inquiry.
169. **Maximilien Robespierre** (1758-1794) was the leader of the
French Jacobins and effective head of state from 1793. He and his fellow
Jacobins, **Louis-Antoine Saint-Just** (1767-1794) and **Georges Couthon** (1755-1794) were overthrown by the counterrevolution of the Ninth
of Thermidor and guillotined.

170. "Optimistic over the Future." From the archives of James P.
Cannon, to whom it was addressed.

171. "A New GPU Attempt." From the archives of James P. Cannon, to
whom it was probably addressed.
172. **Gerard Rosenthal** was a French Trotskyist and Trotsky's lawyer
in France for many years. He is the author of a book, *Avocat de Trotsky*
(Trotsky's Lawyer) (Robert Laffont, 1975).
173. **General Francisco Mujica** was minister of communications and
public works in Cardenas's cabinet. He had helped secure Trotsky's
admission to Mexico.
174. "Their Morals and Ours" was published in *New International* in

June 1938. It is available in the book of the same title from Pathfinder Press. The **Nation** and the **New Republic** were then liberal weeklies strongly influenced by Stalinism. Trotsky's article on their reaction to the Moscow trials, "The Priests of Half-Truth," begins on page 277. **Common Sense** was a liberal monthly published 1932-46.

175. "The Possibility of Foul Play." *Socialist Appeal,* February 26, 1938. Trotsky's elder son, Leon Sedov, died under mysterious circumstances on February 16 in a Paris hospital. Trotsky did not know when he wrote this, nor did he learn later, that the man who arranged for Leon Sedov to go to the hospital where he died was a GPU agent who had infiltrated the Fourth International.

176. "Leon Sedov—Son, Friend, Fighter." This pamphlet, dedicated to the proletarian youth, was published by the Young People's Socialist League (Fourth Internationalists) in March 1938.

177. **The February revolution** in Russia in 1917 overthrew the czar and established the bourgeois Provisional Government, which held power until the **October Revolution** brought the soviets, led by the Bolsheviks, to power.

178. Trotsky's **Criticism of the Draft Program of the Communist International** is included in *The Third International After Lenin* (Pathfinder Press, third edition, 1974).

179. Sedov's article on Stakhanovism was in the February 1936 *New International.*

180. **Karl Liebknecht** (1871-1919) was a left-wing German Social Democrat and antimilitarist. He was the first to vote against war credits in the Reichstag in 1914. Imprisoned for antiwar activity from 1916 to 1918, he was a leader of the Berlin uprising of 1919. He was assassinated by government officers in January 1919.

181. **Alexander F. Kerensky** (1882-1970) was one of the leaders of the Russian Social Revolutionary Party. He became vice-chairman of the Petrograd Soviet, then bolted from its discipline to assume the ministry of justice in the Provisional Government in March 1917. In May he took the post of minister of war and navy, which he continued to hold when he became premier. Later he appointed himself commander-in-chief as well. He fled Petrograd when the Bolsheviks took power.

182. **The July days** of 1917 in Petrograd broke out without any direction and led to bloody encounters. The Bolsheviks were declared responsible, their leaders arrested, and their papers shut down.

183. **Iraklii Tseretelli** (1882-1959), a Menshevik leader who supported the war, held ministerial positions March-August 1917.

184. **Sergei Sedov** (1908-1937?), Trotsky's younger son, was the only one of his children who had no interest in politics. He remained in Russia when Trotsky was deported, as a lecturer in technical subjects until 1934. In 1935 he was arrested after refusing to sign a statement denouncing his father. Unofficial reports say that he was shot in 1937.

185. **Sergei Mrachkovsky** (1883-1936) was a famous civil war commander who had also organized the insurrection in the Urals in 1917. Expelled from the party as an Oppositionist, he capitulated in 1929 but was exiled in 1933 and sentenced to death in the first Moscow trial. **Alexander Beloborodov** (1891-1938) was a member of the Revolutionary Military Committee of the Ninth Army and a member of the Central Committee. He was also a Left Oppositionist who was arrested and deported to Siberia. He capitulated but perished after the third Moscow trial.

186. "After Sedov's Death." From the archives of James P. Cannon. This letter was sent to the leaders of the SWP.

187. **John Glenner** was the pen name of Jan Frankel, one of Trotsky's secretaries. He was a Czech and was a witness at the Dewey Commission hearings.

188. "A Fresh Attack on Asylum." *Socialist Appeal,* March 5, 1938. On February 23, 1938, the first annual congress of the Stalinist-dominated CTM (Mexican Confederation of Workers) adopted a resolution presented by Vicente Lombardo Toledano condemning Trotsky and repeating the Moscow trial slanders. It was not coincidental that Toledano's move came only a week before the opening of the third Moscow trial. The resolution was published in English as a pamphlet by International Publishers in 1938 under the title "Labor Condemns Trotskyism."

189. **Henry Yagoda** (1891-1938) was the head of the Soviet secret police until he was himself made a defendant and shot.

190. **Rosa Luxemburg** (1871-1919), an outstanding leader of the Marxist movement and a prominent opponent of revisionism and opportunism before World War I, was jailed for antiwar activity at the outbreak of the war, but was freed by the November 1918 uprising. Together with Karl Liebknecht she organized the German CP. In January 1919 she was assassinated by officers of the Social Democratic government.

191. **General Lazaro Cardenas** (1895-1970) was president of Mexico from 1934 until 1940. His administration was marked by plans for the redistribution of the land, industrial and transportation development, renewal of struggle with the Roman Catholic church, and, in 1938, expropriations of foreign-owned oil properties. His was the only government in the world that would grant Trotsky asylum in the last years of his life. Trotsky made a pledge not to participate in Mexican politics, but he also made sure that his views on Mexican affairs found expression, by writing editorially or with pen names in the press of his Latin American cothinkers.

192. "The Trial of the Twenty-One." *Socialist Appeal,* March 12, 1938, where it appeared under the title "Elements of New Trial Examined." This was the first of the many articles and statements to the press that

Trotsky wrote about the third big Moscow trial, which was announced on February 27, opened on March 2, and ended on March 13, 1938.

193. **Nikolai Bukharin** (1888-1939) and **Alexei Rykov** (1881-1938) led the Right Opposition in the Russian CP. When it was expelled in 1929 they both capitulated, but they were defendants in the third Moscow trial and were executed. Bukharin succeeded Zinoviev as head of the Comintern (1926-29) and Rykov succeeded Lenin as chairman of the Council of People's Commissars.

194. **Arkady P. Rosengolts** (1889-1938) was a Left Oppositionist for a short time, but capitulated to Stalin by 1927. In 1928 he became people's commissar of state control, and in 1937 he was head of the Administration of State Reserves, but in 1938 he was made a defendant in the third Moscow trial and was shot.

195. **Dimitry Pletnev** (1872-1953) had long been regarded as Russia's leading doctor. Before the revolution he had been a member of the liberal Cadet Party. His arrest, and that of the other doctors who were his codefendants, represented the spread of the worst aspects of the Moscow trials to the nonparty population. Pletnev received a sentence of 25 years, later reduced to 10 years, but he died in a labor camp in 1953.

196. "Eight Ministers." *Socialist Appeal,* March 12, 1938.

197. **Sergei Kirov** (1886-1934) was a member of the Central Committee from 1923 and was party secretary in Leningrad from 1926. His assassination signaled the start of the purges that culminated in the Moscow trials and the extermination of the entire remaining leadership of the Russian Revolution. **Leonid Nikolaev,** Kirov's assassin, was tried behind closed doors and shot in 1934.

198. "Trial Seen as Reply to Dewey Commission." *New York Times,* March 3, 1938, which omitted a few sentences and confused Rakovsky with Mrachkovsky. The complete, correct version is supplied here, by permission of the Harvard College Library.

199. **A.A. Slutsky** was the head of the Foreign Department of the GPU. On February 17, 1938, Slutsky was poisoned with cyanide in the office of a superior. His death was labeled a heart attack.

200. **Lev Karakhan** (1889-1937) had been part of the Soviet delegation to the Brest-Litovsk peace negotiations and was later ambassador to Berlin. He was shot without trial in late 1937. **Abel Yenukidze** (1877-1937) became secretary of the All-Russian Central Executive Committee of the Soviets before his execution. Trotsky's article about him, "Behind the Kremlin Walls" (January 8, 1938), is in *Political Portraits* (Pathfinder, 1977).

201. "To the Attention of Thinking People." From the archives of Joseph Hansen.

202. "Behind the Moscow Trials." London *Sunday Express,* March 6, 1938, where several paragraphs and parts of paragraphs throughout the

article were omitted. Those were translated for this volume from the Norwegian newspaper *Tidens Tegn* (Oslo) by Russell Block.

203. **Isaac Zelensky** (1890-1938) was chairman of the consumer cooperative system and a Central Committee member. A defendant in the third Moscow trial, he was accused of mixing glass and nails with butter. He was sentenced to death and executed, but was posthumously "rehabilitated."

204. **V.I. Ivanov** (1893-1938), commissar of the timber industry, **G.F. Grinko** (1890-1938), commissar of finance, and **M.A. Chernov** (1891-1938), commissar of agriculture, had all been uncritical servitors of Stalin until their arrest. Ivanov was also a full member of the Central Committee. He was accused of sabotaging the timber industry in collaboration with the British intelligence service. Grinko, a Ukrainian, was accused of being a member of a "National Fascist Organization," but his main activity was said to be financial sabotage. Chernov, a former Menshevik, had been in charge of grain collection in the Ukraine in 1929-30. He was blamed for agricultural failures and livestock mortality. All were executed after the third Moscow trial.

205. **Akmal Ikramov** (1898-1938), **Faizul Khodzhaev** (1896-1938), both Uzbek leaders, and **Vasily F. Sharangovich** (1897-1938), first secretary in Belorussia, were accused of "bourgeois nationalism" and executed after the third Moscow trial.

206. **Pyotr P. Kryuchkov** (1889-1938), Gorky's personal secretary, **V.A. Maximov-Dikovsky** (1900-1938), Kuibyshev's secretary, and **Pavel P. Bulanov** (1895-1938), Yagoda's secretary, were accused of complicity in the murders of Gorky and Gorky's son, and were shot after the third Moscow trial. **Sergei Bessonov** (1892-1941) had worked in the Soviet trade delegation in Berlin. Arrested in February 1937, he finally confessed to the charges against him in December, and agreed to testify for the prosecution at the impending trial. He was sentenced to fifteen years, but was shot in 1941. **Prokopy T. Zubarev** (1886-1938), a minor official in the Commissariat of Agriculture, was accused of disrupting the food supply and of having been an agent of the czarist secret police in 1908, and was shot after the third Moscow trial.

207. **L.G. Levin** (1870-1938) was an eminent Kremlin doctor from 1920 until he was accused of killing Gorky's son, Gorky, and Kuibyshev and of complicity in the death of Menzhinsky.

208. **I.N. Kazakov** (1870-1938) was Menzhinsky's doctor but was not otherwise a well-known figure. **A.I. Vinogradov** (d. 1938), a doctor in the medical service of the GPU, never came to trial; proceedings against him were "terminated owing to his death" in the hands of the GPU after his arrest for complicity in the murder of Gorky.

209. **Valerian Kuibyshev** (1888-1935) held a variety of posts before becoming chairman of the Supreme Council of National Economy in 1926. **Vladimir Menzhinsky** (1874-1934) was Yagoda's predecessor as head of the GPU. **Maxim Gorky** (1868-1936), the Russian writer of popular short stories, novels, and plays, was hostile to the October Revolution in 1917 but gave support to the government under Stalin.

210. **Iona E. Yakir** (1896-1937), a full member of the Central Committee, and **I.P. Uborevich** (1896-1937) were among the Red Army commanders charged with treason and executed in 1937. Both had commanded armies with distinction during the civil war. **Konstantin Yurenev** (1889-1938) was the ambassador to Japan until his arrest and execution after the third Moscow trial.

211. **Prince George E. Lvov** (1861-1925) was a Russian politician and large landowner. After the overthrow of the czar, he became prime minister of the first Provisional Government, March-July 1917.

212. **Lenin's "testament,"** written between December 25, 1922, and January 4, 1923, is in *Lenin's Fight Against Stalinism* (Pathfinder, 1975).

213. **Benito Mussolini** (1883-1945), the founder of Italian fascism, had been a member of the antiwar wing of the SP in 1914. He organized the fascist movement in 1919, became dictator in 1922, and set the pattern of repression on which the German Nazis modeled their regime. He was overthrown in 1943 and executed by partisans two years later. **Jozef Pilsudski** (1867-1935), a Polish nationalist, organized his own army to fight against Russia during World War I, and was a leader of counterrevolutionary interventionist forces during the Russian civil war. He moved his troops into Warsaw in May 1926 and became virtual dictator of Poland until his death.

214. "Four Doctors Knew Too Much." *New York Times,* March 4, 1938.

215. **Felix Dzerzhinsky** (1877-1926) was a founder of the Social Democratic Party of Poland and Lithuania. In 1906 he was elected to the Bolshevik Central Committee. After the revolution he became the commissar for internal affairs and first chairman of the All-Russian Extraordinary Commission for Combating Counterrevolution and Sabotage (Cheka), later called the GPU.

216. **G.K. Ordzhonikidze** (1886-1937), an organizer of the Stalin faction, was later put in charge of heavy industry. Although he remained a faithful Stalinist, the circumstances of his death are still not publicly known.

217. "The Secret Alliance with Germany." *New York Times,* March 5, 1938, where it was entitled "Vyshinsky's Tactics Forecast." That version, which was reprinted in the first edition of *Writings 37-38,* omitted the first five and a half paragraphs. The full text is here published for the first time, by permission of the Harvard College Library.

218. Trotsky's "Report on the World Economic Crisis and the New Tasks of the Communist International," delivered June 23, 1921, to the Third Congress of the Comintern, is in *The First Five Years of the Communist International,* Vol. 1.

219. **The Versailles treaty** was imposed by the victors in World War I. It was based on heavy reparations payments by the defeated countries.

220. **Hans von Seeckt** (1866-1936) was commander in chief of the German Reichswehr, 1918-26. Between 1932 and 1935 he was in China as a military adviser to Chiang Kai-shek.

221. **Hohenzollern** was the name of the ruling family of Prussia and Germany until 1918.

222. **The Treaty of Rapallo** (April 1922) made the German government the first in the world to extend diplomatic recognition to the USSR. In addition, it canceled all prewar debts and all war claims between the two governments. Germany, which was then laboring under the Versailles system, was accorded most-favored-nation status and significant trade concessions in return for its technological assistance to the young Soviet government.

223. **Vyacheslav Molotov** (1890-     ), an early supporter of Stalin and a member of the Central Committee from 1920, was president of the Council of People's Commissars, 1930-41, and minister of foreign affairs after Litvinov (beginning 1939). He was eliminated from the leadership by Khrushchev in 1957 when he opposed "de-Stalinization."

224. "Corrections and Observations on the Testimony of the Accused." *Biulleten Oppozitsii,* no. 65, April 1938. Translated for the first edition of *Writings 37-38* by John Fairlie.

225. "The 'Million Dollars.'" From the archives of Joseph Hansen. A portion was quoted in the *New York Times,* March 6, 1938.

226. **The League of Nations,** which Lenin referred to as the "thieves' kitchen," was created by the Versailles Peace Conference in 1919, ostensibly as a form of world government and cooperation that would prevent future wars. Its complete bankruptcy became clear when it was unable to have any effect on the Japanese invasion of China, the Italian invasion of Ethiopia, and other links in the chain that led to World War II.

227. "Army Opposed to Stalin." *New York Times,* May 7, 1938.

228. **A.I. Kork** (1887-1937) was one of the Red Army generals charged with treason and executed in 1937.

229. **Ernst Roehm** (1887-1934), a Nazi leader who was secretary of state in Bavaria, was charged with conspiracy to overthrow Hitler and executed in the "blood purge" of June 1934.

230. **T.I. Alksnis** (1898-1938), an air force commander and a member of the court that sentenced the first batch of Red Army commanders, was himself arrested and executed in 1938. **V.K. Bluecher** (1889-1938) was a candidate member of the Central Committee when he was arrested and charged with treason. **Semyon M. Budenny** (1883-1973) and **Boris M. Shaposhnikov** (1882-1945) were among the few leading army commanders to escape execution or imprisonment during the purges.

231. **Ian Gamarnik** (1894-1937) committed suicide at the prospect of arrest.

232. Tukhachevsky had been a subaltern in the Semeonovsky **Guards** Regiment during World War I.

233. **Adolph A. Rubens** was the real name of Robinson (see note 126).

234. **Earl Browder** (1891-1973) became general secretary of the

American CP by Stalin's directive in 1930 and was similarly deposed in 1945 and expelled from the party in 1946. He was the party's presidential candidate in 1936 and 1940. **William Z. Foster** (1881-1961) was a leader of the American CP, its presidential candidate in 1924, 1928, and 1932, and its chairman after World War II.

235. "Why So Many Centers? Why Do They All Submit to Trotsky?" By permission of the Harvard College Library.

236. **Jakob Blumkin** (1899-1929) had been a Left Social Revolutionary terrorist who became a Communist and a GPU official. He was the first Russian supporter of the Left Opposition to visit Trotsky in exile in Turkey. Bringing back a message from Trotsky to the Opposition, he was betrayed to the GPU and shot in December 1929, the first Oppositionist to be directly executed by the Stalinists. A few weeks later the GPU also executed Oppositionists **Silov** and **Rabinovich,** allegedly for "sabotage of railway transport."

237. "The Role of Yagoda." *New York Times,* March 8, 1938, where it was entitled "Trotsky Accuses Stalin in Murder."

238. **The Okhrana** was the czarist secret police.

239. At the end of 1934, the consul general of Latvia, **George Bissenieks,** was expelled from the USSR. The Latvian government continued to insist that he had nothing to do with the Kirov assassination.

240. **Filip Medved** (d. 1937) was the head of the Leningrad GPU. He and the other secret police involved were given light prison sentences for failure to provide adequate protection to Kirov, but in 1937 they were all shot.

241. "Strange New Developments." By permission of the Harvard College Library. It is not known whether this item was printed anywhere. Its second paragraph is taken from "Army Opposed to Stalin."

242. **Suzanne La Follette,** author and former editor of *The New Freeman,* was secretary of the Dewey Commission.

243. During the second Moscow trial, in January 1937, Pyatakov "confessed" to having flown to Oslo in December 1935 to get "instructions" for terrorist activity from Trotsky, who was then in Norway. It was subsequently proven that no airplanes had landed in Oslo during the whole month of December because of weather conditions.

244. **Brest-Litovsk** was a town on the Russo-Polish border where a treaty ending hostilities between Russia and Germany was signed in March 1918. The terms were exceedingly unfavorable to the new Soviet government, and there were sharp differences among its leaders about whether to accept them until Lenin's proposal to do so was adopted. Bukharin led a group of "Left Communists" who opposed signing the treaty. It was rumored that when he failed to win a majority to his position, Bukharin spoke of "arresting" Lenin's government, which included **Yakov Sverdlov** (1885-1919), chairman of the Central Execu-

tive Committee of the Soviets, secretary of the Bolshevik Central Committee, and first president of the Russian Soviet Republic.

245. **V.V. Osinsky** (1887-1938) held a post in the Commissariat of Agriculture and was a candidate member of the Central Committee at the time of his arrest. **Varvara Yakovleva** (d. 1944) had been a candidate member of the 1917 Central Committee and a Left Communist in 1918. She gave state's evidence in the trial of Bukharin. **Vasily Mantsev** (1888-1939), like Bukharin, denied the charge of plotting to kill Lenin. All three were convicted and sentenced to death, but Yakovleva was not executed until 1944.

246. **Emelyan Yaroslavsky** (1878-1943) was a top Stalinist specialist in the campaign against Trotskyism and was part of the team that brought charges against him and demanded his expulsion from the party in 1927.

247. "Anachronisms." From the archives of Joseph Hansen.

248. **E.S. Goltsman** (1882-1936), a former Oppositionist, was executed after the first Moscow trial for allegedly meeting Leon Sedov in Copenhagen to receive Trotsky's "instructions" to assassinate Stalin and Voroshilov. Not only had their alleged meeting place, the Hotel Bristol, been torn down years earlier, but Sedov had been taking examinations in Berlin at the time, and the Soviet government declined to document Holtsman's entry into Denmark.

249. **Kliment Voroshilov** (1881-1969) was an early supporter of Stalin, a member of the Politburo from 1926, and commissar of defense, 1925-40. During the civil war he was the commander of the Russian Tenth Army, which became the seat of the "military opposition" that Trotsky describes. The Eighth Party Congress in March 1919 rebuffed the military opposition and reaffirmed Trotsky's military policy.

250. "Moscow's Diplomatic Plans and the Trials." *New York Times,* March 9, 1938, where it had the title "Trotsky Sees Plots Dictated by Policy."

251. Edward Frederick Lindley Wood, **Lord Halifax** (1881-1959), was British foreign secretary, 1938-40, replacing **Anthony Eden,** Earl of Avon (1897-     ), who held that position 1935-38.

252. **Neville Chamberlain** (1869-1940) was Conservative prime minister of Britain from 1937 until May 1940, when he resigned after failing to receive a vote of confidence in Parliament for his prosecution of the war.

253. **Colonel Jozef Beck** (1894-1944) was Polish minister of foreign affairs, 1932-39.

254. **The Menshevik-Industrial Party "wreckers'" trials,** where the defendants confessed to sabotage of the economy, were held in 1930 and 1931. At the time, Trotsky accepted these confessions as valid (see *Writings 1930-31*), a view he held until shortly before the first Moscow trial in 1936, when he admitted he had made an error in accepting the official Moscow version of these frame-ups.

255. **Winston Churchill** (1874-1965) was British prime minister, 1940-45 and 1951-55.

256. "Stalin's Article on World Revolution." *Biulleten Oppozitsii,* no. 65, April 1938. Translated for the first edition of *Writings 37-38* by John Fairlie.

257. "Message to New York Protest Meeting." *Socialist Appeal,* March 19, 1938. This telegram was sent to a protest rally held the same day at Hotel Center, New York, under the auspices of the American Committee for the Defense of Leon Trotsky (ACDLT) to protest the third Moscow trial. The speakers were Suzanne La Follette, Eugene Lyons, Carlo Tresca, Bertram D. Wolfe, Max Shachtman, and ACDLT secretary George Novack.

258. "A Key to the Russian Trials." Scottish *Forward,* April 16, 1938, which had omitted the first three paragraphs and a few sentences throughout the text and had scrambled many of the Russian names. Those parts were translated for this volume from the Norwegian *Tidens Tegn,* no. 73, March 25, 1938, by Russell Block.

259. **Jakob Surits** (1881-1952) was Stalin's ambassador first to Berlin and then to Paris, and was one of the few diplomats to survive the purges.

260. **Jan E. Rudzutak** (1887-1938), an early partisan of Stalin, was people's commissar for railways, 1924-30, chairman of the Central Control Commission and of the Workers and Peasants Inspection from 1932 until he became a victim of the third Moscow trial. **Yakov A. Yakovlev** (1896-1939), former commissar of agriculture and a Central Committee member, also was accused in the Bukharin trial and shot in March 1939.

261. **Bogomolov** was ambassador to China.

262. **Yakov Lifshits** (1896-1938), a former Oppositionist, was assistant people's commissar of communications.

263. **Admiral Vladimir Orlov** (1895-1938), the naval commander in chief, was arrested in November 1937. **Nikolai Muralov** (1877-1937) was executed with the other Red Army generals in May 1937.

264. **G.E. Yevdokimov** (1884-1936), secretary of the Central Committee, was removed from the secretariat in 1926 because he·was a supporter of Zinoviev, and was expelled from the Central Committee in 1927. He and **Ivan P. Bakaev** (1887-1936) were arrested in connection with the Kirov assassination and sentenced to prison. They then became defendants in the Zinoviev-Kamenev trial and were executed. **M.S. Boguslavsky** (1886-1936), a veteran of the underground and civil war and a former Oppositionist, was arrested in August 1936, charged with sabotaging the railways and executed after the first Moscow trial.

265. **D.E. Sulimov** (1890-1939), former chairman of the Council of People's Commissars of the Russian Republic and a full member of the Central Committee, was arrested in 1937 and executed in 1939.

266. **Budu Mdivani** (d. 1937), former premier of Soviet Georgia, was

sentenced to death by the Georgian Supreme Court in July 1937 and shot. **M. Okudzhava** perished with him. **Sergei I. Kavtaradze** (1885-1971), chairman of the Council of People's Commissars in Georgia from 1921 to 1922, was expelled from the party as a Left Oppositionist in 1927 and was arrested during the mid-thirties and sent to a labor camp. He was rehabilitated in 1940 and became assistant people's commissar of foreign affairs and then ambassador to Rumania. **Alexander G. Chervyakov** (1892-1937) had been chairman of the Belorussian Supreme Soviet. He committed suicide when the destruction of the Belorussian party was begun in 1937. He was posthumously accused of "national fascism." **Nikolai M. Goloded** (1894-1937), chairman of the Belorussian Council of People's Commissars, also resisted the purge and was charged with bourgeois nationalism, arrested on the way to Moscow, and shot. **Nikolai A. Skrypnik** (1872-1933) was a member of the Central Committee of the Ukrainian party. He was driven to suicide in 1933 for alleged excessive patronage of nationalist tendencies. **Panas Lyubchenko** (1897-1937) became chairman of the Ukrainian Council of People's Commissars. In 1937, he committed suicide to avoid arrest.

267. **Grigory Rasputin** (1871-1916), a monk from a family of poor peasants, gained such ascendancy over the czar and czarina that he became a major influence in court politics. His ignorance and debauchery were legendary. He was assassinated by a group of desperate Russian noblemen in an effort to rid the royal family of his influence.

268. "The Case of Professor Pletnev." *Socialist Appeal,* March 26, 1938. Signed "L.T."

269. **Nadezhda K. Krupskaya** (1869-1939) was an Old Bolshevik and the companion of Lenin. She played a central role in the underground and emigre organization of the Russian Social Democracy. After the revolution she worked in the Commissariat of Education. She adhered to the United Opposition for a brief time in 1926.

270. "Letter to Jeanne Martin." *La Verite,* May 5, 1939, in a special supplement devoted to Trotsky's efforts to gain legal custody of his only surviving grandchild, Vsievolod Volkov ("Sieva"). Translated for this volume from the French by Russell Block. **La Verite** was at this time the newspaper of the "Molinier group." **Jeanne Martin des Pallieres** was the widow of Trotsky's elder son, Leon Sedov, and a member of the Molinier group.

271. "The Defendants Zelensky and Ivanov." *Biulleten Oppozitsii,* no. 65, April 1938. Signed "L.T." Translated for the first edition of *Writings 37-38* by John Fairlie.

272. "Again on the Reiss Case." *Bulletin Interieur,* Parti Socialiste Revolutionaire (PSR), no. 14, May 1938, where it was entitled "Letter from Trotsky to the International Secretariat." Translated for this volume from

the French by J.R. Fidler. The PSR was the Belgian section of the MFI.

273. "Hitler's Austria Coup Aided by Moscow Trial." *Socialist Appeal,* March 26, 1938. German troops occupied Austria on March 11, 1938; on March 13, the two countries were proclaimed to be one (the "Anschluss"); and on April 10 a plebiscite ratified this decision.

274. "On Hearst." *Socialist Appeal,* March 19, 1938. **William Randolph Hearst** (1863-1951) was the publisher of a chain of right-wing newspapers often cited as examples of yellow journalism for their sensational character.

275. "An Explanation for Freda Kirchwey." *Socialist Appeal,* March 26, 1938. **Freda Kirchwey** (1893-1976), editor of the *Nation,* had asked Trotsky to write an article expounding his philosophy.

276. "Notes in the Margin of *Pravda*'s Accounts." *Biulleten Oppozitsii,* no. 64, March 1938. Unsigned. Translated for the first edition of *Writings 37-38* by John Fairlie.

277. **Boris Kamkov** (1885-1938) had been imprisoned in the twenties for being a Social Revolutionary, was released but was rearrested in 1933. Kamkov apparently denied on the stand that the Left SRs had made a plot to kill Lenin. **Vladimir Karelin** (1891-1938), also an old SR, confirmed the plot.

278. "Cain-Dzhugashvili Goes the Whole Way." *Biulleten Oppozitsii,* no. 65, April 1938. Unsigned. Translated by John Fairlie for the first edition of *Writings 37-38,* where it was dated April 1938. The correct date was found by consulting the manuscript at Harvard College Library. **Dzhugashvili** was Stalin's original name, **Tiflis,** the capital of Georgia, his birthplace.

279. "A Reply to Ambassador Bilmanis." *New York Times,* March 21, 1938. The *Times* made several minor changes and omitted one entire paragraph. The article is here restored to its original form, by permission of the Harvard College Library.

280. "New Defectors." *Biulleten Oppozitsii,* no. 65, April 1938. Unsigned. Translated for the first edition of *Writings 37-38* by John Fairlie.

281. "The Priests of Half-Truth." *Socialist Appeal,* April 16, 1938.

282. **John Reed** (1887-1920) was an American journalist and radical who supported the Russian Revolution and wrote the stirring book, *Ten Days That Shook the World.*

283. **William Pitt** (1759-1806) was prime minister of Britain from 1783 until 1801 and 1803 until his death.

284. **The New Masses** was a monthly literary journal under Stalinist influence, published between 1926 and 1948.

285. "Discussions with Trotsky: I– The International Conference." By permission of the Harvard College Library. This is a stenogram of the first of six discussions Trotsky had with SWP leaders at his home in Mexico between March 20 and March 25, 1938. These discussions were part of the collaborative work preparatory to the founding conference of the FI. The SWP delegation went to Mexico for several reasons. Foremost was their desire to reach agreement with Trotsky about the nature and timing of the international conference. They quickly agreed to jointly propose the end of June or early July for the conference date (although it was not actually held until September) and spent most of the week discussing the programmatic documents to be prepared for the conference. They also examined in detail a number of important questions facing the newly formed SWP (whether it should change its position on advocacy of a labor party in the U.S., whether it should give critical support to the Ludlow Amendment, what steps it should take to help create a new defense organization, etc.). In addition, participants Cannon, Shachtman, and Vincent R. Dunne had been sent by the Pan-American Commission of the IS to help resolve internal problems in the Mexican section. **Dunne** (1890-1970) was a founding member of the American Left Opposition and a leader in the Minneapolis teamsters' struggles. He was one of the eighteen prisoners in the 1941 Minneapolis trial, and remained active in the SWP leadership until his death. Rose Karsner and Diego Rivera also participated in at least several of the discussions with Trotsky. **Karsner** (1889-1968) was a founder of both the CP and the Left Opposition in the U.S. She was Cannon's close political collaborator and companion from 1924. The stenographer noted that all six transcripts consisted of "rough notes" that had not been corrected by the participants. Pseudonyms used in the stenograms for security purposes ("Crux" for Trotsky) have been replaced with the real names. Only the March 20, 24, and 25 discussions are printed in this volume. The others—March 21, on the labor party; March 22, on the Ludlow Amendment; and March 23, on transitional demands—are available in the second edition of *The Transitional Program for Socialist Revolution* (Pathfinder, 1974).

286. The founding convention of the SWP, held in Chicago December 31, 1937–January 3, 1938, adopted a declaration of principles, a constitution, and a series of resolutions ("theses") on contemporary political problems, many of which were subsequently printed in *Socialist Appeal*. The second congress of the POI, held in Paris October 30-November 1, 1937, adopted a number of resolutions on the important issues facing the MFI and its French section.

287. **Adolphe** was Rudolf Klement (1910-1938), Trotsky's secretary in Turkey and France and secretary of the committee preparing the founding conference of the Fourth International. He was kidnaped and murdered by the GPU in Paris shortly before the conference was held.

288. **Unser Wort** (Our Word) was the paper of the German section of the MFI, published abroad and smuggled into Germany.

289. Diego Rivera's draft thesis on problems of development in Latin

America was printed in the first issue (October 1938) of *Clave,* a
theoretical magazine supported by the Mexican section of the FI.

290. One of Trotsky's most important contributions to Marxist theory
and practice was his development in 1938 of the concept of **transitional
demands and slogans,** which became the central feature of the
programmatic document he wrote in April for the founding conference.
Entitled "The Death Agony of Capitalism and the Tasks of the Fourth
International," it became known as the Transitional Program, was
debated throughout the MFI for several months, and was adopted by the
founding conference. Briefly stated, transitional demands are those that
cannot be granted under capitalism or can be granted only partially, and
are designed to bridge the gap between the current level of consciousness
of the masses and the needs of the socialist revolution, by drawing the
masses into action around them. Trotsky's major document on the
subject, along with the discussions he held before and after it, is in *The
Transitional Program for Socialist Revolution.*

291. **Joaquin Maurin Julia** (1897-1973) was a leader of the Spanish
Workers and Peasants Bloc, which merged in 1935 with the former Left
Oppositionists led by Andres Nin to create the POUM. Maurin was
elected to parliament in February 1936. When the civil war broke out he
was arrested by Franco's troops, but escaped execution because the
fascists couldn't identify him. Upon his release, he went into exile and
withdrew from politics.

292. **Hendrik Colijn** (1869-1944) was conservative premier of the
Netherlands, 1925-26 and 1933-39.

293. **Walter Dauge** was a leader of the Belgian Trotskyist movement
during the thirties and was elected to the International Executive
Committee at the FI's founding conference. He left the movement during
World War II.

294. **Leon Lesoil** (1892-1942), a founder of the Belgian CP and a
member of its Central Committee, helped organize the Belgian section of
the Opposition and remained one of its leaders for the rest of his life.
Arrested by the Gestapo in June 1941, he died in a concentration camp.

295. **Fred Zeller** had been a leader of the Socialist Youth in France
and International Youth Secretary of the International Communist
League (predecessor of the MFI). Later he became a Freemason. He and
**Mathias Corvin** were expelled from the French section in November
1937 for illicit dealings with the Stalinists.

296. **R.** was probably Vincent R. Dunne, or Rose Karsner, although it
could have been Rae Spiegel, who took the shorthand notes at this
meeting.

297. **Marius Moutet** (1876-1968), the Socialist minister of colonies in
the French People's Front government in 1938, was responsible for jailing
Ta Thu Thau, the leader of the Indochinese Trotskyists.

298. **Walter Held** (d. 1941) was a German Trotskyist who emigrated to
Norway after Hitler came to power in Germany. When Trotsky was in
Norway, Held was one of his secretaries. While traveling legally through

the USSR, he was taken off the train by the Soviet secret police and executed.

299. **A. Johre** and **Oskar Fischer** (Otto Schuessler) were leaders of the German Trotskyists in emigration. Fischer served as a secretary to Trotsky in Turkey and again in Mexico. Both broke with the FI during or after World War II.

300. **Arkady Maslow** (1891-1941) and **Ruth Fischer** (1895-1961) were central leaders of the German CP in the 1920s. They were expelled by the Stalinists in 1927 because as supporters of Zinoviev they had defended the Russian United Opposition. In 1928 they helped to found the German Leninbund, which collaborated with the Left Opposition until 1930. Maslow and Fischer withdrew from the Leninbund and in the mid-thirties drew closer to the Left Opposition. In 1935 Trotsky nominated Fischer for co-optation on the IS, where she served for at least a year. By 1938, however, both of them were withdrawing from the Trotskyist movement.

301. "Discussions with Trotsky: II—Defense Organization and Attitude Toward Intellectuals." By permission of the Harvard College Library. This is the stenogram of the fifth of six discussions between the SWP delegation and Trotsky. This discussion began around the problems connected with organizing a defense organization in the U.S. to mobilize support for the SWP and MFI against both capitalist and Stalinist frame-ups and attacks. The American Committee for the Defense of Leon Trotsky, which had been active since 1936 and had helped bring into existence the Dewey Commission of Inquiry in 1937, was officially dissolved early in March 1938. Some of the intellectuals active in it were expressing disagreements with the SWP's proposals on its replacement.

302. **Herbert Solow** (1903-1964), a labor journalist in the 1930s and briefly a Trotskyist, supported the Dewey Commission of Inquiry into the Moscow trials. He later became an editor of *Fortune* magazine.

303. The Non-Partisan Labor Defense (**NPLD**) was a defense organization, led by the Trotskyists and their allies, that defended victims of capitalist and racist injustice whom the larger Stalinist-led International Labor Defense refused to help because of their political views. It was merged with the Socialist-led Workers Defense League in 1936, when the Trotskyists joined the SP.

304. **Philip Rahv** (1908-1973) was among the current of American intellectuals who were shocked by the Moscow trials and attracted for a brief time, until the outbreak of World War II, to Trotskyism. A prolific writer and critic, Rahv edited *Partisan Review,* which, under his auspices, strove to free itself from Stalinist control and become an independent leftist literary journal.

305. **Sidney Hook** (1902-     ), a former leftist, became a supporter of the cold war and witch hunt in the fifties.

306. **George Novack** (1905-     ), who became a Trotskyist in 1933, played a leading role in many important civil liberties and civil rights cases. Among those for whom he campaigned were the Scottsboro

defendants, Tom Mooney, Trotsky, the Minneapolis defendants, Carl
Skoglund, James Kutcher, Robert F. Williams, the Bloomington defendants, the Fort Jackson Eight, and the SWP and Young Socialist Alliance
in their suit against the FBI and the government. This Marxist scholar
has written many books on history, philosophy, and political subjects,
including *Democracy and Revolution* (1971) and *Pragmatism versus
Marxism: An Appraisal of John Dewey's Philosophy* (1975).

307. **Eugene Lyons** (1898-    ) was a United Press correspondent
in Moscow and the author of *Assignment in Utopia* (1937). Formerly a
Communist sympathizer, in 1938 he was working with the American
Labor Party. Soon after rejecting Stalinism he broke with Marxism.

308. **Liston Oak,** a journalist, broke with Stalinism over the Spanish
Civil War in 1937; he wrote for the Trotskyist press briefly before he
shifted to the Social Democracy.

309. **Vanguard** was an anarchist monthly published in New York,
1932-39.

310. **Anton Ciliga** was a leader of the Yugoslav CP imprisoned by
Stalin but allowed to leave the USSR in the mid-thirties. He revealed
much about conditions in Soviet prisons before breaking with Marxism.

311. **The Workers Party of the U.S.** was the name of the American
Trotskyist movement in 1936, when it entered the Socialist Party to reach
the growing left wing there.

312. **Homer Martin** (1902-1968), a former preacher, was appointed
vice-president of the United Auto Workers in 1935, and became president
in 1936. He tried to lead the UAW back into the AFL, and when he was
prevented from doing so by the union membership he led a small split-off
in 1939, which eventually degenerated into a racket run by outright
gangsters.

313. "Discussions with Trotsky: III—The Russian Question." By
permission of the Harvard College Library.

314. **Martin Abern** (1898-1949) was a leader of the American CP and a
founder of the Communist League of America and the SWP. In 1940 he
split from the SWP with Shachtman and helped found the Workers Party.

315. **Ernest R. McKinney,** a member of the SWP Political Committee
in 1938, insisted that the PC had not changed its position on the Ludlow
Amendment in February when it moved from opposition to abstentionism. The National Committee statement supporting the amendment was
printed in the May 21, 1938, *Socialist Appeal.* McKinney left the SWP in
1940 and became the secretary of the Shachtmanite Workers Party.

316. **Franklin D. Roosevelt** (1882-1945) was Democratic president of
the United States from 1933 until his death.

317. "Roosevelt's Statement on Trotskyists in Russia." By permission
of the Harvard College Library.

318. "Letter to the League of Nations." *Socialist Appeal,* April 23, 1938.

319. **Kurt Landau,** an Austrian, became a leader of the German Left

Opposition. In 1931 he split from the Opposition and formed his own group. He went to Spain and supported the POUM, was kidnaped and killed by Stalin's police.

320. "For the Reorganization of the Mexican Section." From the archives of James P. Cannon.

321. In March 1938, the Mexican government nationalized foreign-owned oil properties. In retaliation, an embargo on Mexican oil was imposed by the British and U.S. governments and by the oil companies that owned the tankers for shipping oil abroad. At the same time, they initiated a slander campaign in Britain and the U.S. that would facilitate armed intervention in Mexico. In 1941 the Mexican and U.S. governments reached an agreement for indemnification of U.S. oil companies; in 1947 a similar agreement was concluded with Britain. **The British Labour Party,** founded in 1906 and affiliated to the Second International, was the chief oppositional force to the Conservative majority in Parliament.

322. **Luciano Galicia** was the leader of the **Internationalist Communist League** (LCI, the Mexican section of the MFI), which pursued a sectarian policy in the trade unions and issued irresponsible and adventuristic slogans. Galicia dissolved the LCI a few days before the arrival of the SWP fact-finding commission (Cannon, Shachtman, Dunne) sent by the Pan-American Commission. Subsequently, after the delegation had left, he reconstituted the LCI, but it was not recognized by the founding conference. **The Casa del Pueblo** was a bakers' union headquarters that served as a left-wing union center in Mexico City.

323. The Pan-American Conference declared that there was no section of the Fourth International existing in Mexico. The founding conference of the Fourth International in September mandated the IS to reorganize the Mexican section on the basis of acceptance of the decisions of the founding conference and the discipline of the Fourth International. The Pan-American Conference decided to send Charles Curtiss to Mexico as a representative of the preconference and of the SWP and IS. He was there from July 1938 to July 1939.

324. The Pan-American Committee established the theoretical magazine *Clave* as the review of all the Spanish-speaking sections of the Fourth International. **Adolfo and Francisco Zamora,** Jose Ferrel, and Trotsky (who used the name "Crux" to avoid the charge of interference in Mexico's internal affairs) were its editors.

325. "Toward a Genuine British Section." From the archives of James P. Cannon. This letter to Charles Sumner, secretary of the British Revolutionary Socialist League in 1938, was part of Trotsky's attempts to insure that Cannon and Shachtman would go to England and France well in advance of the international conference. They had agreed during the talks in March that they would undertake these assignments to strengthen the British and French sections but their departures were delayed by other assignments and a shortage of funds.

326. **Frank Maitland** (1910-      ), a journalist and leader of the

Scottish Revolutionary Socialist Party, did not enter the British Trotskyist organization that emerged from fusion negotiations later in 1938. The article Trotsky refers to is "The Lessons of Spain—The Last Warning," in *The Spanish Revolution (1931-39)*.

327. "Letter to James P. Cannon." From the archives of James P. Cannon.

328. Eastman's letter to Corliss Lamont, the national chairman of the Friends of Soviet Russia, was in the April 1938 *New International.* The June issue carried an article by James Burnham, entitled "Max Eastman as Scientist," which critically reviewed Eastman's article in the March *Harpers Magazine,* "Russia and the Socialist Ideal," charging that Eastman "takes up arms against the socialist ideal." This was followed by an exchange in the August issue: "Burnham Dodges My Views," by Eastman, and "A Little Wool-Pulling," by Burnham.

329. "Thoughts on the French Section." From the archives of James P. Cannon. This letter to Cannon and Shachtman suggested a line of action to be followed in dealing with the group led by Raymond Molinier, which had been expelled from the French section in 1935 for publishing its own paper, *La Commune.* The Molinier group was now engaged in an effort to achieve reunification on its own terms. These terms were rejected at the founding conference.

330. "More on European Problems." From the archives of James P. Cannon. This was another letter to Cannon and Shachtman.

331. "The Mexican Oil Expropriations." *Socialist Appeal,* May 14, 1938. A letter to the *Daily Herald,* the newspaper of the British Labour Party.

332. "Europe or San Francisco?" From the archives of James P. Cannon, to whom this letter was sent.

333. **B.J. Widick** (1910-     ) was labor secretary of the SWP in 1938. He left the SWP in the Shachtmanite split of 1940. **Farrell Dobbs** (1907-     ) was at this time a Teamsters union official in Minneapolis, engaged in organizing over-the-road drivers and warehousemen in an eleven-state area of the Midwest. He resigned this post to become SWP labor secretary in 1940, and was one of the eighteen defendants imprisoned in the Minneapolis labor trial. He became national secretary of the SWP in 1953, and is the author of *Teamster Rebellion* (1973) and three other books about the Teamsters and the SWP in the thirties and forties.

334. **The turn on the labor party question** refers to the decision by the SWP National Committee plenum in April 1938 to begin advocating a labor party in the U.S. For Trotsky's arguments in favor of this course, see his talks with the SWP leaders in March 1938 in *The Transitional Program for Socialist Revolution.* After the plenum, a discussion of the new proposal was opened in the SWP internal bulletin and branch

meetings and the columns of *New International.* Instead of following the usual procedure of having important political issues resolved by a national convention, the SWP leaders decided to settle it through a membership referendum vote. At the end of a three-month discussion a majority of the membership adopted a resolution favoring the new proposal, printed in the October 1, 1938, *Socialist Appeal.*

335. "For an Immediate Trip to Europe." From the archives of James P. Cannon.

336. **Paul Eiffel** led a small split-off from the Oehlerite Revolutionary Workers League in 1936. He advocated sabotage of the Loyalist struggle against Franco and the Chinese nationalist struggle against Japan. Eiffel endorsed Galicia's complaints against the FI leadership, and in general all complaints of dissatisfied groupings throughout the FI.

337. "On C.L.R. James." From the archives of James P. Cannon, to whom it was addressed. **C.L.R. James** (1901-      ) is the West Indian author of *Black Jacobins* and *World Revolution* (the book Trotsky refers to here). He later left the FI.

338. "Learn to Think." *New International,* July 1938.

339. **Simone Weil** (1909-1943) was a French radical intellectual who was converted to mysticism and Catholicism before starving herself to death in England during World War II. **Georgi Plekhanov** (1856-1918), the founder of Russian Marxism, became a leader of the Menshevik faction in 1903. When World War I broke out in 1914, he supported the czarist government, and later opposed the Bolshevik Revolution.

340. "Once More on Comrades Sneevliet and Vereecken." By permission of the Harvard College Library. Translated for this volume from the French by Tom Barrett.

341. **Etienne** was the pseudonym of Marc Zborowski, a Polish-Ukrainian who was a member of the Russian section of the MFI and helped publish the *Biulleten Oppozitsii.* It later came to light that the whole time Etienne was Leon Sedov's most trusted co-worker he was also a GPU agent. Zborowski admitted this in his December 1955 perjury trial in the U.S. after which he was sentenced to five years in prison.

342. **A.J. Muste** (1885-1967), a pacifist and former minister, was head of the American Workers Party, which merged with the Communist League of America to form the Workers Party of the U.S., of which Muste was secretary. In 1936, after the Workers Party had voted to enter the SP, Muste broke with Marxism and returned to pacifism and the church. Toward the end of his life he became a builder and leader of the anti-Vietnam War movement.

343. "No Obstacle to Common Vote." From the archives of James P. Cannon, to whom it was addressed. The SWP's central leaders had been unable, at their National Committee plenum in April 1938, to reach

agreement on resolutions approving the Transitional Program ("draft program") and advocating a labor party in the U.S., although the differences among them were over formulations rather than principle or tactics. By the time Trotsky's letter arrived, they were themselves realizing that there were no real obstacles to their writing common resolutions, which they then wrote and presented to the SWP membership for referendum vote.

344. " 'For' the Fourth International? No! The Fourth International!" *Internal Bulletin,* SWP, no. 3, 1938. A letter to a Belgian comrade.

345. "Revolutionary Art and the Fourth International." *Litterature et Revolution,* edited by Maurice Nadeau (Julliard, 1964). Translated for the first edition of *Writings 37-38* from the French by Constance Weissman. A letter to the founding conference of the Fourth International.

346. "Remarks on Czechoslovakia." *Internal Bulletin,* SWP, no. 3, 1938. When this uncorrected transcript first appeared in print, Trotsky, for security reasons, was designated by the pen name "Crux." At this time there was widespread unrest in Czechoslovakia, particularly in the Sudetenland, which was largely German-speaking, and which would be ceded to Germany in three months.
347. **Konrad Henlein** (1898-1945) was the head of the right-wing Sudetendeutsche Partei, which demanded union with Germany. He committed suicide after the war.

348. "Mexico and British Imperialism." *Socialist Appeal,* June 25, 1938.
349. Through the **Monroe Doctrine** (1823) the U.S. banned European intervention in the Western hemisphere under the pretext of protecting Latin America against military and political domination by Europe.

350. "On the Edge of a Precipice." Minutes of the Parti Socialiste Revolutionnaire, June 23, 1938. Translated for this volume from the French by Russell Block. A letter to Leon Lesoil.
351. **Henri M.** was Henri Molinier (1898-1944), Raymond's brother, an engineer who was killed in the fighting for the liberation of Paris. **Pierre Frank** (1905-      ) was a founder of the French section and a member of the IS; he was Trotsky's secretary in Turkey, 1932-33. **Jean Meichler** (1899-1944), like the Moliniers and Frank a founder of *La Verite* in 1929, was executed as a hostage by the Nazis during their occupation of France.

352. "No, It Is Not the Same." *Socialist Appeal,* July 2, 1938. A reply to an article in *Workers Age,* the weekly paper of the Lovestoneite Independent Labor League.

353. "To the Congress of the Revolutionary Socialist Party of Belgium." By permission of the Harvard College Library. Translated for this volume from the French by Tom Barrett.

354. **Paul van Zeeland** (1893-    ) was a Belgian economist and statesman, and was prime minister of Belgium, 1935-37.

355. "For an Open Polemic with the Liberals." From the archives of James P. Cannon. A letter to Rae Spiegel (Raya Dunayevskaya), one of Trotsky's secretaries in Mexico.

356. "Stalin and Accomplices Condemned." Under this title, the last part of this article was published unsigned in the *Biulleten Oppozitsii,* no. 68-69, August-September, 1938, and was translated for the first edition of *Writings 37-38* by John Fairlie. The complete article, apparently an interview granted the Norwegian journalist Ola Apenas, appeared in the Oslo newspaper *Aftenposten,* August 12, 1938. The first eight paragraphs, and the very last one, which did not appear in the *Biulleten* version, were translated for this volume from the Norwegian by Russell Block.

357. **Nicola Sacco** (1891-1927) and **Bartolomeo Vanzetti** (1888-1927) were Italian immigrants and anarchists framed up on charges of murder and theft and executed despite international protests. **Tom Mooney** (1882-1942) was an American labor leader convicted in 1916 of throwing a bomb that killed nine persons. He was condemned to death but his sentence was commuted to life imprisonment. He was pardoned and released in 1939.

358. "More on the Suppression of Kronstadt." *New International,* August 1938.

359. **Boris Souvarine** (1893-    ) was a founder of the French CP and one of the first serious biographers of Stalin. He was expelled from the French party as a Trotskyist in 1924. In the 1930s he turned against Marxism.

360. "For Freedom in Education." *IV Internacional* (Mexico), August 1938. Translated from the Spanish for Trotsky's *Problems of Everyday Life* (Pathfinder, 1973) by Iain Fraser. This was a letter to *Vida,* the newspaper of the teachers of Michoacan, Mexico. **IV Internacional** was the newspaper of the Mexican section of the MFI.

361. "On the Anniversary of Reiss's Death." *Biulleten Oppozitsii,* no. 68-69, August-September 1938. Translated for the first edition of *Writings 37-38* by John Fairlie.

362. "To the Conference of the Young People's Socialist League." By permission of the Harvard College Library. These greetings were sent for a YPSL convention that was originally slated for September but was not held until November 1938.

363. "The Disappearance of Rudolf Klement." *Socialist Appeal,* July 30, 1938. Klement's mutilated body was found shortly before the founding conference of the FI was held.

364. "Was Leon Sedov Murdered?" *Socialist Appeal,* August 13, 1938.
365. **Jean Rous** (1908-      ) was a leader of the POI and had been the delegate of the IS in Spain in 1936. He left the FI during the war and joined a series of centrist groups.

366. "My Conspiracy." *Socialist Appeal,* July 30, 1938.
367. **Dr. Atl** was Gerardo Murillo, painter and teacher of Diego Rivera. Formerly a revolutionary, by the late thirties he had become a fascist sympathizer.

368. "Financing the Revolutionary Movement." By permission of the Harvard College Library. These were the concluding remarks of Trotsky in the transcript of a discussion with members of the SWP and YPSL. The ranks of both these organizations were engaged in a discussion of the Transitional Program and the proposal to advocate a labor party, with considerable opposition to the labor party being expressed, particularly in the YPSL. Trotsky's preceding remarks, entirely devoted to the labor party dispute, have been printed in full under the title "Three Possibilities with a Labor Party" in *The Transitional Program for Socialist Revolution.* A stenographer's note described the transcript as a "rough draft."

369. "The Forthcoming Trial of the Diplomats." Scottish *Forward,* August 20, 1938. Signed "L.T."
370. **Vladimir Antonov-Ovseenko** (1884-1938) was Russian consul general in Barcelona during the Spanish Civil War. He was made a scapegoat for the defeat of Stalinist policy in Spain and disappeared. **M. Rosenberg** was Soviet ambassador to the Spanish Republican government.

371. "A 'Letter' from Rudolf Klement." *Socialist Appeal,* August 13, 1938.

372. "On the Fate of Rudolf Klement." *Socialist Appeal,* August 20, 1938, where it was entitled "Trotsky Brands 'Klement Letter' as GPU Forgery."
373. **Roman Well** was a pseudonym of one of the Sobolevicius brothers. He was a Stalinist agent in the Trotskyist movement who led a group into the German CP in 1933. Under the name of Robert Soblen, Well committed suicide in 1962 when under prosecution as a Soviet espionage agent in the U.S. **Jacob Frank,** also known as Ya. Graef, was briefly a member of a Left Oppositional group in Austria, 1929-31, before rejoining the Stalinists.

374. **Jan Bur** was a Czech Oppositionist who split from the Opposition shortly after Trotsky was exiled from the USSR.

375. In October 1938, after months of incarceration, leaders of the Spanish POUM were brought to trial on charges of treason and espionage, in a Spanish version of the Moscow trials. As in Moscow, they and all other opponents of Stalinism were called "Trotskyists." They were acquitted of the charges against them, but were imprisoned anyway for their role in the May 1937 uprising in Barcelona.

376. Sobolevicius-**Senin,** alias Jack Soble, like his brother, Roman Well, was a Stalinist infiltrator in the Trotskyist movement.

377. "The Sino-Japanese Struggle." By permission of the Harvard College Library. Signed "L.T." This press release was published in *El Universal, Excelsior,* and *El Nacional,* August 12, 1938.

378. "The USSR and Japan." *Socialist Appeal,* August 27, 1938, where it was entitled "Soviet-Japanese War Inevitable."

379. "Answers to the Questions of Lloyd Tupling." By permission of the Harvard College Library. This interview was also incorporated into an article about Trotsky by Lloyd Tupling, a student at the University of Oregon, in the *Sunday Oregonian,* September 4, 1938.

380. "Freedom of the Press and the Working Class." *Clave* (Mexico), October 1938. Unsigned. Translated for this volume from the Spanish by Gerry Foley.

381. "Further Evidence of GPU Guilt in Sedov Death." *Socialist Appeal,* September 10, 1938. This was another letter to Joseph Pagenel, the examining magistrate in the inquiry into Sedov's death.

382. Trotsky's younger daughter Nina died of tuberculosis in 1928, at the age of twenty-six, after the imprisonment and deportation of her husband, Nevelson. His elder daughter, Zinaida, also tubercular, was allowed to leave Russia without her husband and with only one of her two children (Sieva) and then prohibited from returning; she committed suicide in Berlin in 1933 at the age of thirty.

383. **Mikhailo Glazman** and **Georgi Butov** were two of Trotsky's secretaries during the Russian civil war. Hounded by the Stalinists because he was an Oppositionist, Glazman committed suicide in 1924. Butov was arrested for refusing to sign false charges against Trotsky and died after a hunger strike in prison in 1928.

384. **I. Poznansky,** another of Trotsky's secretaries, was arrested and deported when he followed Trotsky into exile. **N. Sermuks** was expelled with Trotsky from the CP and followed him into exile, but was arrested and deported.

385. "Trade Union Congress Staged by CP." *Socialist Appeal,* September 10, 1938. This press release, in question-and-answer form, was

prepared by Trotsky in the name of Diego Rivera to avoid charges of meddling in Mexican politics, and was released by Rivera at San Angel, Mexico City. **The Pan-American Trade Union Congress** was held in Mexico City September 6-8, 1938, and was attended by delegates from most Latin American countries, as well as by John L. Lewis from the U.S., Leon Jouhaux from France, and Gonzales Pena, Spanish minister of justice. It resulted in the formation of the Confederation of Latin American Workers (CTAL), with headquarters in Mexico and Lombardo Toledano as president. Trotsky's assessment after the congress will be found in the second edition of *Writings 38-39*.

386. **John L. Lewis** (1880-1969) was president of the United Mine Workers of America from 1920 until his death. He headed the minority in the AFL executive council in the mid-thirties which favored industrial unionism, and he was the principal founder of the CIO in 1935 and its main leader until 1940, when he resigned.

387. "The Congress Against War and Fascism." By permission of the Harvard College Library. Unsigned. Translated for this volume from the Russian by Marilyn Vogt. **The Congress Against War and Fascism** took place on September 12 in Mexico City. Its Stalinist sponsors attempted to recruit the international labor movement to the defense of the "democratic" imperialists against the fascist countries in the coming war, and the delegates were handpicked accordingly. However, Mexican, Puerto Rican, and Peruvian delegates argued that the Allied governments shared responsibility for the coming war.

388. "Fascism and the Colonial World." By permission of the Harvard College Library. Unsigned. Translated for this volume from the Russian by Marilyn Vogt. This appears to be a document written to provide a common approach for militant anti-Stalinist delegates and would-be delegates to the coming Congress Against War and Fascism. The Russian manuscript did not contain a point 5.

389. "A Great Achievement." *New International,* October 1938. This evaluation of the significance of the founding conference of the FI was written four days before the conference was held.

390. **Alexander Nevski** (1220?-1263), a legendary Russian hero, defeated the Swedes (1240) in a great battle near the site of present-day Leningrad, on the Neva river (whence the name Nevski). In his honor Peter the Great founded the Order of Alexander Nevski in 1725. **General Alexander V. Suvorov** (1730-1800) and **Prince Mikhail I. Kutuzov** (1745-1812), were both founders of Russian military science who had orders named after them during World War II.

391. "Another Stalinist Ploy." By permission of the Harvard College Library. This "strictly confidential" letter was addressed to Albert Goldman, Martin Abern, and Jack Weber because James P. Cannon and Max Shachtman were at the time still in Europe, following the FI's

founding conference. Goldman, Trotsky's attorney in the U.S., held a press conference raising a number of embarrassing questions for the Stalinists.

392. "The Totalitarian Defeatist in the Kremlin." By permission of the Harvard College Library. The first edition of *Writings 38-39* reprinted the undated version of this article from *Liberty,* November 26, 1938, under the title "Why Russia Is Powerless." Here that version, somewhat altered by *Liberty* from the original manuscript, is replaced by the text in the Trotsky Archives.

393. **Lev Z. Mekhlis** (1889-1953) was a member of the editorial board of *Pravda* from 1930 on. In 1937 he became the head of the political administration of the Red Army.

394. "Letter to Rose Karsner." From the archives of James P. Cannon.

395. **The news concerning the Greek section** was that on the eve of the FI's founding conference the forces formerly around the Spartakos group and the Archio-Marxists had united into a single organization, which the conference recognized as the official Greek affiliate of the FI.

396. "Yes or No?" By permission of the Harvard College Library. Part of this was printed in *Socialist Appeal,* October 1, 1938. Trotsky issued this press release in the name of Diego Rivera.

397. " 'Toward a Decision.' " *New International,* November 1938. A review of *Der Entscheidung Entgegen,* by Jaroslav Cerny (Prague, 1938).

398. **Otto Bauer** (1882-1938) was the chief theoretician of Austro-Marxism and a leader of the Austrian Social Democracy.

399. **Jacob Walcher** (1887-   ) was a founder of the German CP who was expelled in 1929 as a supporter of the Brandlerite Right Opposition (KPO). In 1932 he left the KPO and joined the Socialist Workers Party of Germany (SAP). The SAP under his leadership endorsed the idea of the FI in 1933, then retreated back into centrism. In January 1937 the SAP swung further to the right by endorsing a People's Front for Germany.

# INDEX

Abbiatte, Roland ("Rossi"), 312
Abern, Martin, 300 (pic), 306, 490n
"Adolphe," see Klement, Rudolf
AFL (American Federation of Labor), 64-65, 427-28, 464n
Afrikaans, 469n
*Aftenposten* (Oslo), 372
Alexander, 329
Alksnis, T.I., 219, 247, 481n
"Amalgam," 201, 208, 209, 230
American Committee for the Defense of Leon Trotsky, 119-20, 266, 294-95, 489n
American Federation of Labor, see AFL
*America's Sixty Families* (Lundberg), 47-48, 284, 461n
Amsterdam International (International Federation of Trade Unions), 74, 112, 369, 465n
Anarchists, 135, 136, 137, 140-44; Spanish, 28, 135, 143, 144, 335, 349-50
Anarcho-syndicalism, 20, 28, 374
Anti-Semitism, Soviet, 131
Antonov-Ovseenko, Vladimir, 372, 396, 496n
Apenas, Ola, 495n
*Arbeiderbladet* (Oslo), 373
Archio-Marxists (Greece), 448, 499n
Archives, theft of, 52, 53, 178, 425, 462n
*Assignment in Utopia* (Lyons), 131
"Atl, Dr." (Gerardo Murillo), 393, 496n
Australia, 116-17
Austria, 141, 183, 262, 292

Bakaev, Ivan, 248, 484n
Barbusse, Henri, 31, 458n
Barmin, Alexander, 92-93, 119, 146, 183, 191, 275, 303, 336
Basch, Victor, 113, 470n
Bauer, Otto, 452, 499n
Beals, Carleton, 97, 121, 405, 406, 409, 468n

Beatty, Henry, 31, 309
Beck, Jozef, 238, 483n
Belgian Labor Party, see POB
Belgian section of Fourth International, see PSR
Belgium, 110, 159, 322, 341-42, 346
Beloborodov, Alexander, 175, 477n
Berkman, Alexander, 139, 473n
Berman-Yurin, Konon, 45, 460-61n
Bernstein, Eduard, 20, 454n
Bessonov, Sergei, 199, 264, 267, 479n
Bilmanis, Alfred, 272, 274
Bissenieks, George, 229, 272-74, 482n
*Biulleten Oppozitsii* (Bulletin of the Opposition, Paris), 172-73, 216, 218, 227, 229, 298, 457n
"Bloc of Rights and Trotskyites," see "Right-Trotskyite Center"
Blood purge (June 1934, Germany), 219
Bluecher, V.I., 219-20, 481n
Blum, Leon, 20, 31, 43, 44, 110, 111, 349, 364, 454n
Blumkin, Jakob, 226, 227, 482n
Bogomolov, 247, 396, 484n
Boguslavsky, M.S., 248, 484n
Bolsheviks, 199, 245, 247; in civil war, 137, 141, 143; Old Guard of, 201, 205, 210, 259; and terrorism, 305
Bonapartism: Soviet, 21, 32, 58, 404, 455n; bourgeois, 455n
Bordiga, Amadeo, 125, 472n
Bourgeois democracy, 284, 417-20, 430
Bourgeois revolution, 24-25, 41
Brandler, Heinrich, 56, 59, 299, 364, 365, 405, 463n
"Braun, Nicolle," see Wolf, Erwin
Brenner, Anita, 122, 471n
Brest-Litovsk treaty, 232, 233, 482n
Breton, Andre, 350 (pic)
Britain, 23, 24, 30, 74-75, 237, 284, 314, 323-25, 358-61, 443, 491n; Trotskyism in, 315-16, 329

500

*Writings of Leon Trotsky (1937-38)*

Weber, Sara, 78, 371, 466n
Weil, Simone, 331n 493n
Weisbord, Albert, 86, 91, 467n
"Well, Roman," *see* Soblen, Dr.
White Guards, 30, 140, 187, 189, 190, 247, 262, 304, 457n
Widick, B.J., 326, 492n
Wolf, Erwin ("Nicolle Braun"), 29, 155, 313, 385, 425, 457n, 475n
Wolfe, Bertram, 56-59, 299, 463n
Woll, Matthew, 64, 464n
*Workers Age* (New York), 364, 366, 494n
Workers and Peasants Bloc (Spain), 286
Workers' control, 24, 284
Workers Defense League (U.S.), 295
Workers Party of the U.S., 81-82, 85-91, 156-57, 283, 295, 298, 340, 490n; democracy in, 86, 89-91, 105-06; *see also* Socialist Workers Party
*World Revolution* (C.L.R. James), 329
*World Telegram* (New York), 308, 309
World War I, 174, 349
Wright, John G., 136, 178, 473n
"W. St.," *see* Klement, Rudolf

Yagoda, Henry, 182, 187, 198, 207, 213, 225-30, 248, 250-52, 254, 366, 387, 406, 424-25, 477n
Yakir, Iona, 199, 207, 219, 247, 480n
Yakovlev, Yakov, 247, 484n
Yakovleva, Varvara, 233, 248, 269, 483n
Yakubovich, 372-73, 396-98
Yaroslavsky, Emelyan, 233, 483n

Yenukidze, Abel, 192-93, 205, 478n
Yevdokimov, G.E., 248, 484n
Yezhov, Nikolas, 75, 101, 102, 131, 185, 196,198, 251, 263, 270, 276, 281, 303, 404, 406, 424, 465n
Young Communist League (U.S.), 298, 299, 398
Young Communist League (USSR), 167
*Young Lenin,* 414
Young People's Socialist League (U.S.), 297, 298-99, 309, 383-84, 394-95, 463n, 495n
Yudenich, Nikolai, 138, 473n
Yurenev, Konstantin, 199, 247, 372, 396-97, 480n
Yvon, M., 41, 460n

Zamora, Adolfo and Francisco, 374, 491n
Zaslavsky, David, 30, 457n
Zborowski, Marc, *see* "Etienne"
Zelensky, Isaac, 198-99, 257-60, 479n
Zeller, Fred, 291, 307, 488n
Zhelezniakov, 137
Zhirmunsky, 422-24
Zhuk, 137
Zinoviev, Gregory, 132, 197, 202, 203, 225, 243, 247, 248, 262, 282, 365, 366, 377, 456n; *see also* Moscow trials
Zola, Emile, 98, 468n
Zubarev, Prokopy, 199, 227, 479n
Zyromsky, Jean, 111, 470n

# OTHER WRITINGS OF 1937-38

In addition to the material in the present volume, the following writings by Trotsky during the period covered here have been published:

**The Spanish Revolution (1931-39).** 1973. Includes "The Lessons of Spain—The Last Warning" (December 17, 1937) and "The Fifth Wheel" (January 27, 1938).

**Leon Trotsky on China.** 1976. Includes "Revolution and War in China" (January 5, 1938), Trotsky's introduction to the first edition of Harold J. Isaacs' *The Tragedy of the Chinese Revolution.*

**Political Portraits.** 1976. Includes "Behind the Kremlin Walls" (January 8, 1938).

**Leon Trotsky on Literature and Art.** 1970. Includes "The Future of *Partisan Review*" (January 20, 1938), "Art and Politics in Our Epoch" (June 18, 1938), and "Manifesto: Towards a Free Revolutionary Art" (July 25, 1938).

**Their Morals and Ours: Marxist versus Liberal Views on Morality.** 1966. Includes "Their Morals and Ours" (February 16, 1938).

**The Transitional Program for Socialist Revolution.** Second, expanded edition, 1974. Includes "The Death Agony of Capitalism and the Tasks of the Fourth International" (April 1938) and twelve stenograms and statements on the transitional program between March and July 1938.

**Problems of Everyday Life.** 1973. Includes the April 18, 1938, introduction to the 1925 essay "Dialectical Materialism and Science."

During this period Trotsky was also working on the biography *Stalin,* which was incomplete at his death in 1940.

# BOOKS AND PAMPHLETS BY LEON TROTSKY*

Against Individual Terrorism
The Age of Permanent Revolution
Between Red and White
The Bolsheviki and World Peace (War and the International)
The Case of Leon Trotsky
The Challenge of the Left Opposition (1923-25) (incl. The New Course, Lessons of October, Problems of Civil War, and Toward Socialism or Capitalism?)
Europe and America: Two Speeches on Imperialism
Fascism: What It Is and How to Fight It
The First Five Years of the Communist International (2 vols.)
The History of the Russian Revolution (3 vols.)
In Defense of Marxism
Lenin: Notes for a Biographer
Lenin's Fight Against Stalinism (with V.I. Lenin; incl. On the Suppressed Testament of Lenin)
Leon Trotsky Speaks
Literature and Revolution
Marxism in Our Time
Military Writings
My Life
1905
On Black Nationalism and Self-Determination
On Britain (incl. Where Is Britain Going?)
On China (incl. Problems of the Chinese Revolution)
On the Jewish Question
On Literature and Art
On the Paris Commune

On the Trade Unions
Our Revolution
The Permanent Revolution and Results and Prospects
Problems of Everyday Life and Other Writings on Culture and Science
The Revolution Betrayed
The Spanish Revolution (1931-39)
Stalin
The Stalin School of Falsification
The Struggle Against Fascism in Germany
Terrorism and Communism
Their Morals and Ours (with essays by John Dewey and George Novack)
The Third International After Lenin
The Transitional Program for Socialist Revolution (incl. The Death Agony of Capitalism and the Tasks of the Fourth International and On the Labor Party in the U.S.)
Trotsky's Diary in Exile, 1935
Women and the Family
Writings of Leon Trotsky (1929-40) (12 vols., to be completed in 1977)
The Young Lenin

In preparation:
The Challenge of the Left Opposition (1926-29) (incl. The Platform of the Opposition)
On France (incl. Whither France?)
Political Portraits
The War Correspondence of Leon Trotsky

*This list includes only books and pamphlets by Leon Trotsky published in the United States and in print as of 1976.